*EMPIRICAL STUDIES
OF PROGRAMMERS:
SECOND WORKSHOP*

HUMAN/COMPUTER INTERACTION

A Series of Monographs, Edited Volumes, and Texts

SERIES EDITOR

BEN SHNEIDERMAN

EMPIRICAL STUDIES
OF
PROGRAMMERS:
SECOND WORKSHOP

edited by

GARY M. OLSON

University of Michigan

SYLVIA SHEPPARD

Computer Technology Associates, Inc.

ELLIOT SOLOWAY

Yale University

ABLEX PUBLISHING CORPORATION
NORWOOD, NEW JERSEY

Library of Congress Cataloging-in-Publication Data

Empirical studies of programmers : second workshop / edited by Gary M.
  Olson, Sylvia Sheppard, and Elliot Soloway.
      p.   cm. — (Human/computer interaction)
  Papers presented at the Second Workshop on Empirical Studies of
Programmers held in Washington, D.C. on Dec. 7–8, 1987.
  Bibliography: p.
  ISBN 0-89391-461-4.   ISBN 0-89391-462-2 (pbk.)
  1. Computer programmers—Congresses.   I. Olson, Gary M.
II. Sheppard, Sylvia.   III. Soloway, Elliot.   IV. Workshop on
Empirical Studies of Programmers (2nd : 1987 : Washington, D.C.)
V. Series: Human/computer interaction (Norwood, N.J.)
  HD8039.D37E46   1987   87-25942
  331.7'610051—dc19   CIP

Ablex Publishing Corporation
355 Chestnut Street
Norwood, New Jersey 07648

Contents

Preface

In June of 1986 the First Workshop on Empirical Studies of Programmers was held in Washington, D.C. The goal was to bring together people who were conducting empirical research on programmers, a particular community that up until then had had at best a loose and scattered kind of existence. The hard work of Elliot Soloway, Ben Shneiderman, Ram Iyengar, the program committee, and the participants produced a workshop that was high in quality, extremely useful, and just plain interesting.

On the second day of this Workshop a group convened over lunch to discuss the possibility of holding a second one. Various people "volunteered" for specific roles, and what eventually emerged was a Second Workshop, held again in Washington, D.C., December 7-8, 1987. The eighteen month delay was intentional, giving people time to move on in their research programs. We were amply rewarded. As in the First Workshop, over 50 papers were submitted, from which the 15 papers presented in this volume were selected.. In addition, a working paper by Clayton Lewis and Gary Olson that was the basis of a symposium on cognition and programming is presented here. Another roughly dozen papers were presented in a poster session at the Workshop itself.

In the Preface to the First Workshop the editors noted that the research presented there focused on "programming in the small." Both the editors and the participants in the invited panel session lamented the absence of studies of "programming in the large" and of the behavior of "real" expert programmers, who often work as parts of programming teams. Well, we no longer need those lamentations. A number of papers were submitted to the Second Workshop that reported studies of programmer behavior involved in the writing and maintaining of the large programs found in the "real world." Several of these papers have made it into this volume. We are heartened by this tendency. At the same time, there continues to be an important and necessary tradition of studies of small programs and relatively novice programmers that also adds to our understanding of the people part of programming. It is only through a blend of different kinds of studies of different kinds of programmers and programming situations that we can construct a body of empirical knowledge that will help us formulate advice and guidelines for programmers and managers of programming projects.

Once again, we had the help--financial and moral--of several organizations. The primary sponsor for the Workshop is the recently established Foundation for Empirical Studies of Programmers. This Foundation will provide a vehicle for continuing the Workshops and any other activities the Board of the Foundation feels will further the advancement of the empirical study of programmers. Stan Rifkin serves as the Secretary-Treasurer of the Foundation, and is the person who has ably handled all of the administrative and financial arrangements for the first two workshops. We also had support from the University of Michigan, Yale University, and the Software Psychology Society. The three editors of this volume contributed lots of time to preparing the workshop, as did Bill Curtis and Ben Shneiderman. We had an excellent program committee, who carefully reviewed our submissions and over half of whom met in Laurel, Maryland in June of 1987 to put together the program. The members, in addition to those already named, were Victor Basili, Deborah Boehm-Davis, Ruven Brooks, Marc Eisenstadt, Thomas Green, Jean-Michel Hoc, S. Sitharama Iyengar, Clayton Lewis, Tony Norcio, Roy Pea, Kathleen Swigger, Marvin Zelkowitz, Nicholas Zvengintzov, and Stuart Zweben. Sharon Doyle, Mary Jo Blahna, and Suzanne Visel helped in handling the manuscripts and reviews at Michigan. Barbara Bernstein, Carol Davidson, Karen Kronman, and Walter Johnson from Ablex were all helpful in making this volume a reality.

CHAPTER 1

Programming and Algebra Word Problems:
A Failure to Transfer

Gary M. Olson
Richard Catrambone
Department of Psychology
University of Michigan
330 Packard
Ann Arbor, MI 48104

Elliot Soloway
Department of Computer Science
Yale University
New Haven, CT 06520

ABSTRACT

Prior work has suggested that learning to program may provide students with skills that help them in algebra. However, this work was only preliminary. An extensive experiment was conducted in order to examine the contribution of programming to students' algebra word problem performance. Students taking an introductory programming course in Pascal were compared to a control group of students (taking an introductory statistics course) with a similar mathematics background. Subjects were tested on algebra word problems at the beginning of the semester and either one week later or at the end of the semester (12 weeks later). Subjects performance on the algebra word problems improved from the first test to the second. However, contrary to expectations, the programming students did not improve more than the control subjects. In addition, those subjects who took the second test one week after the first test improved more than subjects who took the second test at the end of the semester. The results suggest that programming does not provide general benefits that transfer to algebra word problems, but that there is specific transfer due to practicing algebra problems.

INTRODUCTION

When students learn computer programming do they also learn general problem solving skills that are useful in domains such as mathematics (Papert, 1980)? A series of investigations by Soloway and his associates have provided suggestive evidence for transfer from programming to solving algebra word problems (Soloway, Lochhead & Clement, 1982; Ehrlich, Soloway & Abbott, 1982; Ehrlich, Abbott, Salter & Soloway, unpublished). However, none of these earlier studies was definitive. In this paper we report the results of an ambitious study of transfer from computer programming to algebra word problems. Our data are quite clear: there was no selective improvement across a semester on algebra tests for subjects taking programming courses when compared to appropriate control subjects.

Why should programming affect how well students solve algebra word problems? We start with the well-established finding that word problems are exceptionally difficult (Clement, Lochhead & Monk, 1981.). In particular, there is a classic set of problems that even college students have great difficulty solving. Here are two examples of such problems:

For every 6 students at this university, there is 1 professor. Please write an equation which represents this statement. Use S for the number of students, and P for the number of professors.

Correct Answer: $S = 6P$

Most Frequent Incorrect Answer: $6S = P$

> For every 5 people who order cheesecake, 4 people order strudel. Please write an equation which represents this statement. Use C for the number of people who order cheesecake, and S for the number of people who order strudel.

Correct Answer: $5S = 4C$

Most Frequent Incorrect Answer: $5C = 4S$

Why should these problems be so difficult? Clement et al (1981) have argued that the students were writing down the reversed answer because they were not viewing the algebra in general, and their specific equation in particular, as a command to act (i.e., to calculate a value), but rather as a passive description of a state. This would lead them to make the reversal mistake that is so common with these problems. The reversal error is a descriptive mapping of algebraic terms onto the word order of the problem, but reverses the algebraic structure of the problem.

If students had a more active, procedural view of the algebra, one might expect that the reversal error would be less common. An active, procedural approach would lead students to focus on computing a value rather than describing the state of affairs. How might students come to have such an active view of algebra? Learning to program computers would seem to be one means to this end. For example, the actual equation that must be written in the "students and professors" problem above $(S = 6 * P)$ is the same from both an algebra and programming perspective. However, in programming, instruction focuses a great deal of attention on the fact that some number is being computed on the right-hand side of the equation and that this number is then stored in a memory location named by the variable on the left-hand side. Thus, students who had this view might be less likely to make the common kind of error shown above. They have clearly differentiated the roles of the two variables.

The above example is a specific instance of the general hypothesis that computer programming improves general problem solving skills. What is the evidence for it? In several studies, Soloway and his colleagues explored this question. One kind of evidence came from studies in which programming students either wrote programs or wrote algebraic expressions (Soloway et al., 1982). Students were more often correct when asked to write a program to compute a value than when they were asked to write the algebraic equation. This is a striking result since, as discussed above, the equations in both cases are the same--it is simply the view taken of the equations that is different. In a later study, students who had just finished a programming course were more often correct on such problems than those who had never taken a programming course (Ehrlich et al., 1982). Finally, in a study in which programming and non-programming students were measured both at the beginning and at the end of a semester, there was suggestive evidence of transfer, especially on certain kinds of algebra word problems (Ehrlich et al., unpublished).

While encouraging, the above studies did not conclusively support the hypothesis that programming provides a context for viewing solutions to problems in a more active, procedural manner. Nonetheless, these results were sufficiently intriguing to us to warrant the commitment to a more major study. Experimental subjects would be tested before and after learning to program, and would be compared to control subjects who were tested under identical conditions and whose background was identical to the experimental subjects' in as many ways as possible.

We focused on university students who were taking their first serious programming course (Pascal). Since we could not randomly assign subjects to experimental and control conditions, we looked for control subjects who were similar in background and ability to our programming subjects. Our control sample initially consisted of undergraduates taking a physiological psychology course or an introductory statistics course. Both classes were chosen on the assumption that they would contain students of approximately the same class as the programming course (i.e., sophomores and juniors). Furthermore, since these control subjects were taking science courses, we assumed they would be approximately equal to programming students in math ability and background. We oversampled control subjects so we could select various matched groups to compare to our experimental ones. To assess whether there were test-retest effects that we needed to take into account to interpret our findings, approximately one-fourth of the experimental and control subjects took the second test a week after taking the first test. The rest of the subjects took the second test at the end of the semester.

Ehrlich et al. (1982) constructed an impressive battery of algebra word problems of the general type discussed earlier. A number of specific factors were varied in producing problems. For instance, some problems required numerical calculation while others only required equations to be set up. The full range of problem types is described in the Method section. By having a broad range of problem types we had an increased ability to both find and understand positive transfer from programming to algebra. Some problem types would be expected to be much more difficult for non-programmers compared to programmers while other problem types would not be expected to produce highly differential performance.

METHOD

Design and Procedure

Each subject was tested in two sessions. The first session took place at the beginning of the academic semester. Subjects provided background information and then received a booklet of problems. The front page contained two sample problems for subjects to study in order to become familiar with the nature of the problems and the type of solutions required. The remaining 18 pages contained the 36 experimental problems, two to a page. Subjects were asked to solve as many problems as they could in a one-hour time period and to show all their work. Almost all subjects were able to finish the booklet in the one-hour time period.

The second session took place either one week after the first session or at the end of the semester. Subjects were randomly assigned to the "week" condition or the "semester" condition with the constraint that approximately 75% of the subjects would be in the semester condition. Subjects were again given an hour to complete a booklet with 36 algebra word problems to solve. The same types of problems were given as in the pre-test, but the specific content differed from the first testing.

Materials

To accommodate the test-retest design there were two test booklets (A & B) used in the experiment. Each booklet contained the same 36 unique problem types. Roughly half the subjects were given the booklets in the order A - B while the rest of the subjects received B - A. The specific booklet did not affect performance, so this factor will not be discussed further.

The problem types were constructed to allow a range of specific predictions to be tested regarding the potential benefits of learning to program. We also wanted a number of different problem types to help us check the generality of our findings. Below, we identify the various question types, and the factors being manipulated in each one.

(1) Generation versus completion. Each test booklet consisted of 24 generation problems and 12 completion problems. Generation problems required the student to solve the word problem from scratch while completion problems provided a partial answer and asked the student to fill in the missing information. Completion problems should be easier than generation problems. Further, if all subjects had difficulty determining the correct form of equations, but computer science students were better able to place the variables or numbers in the correct slots (after having taken the programming course), then, on the post-test, they would do better than control subjects (described later in this section) on the completion problems but not necessarily on the generation problems.

(2) Ratio versus percent (generation). Of the 24 generation problems, 12 were ratio problems and 12 were percent problems. Ratio problems expressed the relationship among the variables as ratios while percent problems expressed the relationship as percentages. Table 1 presents an example of each. Percent problems should be easier to solve than ratio problems because they involve fewer transformations of the surface structure of a word problem to its underlying algebraic representation. Thus we might expect that, on the post-test, programming students would do quite a bit better than the control subjects on the ratio problems since the programming students would have learned how to go beyond the surface structure of the problems and focus on the equations. The control subjects should do about as well as the programmers on the percent problems though since the word order of percent problems typically corresponds to the underlying algebraic order.

Table 1
Examples of Ratio and Percent Problems

Ratio Problem
Given the following statement:
"In the animal pound there are 6 dogs for every cat."
Calculate the number of dogs when there are 18 cats.

Percent Problem
Given the following statement:
"Mr. Steward invested 40% of his savings with the First National Bank."
Calculate the amount of savings Mr. Steward has if he invests $200 with the First National Bank.

(3) Integral versus non-integral versus combination. Of the 24 generation problems, there were eight each of integral, non-integral, and combination problems. Of the 12 completion problems, 6 were integral and 6 were non-integral. This manipulation had to do with whether one variable was expressed as a simple multiple of another variable (integral problems), or whether two variables were expressed as multiples of each other (non-integral problems), or whether one variable was expressed as a simple multiple of a second variable and the second and third variables were then expressed as multiples of each other (combination problems). Table 2 gives an example of each (all three examples are generation problems). If programming teaches students how to set up relations among variables and to view the variables in a more procedural way, then programming subjects should show more improvement (from pre-test to post-test) on the (more difficult) non-integral and combination problems compared to the control subjects since these problems represent the most complex relationships.

Table 2
Examples of Integral, Non-integral, and Combination Problems

Integral Problem
Given the following statement:
"In the animal pound there are 6 dogs for every cat."
Calculate the number of dogs when there are 18 cats.

Non-integral Problem
Given the following statement:
"At the airport there are 5 PanAm flights for every 6 TWA flights."
Calculate the number of PanAm flights when there are 60 TWA flights.

Combination Problem
Given the following statement:
"At the conference there were 4 times as many linguists as computer scientists and there were also 7 linguists for every 5 psychologists."
Calculate the number of psychologists at the conference given that there were 140 computer scientists at the conference.

(4) Equation versus numerical-answer (generation). Of the 24 generation problems, 12 required students to generate an equation while 12 required them to generate a numerical answer. Table 3 shows examples. Equation problems might be considered more difficult since they do not foster an active approach, rather, they are more abstract than numerical-answer problems. If computer science students acquire an active approach to algebraic relations, then they should demonstrate more improvement on the equation problems compared to the control subjects.

Table 3
Examples of Equation versus Numerical Answer Problems

Equation Problem
Given the following statement:
"At Marcellos store, there were 6 oranges sold for every pear that was sold."
Write a mathematical function (or functions) which can be used to calculate the number of oranges sold when supplied with the number of pears that were sold.

Numerical Answer Problem
Given the following statement:
"In the animal pound there are 6 dogs for every cat."
Calculate the number of dogs when there are 18 cats.

(5) Procedural versus non-procedural (generation). Of the 24 generation problems, 12 were procedurally worded and 12 were non-procedurally worded. Procedurally worded problems directed the student to calculate a particular value or write a particular equation whereas the non-procedurally worded problems did not specifically indicate which variable to solve for or to set up the equation for. Table 4 shows examples. Ehrlich et al. (unpublished) found that students who had taken programming benefitted from the procedural wording of the problems: programming students were better able to solve algebra word problems when they were expressed in a procedural form. It was as if programming allowed students to take advantage of the call to act. Students who had not taken programming did no better on the procedurally worded problems than on the non-procedurally worded ones.

Table 4
Examples of Procedural and Non-procedural Problems

Procedural Problem
Given the following statement:
"In the animal pound there are 6 dogs for every cat."
Calculate the number of dogs when there are 18 cats.

Non-procedural Problem
Given the following statement:
"In the museum, there are 9 Picassos for every Rembrandt."
If there are 18 Picassos, how many Rembrandts are there in the museum?

(6) Single-variable versus ratio versus combination (completion). Of the 12 completion problems, there were four each of single-variable, ratio, and combination problems. Single-variable problems expressed one variable as a multiple or fraction of another variable. Ratio problems expressed the relationship of two variables as a ratio. Combination problems expressed two variables as multiples of each other. Table 5 shows these three types. Prior work (Clement et al., 1981) suggests that students have more difficulty solving problems that express relationships between variables as multiples of each other. They are more successful on the single-variable and ratio problems. In addition, students with programming tended to do better than non-programmers on problems in which one variable was expressed as a multiple or fraction of another (Ehrlich et al., unpublished). Thus, we might expect programmers to improve more than non-programmers on the single-variable and ratio problems and to improve the most on the more difficult combination problems (although the overall performance on the combination problems might be lower than for single-variable and ratio problems).

Table 5
Examples of Single-variable, Ratio, and Combination Problems

Single-variable Problem
Given the following statement:
"In the park, there are 4 times as many joggers as bicyclists."
Let J represent the number of joggers and let B represent the number of bicyclists.
Complete the equation given below by replacing the question marks.

VARIABLE stands for WHAT   SOLUTION
J stands for number of joggers

$$J = \frac{?}{?} B$$

B stands for number of bicyclists

Ratio Problem
Given the following statement:
"There are 4 times as many minnows as trout in the river."
Let M represent the number of minnows and let T represent the number of trout.
Complete the equation given below by replacing the question marks.

VARIABLE stands for WHAT   SOLUTION
M stands for number of minnows

$$\frac{?}{?} = \frac{M}{T}$$

T stands for number of trout

Combination Problem
Given the following statement:
"The department store sells 4 times as many televisions as radios."
Let T represent the number of televisions that are sold and let R represent the number of
radios that are sold. Complete the equation given below by replacing the question marks.

VARIABLE stands for WHAT   SOLUTION
T stands for number of televisions

$$? T = ? R$$

R stands for number of radios

Subjects

The final sample consisted of 163 control subjects and 78 treatment subjects. Of the 163 control subjects, 44 were tested after one week and 119 were tested after a full semester. Of the 78 treatment subjects, 24 were in the week condition and 54 were in the semester condition.

A total of 369 students were initially recruited from three undergraduate courses in order to get this final sample. Treatment subjects came from an introductory PASCAL programming course. Candidates for control subjects came from a physiological psychology course and an introductory statistics course. Subjects were paid $20 for their participation in the experiment.

We wanted to find control subjects that were in as many ways possible similar to the treatment subjects on various background measures. We queried subjects on such factors as prior computer experience and math background, and we obtained the permission of subjects to get their SAT scores from the University. Computer science students had significantly higher Math SAT scores than the psychology students, but were comparable to the statistics students. Thus, we choose to exclude the psychology students from the analyses. In addition, we chose to exclude from the analyses students who had any prior college computer classes. Thus, our final control group consisted of statistics students who had no prior college computer classes while the treatment group consisted of computer science students who had no prior college computer classes.

Computer science students tended to have more math background than statistics students, but in preliminary analyses we found that controlling for this difference did not make a difference in the results. The proportion of males and females in each group was roughly the same. In addition, sex never produced a main effect in any of our analyses and only rarely interacted with any other variable. Thus, all analyses reported below collapse across sex.

Some subjects came to the pre-test but failed to return for the post-test. We found no difference in the pre-test performance of these subjects compared to the pre-test performance of subjects who did return for the post-test. The data from subjects who did not return for the post-test were not included in the analyses below.

We interviewed the instructors of the programming and statistics courses to learn more about the content of these courses and the kinds of assignments given to students. The instructor of the programming class typically introduced a concept in lecture and then presented a number of examples demonstrating the concept. As the semester progressed, he would present a problem and demonstrate how earlier concepts were not well-suited for the new problem. Then he would introduce a new concept and show its usefulness for the current problem. For example, arrays were introduced in the context of creating a data file when it became clear that a simple linear indexing of a variable would be clumsy. Homework assignments typically consisted of applying the new concept to a programming problem that was similar to one shown in class. Students practiced using new data or control structures in their homework assignments. At least one assignment explicitly involved setting up a number of equations such that certain values could be input to a program and it would output new values. In general, of course, many assignments would involve assigning values to variables and manipulating those values in some way. Thus, students received practice in setting up equations and equivalences.

The instructor of the statistics course also taught concepts through many examples. Typically, a concept was presented and then examples were used to supplement the explanation. For instance, the issue of sampling bias was illustrated by examples dealing with various polls which, due to the way they sampled, lead to incorrect predictions in certain political races. Weekly homework assignments typically consisted of about 10 questions. Some questions involved using certain statistical formulas while others were more "thinking" problems; that is, they required students to consider various concepts and their relationships without using numbers or equations.

It is clear that students in the statistics class received practice using equations (such as in calculating standard deviations). However, these students did not necessarily receive practice on how to express new relationships through equations. Programming students received experience creating equations for novel situations.

Scoring

We assessed students' performance on the algebra word problem tests using strict and lenient criteria. Under the strict criterion, an answer was scored correct only if there were no mistakes. For problems that had several parts, a student only got credit for the problem if every part was correct. The danger of using a strict criterion is that subtle differences between the groups' performance could be missed. For example, computer science students may become good at setting up equations for algebra problems but fail to put them in the form requested by the problems. Under the strict criterion, their answers would be counted incorrect. Meanwhile, statistics students may have fundamental difficulties with the problems that would not be differentiated from the difficulties of the computer science students. Thus, a lenient scoring criterion was also used to assess subjects' performance.

Under the lenient criterion, a problem would be scored correct if the student solved the problem correctly or made one of two mistakes. One mistake was to set up the equations in the problem correctly but fail to perform a required computation. The second mistake was to fail to express the relationship of the variables in the correct pattern. For example, suppose a problem asked the student to provide a final equation which would give the number of females (F) in a class given that the total number of people over five feet was T. Suppose the correct answer was $F=T/3$, but the student wrote $3F=T$. Under the strict criterion the answer would be counted as incorrect since the equation is not set up to calculate F given T. However, under the lenient criterion the answer would be counted correct since the relationship between the variables is correct.

It turns out that lenient scoring boosted subjects' score on the tests (compared to the "strict" score) by the same amount regardless of whether a subject was in the control or treatment group, and regardless of problem type. Thus, all analyses below will be based on strict scoring.

RESULTS

Table 6 lists students' overall scores on the pre- and post-tests. The maximum score a subject could get on either test was 36. The data from the students in the psychology class are included for comparison. (There were 25 of these subjects; 17 in the semester condition and eight in the week condition.) The ANOVA used to analyze the data from this table had two between-subjects variables: class (computer science versus statistics versus psychology) and timing of post-test (either one week after the pre-test or at the end of the semester). There was also one within-subjects variable: pre- versus post-test score. Computer science students outperformed both the statistics and psychology students on both tests, $F(2,260) = 8.65$, $p = .0002$. Subjects did better on the post-test than the pre-test, $F(1,260) = 36.87$, $p < .0001$. If computer science students learned something in their class over the course of a semester which would help them solve algebra problems, then the effect of interest would be found in the triple interaction term of class, pre- versus post-test, and timing of post-test (week versus semester). A significant interaction (with results in the expected direction) would show that computer science students' improvement on the post-test was greater than the improvement by statistics and psychology students and that this result is only found for the semester subjects. The triple interaction was not significant, $F(2, 260) < 1$. Surprisingly, there was a tendency for week subjects to do better on the post-test than semester subjects, $F(1,260) = 3.10$, $p < 08$. This suggests that the practice effect of taking two tests close together in time may be more effective than taking a programming course in helping students learn to solve algebra word problems.

The above analyses were repeated considering only computer science and statistics students since they were closely matched on prior mathematics experience and Math SAT scores. The results mirror what was reported above. There was a significant improvement from pre- to post-test, $F(1,237) = 38.92$, $p < .0001$. Computer science students did better overall than statistics students, $F(1,237) = 16.49$, $p = .0001$. The triple interaction that tested the hypothesis that computer science students would show the most improvement after a semester of programming was not supported, $F(1,237) < 1$. Finally, week subjects tended to do better on the post-test than semester subjects, $F(1,237) = 3.35$, $p < .07$.

Table 6

Average Number of Problems Correct on Pre- and Post-Tests as a

Function of Subject Type and Timing of Post-Test[1]

	Post-test one week after pre-test			Post-test at end of semester		
	Psych	Statistics	Computer Science	Psych	Statistics	Computer Science
Pre-test	15.5 (7.7)	18.2 (9.3)	23.2 (9.3)	20.1 (7.2)	17.8 (9.5)	22.4 (8.4)
Post-test	21.0 (8.2)	21.2 (10.2)	28.2 (7.6)	23.1 (8.7)	19.8 (10.0)	24.8 (9.4)

[1]Maximum value for each cell is 36. Standard deviations in parentheses.

In order to simplify the rest of the results, the remainder of the analyses will deal only with computer science and statistics subjects. In addition, we will focus only on subjects who took the post-test at the end of the semester (although all tables will also contain the results for the week subjects). The week subjects' role was to assess the test-retest effect. In most cases, the improvement in performance of the week subjects was greater than or equal to the improvement of the semester subjects. Differences in performance (between groups, problem types, pre versus post tests, or any of the interactions), when significant, were typically at the .005 level or better. Thus, when differences are reported below, they should be assumed to be significant at the .005 level or better. If the significance level is less than .005, then it will be explicitly reported.

One consistent finding in the analyses below is that while computer science students tended to outperform statistics students on the various problem types, they did not improve their performance more than the statistics students from the pre-test to the post-test. Both groups did better on the post-test than the pre-test, but computer science students failed to produce a larger degree of improvement.

Table 7 presents the proportion of generation and completion problems subjects solved correctly. We had to compare proportions instead of number of problems correct because there were 24 generation problems and only 12 completion problems per test. An analysis of variance was performed on the arcsine transformations of the proportions. Computer science students did better than statistics students and both groups did better on the post-test than the pre-test. However, there was no overall difference in performance on generation versus completion problems.

Table 7

Proportion of Generation and Completion Problems Correct on Pre- and Post-Tests as a Function of Subject Type and Timing of Post-Test

Problem Type	Post-test one week after pre-test		Post-test at end of semester	
	Statistics	Computer Science	Statistics	Computer Science
Generation				
Pre-test	.50	.63	.49	.62
Post-test	.58	.75	.55	.69
Completion				
Pre-test	.51	.65	.50	.62
Post-test	.60	.86	.55	.70

Table 8 presents the number of ratio and percent problems (generation type only) subjects solved correctly. Computer science students did better than statistics students and both groups did better on the post-test than the pre-test. Both groups did better on percent problems than ratio problems.

Table 8

Average Number of Ratio and Percent Problems Correct on Pre- and Post-Tests as a Function of Subject Type and Time of Post-Test[2]

Problem Type	Post-test one week after pre-test		Post-test at end of semester	
	Statistics	Computer Science	Statistics	Computer Science
Ratio				
Pre-test	5.78 (3.6)	7.04 (3.6)	5.64 (3.7)	6.72 (3.7)
Post-test	7.02 (3.9)	9.33 (3.2)	6.08 (4.2)	7.70 (4.0)
Percent				
Pre-test	6.11 (2.7)	8.12 (3.0)	6.02 (2.4)	8.11 (2.9)
Post-test	6.77 (2.9)	8.75 (2.8)	7.12 (2.8)	8.78 (2.7)

[2]Maximum value for each cell is 12. Standard deviations in parentheses.

Table 9 presents the number of integral, non-integral, and combination problems (generation type only) subjects solved correctly. Computer science students did better than statistics students and both groups did better on the post-test than the pre-test. Students did best on the integral problems and worst on combination problems. Finally, there was an interaction of problem type and pre/post test such that subjects improved most on the non-integral and combination problems and least on the integral problems, $F(2,342) = 3.2$, $p < .05$.

Table 9
Average Number of Integral, Non-integral, and Combination Problems Correct on
Pre- and Post-Tests as a Function of Subject Type and Timing of Post-Test[3]

Problem Type	Post-test one week after pre-test		Post-test at end of semester	
	Statistics	Computer Science	Statistics	Computer Science
Integral				
Pre-test	4.98 (2.0)	5.79 (1.9)	5.00 (2.0)	5.93 (1.6)
Post-test	5.48 (1.7)	6.21 (1.6)	5.24 (2.0)	6.24 (1.8)
Non-integral				
Pre-test	3.95 (2.1)	5.04 (2.3)	3.94 (2.3)	4.91 (2.1)
Post-test	4.82 (2.2)	6.46 (2.0)	4.58 (2.2)	5.72 (2.1)
Combination				
Pre-test	2.95 (2.4)	4.33 (2.2)	2.71 (2.0)	4.00 (2.2)
Post-test	3.50 (2.6)	5.42 (2.0)	3.38 (2.4)	4.52 (2.2)

[3]Maximum value for each cell is 8. Standard deviations in parentheses.

Table 10 presents the number of equation and numerical-answer problems (generation type only) subjects solved correctly. Computer science students did better than statistics students and both groups did better on the post-test than the pre-test. Students did better on the numerical-answer problems than the equation problems. There was an interaction of problem type and pre/post test such that subjects improved more on the equation problems than the numerical-answer problems, $F(1,171) = 6.74$, $p < .02$.

Table 10
Average Number of Equation and Numerical-answer Problems Correct on
Pre- and Post-Tests as a Function of Subject Type and Timing of Post-Test[4]

Problem Type	Post-test one week after pre-test		Post-test at end of semester	
	Statistics	Computer Science	Statistics	Computer Science
Equation				
Pre-test	4.75 (3.0)	7.21 (3.2)	5.05 (3.1)	6.69 (2.9)
Post-test	6.09 (3.5)	8.79 (2.5)	6.00 (3.2)	7.89 (2.9)
Numerical-answer				
Pre-test	7.14 (3.1)	7.96 (2.9)	6.61 (3.0)	8.15 (2.8)
Post-test	7.70 (3.0)	9.29 (3.1)	7.19 (3.1)	8.59 (2.9)

[4]Maximum value for each cell is 12. Standard deviations in parentheses.

Table 11 presents the number of procedurally worded and non-procedurally worded problems (generation type only) subjects solved correctly. Computer science students did better than statistics students and both groups did better on the post-test than the pre-test. Contrary to expectations, students did better on the non-procedurally worded problems than the procedurally worded problems.

Table 11

Average Number of Procedurally and Non-Procedurally Worded Problems Correct on

Pre- and Post-Tests as a Function of Subject Type and Timing of Post-Test[5]

Problem Type	Post-test one week after pre-test		Post-test at end of semester	
	Statistics	Computer Science	Statistics	Computer Science
Procedurally worded				
Pre-test	5.23 (3.0)	6.83 (3.2)	5.14 (3.0)	6.80 (2.9)
Post-test	6.07 (3.1)	8.25 (2.7)	5.85 (3.2)	7.74 (3.0)
Non-procedurally worded				
Pre-test	6.66 (3.0)	8.33 (2.7)	6.52 (3.0)	8.04 (2.7)
Post-test	7.73 (3.3)	9.83 (2.6)	7.35 (3.0)	8.74 (2.8)

[5]Maximum value for each cell is 12. Standard deviations in parentheses.

Table 12 presents the number of integral and non-integral problems (completion type only) subjects solved correctly. Computer science students did better than statistics students, $F(1,171) = 5.88$, $p < .02$, and both groups did better on the post-test than the pre-test, $F(1,171) = 4.66$, $p < .04$. Students did better on the integral problems than the non-integral problems, $F(1,171) = 4.37$, $p < .04$. Computer science students outperformed the statistics students (indicated by an interaction of class and problem type) more on the non-integral problems than the integral problems, $F(1,171) = 4.96$, $p < .03$.

Table 12

Average Number of Integral and Non-integral Problems Correct on Pre- and

Post-Tests as a Function of Subject Type and Timing of Post-Test[6]

Problem Type	Post-test one week after pre-test		Post-test at end of semester	
	Statistics	Computer Science	Statistics	Computer Science
Integral				
Pre-test	3.18 (2.2)	3.96 (2.1)	3.21 (2.2)	3.70 (2.0)
Post-test	3.48 (2.5)	5.08 (1.6)	3.45 (2.3)	4.22 (2.2)
Non-integral				
Pre-test	3.09 (2.1)	4.04 (2.3)	2.92 (2.2)	3.85 (2.1)
Post-test	3.89 (2.3)	5.08 (1.6)	3.15 (2.4)	4.09 (2.2)

[6]Maximum value for each cell is 6. Standard deviations in parentheses.

Table 13 presents the number of single-variable, ratio, and combination problems (completion type only) subjects solved correctly. Computer science students did better than statistics students, $F(1,171) = 5.88$, $p < .02$, and both groups did better on the post-test than the pre-test, $F(1,171) = 4.66$, $p < .04$. Students did best on the ratio problems and less well on the single-variable and combination problems. There was also a marginally significant interaction of class and problem-type, $F(2,342) = 2.66$, $p < .08$, which reflects the fact that the computer science students tended to outperform the statistics students especially on the combination problems and less so on the other two types.

Table 13

Average Number of Single-variable, Ratio, and Combination Problems Correct on

Pre- and Post-Tests as a Function of Subject Type and Timing of Post-Test[7]

Problem Type	Post-test one week after pre-test		Post-test at end of semester	
	Statistics	Computer Science	Statistics	Computer Science
Single-variable				
Pre-test	2.00 (1.6)	2.58 (1.5)	1.90 (1.7)	2.31 (1.6)
Post-test	2.43 (1.6)	3.12 (1.4)	2.00 (1.7)	2.72 (1.5)
Ratio				
Pre-test	2.55 (1.4)	2.92 (1.3)	2.60 (1.5)	2.87 (1.4)
Post-test	2.64 (1.8)	3.58 (0.9)	2.63 (1.6)	2.98 (1.5)
Combination				
Pre-test	1.73 (1.7)	2.50 (1.7)	1.63 (1.6)	2.37 (1.6)
Post-test	2.30 (1.8)	3.46 (1.4)	1.96 (1.7)	2.61 (1.7)

[7]Maximum value for each cell is 4. Standard deviations in parentheses.

DISCUSSION

Our results show that students who had taken an introductory Pascal programming course showed no differential improvement (from pre-test to post-test) in their solving of algebra word problems than did control subjects. We never found an interaction of class by pre-/post-test for the various problem types for the semester subjects. This interaction would have indicated that computer science students improved more than control subjects from pre- to post-test. Instead, we found that computer science students were better than the control subjects both before and after having taken the programming course. Both groups improved from pre- to post-test, especially on the more difficult problem types. Even psychology students, who had lower Math SAT scores, improved as much as the other two groups. These students did not spend the semester studying a mathematics or programming related subject, so their improvement cannot be attributed to formal instruction in those domains. We also found that, as predicted, some problem types were more difficult than others and that computer science students tended to outperform control subjects especially on the harder types. The differential performance on the various problem types indicates that the tests were sensitive to subjects' difficulties. Nevertheless, we found no effects on subjects' performance of having taken the programming course.

It is important to place our findings in perspective. We examined one class of algebra word problems and one type of programming experience. It is conceivable that other types of algebra problems, other types of mathematical problem solving, or other types of cognition would be affected by learning to program. Similarly, other kinds of programming experiences might affect mathematical problem solving. Pea and Kurland (1984) have provided a particularly useful discussion of these kinds of issues pertaining to the effects of programming on cognition. We chose to examine the circumstances used in this experiment because there had been a fair amount of prior research on them, much of which had been suggestive but none of which had been conclusive. We wanted to carry out a definitive study of this kind of problem solving and this kind of programming experience to find out once and for all where this particular line of work was leading. We think we have produced a definitive answer.

The obvious question, then, is: where does this leave us? To reiterate the point just made: these findings do not destroy the case for transfer of problem solving skills from learning to program to other domains. We have examined one plausible candidate for transfer--algebra word problems of a certain restricted set of types--and have found no positive evidence. In addition, we obviously could not control what subjects were taught in their programming and statistics classes. Consistent with Pea and Kurland's (1984) analysis of the issues involved in transfer, it is useful to look at various specific skills that might transfer and investigate them in a focused way.

As one concrete example, let us briefly mention the work of Soloway, Spohrer and Littman (1987). They are teaching students learning to program the skill of generating more than one solution to a problem. In most disciplines, students tend to think that once they have found an answer, any answer, they can stop. In fact, expert problem solvers know that all answers are not created equal -- some are better than others. Experts use heuristics to generate alternatives. If this skill of generating alternative answers is taught in the context of learning to program, will it generalize to other domains?

Programming is a complex skill, whose components are only slowly being explicated. Whether any of the component skills of programming affect other domains of problem solving is an interesting and important possibility. So far, despite a lot of excitement over this prospect, little careful empirical work exists which shows positive transfer. Research on both the cognitive prerequisites and the cognitive consequences of learning to program will help us better understand what is actually learned.

ACKNOWLEDGMENTS

This research was supported by grant #MDR-84-70150 from the National Science Foundation.

The authors would like to acknowledge the assistance of Nancy Johnson, Mark McClellan, and Stirling Olson in collecting and coding the data. The authors would also like to thank the instructors of the courses that provided subjects for the experiment.

REFERENCES

1. Papert, S. (1980). *Mindstorms*. New York: Basic Books.

2. Soloway, E., Lochhead, J., & Clement, J. (1982). Does computer programming enhance problem solving ability? Some positive evidence on algebra word problems. In R.J. Seidel, R.E. Anderson & B. Hunter (Eds.), *Computer literacy*. New York: Academic Press.

3. Ehrlich, K., Soloway, E., & Abbott, V. (1982). Styles of thinking: From algebra word problems to programming via procedurality. Proceedings of the 4th Meeting of the Cognitive Science Society, Ann Arbor, Michigan.

4. Ehrlich, K., Abbott, V., Salter, W., & Soloway, E. Issues and problems in studying transfer effects of programming. Unpublished paper.

5. Clement, J., Lochhead, J., & Monk, G. (1981). Translation difficulties in learning mathematics. *American Mathematical Monthly, 88*, 26-40.

6. Pea, R.D., & Kurland, M. (1984). On the cognitive effects of learning computer programming. *New Ideas in Psychology, 2*, 137-168.

7. Soloway, E., Spohrer, J., & Littman, D. (1987). E unum pluribus: Generating alternative designs. Invited Paper, Cognitive Science Society, University of Washington.

CHAPTER 2

Understanding Procedures as Objects

Michael Eisenberg
Mitchel Resnick
Franklyn Turbak
Laboratory for Computer Science
Massachusetts Institute of Technology
Cambridge, MA 02139

Abstract

Programming languages that treat procedures as "object-like" entities (for example, allowing procedures to be passed as arguments to other procedures) offer major advantages in semantic power and syntactic elegance. In this paper, we examine how novice programmers appropriate the idea of procedures as objects. Based on a series of structured interviews with students in the introductory computer-science course at MIT, we develop a model of the students' ontology of procedures. We conclude that many students view procedures as inherently active entities, with few "object-like" properties. We speculate on the implications of these results for the design and teaching of languages that treat procedures as objects.

1. Introduction

Most programming languages (as well as the courses that teach them) encourage a sharp distinction between procedures and data. In this paradigm, procedures and data are typically viewed, respectively, as actions and objects: just as actions manipulate and transform objects in the physical world, procedures manipulate and transform data in computer programs.

This procedure-data distinction, however, is both artificial and limiting. In fact, procedures are *not* active entities at all: they are merely *descriptions* of processes. As such, procedures *are* data. Moreover, languages that treat procedures as data objects can realize tremendous benefits in semantic power and syntactic elegance.

Scheme, a dialect of Lisp, is a prime example of this approach. In Scheme, procedures are "first-class objects." That is, they have all of the same "object traits" as traditional data objects like numbers, lists, and vectors. For example,

Scheme procedures can be passed as arguments to other procedures, and they can be returned as the results of procedure calls. These first-class properties of procedures make possible simple and elegant implementations of object-oriented programming and delayed evaluation *(1)*, and continuation-passing models of programming *(2)*. Indeed, there is a growing recognition within the computer-science community of the importance of first-class procedures, and the concept is likely to influence the design of future programming languages *(3)*.

In this study, we interviewed a group of students learning Scheme in order to examine how novice programmers think about procedures. Most empirical studies of programmers have focused on syntactic issues and higher-level planning skills. Our aim here is somewhat different: we focus on programmers' semantic models, on their *ontology* of procedures. In particular: what characteristics do novice programmers attribute to procedures, and how does that ontology affect their ability to think of procedures as objects?

We believe that research in this area might provide a theoretical foundation for changes in language design and pedagogy. Only by more fully understanding "naive ontologies" of procedures can we hope to develop improved methods for helping students learn about the use of procedures as first-class objects.

Section 2 of the paper provides a brief background on first-class objects and Scheme procedures. Section 3 describes the methodology of the empirical study. Section 4 uses results from the study to develop a model of the subjects' ontology of procedures. The section also explores this ontology more deeply by focusing on several extended examples from the interviews. Section 5 suggests language-design and pedagogic changes that might help students to learn to think about procedures as objects. Section 6 suggests directions for future work.

2. Background

This section provides a brief discussion of first-class objects and Scheme procedures.[1]

2.1 First-Class Objects

In the semantics of programming languages, certain types of objects are classified as *first-class* [cf. Stoy *(6)*]. A first-class object has the following properties:

1. Variable names may be bound to it;
2. It may be passed as an argument to procedures;
3. It may be returned as the value of a procedure call;

---

[1] Readers interested in a more thorough treatment of these subjects should refer to *Structure and Interpretation of Computer Programs* by Abelson and Sussman with Sussman *(1)*. This text is used in the MIT introductory computer-science course that our subjects were taking. Eisenberg *(4)* provides a more elementary introduction to this material, while Rees and Clinger *(5)* gives a formal definition of the Scheme language.

4. It may be stored as an element of compound data structures (such as lists or arrays).

Numbers are first-class objects in virtually every programming language. For instance, the following line of Pascal code illustrates the first three properties of first-class objects as they apply to Pascal integers:

```
x := double(3)
```

Here, the double function (which we have presumably written earlier) takes an integer as an argument and returns an integer as its result; the value of the call to double is now associated with the variable name x. We could illustrate the fourth "first-class" property by assigning the result to an array location — e.g., x[1] instead of x.

2.2 Scheme Procedures

In Scheme, numbers and procedures are both first-class objects.[2] The define construct binds a variable name to an object, as in the following examples:[3]

```
(define a 1)
(define b (+ 2 3))
(define stuff (lambda (x) (/ x 3)))
```

In each of these examples, the Scheme interpreter *evaluates* (i.e., finds the object designated by) the rightmost subexpression and binds the specified name to the resulting object. In the first case, the Scheme interpreter evaluates 1 and binds the name a to the result (the number 1). In the second example, the interpreter evaluates the subexpression (+ 2 3) and binds the variable name b to the result (the number 5).

The third example uses the lambda construct, Scheme's method for creating a procedure object. In this case, the lambda expression creates a procedure that takes one argument and returns the value of that argument divided by 3. The interpreter first evaluates the lambda expression, then binds the name stuff to the resulting procedure object.

Scheme includes an alternative syntax for defining procedures. The stuff definition could also be written as:

```
(define (stuff x) (/ x 3))
```

The association of names with objects is shown in Figure 1. Note that both primitive and compound (i.e., user-defined) procedures are named in exactly the same way as other Scheme objects.

---

[2] Scheme supports other first-class objects, including lists, symbols, booleans, and strings. The examples in our study use only numbers and procedures.

[3] Most of the examples in this section were used in the student interviews. See the Appendix for a listing of all expressions used in the interviews.

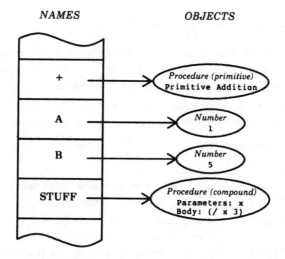

Figure 1: Bindings between names and objects in Scheme.

When the Scheme interpreter evaluates a name, it returns the object bound to that name. For example:[4]

```
a       ⟹      1
b       ⟹      5
stuff   ⟹      [COMPOUND-PROCEDURE STUFF]
```

Procedure calls in Scheme are illustrated by the following example:

```
(stuff b) ⟹  1.66666
```

The Scheme interpreter first evaluates each of the subexpressions. Stuff evaluates to a procedure object – namely, the divide-by-3 procedure created earlier. The other subexpression, b, evaluates to the number 5. The interpreter then applies the procedure object to 5, and returns the result.

The above examples demonstrate the first property of first-class procedures – that variable names can be bound to procedures. The second property – that procedures may be passed as arguments to other procedures – is illustrated in the following example:

```
(define (apply-to-5 f)
  (f 5))
```

Evaluating this expression binds the name apply-to-5 to a procedure that takes one argument. When the procedure named by apply-to-5 is called with a procedure as an argument, the interpreter will apply the argument to the number 5 and return the result:

---

[4] We use the arrow character "⟹" to mean "evaluates to."

```
(apply-to-5 stuff) ⟹  1.66666
```

```
(apply-to-5 (lambda (x) (* x x))) ⟹  25
```

In the first expression, the argument to `apply-to-5` is the procedure bound to `stuff`. In the second expression, the argument to `apply-to-5` is the "squaring" procedure returned by evaluating the `lambda` expression.

The third property of first-class procedures – that they may be returned as the result of procedure calls – is illustrated by the following example:

```
(define (create-subtracter n)
  (lambda (x) (- x n)))
```

Evaluating this expression binds the name `create-subtracter` to a procedure which, when applied to an object, returns *another* procedure. This new procedure takes one argument and subtracts from it the value of n, where n refers to the original argument to `create-subtracter`. Thus, calling `create-subtracter` with an argument of 1 will return a "decrement" procedure – a procedure that takes one argument and subtracts 1 from it. Similarly, calling `create-subtracter` with an argument of 10 will return a "subtract-10" procedure. Here are some examples:

```
(create-subtracter 1) ⟹  [COMPOUND-PROCEDURE 23407230]
```

```
((create-subtracter 1) 5) ⟹  4
```

```
(define increment (create-subtracter -1)) ⟹  INCREMENT
```

```
(increment 7) ⟹  8
```

```
(apply-to-5 (create-subtracter 3)) ⟹  2
```

```
((apply-to-5 create-subtracter) 3) ⟹  -2
```

The final property of first-class procedures – namely, that they may be used as elements of compound data structures – was not within the scope of our investigation and will not be discussed further.

As a concluding example, we present a procedure more elaborate than any used in our interview; we include it here to provide a brief illustration of the power of the first-class procedure concept. Our example, `derivative`, takes one argument (a procedure), and returns as its result the procedure corresponding to the derivative of the argument:

```
(define (derivative f)
  (lambda (x)
    (/ (- (f (+ x 0.0001))
          (f x))
       0.0001))
  )
```

Programmers with experience in other languages will recognize how difficult it would be to implement `derivative` without first-class procedures. Using the `derivative` procedure is straightforward:

```
(define double (derivative (lambda (x) (* x x)))) ⟹ DOUBLE

(double 5) ⟹ 10.

((derivative double) 5) ⟹ 2.
```

3. Methodology

3.1 Subjects

The subjects in the study were 16 MIT undergraduates enrolled in MIT's introductory computer-science course (6.001). A sign-up sheet was placed in the course laboratory, and students were selected randomly from among those who signed up. All the subjects had some programming experience prior to the course.[5] We conducted the interviews during the fifth and sixth weeks of the semester; first-class procedures had been introduced during the second week of the course. By the time of the interview, all students had completed a laboratory problem set that made heavy use of first-class procedures.

3.2 Task

In each interview, we provided the subject with a written sequence of Scheme expressions. We instructed the subject to evaluate each expression in order and to write his[6] response (as well as any scratch notes) below the expression. The subject was informed that some expressions might result in an error message. We encouraged the subject to talk about the rationale behind his answers. On occasion, we asked additional questions or requested that the subject elaborate on an answer. During the interview, the subject had the opportunity to review and rethink previous answers. We told the subject that answers would not be provided during the interview itself, but offered to provide an informal tutorial at the completion of the interview. The Appendix includes the complete sequence of Scheme expressions used in the interviews.

Two of the authors were present at each interview. Our data for each interview included: a tape recording of the interview, the subject's written responses, and our own written notes. (One tape recording was lost due to equipment failure.)

---

[5] All had programmed in BASIC, and several had programmed in Pascal (6), Fortran (5), C (5), and Logo (3). A few listed other programming languages as well.

[6] We use the masculine pronoun for both male and female subjects.

4. Analysis of Results

In this section, we first present a framework for understanding the subjects' responses. We then present a series of extended examples to support that framework. Finally, we discuss some of the issues raised by our results.

4.1 A Naive Ontology of Procedures

Although student responses varied over a wide range, most subjects seemed to share a common mental map of procedures. This mental map, while consistent among the subjects, is seriously at odds with the semantics of Scheme.

As described in Section 2, Scheme procedures are properly categorized as first-class objects. Of course, each type of object has its own special properties: number objects can be added together, procedure objects can be applied to arguments, and so on. But all first-class objects share the four "first-class properties." Figure 2 illustrates this "correct" ontology of Scheme objects.

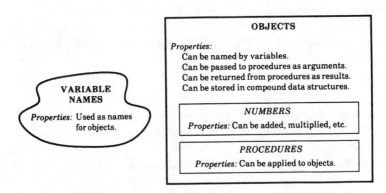

Figure 2: The "correct" ontology for Scheme objects.

Although a few of the subjects viewed procedures in this way, the majority seemed to categorize procedures very differently. Most important, students ascribed to procedures two essential traits:

Activity. The subjects tended to view procedures as the active manipulators of passive data (such as numbers). They associated activity with several aspects of a procedure call: finding and evaluating arguments, working to compute a result, and actually returning the result. Even when procedures were not in the operator position of a procedure call, subjects commonly viewed them not as static data structures, but as bundled up "computational energy" waiting to be unleashed.

Incompleteness. Subjects commonly saw procedures as incomplete entities that needed "additional parts" before they could be successfully used. The missing parts were usually the formal parameters of the procedure or other variables used within the body of the procedure. On occasion, subjects also regarded the parentheses that specify a Scheme procedure call as parts required to "complete" a procedure. As the examples in Section 4.2 illustrate, subjects often had problems with procedures that they viewed as having too few or too many parts.

We distinguish between these two properties mainly for the sake of exposition. In practice these properties blur together. Indeed, the act of finding and using missing parts is a main component of a procedure's activity. Again and again, subjects referred to a procedure "needing," "wanting," "expecting," "demanding," and "requiring" its arguments. A classic example is Subject 14's statement that he thought of "lambda as like a hungry monster that wants food." There are clear traces here of both activity and incompleteness.

The focus on activity and incompleteness seemed to lead students to associate procedures more with the processes they describe rather than with the objects they are. Indeed, many students placed procedures in a category separate from other objects, viewing procedures as a different sort of thing – or, perhaps, not as a "thing" at all.

We can gain some insight into what the students thought procedures *are* by looking at what they said procedures are *not*: they are *not* objects, *not* values, *not* variables. Consider the following quotes, each made by a different subject:

> Junk is a bound variable, it's not a procedure. [Subject 3]
> B has a value rather than being a procedure. [Subject 9]
> A is not a procedure, it is just a thing. [Subject 10]
> What-not is really not a procedure – it's just a name, a variable name. [Subject 13]
> I often get tripped up whether these are procedures or variables [Subject 15]

Statements like these could be slips of the tongue, or simply loose use of terminology. But such comments were so common in the interviews that we believe they provide evidence of a faulty model of procedures, a model in which procedures and their names are fundamentally different from other objects and the variables that name them.[7]

Even subjects who had some sense of procedures as objects tended to view them as less "object-like" than numbers. One subject [Subject 5], for example, described an "abstraction" hierarchy among objects. In his view, numbers are the "most primitive objects." Accordingly, he described sub-1 (bound to a procedure) as "much more of an abstraction" than b (which he saw as bound to the expression (+ 2 3)). In turn, b was more abstract than a (bound to 1), since "you're setting [a] actually equal to a value."

The salient features of the students' naive ontology are captured in Figure 3. The figure depicts procedures as active, incomplete entities that comprise a class distinct from other Scheme objects.

The naive ontology in Figure 3 reflects the subjects' reliance on functional, as opposed to structural, models *(7)*. That is, the subjects were much more concerned

---

[7] As mentioned before, procedures *are* different than other objects in some ways. For example, procedures, unlike numbers, can be applied to arguments. But most subjects see the differences as more fundamental.

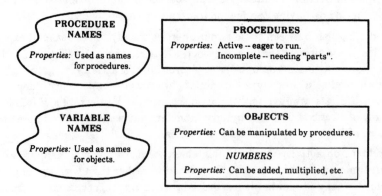

Figure 3: A "naive" ontology for Scheme objects.

with what procedures *do* or how they are *used*, rather than with what they are or the mechanism by which they work. While functional models can be a powerful approach for reasoning about programs, the examples below show how they can lead to serious misconceptions in the absence of a robust structural understanding.

4.2 Extended Examples

This section probes the naive ontology more deeply by focusing on several specific expressions from the interviews.

4.2.1 Decrement

Early in the interviews, we defined b and decrement as follows:

```
(define b (+ 2 3))
(define (decrement x) (- x 1))
```

Then we asked subjects to evaluate three expressions:

```
(decrement b)
b
decrement
```

All 16 students gave the correct response (namely, 4) for (decrement b), and 15 students gave the correct response (5) for b.[8] But subjects had more trouble evaluating decrement alone. Four subjects – at least as their first response[9] – said that decrement would return an error (when, in fact, it returns a procedure object, with printed representation [COMPOUND-PROCEDURE DECREMENT]).

---

[8] One student fell into the trap of thinking that evaluation of (decrement b) would change the value of b.

[9] One subject later changed his answer.

The responses of these four students exhibit many aspects of the naive ontology. All four attributed the error to a lack of arguments for decrement; they interpreted decrement as the name of a procedure that must be applied, rather than the name of an object that can be returned. The notions of "activity" and "incompleteness" were evident in their reasoning. Subject 13, for example, explained: "[Decrement] has no arguments to evaluate, nothing to evaluate." Subject 1 used similar reasoning: "You're just calling decrement and you're not giving the arguments with it . . . because decrement is a procedure which requires an argument."

Significantly, several students who gave the *correct* answer for the evaluation of decrement revealed in their explanations that they, too, viewed the evaluation of decrement as fundamentally different from the evaluation of b. In fact, many of them did not see the question as a matter of evaluating decrement at all.

As Subject 15 explained: "You haven't asked it to evaluate [decrement]. You've just asked it about decrement, you haven't asked it to evaluate it or anything." Similarly, Subject 5 explained: "It doesn't return a value, it just returns that it is a procedure. So this doesn't evaluate an expression. It more just confirms the fact that it is a procedure."

In their laboratory experience with the Scheme interpreter, these students had no doubt seen that evaluating a "naked" procedure name like decrement gives a printed result of the form [COMPOUND-PROCEDURE *name*]. But since they did not view procedures as objects, they did not see this phenomenon as the evaluation of a name. Rather than modifying their mental map of procedures to explain this behavior, they simply inferred that the interpreter had a special-case rule for handling naked procedure names — something like, "Inform the user that this is the name of a procedure."

Subjects gave similar responses to the three other examples of naked procedures in the interview (see sub-1, thing, and stuff in the Appendix). In each case, between 3 and 6 students expected the naked procedure to return an error, explaining that procedures need arguments and/or parentheses to be meaningful.

4.2.2 Apply-to-5 and Create-Subtracter

The decrement example highlighted students' difficulties with the first (i.e., naming) property of first-class procedures. Apply-to-5 and create-subtracter probed students' understanding of other first-class properties. These procedures were discussed in Section 2 of this paper; their definitions are repeated below.

```
(define (apply-to-5 f)
  (f 5))
```

```
(define (create-subtracter n)
  (lambda (x) (- x n)))
```

Apply-to-5 takes a procedure as an argument; create-subtracter returns a procedure as a result.

The following expression, using both of these procedures, is particularly useful for illuminating students' models of procedures:

```
(apply-to-5 create-subtracter)
```

The evaluation process for this expression may be summarized as follows: the `apply-to-5` procedure takes as its argument a procedure, and applies that procedure to the number 5. In this instance, the argument to `apply-to-5` is the `create-subtracter` procedure; thus, the `create-subtracter` procedure is applied to 5, and the result is a "subtract-5" procedure — i.e., a procedure which, when applied to some argument, will subtract 5 from that argument.

Although (`apply-to-5 create-subtracter`) is a perfectly valid Scheme expression, nine of the sixteen students stated – at least as their first response[10] – that the expression was in error; one remained unsure of the result. Here is a sampling of quotes from the interviews:

> I don't think this'll work... Because create-subtracter when you use, you have to have two arguments, I mean you have to have an argument to create-subtracter which is n... and then you have to apply it to some... I mean, you have to give it an argument for x... So I mean create-subtracter will only have one parameter in it, it needs another one. [Subject 1]

> ... with create-subtracter, you haven't given that any arguments. [Subject 2]

> Create-subtracter doesn't have an argument which it needs, cause when you defined it you define create-subtracter of n, so you don't have an argument. [Subject 4]

> I can't picture where the argument x comes from... it has the expression x minus 5, but it doesn't have any value for x, so it can't evaluate the expression minus x 5. [Subject 9]

> Probably an unbound variable... it's either x or n. [Subject 10]

> Possibly error... since n doesn't have a value. [Subject 12]

> I'm confused as to where both variables – the x or the n – are coming from... [Subject 13]

> ... I think that this would... give a wrong number of arguments error. Because create-subtracter needs one argument and isn't given one argument. [Subject 15]

These comments reveal a remarkable consistency. Eight of the ten students who had difficulty with the expression tended to focus on the "missing" argument values for either n or x. For some students (Subjects 2, 4, 12, and 15), the problem was that `create-subtracter` had not explicitly been given an argument. By fixating on the absence of an argument for `create-subtracter`, these students were unable to consider passing that procedure as an argument to `apply-to-5`. For others (Subjects 1 and 9) the problem was that, after `create-subtracter` was applied to 5, there was no value to be bound to x; these students were uncomfortable with the idea of a procedure being returned as the result of a procedure call. Still other students (Subjects 10 and 13) mentioned both "missing" variables in their discussion.

In all these cases, subjects focussed on finding the arguments for a procedure, regardless of whether the procedure is actually being invoked. This illustrates yet again that they saw procedures as active (always eager to run) and incomplete (requiring arguments in order to run).

---

[10] Two subjects later changed their answers.

Other examples involving `apply-to-5` and `create-subtracter` provide further evidence that subjects ascribed these traits to procedures. For example, consider the following expression:

```
(apply-to-5 (create-subtracter 3))
```

Since both `create-subtracter` and `apply-to-5` are actually being invoked and since all "parts" needed by both procedures are available, this expression was much less problematic for students than the previous one. In fact, 14 of the 16 subjects responded correctly that this expression would evaluate to 2.

A more complicated example is the following:

```
((apply-to-5 create-subtracter) 3)
```

Note how this contains (apply-to-5 create-subtracter) as a subexpression. As we have seen, this subexpression evaluates to a "subtract-5" procedure; the application of this procedure to 3 gives the number -2 as the result.

As with (apply-to-5 (create-subtracter 3)), the expression ((apply-to-5 create-subtracter) 3) supplies all "parts" needed to complete both procedures. Even though subjects had more difficulty with this expression, 11 of the 16 converged upon the correct answer. Interestingly, 4 of these 11 subjects had previously concluded that (apply-to-5 create-subtracter) was an error.

The fact that ((apply-to-5 create-subtracter) 3) had all its parts available presumably simplified reasoning about the expression. For a number of the subjects, a crucial step was noticing that both a 3 and a 5 were available to be used as arguments. Subject 13, who never converged on the correct answer, provided a particularly interesting example of reasoning by parts. His comments clearly show that he was keying in on the 3 and the 5 as the relevant parts to match to the arguments n and x, but he wasn't sure whether the expression resulted in 2 or -2. It appears that his structural models were not well-developed enough to say which number corresponded to which variable.

4.2.3 Junk

The junk example proved especially troublesome for the subjects. Only four of the sixteen subjects were correct in their initial answers; two more eventually arrived at the correct answer. The example consists of two expressions:

```
(define junk ((lambda (y) (- 3 y)) 5))
```

```
(junk b)
```

where b has previously been bound to 5.[11]

---

[11] The use of 5 in the expression for defining junk was unfortunate because b is also bound to 5. During the interviews, we asked most subjects to consider scenarios where either the 5 or the value of b had been changed. This allowed us to distinguish between the two values in analyzing their protocols.

The first expression applies a "subtract-from-3" procedure to 5 and gives the name junk to the resulting number (i.e. -2). Thus, the first expression is equivalent to (define junk -2). The second expression tries to apply the object named by junk to the object named by b, and is thus equivalent to the expression (-2 5). Since -2 is a number, not a procedure, this attempted application results in an "application of a non-procedural object" error. This is a type error; the value of the first subexpression of a procedure call must be of type procedure.

Most subjects expressed confusion about the definition of junk. Indeed, the definition does not match the common patterns of definition generally encountered in the course. Nine students explicitly stated that junk was a procedure or function, and three more, while making no similar claim, clearly used junk as a procedure. Most probably, the presence of an explicit lambda led students to think that junk was a procedure.

A major source of students' confusion with (junk b) was the mismatch between the number of parts needed and the number of parts supplied. The procedure specified by the lambda takes only one argument, but there are two numbers available – the 5 in the definition of junk and the one specified by b. This confusion is clear in a number of the protocols:

I'm trying to figure out what this 5 does. [Subject 1]

I can't remember what the term 5 is supposed to do. [Subject 2]

Even if you put b in for y, this [the procedure specified by the lambda] is going to give you a number and just this other number [5] is standing right there, doing nothing. If junk does put this 5 in the junk definition, then you have this extraneous argument [b] here . . . [Subject 6]

And if you say the junk of 10 [if the value of b were 10], then my first thought would be to subtract 10 from 3, but then I don't really know what you do with the 5, but you can't really get rid of the 5, because it's there . . . [Subject 13]

I really don't know what the 5 is doing out there. [Subject 12]

I don't know what the 5 is for, exactly. [Subject 15]

As is evident from the above quotes, the "extra" 5 in the definition of junk was disconcerting for many students. The subjects displayed a great amount of inventiveness in circumventing the "mismatch in number of parts" impasse. Four students viewed junk as a procedure whose argument had been already "supplied", but which had not been properly activated. For them, junk could be activated by a pair of parentheses (Scheme's method of procedure invocation). Thus, these students claimed that (junk) evaluated to -2, and (junk b) gave an error (usually a "wrong number of arguments" error). For example, Subject 5 went so far as to claim (correctly) that the definition was equivalent to (define junk -2), but reasoned later that junk "is a procedure of no arguments. There's a lambda in there, yes, but it's already being evaluated. You're already assigning it 5. It doesn't take any other arguments."

In another set of interpretations, eight subjects treated junk — at least at one point — as a procedure of one argument. In these interpretations, calling junk on b was an appropriate use of the procedure. These subjects handled the problem of "too many parts" in a variety of ways. One heuristic was to ignore the "extra" information. Thus, two subjects chose to disregard the 5 in the definition of junk, and treated junk as simply the procedure specified by the lambda expression. Another treated 5 as the argument to the procedure specified by the lambda expression regardless of what the value of b was.

Four subjects did not ignore the "extra" information, and found a way to use both the value of b and the 5 in the definition of junk. One of these four saw the lambda expression and the 5 in the junk definition as the two elements of a sequential expression. The lambda expression was applied to the value of b, but the result of this application was ignored, and the 5 (the second element of the sequence) was always returned.[12] The remaining three subjects also applied the procedure specified by the lambda expression to the value of b, but further tried to apply the returned object (presumably a number) to the 5. Although this approach ultimately leads to the right kind of error (the object being applied to 5 is a number, not a procedure), it is for altogether the wrong reasons.

4.3 Discussion

The analysis of the above examples admittedly ignores some subtleties in the subjects' reasoning. Many subjects displayed uncertainty about their answers. They often altered answers to particular expressions, and their reasoning about procedures commonly evolved during the course of their interviews.

Nevertheless, when the students used incorrect reasoning, there was a marked consistency in the nature — and even wording — of their explanations. The commonality is particularly striking considering that these explanations were *wrong*. The students were not mimicking the reasoning presented by an instructor or textbook; they were responding to the expression with a rationale of their own creation. We can only conclude that the difficulty in seeing a procedure as an object is both widespread and (at least to some degree) consistent in its symptoms.

This difficulty is indicative of the students' reliance on functional, rather than structural, reasoning in evaluating Scheme expressions. In the absence of a firm grasp of Scheme's objects and interpretation rules, subjects appealed to numerous special-case evaluation strategies. The decrement example — in which students expected the interpreter to treat "naked" procedure names using some informative *ad hoc* rule — is a clear case of this behavior. (This phenomenon is not unlike what Pea *(8)* refers to as the "conversational metaphor" in novices' interactions with interpreted languages.)

Finally, it should be noted that the central concerns of many other programming studies, though important, are not at issue in these examples. The students were *not* required to assimilate or "chunk" large sections of code; no expression was longer than two lines, and students never needed to look back at more than two definitions to evaluate an expression. Thus, the sample expressions placed no burden on the students' memorization skills, nor did they require recourse to higher-order notions of goals or plans [cf. *(9)*, *(10)*, *(11)*]. Moreover, none of the procedures had misleading names; many of the names (such as apply-to-5 and

---

[12] The subjects were apparently making use of the fact that the value of a sequence of expressions in Scheme is the value of the last expression in the sequence.

create-subtracter) are, in fact, suggestive of the procedures' purposes. Thus, no expression violated any implicit rules of programming etiquette [cf. *(12)*, *(13)*].

Rather, our questions were designed to focus on students' ontologies of procedures. For the novice, a firm grasp of the nature of the objects in a programming language is arguably a prerequisite to mastering higher-level programming techniques. Exploring how students view objects can thus provide an important window into how they learn and understand programming.

5. Pedagogical and Language Design Issues

One of the important benefits of studying the learnability of programming languages is that such investigation can lead to improvements in the teaching and design of programming languages. Our results suggest some possible avenues of exploration in these areas.

At the very least, teachers of Scheme (and presumably other languages with first-class procedures) should be aware of the special difficulties inherent in the first-class procedure concept. For example, upon introducing the concept of a procedure as argument, teachers might lay particular emphasis on the fact that the argument value, although a procedure, is not "looking for" any arguments. In addition, we noticed that the interview format (a sequence of expressions covering a broad range of uses of procedures) forced students to reconsider their models in the interest of consistency. This format could be profitably used in instruction.

In the interviews, we observed that students' textual and graphical representations of procedures were flawed — or non-existent. This is hardly surprising given that the computer's printed representation is the rather abstruse [COMPOUND-PROCEDURE *name*], and the MIT course does not provide an explicit representation for procedure objects until later in the course. It is difficult to view something as an object if you don't have a way to envision it. Thus, one possible teaching strategy would be to provide, early in the course, an abstract representation for procedures that stresses their "object-like" character; this representation could then be made more concrete and realistic over time.

The procedure-representation problem could also be addressed through changes in language design (or perhaps more accurately, language interface design). MIT Scheme's printed representation is unhelpful for novices striving to understand what a procedure might be. It would be worthwhile to explore some alternative printed representations of procedures. For example, a procedure might be displayed as a picture of a script or recipe; these are images which we ourselves use in explaining the nature of procedures [cf. *(14)*, *(15)*].

The existence of two syntaxes for defining procedures is another potential source of confusion, inasmuch as it perpetuates the mistaken distinction between procedures and other objects. Although removing the procedure-specific form from the language might be too radical a change, programming courses could stress the more general form, at least in the beginning of the course.

Further, we believe that **define** expressions could return more informative results.[13] In the MIT version of Scheme, `define` expressions return the name being bound. It would be more useful if Scheme printed some representation of both the name and the object to which it is bound. Such a representation would underscore that names are bound to procedures in the same way that they are bound to all other first-class objects.

6. Future Research

In conclusion, we suggest a number of directions for future research:

Generality of the results. We believe that the results of this study are meaningful for any language with first-class procedures, but this issue should be resolved empirically. In other words, how "Scheme-specific" are our results? Do students' difficulties with first-class procedures transcend the particular language in which they are working?

Procedures in other domains. Do mathematics students dealing with concepts such as "groups of operators" or "function spaces" experience the same problems as students of Scheme? Is there any transfer between domains – that is, after students have mastered the concept of first-class procedures in Scheme, can they transfer the concept to work in mathematics?

Origins. What are the origins of the naive ontology of procedures? Is the ontology related to linguistic structures (e.g. noun/verb distinctions) in English? Is it related to experience with other programming languages?

Finer-grained models. How do students view the first position of a procedure-call expression? In what ways do students see "naked" procedure names as different from names bound to other objects? How do variations in Scheme syntax affect students' ontological models?

Other first-class objects. What difficulties do students have in understanding languages in which other objects, such as environments and continuations, are first-class?

Acknowledgments

We would like to thank Andy diSessa, Hal Abelson, Gerry Sussman, and Roy Pea for providing suggestions and advice during the course of the study. We'd also like to thank Louis Braida and Rod Brooks for helping us to obtain subjects from their course.

The sole criterion used in listing the authors' names was alphabetical order.

---

[13] Since defining is done for effect rather than value, its return value is arbitrary in terms of program semantics.

References

1. Abelson, Harold and Sussman, Gerald Jay with Sussman, Julie. *Structure and Interpretation of Computer Programs*. MIT Press, 1985.

2. Steele, Guy Lewis, Jr. and Sussman, Gerald Jay. *Lambda: the Ultimate Imperative*. AI Memo 353, MIT AI Lab (1976).

3. Atkinson, Malcolm P. and Morrison, Ronald. *Procedures as Persistent Data Objects*. ACM Transactions on Programming Languages and Systems, 7:4, October 1985.

4. Eisenberg, Michael. *Programming in Scheme: an Introduction*. Scientific Press, 1988 (in preparation).

5. Rees, Jonathan and Clinger, William (eds.). *Revised³ Report on the Algorithmic Language Scheme*. ACM Sigplan Notices, 21:12, December 1986.

6. Stoy, Joseph S. *Denotational Semantics: The Scott-Strachey Approach to Programming Language Theory*. MIT Press, 1977.

7. diSessa, Andrea. *Models of Computation*. In *User Centered System Design*, Norman, Donald and Draper, Stephen, eds. Lawrence Erlbaum, 1986.

8. Pea, Roy. *Language-Independent Conceptual "Bugs" in Novice Programming*. J. Educational Computing Research, 2:1 1986.

9. Anderson, John R. and Jeffries, Robin. *Novice LISP Errors: Undetected Losses of Information from Working Memory*. Human-Computer Interaction, 1:2 (1985) 107-131.

10. Rist, Robert S. *Plans in Programming: Definition, Demonstration and Development*. In *Empirical Studies of Programmers*, Soloway, E. and Iyengar, S. (eds.). Ablex, 1986.

11. Spohrer, James C.; Soloway, Elliot; and Pope, Edgar. *A Goal/Plan Analysis of Buggy Pascal Programs*. Human-Computer Interaction, 1:2 (1985) 163-207.

12. Soloway, Elliot; Ehrlich, Kate; and Black, John. *Beyond Numbers: Don't Ask "How Many"... Ask Why*. In *Human Factors in Computing Systems*, CHI'83 Conference Proceedings, 1983.

13. Soloway, Elliot and Ehrlich, Kate. *Empirical Studies of Programming Knowledge*. IEEE Transactions on Software Engineering, Sept. 1984.

14. Turbak, Franklyn. *Grasp: a Visible and Manipulable Model for Procedural Programs*. Master's Thesis, MIT 1986.

15. Eisenberg, Michael. *Bochser: an Integrated Scheme Programming System*. MIT Laboratory for Computer Science Technical Report 349, October 1985.

Appendix

This appendix presents the expressions used in the interviews. The expressions are to be treated as if they were evaluated one after the other in a single session with the Scheme interpreter. Subjects were asked to describe the value returned by each expression; they were informed that some expressions might lead to errors. Whenever a subject said that an expression would lead to an error, we asked him to describe the type of error; in certain cases, we also asked the subject to generate a similar expression that would not give an error.

The results of evaluating the expressions are also provided below (these, of course, were not presented to subjects).

```
(define a 1)  ⟹  A

a ⟹ 1

(define b (+ 2 3))  ⟹  B

b ⟹ 5

(- b 1) ⟹ 4

(define c b)  ⟹  C

c ⟹ 5

(define d (- b 1))  ⟹  D

d ⟹ 4

(b + 3)  ⟹  Error! Object being applied is not a procedure: 5

(define (square x)
   (* x x))          ⟹  SQUARE

(square b)  ⟹  25

b ⟹ 5

(define (mul-by-self) square)  ⟹  MUL-BY-SELF

(mul-by-self 4)  ⟹  Error! Wrong number of arguments: 1

(define (decrement x)
   (- x 1))           ⟹  DECREMENT

(decrement b)  ⟹  4

b ⟹ 5

decrement  ⟹  [COMPOUND-PROCEDURE DECREMENT]
```

```
(define sub-1 decrement) ⟹  SUB-1

(sub-1 b) ⟹  4

sub-1 ⟹  [COMPOUND-PROCEDURE DECREMENT]

(define (what-not x) 1) ⟹  WHAT-NOT

(what-not) ⟹  Error! Wrong number of arguments: 0

(define (thing) (+ 4 b)) ⟹  THING

thing ⟹  [COMPOUND-PROCEDURE THING]

(thing) ⟹  9

(define stuff (lambda (x) (/ x 3))) ⟹  STUFF

stuff ⟹  [COMPOUND-PROCEDURE STUFF]

(stuff b) ⟹  1.66666

(define junk ((lambda (y) (- 3 y)) 5)) ⟹  JUNK

(junk b) ⟹  Error! Object being applied is not a procedure: -2.

(define something (lambda () (- 9 b))) ⟹  SOMETHING

(something 6) ⟹  Error! Wrong number of arguments: 1

(define (apply-to-5 f)
  (f 5))                  ⟹  APPLY-TO-5

; Give an example of how you would use APPLY-TO-5

(define (create-subtracter n)
  (lambda (x) (- x n)))        ⟹  CREATE-SUBTRACTER

; Give an example of how you would use CREATE-SUBTRACTER

(apply-to-5 create-subtracter) ⟹  [COMPOUND-PROCEDURE 12430420]

(create-subtracter apply-to-5) ⟹  [COMPOUND-PROCEDURE 12437452]

(apply-to-5 (create-subtracter 3)) ⟹  2

((apply-to-5 create-subtracter) 3) ⟹  -2

(((apply-to-5 create-subtracter) 3) 9) ⟹  Error! Object being applied
  is not a procedure: -2
```

CHAPTER 3

Mental Representations of Programs for Student and Professional Programmers

Robert W. Holt
Deborah A. Boehm-Davis
George Mason University
Psychology Department
Fairfax, VA 22030

Alan C. Schultz
Naval Research Laboratory
Navy Center for Applied Research in
Artificial Intelligence
Washington, D.C.

ABSTRACT

This research examined programmers' cognitive representations of software. In this study, student and professional programmers were asked to make either simple or complex modifications to three different programs that had been generated using each of three different design methodologies: in-line code, functional decomposition, and a form of object-oriented design. The programmers' mental models of the programs they had studied were elicited and then scored in several different ways. The results suggest that problem structure, problem type, and ease of modification may affect the mental models formed. Specifically, the data suggest that while the mental models of professional programmers were affected primarily by modification difficulty, the mental models of student programmers were primarily affected by the structure and content of the programs. Performance differences between the two groups of programmers were small because the experience variables which were most strongly related to performance were nearly equal in the two groups, and the experience variables which were very different between the two groups were not related to performance. Across the two groups, the primary aspect of the mental model which was correlated with performance variables was the width or breadth of the mental model structure. The implications of the results for the application of program design methodologies are discussed.

INTRODUCTION

In order to understand and optimize the process of programming, we must consider the way in which knowledge about a computer program is represented cognitively, and the way in which programmers use this cognitive representation. One approach to understanding the programmer's knowledge about a program is to hypothesize that the programmer forms a mental model about the structure and functions of the program.

Mental models. A number of investigators (e.g. Johnson-Laird (1)) have argued that the formation and use of mental models is critical to understanding complex cognition. More specifically, several authors have used the mental models approach to understanding the functioning of devices such as computers or calculators. Young (2) analyzed the adequacy of two different types of mental models (the implied register models and task/action mapping models) to account for the functioning of different types of calculators. Saja (3) suggested that mental models are developed by users of interactive computer systems. Saja further hypothesized that these mental models would be used to set expectations for system performance and guide system-relevant behavior. Mac an Airchinnigh (4) presented a formalization of the concept of user mental models for interactive computer systems that uses Sowa's (5) conceptual graph notation as an intermediate representation between the user's mental model and a computable form of the mental model. Clearly, however, the types of mental models developed in interaction with simple computational devices like a calculator may differ from mental models developed in interaction with complex programs or operating systems. Carroll (6) and Rouse and Morris (7) reviewed a variety of types of mental models in different domains and discussed empirical evidence on the effects of mental models. These reviews illustrate the lack of consensus on a definition of mental models.

Contents of Mental Models. The basic facets of a cognitive representation or knowledge structure are the fundamental elements or entities of which the structure is composed and the relationships among those fundamental elements (Sowa (5)). There are different views, however, on what the fundamental elements and relationships are for the mental models representing programmers' knowledge of computer programs.

Weiser (8) has hypothesized that programmers cognitively deal with segments of programs that are comprised of either contiguous lines of code or of functionally related lines of code. These functional units deal with the same set of variables, forming a mini-program which Weiser calls a program "slice". Recall of programmers for debugged programs indicated that they had stored both chunks of contiguous lines of code and program slices. Thus the fundamental elements may represent either a functional unit such as a program slice or a contiguous block of code.

Adelson (9) studied the recall of both novice and expert programmers for lines of three small computer programs. The clustered recall of the novices suggested that they were clustering lines of code from all three programs on the basis of syntactic categories such as "all IF statements". Experts, on the other hand, used the functional units of the three programs to cluster their recall of the lines of code. Since these three programs contained only 16 lines of code, the size of these programs corresponded to the size of the slices discussed by Weiser (8).

The results for expert programmers in these two studies using small programs are consistent in indicating some functionally-based organization of the program material on the part of professional programmers. However, Adelson's results for novice programmers suggest that syntactic classification can also be used for organizing program material, and Weiser's results suggest that simple contiguity can also be used for organizing program material.

For larger programs there is also conflicting evidence on the contents of the programmers' mental models. Letovsky (10) had 6 professional programmers study a 250-line interactive database program and found evidence that programmers were constructing a multi-layered network based on the goals and functions of the program. Pennington (11), however, had 20 COBOL and 20 FORTRAN programmers study a 200-line industrial plant specification program and found that the summary statements were mostly procedural in nature rather than concerning the functioning and data flow of the program. Since there is little agreement on the specific contents of the mental models of programmers, the procedure used in this study allowed programmers to specify the contents and the structure of their mental representations of the program.

Structure of mental models. The structure organizing the basic elements of program comprehension is generally supposed to be a basic hierarchical structure of larger, more abstract elements subsuming lower-level, more detailed elements (Shneiderman & Mayer (12), Basili and Mills (13)). Besides the inclusion relationship that generates a hierarchical structure, other types of relationships are possible among program chunks, such as causal relationships between a computational subroutine and an I/O subroutine that is invoked by it. Letovsky (10) proposed that the basic mental model contained a top-level specifications layer containing the most general goals of the program which was connected by subgoal or purpose links to lower levels of goals, finally ending in the implementation layer which contained explicit, complete descriptions of the specific actions and data structures used by the program.

Several attempts at describing cognitive representation rely on schema theory as their basic framework (e.g. Boehm-Davis (14)). Within this framework, it is thought that with programming expertise, programmers come to have plans, templates, or schemata, representing rules of programming discourse, language-independent algorithms, and language-dependent rules (Detienne (15); Soloway & Ehrlich (16)). Each of these aspects of programmer knowledge may affect the construction of the mental model. The resulting mental model would still, however, have a definite structure among basic cognitive elements or components of some type.

Since several authors have emphasized a hierarchical structure, the scoring of the mental model information in this study emphasized the following aspects of the structure of the mental models: (a) the number of distinct components specified by the programmer, (b) the number of relationships specified among these components, (c) the height or maximum depth of the structure, (d) the width or maximum branching of the structure, and (e) the connectedness of the elicited structure.

Expert vs. Novice programmers. The more extensive knowledge of more experienced programmers would be apt to create qualitatively different mental models compared to less experienced programmers. Cooke and Schvaneveldt (17) used a pathfinder analysis of psychological distance estimates among generic computer programming terms for naive, novice, intermediate, and expert programmers. They found qualitative changes in the cognitive structures linking these terms as the degree of expertise increased. In comparing expert vs. novice programmers, however, the fundamental question is whether the increased knowledge base and qualitatively different mental models of the expert programmers will give positive transfer or negative transfer to the particular programming task at hand. Clearly the general expectation is that the increased knowledge repertoire and qualitatively better mental models of expert programmers will facilitate the programming process. Kieras and Bovair (18) found that providing operators with a mental model of a moderately complex device facilitated performance. Borgman (19), using an online computer catalog task, found a trend for model-trained subjects to perform slightly better and have a significant superiority in search-state transitions. If these results apply to naturally-evolved mental models of programmers dealing with a computer program, positive transfer would be expected and the performance of experts should exceed that of novices.

Such positive transfer may not always be the case, however. Intuitively, transfer of training from procedural languages like PASCAL to applicative languages such as LISP might be negative. Adelson (20) found that experts tended to form abstract representations of a computer program and were worse in answering concrete questions than novices who tended to form concrete representations of the functions of a computer program. The modification tasks used in this study required concrete modifications of the functions of the programs. Such modifications might cause a negative transfer with the abstract mental models of the professionals and decrease their performance relative to novices. However, Adelson also found that when experts were given an appropriate concrete set they could perform equally well with novices. Thus, if the experts respond to the modification task with a concrete set, their performance may be equal or superior to novices.

The questions derived from the above considerations for this study were (a) would the mental models of the experts and novices be significantly different in any respect, (b) would the mental models of the experts and novices be differentially influenced by the structure and content of the program or the difficulty of the modification to be made to the program, and (c) would the differences between the experts and novices produce positive or negative differences in performance between these two groups.

Study Design. Two types of programmers were examined in this study. Expert programmers were professional programmers proficient in PASCAL solicited from commercial programming jobs. Novice programmers were student programmers proficient in PASCAL solicited from the university. Relevant background information focusing on the variety of experience of both professional and student programmers was elicited by a questionnaire.

The participants were given programs which had been created using each of three design approaches. The three program design forms were straight serial structure (in-line code), structure emphasizing functional units of the program (functional decomposition), and structure emphasizing larger object-oriented modules of the program (object-oriented). These program structures were used to write programs for each of three problems. The problems involved a real-time response system, a database system with files, and a program constructing large linked-list data structures. The programmers were presented with easy or difficult modifications to be made to the functioning of each program and performance was measured in terms of the amount of time required to make those modifications and in terms of the number of editing cycles and editor transactions required to successfully make the modification. The mental models of the programmers were examined by having the programmers write down as many relevant components or aspects of the program as possible and then having them arrange these components and specify the relations among these components. Other reactions of the programmers to the programs were elicited by having the programmers systematically rate each program on several rating scales reflecting relevant aspects of the program for the modification task (e.g. ease of understanding program).

<u>Hypotheses</u>

(1) Are professional programmmers equal or not equal to the student programmers in terms of the variety of their background, the mental models they construct, their reactions to the programs, and their performance in modifying the programs.

(2) For the professional group of programmers, does the structure of the program, program content, or difficulty of the modification task affect the mental models of the programmers or their reactions to the programs.

(3) For the student group of programmers, does the structure of the program, program content, or difficulty of the modification task affect the mental models of the programmers or their reactions to the programs.

(4) For both professionals and students, what is the effect of:

  (4a) Variety of background experience on performance
  (4b) Difficulty of modification on performance
  (4c) Mental Models on performance
  (4d) Reactions to the program on performance

METHOD

<u>Materials</u>

Problems. Three experimental problems and one practice problem were used in this experiment. The three experimental problems involved a military address system, a host-at-sea buoy system, and a student transactions list; all were written in PASCAL.

The military address system maintained a data base of names and postal addresses. From this data base, subsets of names, addresses, and ranks could be drawn according to specified criteria and printed according to a specified format. The host-at-sea problem involved providing navigation and weather data to air and ship traffic at sea. In this problem, buoys are deployed to collect wind, temperature, and location data and they broadcast summaries of this information to passing vessels and aircraft when requested to do so. The student transactions list problem involved storing and maintaining information about students through a transaction file using the data structure of a linked list.

Program form. Each experimental problem was programmed in three basic forms: in-line code, functional decomposition, and object-oriented. The lengths of the resulting nine experimental programs are given in Table 1. The in-line code had no function or procedure calls; the PASCAL top-level definition was the entire program. These programs were generated by expanding all procedure and function calls in line. Although this technique generates unstructured code, there were some advantages which must be noted. Most notably, the number of variables in the program as a whole was greatly reduced, and this might in some cases lead to less confusion than would interpreting formal and actual parameters, etc.

The functionally decomposed code was derived by decomposing the program specifications into separate functions. These functions were further decomposed until each module contained one coherent function of the program.

The object-oriented version of the code attempted to capture the aspects of object-oriented design that focus on the modularity of the code. In essence, the information hiding and abstraction concepts were simulated by using commenting and modularization techniques. For each defined object, all function calls in the object that were available to other objects (visible) were specially named by concatenating the object name and the function name. All function calls that were not available to outside objects (invisible) did not include the object name and were nested within other functions so that they could not be used except by the enclosing function. In addition, data structures were insulated as much as possible by embedding them in functions that were considered invisible. Special function calls were created to manipulate these data structures. The net result was that objects could only alter the data structures of other objects in predefined ways, and could only alter them by sending a request to the object that owned that data structure.

Table 1

Length of programs by type of problem and program form. Length of each program is measured by the lines of code for that program, ignoring comment and documentation lines.

| | Type of Problem: | | |
Program form:	Host-at-Sea	Military Address	Transaction File
In-line	123	280	309
Function decomp.	162	312	223
Object-oriented	233	373	244

Modifications. Two modifications were constructed for each problem: a simple and a complex modification. The simple modification required changing the program in only one location in the code. The complex modification required changing the code in several locations.

Supplemental Materials. Each problem was accompanied by five types of supplemental materials: a program overview, a data dictionary, a program listing, and listings of the current and expected output from the program. The program overview contained the program requirements, a general description of the program design, and the modification to be performed for each program. The data dictionary included the variable names, an English description of the variables, and the data type for each variable. The program listing was a paper printout of the Pascal code which was identical to the code presented on the CRT screen. The listings of the current and expected output provided the programmers with the current output and the output expected from a correct run of the program; this allowed them to determine where they had gone wrong if their modification to the program did not run correctly.

Participants

The participants in this experiment were 36 programmers. Eighteen of the participants were professional programmers; eighteen of the programmers were upper-division computer science majors. Programmers were solicited through advertisements and they were paid for their participation in the research. All of the programmers had previous experience with Pascal.

Procedure

Experimental sessions were conducted on an IBM PC. Initially, the participants were given a half-hour training session in which they had to solve a sample problem. The experimenter also described the procedure for using the text editor to modify the programs during this session. This initial part of the session demonstrated the compiling and program-checking sequence. The participants were first asked to enter the changes from the problem discussed during the training session. This was done to familiarize them with the operation of the experimental system and its editor.

Following the practice program, three selected experimental programs were presented in a unique random order for each subject. These programs were selected in such a way that each programmer worked with a different problem with each of the three program forms (in-line, function, object-oriented). This selection process was counterbalanced over the entire sample of student or professional programmers such that the total frequencies of each of the 9 program content-form combinations was equal. Each programmer was either assigned all three easy modifications or all three difficult modifications for the three programs. Thus, the difficulty of the modification is a between-subjects variable.

An interactive data collection system recorded the participants' responses throughout the session. The system recorded each call for an editor command (e.g. ADD, CHANGE, LIST, or DELETE). From these, the overall time to modify and debug the programs was calculated by summing the times from the individual editing sessions; the number of errors made was also calculated. The time required for compiling, linking, and executing the programs was not included in these measures. The programmers were required to continue working on each program until it was completed successfully or until 1-1/2 hours had passed. They were allowed to take breaks between programs.

After successfully modifying the programs, the programmers completed a questionnaire about their previous programming experience. The information requested included detailed information on their familiarity with programming languages, operating systems, and program design methodologies. The participants were also asked about their educational background and the extent of their professional programming experience. Finally, they were asked to rate several aspects of the programs they had worked with (e.g., difficulty in recognizing program units, difficulty in finding information in the program, difficulty in working with the program).

Following this, the contents and structure of the programmers' mental models of all three programs were elicited by the experimental assistant. A free recall procedure was used to elicit as much of the mental content as possible. This procedure was loosely based on Buschke's (21) two dimensional grid procedure. First, the research assistant encouraged the programmer to recall as many components of the program as possible. These components could be based on program code structure, program functioning, or any other basis the programmer used to encode this information. Each component was written on a separate large index card. Next, the research assistant asked the programmer to specify all the relationships among these units by writing the relationships on small index cards and arranging the structure of the basic units and relationships to correspond to the programmer's mental representation of the structure of the program. These arrangements were recorded by having the experimental assistant number each card and either photograph the arrangement or draw a precise picture of the arrangement of the cards produced by the subject for each program.

These photographs or diagrams were later scored by one of the authors for the number of components, number of relationships, depth and width of the indicated structure. This scoring was done "blind" to the experimental condition of the subjects by separating all the packets of cards from the data folders and reconstructing the arrangement of the cards and scoring these arrangements without knowledge of the experimental condition of the participant. Depth was assessed as the longest chain of linked program segments while width was assessed as the largest number of branches in the structure. The overall degree of connectedness of the structure was calculated by comparing as a ratio the number of given relationships to the maximum number of possible relationships for the number of program components or segments specified. Thus, five variables reflect the mental models of the programmers: number of program segments or chunks, number of relationships, depth of structure, width of structure, and connectedness of structure.

RESULTS

Professional vs. Student programmers

The 18 professional and 18 student programmers in our sample were compared on variables measuring background experience, mental models, reactions to the programs, and average performance modifying the three programs.

Background variables. Professional programmers were slightly, but not significantly, superior to student programmers for four background variables: number of languages known, number of programs written across these languages, number of design methodologies known, and number of programs written across these design methodologies (see Table 2). Professional programmers were significantly superior to the student programmers in the number of operating systems they knew, the number of years they had been programming, and the number of years of post-secondary eduction they had. There were no significant differences for the other four variables; this may reflect the fact that the "student" programmers were advanced students in computer science with a wide variety of programming experience.

Table 2

Comparison of professional and student
programmers on background variables

	Professionals	Students
number of computer languages	6.61	5.44
index of programs per language	15.94	11.06
number of design methodologies used	2.50	2.33
index of programs per design methodology	6.89	4.65
number of operating systems used	5.28	2.78***
years of commercial programming	3.61	0.22***
years of post-secondary education	6.00	3.88**

*** $p < .001$
** $p < .01$

Mental Models variables. No significant differences were found between the professional and student programmers in the overall number of program segments or chunks recalled, number of relationships specified between these chunks, depth of recalled structure, width of recalled structure, and connectedness of recalled structure. Despite this lack of overall difference, the mental models of the two groups were differentially affected by other variables, such as program structure and content (discussed below).

Reactions to the programs. No significant differences were found between the professional and student programmers in their responses on whether the program format was too condensed or on the difficulty of finding information, recognizing program units, comprehending the program, or working with the program code. Once again, the professional and student programmers had an indistinguishable or equivalent pattern of responses to the programs with which they worked.

Performance variables. Overall analyses comparing performance of professional vs. student programmers were not significant. However, due to the strong relation between difficulty of modification and all aspects of performance, we re-analyzed the performance of professional and student programmers using the difficulty of the modification as a covariate. In these analyses of covariance on the performance variables, the average time to complete debugging was significantly different for professionals and students (F (1,33) = 5.59 , p = .024). That is, the difference of 33.3 minutes per problem for professionals vs. 40.2 minutes per problem for students was significant when the effects of simple vs. complex program modification were covaried out.

Professional Programmer Results

Mental models variables. The number of program segments or chunks recalled was significantly affected by the difficulty of the modification (F (1,17) = 6.57, p < .05). The complex modifications caused more chunks to be recalled (4.1) than the simple modifications (3.2).

The number of relationships was similarly affected by the difficulty of the modification (F (1,17) = 12.19, p < .01). The complex modifications caused more relationships to be specified among the program segments (3.1) than the simple modifications (2.0).

There was a trend for the depth of the recalled structure to be affected by the difficulty of the modification in the same way (F (1,17) = 3.32, p < .10). Again the simple modifications caused a less deep mental structure to be constructed (2.56 levels) than did the complex modifications (3.15 levels).

All of these findings are congruent with the principle that a more intense mental effort or a deeper level of processing leads to increasingly complex representation and recall of complex material such as a computer program.

There was a trend for the width of the recalled structure to be influenced by the nature of the modification in conjunction with the type of problem specified (F (2,17) = 3.00, p = .07). The width of the cognitive structure was particularly high for the complex modification of the host-at-sea program (2.33) compared to the width for the simple modification of this problem (1.11) or of any of the other problems.

Reactions to the Programs. For the professional programmers, the structure of the program and the content of the problem did not strongly affect the ratings of the programs made by the professional programmers. The one exception to this pattern is the effect of program structure on the difficulty of recognizing program units (F (2,24) = 3.47, p < .05). Professional programmers had more difficulty recognizing program units in the object-oriented programs (3.33) than in either the functionally decomposed programs (2.28) or the in-line code (2.11).

Student Programmer Results

Mental models variables. In contrast to the professional programmers, the mental representations of the students were not significantly affected by the difficulty of the modification. The student programmers were, however, influenced by the structure of the program.

The structure of the program significantly affected the number of program segments or chunks recalled by the student programmers (F (2,24) = 4.23, p < .05). Students recalled more segments or chunks from the functional (4.06) and object-oriented (4.11) programs than from the in-line code programs (3.22).

The structure of the program also significantly affected the number of relationships specified among the program segments (F (2,24) = 3.73, p < .05). Students specified more relationships among the segments recalled from the functional (2.94) and object-oriented (2.89) programs than from the in-line code programs (2.11).

Program structure also affected the connectivity of the structure recalled by the student programmers (F (2,24) = 3.30, p = .05). Functionally decomposed programs (.535) and object-oriented (.567) programs had a lower average connectedness than the in-line code (.711). Interpreting all three of these results together, it would appear that the student programmers formed a smaller but more tightly connected view of the in-line programs than either of the two forms of structured programs. This is consistent with the view that the lack of structure in the in-line code forced the programmers to build their own coherent cognitive structure as they read through and attempted to comprehend the program.

The nature of the problem also apparently influenced the mental representations of the student programmers. That is, the joint effect of the program content and the nature of the modification that had to be made to the program seemed to affect the number of program segments recalled (F (2,24) = 2.74, p < .10) and the depth of the structure recalled (F = 3.82, p < .05). The pattern for the mean differences in these interactions are similar and are given in Tables 3 and 4. For simple modifications, there was no difference in the number of segments recalled or in depth of structure across the three problems. This is congruent with the idea that simple modifications require only superficial knowledge of the program that does not lead to development of a complex mental structure. For complex modifications, the size and depth of the mental structure constructed while working with the programs depended jointly on the nature of the problem and the nature of the modification.

Table 3

Interaction between type of problem and
difficulty of modification on the
number of program segments recalled
by student programmers.

	Type of Problem:		
Modification:	Host-at-Sea	Military Address	Transaction File
Simple	4.00	4.00	3.89
Complex	2.78	3.89	4.22

Table 4

Interaction between type of problem and
difficulty of modification on the
depth of program structure recalled
by student programmers.

	Type of Problem:		
Modification:	Host-at-Sea	Military Address	Transaction File
Simple	3.11	3.11	3.00
Complex	2.33	3.67	3.67

Reactions to the programs. The structure of the program significantly affected the difficulty of finding information in the program (F (2,24) = 3.72, p < .05), the difficulty in recognizing units in the program (F (2,24) = 3.73, p < .05), and the difficulty in working with the program (F (2,24) = 3.07, p < .10). For finding information, the student programmers felt that the object-oriented program was most difficult (3.17), while both the in-line code (2.44), and the functionally decomposed program were less difficult (2.11). For recognizing program units, the students also felt that it was more difficult in the object-oriented program (3.56) than in either the in-line code (2.50) or the functionally decomposed program (2.39). The same trend was obtained in the ratings of the difficulty in working with the program. Students felt it was more difficult to work with the object-oriented code (3.06) than either the in-line code (2.33) or the functionally decomposed program (2.11). Thus, all these results suggest that something about the implementation of the object-oriented code made it more difficult to use for making the modifications. Possibly this difficulty is due to the increased overhead in extra declarations etc. for the object modules, or possibly the object modules developed for our programs did not match the students' expectations.

The content of the problems also significantly affected the difficulty of finding information in the program (F (2,24) = 5.30, p < .05). For the difficulty of finding information, the host-at-sea problem was most difficult (3.17), the student transactions problem was moderately difficult (2.67), and the military address problem was least difficult (1.89). Thus, both the program structure and the program content were found to affect the difficulty of finding information in a program. Program structure also affected the perceived difficulty in recognizing program units and working with the program.

Performance correlates for professionals and students

A number of correlational analyses were conducted, using the data for each of the 36 subjects as a basis (except where explicitly noted). For performance variables (modification time, number of editing sessions, and number of editor transactions) and subjective reactions to the programs, the performance and reaction data were averaged across the three problems for each subject.

Correlations of performance and background variables. The time required to solve the three problems was negatively related to number of languages known (r = -.422, p < .01), number of programs written in each language (r = -.532, p < .001), number of design methodologies used (r = -.333, p < .05), and number of operating systems used (r = -.493, p < .001). The two background variables that most strongly distinguish our professional from student programmers, years of programming experience and years of postsecondary education, were not significantly correlated with any aspect of performance.

Correlations of performance and modification difficulty. Making a complex vs. a simple modification was strongly related to all three performance variables, correlating with average time, average number of editing cycles, and average number of transactions r = .833, .420, and .748, respectively, p < .01 for all three correlations. These high correlations (especially the first and third) may mask the effects of other variables. Thus, the effects of modification difficulty were partialled out of the remaining correlations with performance.

The difficulty of the modification was also significantly correlated to the rating of the program as more difficult to find information in (r = .378, p = .011) and more difficult to work with (r = .353, p = .017). Apparently, the complex modifications caused a more thorough examination of the program and a lower rating of its "programmer-friendliness".

Correlations of performance and mental models variables. Width or breadth of the mental reconstruction of the program was found to be negatively correlated with time spent on the problem (r = -.313, p < .05) while being positively correlated (r = .304, p < .05) with the number of editing transactions while solving the problem. This intriguing finding may indicate that time spent in pure thinking results in a detailed understanding of specific parts of the program while an active exploration of the program results in a broader knowledge of the program.

Correlations of performance and reactions to each program. For this analysis, the reactions of the programmer to each distinct program served as the basis of the analysis (N = 36 programmers x 3 programs = 108). The programmers' difficulty in finding relevant information and recognize program units were positively related to all three aspects of performance on a program-by-program basis (see Table 5). Perceived difficulty in working with a program was positively related to the time required to debug that program. The feeling that a program was too condensed in format was positively related to the number of editing transactions required to debug the program. Thus, the performance of both professional and student programmers in modifying a program has sensible, systematic relationships to their psychological reactions to the program.

Table 5

Correlations of performance variables and
psychological reactions to each program (N = 108 programs).
Difficulty of bug is partialled from these correlations.

| | Performance Variable: | | |
	Time to Debug	Editing Cycles	#Transactions
Difficulty in finding information in program	.235**	.184*	.237**
Difficulty in recognizing program units	.291***	.177*	.205*
Difficulty in working with code	.210*	NS	NS
Program is too condensed in format	NS	NS	.197*

* $p < .05$
** $p < .01$
*** $p < .001$

Summary of results

Hypothesis 1: Overall differences between student and professional programmers. In comparing our student and professional programmers, it appears that advanced student programmers are similar to professional programmers in their average performance. In part, this similarity in overall performance may be due to the fact that on the background variables, with the exception of the knowledge of different operating systems, the professional programmers were significantly higher on variables such as years programming and years education which did not relate to performance. Conversely, they were not significantly higher on those background variables such as number of languages and number of design methodologies known that did relate to performance. This pattern of differences between professional and student programmers implies that we would be less likely to find differences between our two groups because this pattern of background variables would cause relatively weaker differences between these groups than if the group differences were on the "important" or performance-related background variables.

Hypotheses 2 and 3: Effects of Program Structure, Program Content, and Ease of Modification on Mental Models. The students and professionals are very dissimilar in the types of variables that affect their mental model of the program and their reactions to the program. The mental models of professionals are affected by the difficulty of the modification task, possibly due to the amount of understanding required by the difficult modification, but their mental models are not affected by the structure and content of the task. The mental models of students, on the other hand, are affected by both the structure and the content of the program but not by the difficulty of the modification task. The reactions of students to the programs is similarly affected by the structure and content of the program, while the reactions of the professionals to the programs is much less strongly affected by these variables.

Hypothesis 4: Variables Affecting the Performance of Both Student and Professional Programmers. For the combined student and professional groups, the width of the knowledge structure was associated with faster modification performance and more editing transactions. This may reflect a stylistic individual preference on the part of some programmers to obtain a broad knowledge of the program while other programmers attempt to focus solely on the parts of the program relevant to solving the problem. Such a preference may be an example of the different programmer strategies in comprehending a program discussed by Brooks (22).

DISCUSSION

The results found in this research have several implications for understanding the programmer's performance in comprehending and altering our programs. First, the performance of the programmer depends on critical background variables such as the number of languages known and the number of programs programmed in each language, but not on other background variables such as years of experience or years of education. Our students performed almost as well on average as the professionals except that they were slower. Presumably, this lack of an overall difference can be traced to the fact that the students were similar to the professionals on the critical experience variables.

There were, however, differences in how the students and professionals were affected by different aspects of the experimental design. The mental models of the professionals were primarily affected by the difficulty of the assigned modification, while the mental models of the students were primarily affected by the structure and content of the programs. This may indicate that the professionals are better at getting at the kernel of the task to be performed and are less influenced by "peripheral" aspects of the programming task such as the surface structure of the program or the content of the program. If this is the case, we would expect that professional programmers would also be less distracted by aspects of the situation not centrally related to the programming task. This may also suggest that a relevant part of student programmer training would be training in concentrating on the essential data structures and processes in the program rather than the superficial form of the program. This is a quite different emphasis than emphasizing a particular "true" route to constructing a program, such as those suggested by advocates of program design methodologies.

The ability of programmers to abstract information from the code was also found to be a crucial determinant of how well programmers performed our modification task. In particular, the difficulty in finding information or recognizing program units was negatively related to all three measured aspects of modification performance. These variables were, in turn, significantly affected by the different program structures, with the object-structured program faring the worst in our study.

The students' ability to find and recognize program information was primarily affected by the structure and content of the programs. This is not surprising since the structure and content of the programs were also the major variables affecting the students' mental representations of the program.

Professional programmers, in contrast, were not as affected by the structure and content of the programs in the information gathering process. The only effect for professionals was increased difficulty in recognizing program units in the object-oriented programs. Thus, once again it appears that the professional programmers were less influenced by superficial or peripheral aspects of the programs in the information gathering process.

Thus, the information gathering process seems to be a critical step in forming a correct mental representation of the program. For student programmers, or perhaps less widely experienced programmers in general, solving the problem should be enhanced by a careful attention to having a clear program structure that facilitates finding relevant information and recognizing the functioning of program units. This suggests that two criteria for ease of maintainability of program code ought to be (a) the ease of finding specified information in a program and (b) the ease of recognizing relevant program structures. Further, it suggests that programming techniques such as design methodologies ought to be evaluated in part on the extent to which they foster rather than inhibit these valuable qualities of program code.

In summary, the mental representation of the program and the information-gathering process seem to be the critical aspects of performance in a program maintenance task. The methods of measuring mental models used in this study were first approximations, and future research should revise, refine, augment, and validate these measures. The development of these measures should preserve the flexibility needed to measure strong individual differences in the content and structure of the mental models of programmers. Further refinement in measurement is also necessary to obtain a more precise and complete description of the information-gathering process. The development of better methods in these two areas ought to enable us to more precisely explain and predict programmer performance both on maintenance tasks and possibly other kinds of programming tasks. Finally, developers of programming methodologies or program generators should consider the impact of their design decisions on the difficulty of finding program information and on recognizing program units in order to maximize the comprehensibility and modifiability of the resulting code.

REFERENCES

1. Johnson-Laird, P. N. (1983). Mental Models: towards a cognitive science of language, inference, and consciousness. Cambridge, Mass: Harvard University Press.

2. Young, R. M. (1981) The machine inside the machine: users' models of pocket calculators. International Journal of Man-Machine Studies, 15, 51-85.

3. Saja, A. D. (1985). The cognitive model: an approach to designing the human-computer interface. SIGCHI Bulletin, 16, 3, 36-40.

4. Mac an Airchinnigh, M. (1984). Some notes on the representation of the user's conceptual model. SIGCHI Bulletin, 16, 2, 62-69.

5. Sowa, J.F. (1984). Conceptual Structures: Information Processing in Mind and Machine. Addison-Wesley Publishing Company, Reading MA.

6. Carroll, J. M. (1984). Mental models and software human factors: an overview. Background paper for workshop on mental models organized by the NAS-NRC Committee on Human Factors, May, 1984.

7. Rouse, W. B. and Morris, N. M. (1986). On looking into the black box: prospects and limits in the search for mental models. Psychological Bulletin, 100, 3, 349-363.

8. Weiser, M. (1982). Programmers use slices when debugging. Communications of the ACM, 25, 446-452.

9. Adelson, B. (1981). Problem solving and the development of abstract categories in programming languages. Memory and Cognition, 9, 4, 422-433.

10. Letovsky, S. (1986). Cognitive processes in program comprehension. In E. Soloway and S. Iyengar (Eds.) Empirical Studies of Programmers. Norwood, NJ: Ablex.

11. Pennington, N. (1986). Stimulus structures and mental representations in expert comprehension of computer programs. In press, Cognitive Psychology.

12. Shneiderman, B., and Mayer, R. (1979) Syntactic/semantic interactions in programmer behavior: A model and experimental results. International Journal of Computer and Information Sciences, 7, 219-239.

13. Basili, V.R. and Mills, H.D. (1982). Understanding and documenting programs. <u>IEEE Transactions</u> <u>on</u> <u>Software</u> <u>Engineering</u>, <u>SE-8(3)</u>, 270-283.

14. Boehm-Davis, D.A. (in press) Software comprehension. to appear in M. Helander (Ed.), <u>Handbook</u> <u>of</u> <u>human-computer</u> <u>interaction</u>. Amsterdam: Elsevier Science Publishers.

15. Detienne, F. (1986). Program understanding and knowledge organization. The influence of acquired schemata. In <u>Third</u> <u>European</u> <u>Conference</u> <u>on</u> <u>Cognitive</u> <u>Ergonomics</u>, Paris, September 15-20.

16. Soloway E. and Ehrlich, K. (1984) Empirical studies of programming knowledge. <u>IEEE Transactions</u> <u>on</u> <u>Software</u> <u>Engineering</u>, SE-10, 595-609.

17. Cooke, N. M. and Schvaneveldt, R. W. (1986). The evolution of cognitive networks with computer programming experience. Technical report from University of New Mexico.

18. Kieras, D. E. and Bovair, S. (1984). The role of a mental model in learning to operate a device. <u>Cognitive</u> <u>Science</u>, <u>8</u>, 255-273.

19. Borgman, C. L. (1986). The user's mental model of an information retrieval system: an experiment on a prototype online catalog. <u>International</u> <u>Journal</u> <u>of</u> <u>Man-Machine</u> <u>Studies</u>, <u>24</u>, 47-64.

20. Adelson, B. (1984). When novices surpass experts: the difficulty of a task may increase with expertise. <u>Journal</u> <u>of</u> <u>Experimental</u> <u>Psychology:</u> <u>Learning,</u> <u>Memory,</u> <u>and</u> <u>Cognition</u>, <u>10</u>, 3, 483-495.

21. Buschke, H. (1977). Two-dimensional recall: Immediate identification of clusters in episodic and semantic memory. <u>Journal</u> <u>of</u> <u>Verbal</u> <u>Learning</u> <u>and</u> <u>Verbal</u> <u>Behavior</u>, <u>12</u>, 201-206.

22. Brooks, Ruven. (1983). Towards a theory of the comprehension of computer programs. <u>Int.</u> <u>J.</u> <u>Man-Machine</u> <u>Studies</u>, <u>18</u>, 543-554.

CHAPTER 4

Communication Breakdowns and Boundary Spanning Activities on Large Programming Projects

Herb Krasner
Bill Curtis
Neil Iscoe

MCC Software Technology Program
P.O. Box 200195
Austin, Texas 78720

ABSTRACT

Detailed interviews were conducted with personnel from 19 large software development projects to better understand team and project level problems to be addressed in MCC's research on software design environments. This paper reports observations of project communication phenomena that help bridge the gap between our understanding of programming–in–the–small and programming–in–the–large. We describe 1) the typical communications breakdowns in large programming projects, 2) the cultural and environmental differences that create barriers to effective intergroup communications, and 3) the boundary spanning activities that coordinate five crucial topical networks of communication. The identification of these processes and breakdowns provide a basis for more effective project coordination, including the use of tools for computer supported collaborative software design.

1. INTRODUCTION

In large software development projects, the preponderance of an individual programmer's time is spent in communication rather than programming. Results of a Bell Labs study (Bairdain, 1964) presented in Table 1 show that less than 30% of a programmer's time on the project studied was spent on traditional programming tasks, and only 13% involved coding. Similar percentages have been published more recently by Barstow (1987). Although much of the programmer's task in large systems development involves communications, there is little data characterizing these communication processes or the breakdowns to which they are susceptible. This paper presents some exploratory observations on the communication behavior of large software development projects.

Table 1
Programmer's Time Allocation

%	Task
13%	Writing code
16%	Reading code (code reviews)
32%	Job communications
13%	Personal calls and business
6%	Training
5%	Electronic mail
15%	Miscellaneous

Previous research on large scale programming projects concentrated on identifying factors affecting software productivity and quality (Walston and Felix, 1977; Boehm, 1981; Brooks, 1981; McGarry, 1982 Vosburgh, Curtis, Wolverton, Albert, Malec, Hoben, & Liu, 1984; Jeffrey & Lawrence, 1985), the differences between the state-of-the-art and the state-of-practice (Thayer, 1980; Beck and Leland, 1983; Zelkowitz, Yeh, Hamlet, Gannon, & Basili, 1984), and project management problems (Musa & Woomer, 1975). In order to gain greater insight into the processes by which productivity and quality factors exert their influence, we conducted a field study to investigate the processes underlying large systems design.

Although individual differences among programmers account for a substantial amount of the variance in software productivity (Boehm, 1981; Curtis, 1981; McGarry, 1982), there is evidence that the addition of social processes, especially those related to the communication of technical information, will help explain some of the remaining variance in productivity (Walston & Felix, 1977; Vosburgh et al., 1984). Because large systems cannot be designed by any single individual, teams of experts are needed. As the number of teams that must handle and transform design information increases, additional processes begin to impact design decision making, and therefore the productivity and quality of the project. These processes can be categorized in the layered model presented in Figure 1. As projects grow larger, the addition of more people is related to the addition of processes, especially those involving communication, that do not occur when individuals are programming alone or in laboratory environments where the tasks are brief and involve no more than a few people.

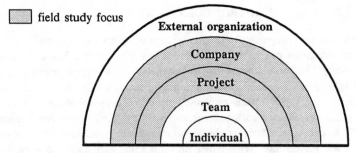

Figure 1. Levels of processes affecting software development.

Large software projects are typically organized and managed (cf. Metzger, 1972; Burrill & Ellsworth, 1980) according to guidelines adapted from other fields. The goal of these structures is to control the responsibilities, authority, and communications of a project team and not necessarily to coordinate the flow of technical information needed for making design decisions. Figure 2 presents a project organization structure that displays the usual hierarchy of management reporting relationships.

The subdivision of labor on large software projects usually causes the creation of specialist groups such as technical programming teams, configuration management, quality assurance, technical writing, contract management, customer representatives, systems engineering, hardware engineering, and integration/test. Most of these specialists do not "program", but perform functions that are required for overall project success. The project management hierarchy and its associated work breakdown structure provide a formal structure for project communication, but one directed solely at management reporting issues.

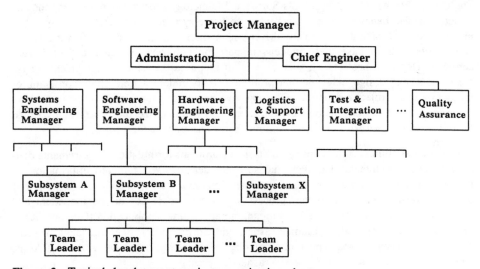

Figure 2. Typical development project organization chart.

In modeling a large software development project as a communications system, attention is focused on the information flow relationships between organizational components. Figure 3 presents a sample of the technical information flow that constitutes part of a formal communication plan for the project structure pictured in Figure 2. Although the structure of these communication paths assumes that the formal artifacts produced by one group are sufficient to convey all of the information needed by another group, this has rarely been the case. Furthermore, the organizational separation of such groups as systems engineering, hardware engineering, and software development can inhibit the ability of different experts to communicate technical information, resulting in potential system interface problems. This paper will report observations from our field study regarding formal and informal communication processes and how breakdowns occur.

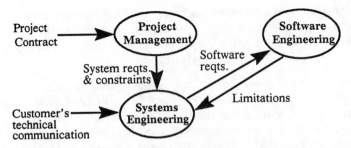

Figure 3. Technical information flow within a project.

2. THE MCC FIELD STUDY

The Design Process Group in MCC's Software Technology Program is developing models of actual design behavior on large, complex, software systems to ensure that our research in software environments is problem–driven rather than technology–driven (Myers, 1985). Our approach is to base these models, in part, on empirical evidence collected from actual development projects. It was the lack of empirical information on which to base these models of design behavior that prompted us to initiate a field study consisting of interviews with project personnel. Our objective was to examine large software projects embedded in the culture of their organizations and characterize the processes by which technical decisions were made and communicated throughout the project.

We focused attention on the "upstream" tasks of problem formulation, requirements definition, system architectural design, and software design. We gathered information on how design decisions were made, represented, communicated, changed, and how they impacted subsequent development processes. Design processes at the individual and team levels are characterized in the companion papers in this publication (Guindon, Krasner, and Curtis, 1987; Walz, Elam, Krasner, and Curtis, 1987). The modeling of processes at the organizational and multi–organization level is further described in (Curtis, Krasner, Shen, and Iscoe, 1987) and Krasner (in press).

From May through August, 1986, we visited 19 projects from nine companies ranging from aerospace contractors to computer manufacturers. The original guidelines for selecting projects included the following criteria: 1) projects with at least 10 people, 2) projects that had passed the design phase but had not been delivered, and, when possible, 3) projects that dealt with real–time, distributed, or embedded applications. Most projects selected conformed to some, but not all of these criteria. Occasional deviations from these criteria actually provided a richer set of project types to study. Projects studied varied in 1) the stage of development (early definition through maintenance), 2) the estimated or actual size of delivered system (25K – 100M lines of code), 3) the application domain (system software, transaction processing, telephony, computer–aided engineering, command and control, process control, etc.), 4) the number of personnel associated with the project (6–125), and 5) key project/system characteristics (e.g., real–time, distributed, embedded, defense contract, etc.).

During on–site visits, we conducted hour–long structured interviews with key project personnel such as the senior systems engineer, the software designers, the project manager, the division general manager, customer representatives, and the testing or quality assurance group. We always interviewed individuals from the first three categories, but were able to interview individuals from the last three categories on only one third of the projects. Participants were guaranteed anonymity and these observations have been "sanitized" so that no individual, project, or company can be identified. Although we structured the interviews to cover certain topics, we asked open-ended questions that allowed participants to formulate answers in their own terms and discuss what they thought were important events and challenges during development.

Tape-recordings of the 97 interviews produced over 2,000 pages of transcripts. We began the analysis by building models of the important processes we uncovered in the interviews. We have currently worked through nearly half of the interview transcripts to determine how well these models fit across projects, and are making refinements where necessary. We have also performed an issue-based analysis by selecting quotations that represent *particularly poignant assessments* of the problems. This report concentrates on the larger projects (at least 30 personnel in several teams developing at least 50K lines of code) in our sample and the communications problems they experienced.

3. COMMUNICATION BREAKDOWNS OBSERVED ON LARGE PROJECTS

A model of typical groups that may be associated with large software projects is shown in Figure 4. These groups are clustered into organizational levels where the layers represent increasing levels of communications insulation from the individual programmer. This model implies that it is normally easier for a programmer to communicate with team members, less easy to communicate with other groups on the project, harder to communicate with corporate groups, and very difficult to communicate with external groups. These communication difficulties are due not only to the geographic separation of groups, but also to cultural and environmental factors that differ between levels and that precondition the communication channels in how they filter and interpret various messages.

As an example, communication at the team level is mostly about technical project or personal issues. At the project level, more of the communication is related to the coordination of technical activities and the discussion of constraints on different aspects of the system. Communication at the company level generally concerns the attributes of the product, progress and schedules, or the allocation of resources. Communication with external organizations involves contractual issues, operational characteristics, delivery planning, and future business. Thus, communication to each higher level involves a change in the content of the message, a different set of motivations and context within which the message will be interpreted, and a more restricted channel for transmission (e.g., the removed the level, the less the opportunity for face-to-face transmission). In Section 4 we will discuss the topics of technical communication that are characteristic of the project level.

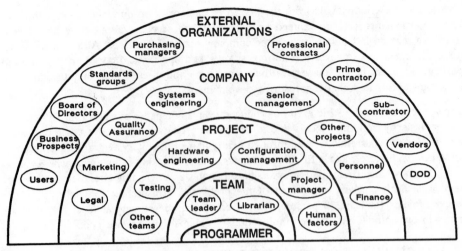

Figure 4. Layers of insulation in communication channels.

3.1 Types of Communications Breakdowns

There were four types of communication breakdowns observed on the projects we studied:
1) no communications between groups that should be communicating, 2) miscommunication between groups, 3) groups receiving conflicting information from multiple sources, and 4) communication problems due to project dynamics. Furthermore, we observed communication breakdowns that were composites of these basic types (e.g., conflicting information absorbed by one group being passed on as miscommunication to another group). We do not claim this list of breakdowns is complete, nor is there any significance to the order in which they are described. We considered communication through any channel, including hallway talk, email, formal documents, memos, meetings, etc. The cultural and environmental factors that contribute to these breakdowns are discussed in Section 3.2. The following examples should clarify how each of these breakdowns occur on large software projects.

No communication between groups – There were many situations where two or more groups needed to communicate but did not, either because of a failure to realize the necessity of communication or because neither group perceived initiating the interaction as their responsibility. Many times the necessary communication had to be forced by an external source, as in this statement by a system engineer:

> *Finally in a level of frustration that was pretty serious, I concluded that given the organizational state, the personalities involved, and what my skills were, the only way that I could achieve the level of communications that we needed was to force the documents...forcing them each to review each other's documents.*

There were occasions when the absence of communication was by policy. For instance, technical information was often compartmentalized to protect classified data or trade secrets. Although it was not surprising that tactical operational information about a weapon system would be classified in a defense environment, this compartmentalization also occurred on commercial projects. When information is selectively denied to those without a "need to know", the design rationale, trade-off analyses, and usage scenarios are sometimes unavailable to resolve questions affecting implementation alternatives. In this quote, a lead software architect stated why certain changes were delayed.

> *Even the product description for this project is a secret document for only people who need to know. I know that there were at least 3 revisions that I didn't hear about until six months after the fact. Some of the changes we are making now might have been avoided if we would have had earlier access to it.*

Miscommunication between groups – One of the most common causes for miscommuniation between groups involved different levels of understanding about the subject of the message. For instance, people in one group often mistakenly assume those in another group shared a common understanding of crucial issues in the system. In this example an on–site customer representative described why a severe system problem was not found for over a year.

> *I think we have had to learn as well as the developers. At the time we wrote the specification, we did not appreciate that it could be interpreted any other way. We assumed that they had the same common knowledge as we did. And then on top of that, this particular thing was so obvious to me as an operator that, you know, its common knowledge. Its one of the basics you teach the uninitiated student. Everyone knows. I should have known* [that they wouldn't know].

In more bureaucratic organizations, we found miscommunications occurring with information "thrown over the wall". For example, when a systems engineering group passed a software requirements document to the software engineering group they often failed to provide the operational context for interpreting the requirements. This problem was exacerbated when systems engineering reported into a different organization and had been reassigned to another project when software implementation began, making inter–group communication even more difficult.

When several groups were negotiating system features or architecture, miscommunication would lead to a state of mutual confusion. Such confusion usually arose when each group held different unstated assumptions. Often these assumptions involved fundamental differences in how the operational system should work. In the next quote, a project's chief engineer describes how multiple contractors using different analysis tools with different sets of assumptions got conflicting answers that stalled the project design.

> *Everybody was doing simulations. We were up there* [at the customer site] *for about four months. The customer was running SLAM II and the prime contractor was running...GPSS, and the other subcontractor, I can't put my finger on what they were running, but it was kind of a kluge of homebrew software that they were playing around with. We had three different simulators all coming up with different answers.*

Conflicting information from multiple sources – When one group receives inconsistent information from other groups, the receiving group may not know how to resolve the conflict. Customer interaction is a critical area subject to the receipt of conflicting information. The customer interface was often cluttered with different organizational components communicating about their particular concerns, not all of which involve the requirements for the product. For instance, in a defense environment developers had to communicate with a contracting agency about progress and finances, an operational engineering agency about the design of the system, a general (rather than the enlisted men who were the actual users) about how the system should operate, a systems program office about delivery and acceptance testing, and a host of other organizations, depending on the project, all of whom consider themselves "the customer". Opportunities for developers to talk with real users were often quite limited, and the needs of users were frequently interpreted to developers by a third party such as a general or a marketing group.

Typically, development organizations said that they would like to have, but could not get, a single point of customer contact to which they could look for a definition of system requirements. Even in the case of commercial projects, development organizations often find that the specifications from their marketing department conflict with the requests from their current users. Sometimes, as the next quote illustrates, the information needed to resolve conflicting specifications comes from channels that are not formally recognized within an organization.

> The original impetus that I got to define something that could be used for all the machines came from, surprisingly enough, some member of the Board of Directors who is not an employee of the corporation, [and] who couldn't understand why we had different [features for each machine]. I'm sympathetic.

MCC: *You just knew him? How did you get the message from him?*

> A dove descended with it. You know how it is...

Occasionally, different parts of the same corporation competed to define system requirements. In several cases, we observed that the requirements, and often even the understanding of the product, varied between strategic planning, marketing, and product planning groups. Consequently, conflicting messages were being sent to the development organization. The resulting uncertainty about system features sometimes caused the development organization to make suboptimal design decisions. In the following quote, a lead software designer described how the system architecture was determined.

> The whole software architecture to begin with was designed around one customer that was going to buy a couple of thousand of these. And it wasn't really designed around the European marketplace at all. Another European customer had another need, so we're trying to rearrange the software to take care of these two customers. And when the third one comes along, we do the same thing. And when the fourth one comes along, we do the same thing.

Communication problems due to project dynamics – Large projects experience changes associated with life cycle phases, and communication breakdowns were observed in transitional states associated with changes in people, goals, technology, and so forth. Often, each of the major phases (definition, development, and delivery – see Figure 5) on a large project was performed by a different group of people, causing problems in the transition between phases when groups handed off intermediate work products to the succeeding group. Major problems occurred later when iteration back through these phases was necessary (e.g., a redesign) and the previous groups had been disassembled or reassigned. Much of the information that was needed had not been recorded. As the project grows over time the potential for communications breakdowns increases, as seen in the following:

> I think this is the way it always turns out with this stupid design of large systems. In the beginning it was easy. Hell, there were three of us. How many lines of communications are there? One, two, three. But once you go to 15 people it can get out of hand...In the beginning, it was easy to keep track of what was going on. It was only after reaching the critical mass ... that things began falling into the cracks, and we were losing track. I mean, I used to religiously keep track of the [change notices]. But now, I don't think I've looked at them in six months. I just couldn't keep up with everything else going on. There was just so much going on.

In Figure 5 we see a typical phased work flow process (phases are numbered 1–11) that identifies the major tasks to be accomplished by the project. Several phase oriented teams such as proposal, design, or testing teams appear at specific points in a project's life, with occasional carry over of personnel from team to team. In typical order of appearance, these teams are the proposal, project management, system definition, system development, system delivery, and maintenance teams. The communication of knowledge about the evolving system is reduced as fewer personnel are rotated between these teams and carried across project phases.

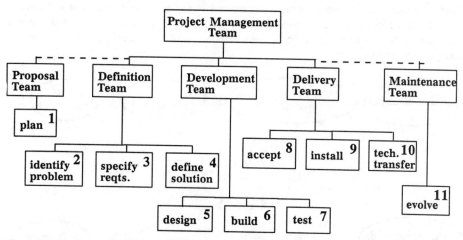

Figure 5. Teams responsible for phases of the life cycle.

The traditional project management focus of software development has been on *controlling* the work flow through the use of identifiable intermediate work products at the end of each phase (e.g. project plan, specification document, integration build plan, etc.). In practice, however, work rarely progresses sequentially, since several phases are performed simultaneously, different subsystems are at different points in their development process, and feedback from prototyping efforts causes changes in plans. Occasionally, the structure of communications among project personnel conflicted with the most efficient decomposition of the system. In this example a chief systems engineer discussed a conflict in decomposing the system.

> First, one of the biggest problems is communication problems that occur among people because of their misunderstanding of the terminology. And the real problem that we found was partitioning the system enough so we could minimize the interfaces required between people. In fact, it was more important to minimize the interfaces between systems engineers than it was to make the system logical from the viewpoint of the user.

It is obvious that management of a large project is quite complex from both the organization and work flow perspectives. The relationship between the project organization and the project task is crucial, yet when projects contain research–like components (e.g. technology prototyping) or become long lived, highly bureaucratic organizations become unsuitable (Mantei, 1981).

3.2 Cultural and Environmental Factors that Affect Communication Channels

There are many potential barriers that inhibit group–to–group communication on a project, and some of the most problematic involved differences among groups in their cul-

tural milieu and the environmental conditions under which they operated. These differences in cultural and environmental milieu involved: 1) communication skills, 2) existing
incentive systems, 3) shared representational formats, 4) conditions of rapid change, 5)
local jargon, 6) the breakdown of information capture, and 7) cultural mores for individual behavior. The individual interpretations of each of these factors, and most importantly the hidden assumptions in each, play a key role in the relationship to communications breakdowns. In Figure 6, we show the one–to–many relationship of these ten factors
to the four types of communications breakdowns of the previous section. We do not
claim that these factors are necessarily complete, nor is there any special significance to
the order in which they are described. They merely represent an exploratory attempt to
explicate the factors that predispose communications problems among groups on software
development projects.

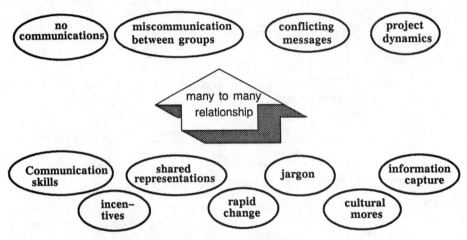

Figure 6. Relationships between breakdowns and factors.

Communication skills – The ability of a group to communicate is determined, in large
part, by the communication skills of the individuals that compose it. Although group
members may be technically skilled, not all of them are also skilled in communications.
Thus, the first barrier to communication can be a lack of relevant skills in translating
information into a form that can be received effectively by other groups. In the following
example, a project manager describes this phenomena:

> The best people are the ones that can organize information and give it to someone
> else...There are also very capable people who cannot give the information to others in
> any way...Their value to the organization is low.

The best system analysts seem to be individuals with both excellent communication
skills and technical competence. See Guinan and Bostrum (1987) for a description of the
types of individual communications behaviors that are most effective for information systems design.

Existing incentive systems – In many projects, individuals receive a number of conflicting
messages about their performance and its relation to group productivity. In some cases,
individual goals are emphasized so that performance can be evaluated and rewarded. In
other cases, although long term group goals are stressed, only short term individual performance is rewarded. Communication requires work which unless properly rewarded

will usually not be performed. Communications, written or oral, were often poorly rewarded, as in this statement from a chief systems engineer:

> *Engineering practices have got to become part of the culture. Senior members of the technical staff have to promote that culture. We have no incentive to document. Management needs to recognize that requirements tracing is important and reward it with bonuses, with raises.*

Often there are strong internal rewards for remaining an "expert" by possessing knowledge that others on a project do not have and by dispersing it slowly. Unless the goal of communicating an individual's project knowledge is made explicit and rewarded, it may not occur, as illustrated by this software engineer's statement:

> *It was quite some time before most of the people had a good understanding of what was going on. There was an attachment of the [system] concept to the personality of <deleted>, and as long as it stayed in his head and he didn't have a particular interest in getting it out to other people. Or at least he wasn't patient enough to communicate those concepts.*

The failure to have incentive systems that stressed intergroup cooperation occasionally caused managers to place a low priority on intergroup communication, as in the following quote.

> *Another big problem was the individual supervisors holding external interactions down to a minimum...Either because they didn't realize that the interaction was crucial or because of the thought that if they forged ahead they could set the standard.*

Shared representational formats – Many different representational methods are used to organize and communicate a shared model of a system. Successful projects almost always had a common representational format to facilitate communication, as in the following example of how a large project was managed.

> *The ER [entity–relationship] diagram means that everybody speaks the same language. Developers, designers, human performance people, we all use the same language. The ER diagram, its the language. It was six months or so before it settled down, but once it did, we could resolve all problems in terms of the diagram.*

In the absence of a common representational format to promote shared knowledge, a group's understanding of the system is often fragmented and uncoordinated. For example, a chief designer told us during one interview that he had,

> *...a folder of what I think are important things to remember about various areas of the system. It's not complete and it's not something that I would hand off to someone else.*

He could not find the time to organize the file so that it would be meaningful to another project member. Yet, this information was critical to the success of the project.

Conditions of rapid change – Change in the system requirements, design concepts, and underlying hardware technology occurred on all the large projects we interviewed. For example, on one project we were told that changes in the underlying hardware technology could cause a redesign every six months. The changes that caused the most problems occurred in the system requirements. In this example, a chief system engineer described the impact of continual requirements change.

The original proposal was rejected because it was not as all encompassing as they had originally perceived a system ought to be. So we made it bigger. Then it was too costly. So we scaled it down. It went through over 20 versions. It keeps expanding and contracting until it cools. It's like the earth.

Under these conditions, it is difficult to track the status of design decisions, and the communication channels were often overloaded with change information. Periods of great instability of requirements or design information was a primary source of conflicting information and miscommunication among groups.

Local jargon – Bringing someone *up to speed* on projects was consistently reported to take between six months and a year. One reason cited was the complicated task of teaching what terms meant, what information was important, and who to communicate with to get more information. For example, technical design and code reviews were used extensively as communication and training mechanisms rather than just as fault detection or quality assurance mechanisms. Several projects achieved major time savings in acclimating new staff by mechanizing or strictly enforcing naming conventions.

It seems simple, but one of the most effective time savers...was a naming convention for subroutines.

Although some projects have glossaries of their own internal jargon, the actual definitions of terms and their use were found to vary within groups working on the same project.

The breakdown of information capture – The massive volume of specification, documentation, and implementation information was controlled by a variety of electronic and manual methods. Finding information in a timely manner was a critical problem. Second-level designers often complained about not knowing what technical commitments had been made, how rigid the commitments were, or what issues were actively being discussed within the project. Many of the comments from programmers concerned their inability to easily access information about the operation of various parts of systems. While several projects had attempted to create on-line documentation systems, most were not heavily used for information capture, nor were they regularly updated.

On the other side, we didn't have enough documentation, enough code review, ANY design review. You have to understand, we don't have any design review. And now we're going into maintenance mode, and the smart guys are going to leave; the poor <expletive deleted> that have to maintain the system are going to suffer.

Regardless of how well a communication system is structured, it may break down due to an overload of information. The breaking point usually occurred during the middle of a project when expectations were high, procedures were being followed, and people had yet to realize that they would eventually be unable to handle the flow of information. This was also the point at which the fewest staff were available for restructuring the system.

Scheduling pressure was a major contributing factor at the point that many information capture systems broke down. There was typically a conflict between the desire to forge ahead with code and to slow down and document it correctly. In many cases, we were told that,

...if we could only have a tool to record our decisions...we could save weeks of rework.

Yet, the same individual told us that,

...there is just no time...to stop to write things down.

Toward the end of most projects, expectations were much more realistic, and certain kinds of information were no longer being transferred. Typical items that got dropped were decision rationales, tradeoffs analyses, and operational usage scenarios, as seen in this statement from a lead software engineer:

> *There were various committee meetings that described various menus and how they worked and I'm not exactly sure where the description of each feature menu is right now...Its not in the software requirements document.*

Cultural mores for individual behavior – Individuals act within the set of cultural values that are defined by their organizations and their peers. Although the model of organizations held hostage by brilliant, unkempt, and socially deviant programmers is popular, it seemed an anachronism from our observations. In fact, we observed some of the best software development taking place in organizations that had created cultures of *egoless* programming (Weinberg, 1971). In these cultures, individuals take pride in both their own work, and the overall achievements of their groups. By carefully selecting new personnel, and then using peer pressure and management to enforce the cultural norms, high degrees of performance were attained by some organizations. Furthermore, strict cultural norms meant that rigorous formal standards, such as documentation standards, need not be strictly maintained. In these cultures, violating a standard became an asocial event, as illustrated by the following quote:

> *We look for bright people, and we look for people who want to be part of the team. And then we go to great lengths that first year to try to teach them the discipline in software engineering...The philosophy of our whole system is peer to peer, it isn't hierarchial, and the organization matches that. If a person isn't performing, its his peers who detect that. He probably gets yelled at by his peers before he gets yelled at by management.*

In summary, these factors create a cultural framework from which a group communicates. In group to group communications, the extent to which two such frameworks differ will precondition the communications channel. Other factors that were not discussed have less of an influence on communications include: standards, policy and procedure, computational and physical environment infrastructure.

4. BOUNDARY SPANNERS AND PROJECT COORDINATION NETWORKS

Some of the potential breakdowns between groups were avoided by having one or more individuals "span the boundary" between groups. An example of a *boundary spanner* is the chief system engineer who translates between the needs of the customers and the capabilities of the software designers. Boundary spanning activities translate information from the form in which it was used by one team to a form that can be used by other teams. Boundary spanners reduce the amount of information lost or miscommunicated between different phases of development and different development teams.

Boundary spanners had good communication skills and a willingness to engage in constant face–to–face interaction. When individuals appointed to formal liaison positions did not have skills that matched the needs of the boundary spanning role, a different person usually emerged to fill it informally. Boundary spanners often became the hubs of information networks that assisted the technical integration of the project.

We will describe the coordination activities of boundary spanners as a collection of intersecting communication networks in an open system in which a node (e.g., a programmer as a processor of information) may exist in several networks simultaneously. As such, a programmer provides both formal work products and also crucial information based on experience and expertise. We will describe the communication networks that we observed in five areas of technical information: application design, system diagnosis, technology awareness, feature and attribute negotiation, and reuse. Communication in each of these areas is characterized by processes of negotiation, conflict analysis, issue formation, and decision making.

Application design network – Informal communication channels were found to be the primary carriers of technical information during the design process. Most of the projects initially had a small team (sometimes just one person) who conceived the architectural concepts underlying the system. This group operated as the hub of the network that communicated design information. They became the hub because of their extreme familiarity with the application area (e.g. telephony, avionics, operating systems, etc.) and their ability to map between the behavior expected of the application system and the high–level computational structures required to automate this behavior in software. The hierarchy of expertise in a project represented a second organizational hierarchy (informal) that exerted great control over the course of a project.

The deep application–specific knowledge required to successfully build most large complex systems was thinly spread through most software development staffs. Many software developers were novices in the application domains represented in the shareholders' business mix. As a result, programmers often spent considerable time learning the application area from the senior staff members. In such cases, the programmer was primarily a consumer of application information for the first 6 months to a year in a new application area (the typical learning period cited across our projects). As one software designer stated:

> Seven years ago each person was learning their own area. There were no real experts, nobody knew the whole big picture because it was such a new and emerging thing.

Chief systems engineers consistently complained about the difficulty of tracking and overseeing the unresolved issues that arose during the design. In fact, a count of the issues raised and the proportion remaining unresolved could be a valuable leading indicator of the progress of the system definition. Issue resolution rates offered one of the few opportunities to provide management visibility into the intellectual progress and conceptual integrity of the design. On most projects there were no tools for capturing issues and tracking the status of their resolution and the failure to resolve them often did not become obvious until integration testing. The systems engineers usually became the hub of networks created by the open issues in the design. However, breakdowns occurred when the number of issues overloaded their tracking capacity and decisions bearing on these issues were made by others without being communicated to the senior systems engineers.

System diagnosis network – The diagnosis of system problems requires a thorough knowledge of a large segment of the program's structure and internal behavior. This expertise was also typically localized in a few individuals (diagnosticians), who could be identified by the occasional queues that formed outside their office. During maintenance and enhancement tasks, knowledge of how system components interacted was needed to assess the impact of multiple changes or enhancements on the system. Such information was rarely contained in the code and documentation. Diagnosticians provided system structural information to programmers, who provided in return the same service regarding their particular subsystem or module. Diagnosticians formed the hub of a network of technical information about the system's structure and its components that was at a level more detailed (implementation rather than design information) than the systems information communicated in the application design network.

Technology awareness network – Throughout the project, developments external to the project (e.g., tools, methods, etc.) that could expedite performance were missed because of deadline pressures. Information about external resources was occasionally provided by technology gatekeepers (often other programmers) in the company that championed particular technologies. However, with respect to software engineering technology, many mangers seemed unaware of the potential benefits, as in this statement by a software engineer:

> The way the managers are getting trained is that the engineers are coming back [from software engineering school] and fighting to keep using some of the tools and techniques they've learned; and fighting against the managers to let them use them, and that's really how the managers are getting their experience.

A network of related technology gatekeepers occasionally formed to match project needs with external technology. Gatekeepers and champions were crucial in the smooth transition of external technology into a project. A model of the technology transfer process is discussed in Krasner (in press).

Feature and attribute negotiation network – As development proceeds, the system–to–be becomes an integration of *functional features* of the delivered system (e.g., switching calls, updating billing data, maintaining lines, etc. in a telephone switching system). Functional features can usually be traced to the existence of one or more system components. However, the mapping of functional features to components can be many–to–many, making them difficult to analyze when they become the foci for cost and schedule negotiations. Sometimes software organizations fell into the flexibility trap, as in this statement by a software team leader:

> One of the pitfalls in our process occurs when [marketing or engineering] says, "Do we have to make the decision on how it is going to operate? Could you [the software team] write it both ways?" We say, "Well its going to cost some resources but we could." The tendency is to not make the decision because we can have it operate both ways. This leads to thinking that we can make everything flexible. In implementation we can do fewer things because we are doing each thing 8 different ways in order to be flexible.

Further, many systems suffer "creeping elegance" when features are continually enhanced by developers beyond the actual requirements and in conflict with scheduled delivery dates. One software team leader told us:

> The most difficult thing was the allocation of features into memory. Prioritizing and making the decisions, getting people to agree to what we are and are not putting in.

As distinguished from features, *operational attributes* are characteristics of system that are often difficult to trace to a particular component, but describe the overall operational behavior of the system, such as response time, reliability, or maintainability. The focus for overseeing attributes was less obvious in practice then for functional features, since there could not be a simple mapping of people to components. Usually operational attributes cannot be traced directly to the existence of particular system components, but are measured during the operation of the total system. Quantitative measures that reliably predict many of these operational characteristics are still in research (Conte, Dunsmore, & Shen, 1986). Thus, experienced personnel were the best source of evaluating operational behavior from static design descriptions at the component level.

In a few organizations the responsibility for overseeing each attribute was delegated to specific individuals, but in most it was centralized in a quality assurance organization. Many negotiations relating to system quality were conducted in design review meetings, before quality assurance had even been assigned to the project. Thus, individuals who became champions for particular operational attributes became the most effective means of communicating concerns for the particular attribute across the project teams.

Reuse network – Programmers often created components whose design or code had the potential to be reused in other systems. However, they would be reused only if they were well enough described that their relevance could be recognized. We found little use of prepackaged components from reuse libraries or from previous projects. Reuse libraries needed additional mechanisms to become effective in capturing the information required to transfer the accumulated technical expertise across projects. Currently, this transfer across projects occurred when people moved to their next assignment. A simple broadcast mechanism for a plea for help could sometimes locate reusable components, but the transfer of design knowledge was accomplished through the network of individuals who remain in a division over a number of projects. Thus, the major source of reusability appeared to be in the communication networks among the professional staff rather than in the search of libraries or documents.

5. CONCLUSIONS

In this paper we have described the typical communications breakdowns observed on large programming projects, the underlying cultural and environmental factors affecting group communications, and how boundary spanning activities created networks that overcame some of these breakdowns. We discussed five communication networks that spanned across the various teams and phases of a large project. Different networks appeared to have different informational topologies, different loci of knowledge, and different diffusion rates. These networks were typically not represented in the formal division of project labor, but became crucial to project success. A more precise definition of these networks could provide a stronger basis for the coordination and management of large projects.

We believe that we have shown the research–like aspect of many large scale software development projects and how that aspect affects the technical communications processes involved. We postulate that as a project gets larger and more research–like, traditional project management strategies begin to inhibit the flow and integration of technical design information. As a counterpoint, the Japanese have demonstrated in their software factories that software development can be separated into a research/engineering (i.e. divergent then convergent) phase followed by a production–like (i.e. manufacturing–like) phase (Belady, 1986). The focus is on technical information and innovation processes in the former phase and resource coordination processes (i.e. traditional project management) in the latter phase.

The relationship between effective communication processes and overall project performance was not specifically addressed in this study. The determinants of such a relationship are only beginning to become understood (cf. Hauptman, 1986). Our analysis of breakdowns, causal factors, and boundary spanning activities can lead to a better understanding of this relationship through future studies.

Tools to augment traditional project management structures with mechanisms to coordinate the communication of technical information across project teams can provide an improvement in productivity and quality separate from that offered by most programming tools. One focus for supporting the coordinated information flow over these networks within a project would be to augment them with tools for computer–supported collaborative design work (Krasner, 1986). Information collection and breakdown detection mechanisms will help in routing informal network communications, as well as formally defined documents, reports, and other artifacts. Features included in such systems might be mediated discussion groups (e.g. technology supported quality circles), integrated mail/scheduler/calendar, issue–based conflict resolution aides, strategic assumption surfacing aides, coordination data collection, and organizational design support tools (e.g. containing reusable coordination protocols).

ACKNOWLEDGMENTS

We thank the remaining members of the MCC STP empirical studies team (Vincent Shen, Diane Walz and Raymonde Guindon) for their contributions to this work, and our colleagues that provided insightful review comments (at MCC – Colin Potts, Peter Marks, Jonathan Grudin and at Yale, Elliot Soloway). We thank the STP liaisons for their efforts in helping us set up the interview trips. We also thank Dani and Jerry Weinberg for their assistance in selecting interviewing strategies. We also wish to thank Les Belady for his continuing support of the Empirical Studies of Design project and to the MCC STP shareholders and participants of the study for their support of this long range research effort.

REFERENCES

Bairdain, E. (1964). *Research Studies of Programmers and Programming* (Unpublished manuscript). New York: AT&T Bell Laboratories. Cited in R. Fairley, *Software Engineering Concepts*. New York: McGraw–Hill, 1986.

Barstow, D. (1987). Artificial intelligence and software engineering. *Proceedings of the 9th International Conference on Software Engineering*. Washington, DC: IEEE Computer Society, 200–211.

Beck, L. & Perkins, T. (1983). A survey of software engineering practice: Tools, methods, and results. *IEEE Transactions on Software Engineering*, 9 (5), 541–561.

Boehm, B. W. (1981). *Software Engineering Economics*. Englewood Cliffs, NJ: Prentice–Hall.

Brooks, W.D. (1981). Software technology payoff: Some statistical evidence. *Journal of Systems and Sofware*, 2 (1), 3–9.

Burrill, C. & Ellsworth, L. (1980). *Modern Project Management: Foundations for Quality and Productivity*. Tenafly, NJ: Burrill–Ellsworth Assoc.

Conte, S.D., Dunsmore, H.E., & Shen, V.Y. (1986). *Software Engineering Metrics and Models*. Menlo Park, CA: Benjamin/Cummings.

Curtis, B. (1981). Substantiating programmer variability. *Proceedings of the IEEE*, 69 (7), 846.

Curtis, B., Krasner, H., Shen, V., & Iscoe, N. (1987). On building software process models under the lamppost. *Proceedings of the 9th International Conference on Software Engineering*. Washington, DC: IEEE Computer Society, 96–103,

Grudin, J. (1987), Social evaluation of the user interface: Who does the work and who gets the benefit. *Proceedings of Interact'87*. Amsterdam: North–Holland.

Guinan, P. & Bostrum, R. (1987). *Communication Behaviors of Higly-Rated vs. Lowly-Rated System Developers: A Field Experiment* (IRMIS Working Paper #W707). Bloomington, IN: Indiana U., School of Business.

Guindon, R., Krasner, H., & Curtis, B. (1987). Cognitive processes in early, upstream design: differences in strategies among experienced designers. *Proceedings of the 2nd Workshop on Empirical Studies of Programmers*. Norwood, NJ: Ablex.

Hauptman, O. (1986), Influence of Task Type on the Relationship between Communication and Performance: The Case of Software Development, in *Journal of R&D Management*, April, 1986.

Jeffrey, D.R. & Lawrence, M.J. (1985). Managing programming productivity. *Journal of Systems and Software*, 5 (1), 49-58.

Krasner, H. (Ed.) (1986). *Proceedings of the Conference on Computer-Supported Cooperative Work*. Austin: MCC Software Technology Program.

Krasner, H. (in press). *Empirical Evidence of Software Engineering Technology Transfer Problems*. Talk presented at the IEEE Workshop on Software Technology Transfer.

Mantei, M. (1981). The effect of programming team structures on programming tasks. *Communications of the ACM*, 24 (3), 106-113.

McGarry, F.E. (1982). What have we learned in the last six years? In *Proceedings of the Seventh Annual Software Engineering Workshop* (SEL-82-007). Greenbelt, MD: NASA-GSFC.

Metzger, P. (1973). *Managing a Programming Project*. Englewood Clifts, NJ: Prentice-Hall.

Musa, J.D. & Woomer, F.N. (1975). SAFEGUARD data-processing system: Software project management. *The Bell System Technical Journal: SAFEGUARD Supplement (1975)*, S245-S259.

Siegal, J., Dubrovsky, V., Kiesler, S., & McGuire, T. (1985). *Group Processes In Computer-Mediated Communication*. CMU Research Report, Pittsburgh: Carnegie-Mellon, Dept. of Social Sciences.

Thayer, R.H. (1980). Organizational structures used in software development by the U.S. aerospace industry. *Journal of Systems and Software*, 1 (4), 283-297.

Vosburgh, J., Curtis, B., Wolverton, R., Albert, B., Malec, H., Hoben, S., & Liu, Y. (1984). Productivity factors and programming environments. *Proceedings of the Seventh International Conference on Software Engineering*. Washington, DC: IEEE Computer Society, 143-152.

Walston, C. E. & Felix, C. P. (1977). A method of programming measurement and estimation. *IBM Systems Journal*, 16 (1), 54-73.

Walz, D., Elam, J., Krasner, H., & Curtis (1987). A methodology for studying software design teams: an investigation of conflict behaviors in the requirements definition phase. *Proceedings of the 2nd Workshop on Empirical Studies of Programmers*. Norwood, NJ: Ablex.

Weinberg, G. (1971). *The Psychology of Computer Programming*. New York: Van Nostrand Reinhold.

Winograd, T. & Flores, F. (1986). *Understanding Computers and Cognition*. Norwood, NJ: Ablex.

Zelkowitz, M., Yeh, R., Hamlet, R., Gannon, J., & Basili, V. (1984). Software engineering practices in the U.S. and Japan. *IEEE Computer*, 17 (6), 57-66.

CHAPTER 5

Breakdowns and Processes During the Early Activities of Software Design by Professionals

Raymonde Guindon
Herb Krasner
Bill Curtis
Microelectronics and Computer Technology Corporation
9390 Research Boulevard
Austin, Texas 78759

ABSTRACT

This chapter summarizes some of the main breakdowns (or difficulties) occurring early in the software design process when professional designers work on a problem of realistic complexity. One class of breakdowns is caused by lack of knowledge and another class is caused by cognitive limitations. A third class of breakdowns is caused by a combination of these two factors. The main breakdowns observed are: 1) lack of specialized design schemas; 2) lack of a meta-schema about the design process leading to poor allocation of resources to the various design activities; 3) poor prioritization of issues leading to poor selection of alternative solutions; 4) difficulty in considering all the stated or inferred constraints in defining a solution; 5) difficulty in performing mental simulations with many steps or test cases; 6) difficulty in keeping track and returning to subproblems whose solution has been postponed; and 7) difficulty in expanding or merging solutions from individual subproblems to form a complete solution. We have also observed *serendipitous design* and the process of understanding and elaborating the requirements through exploration of the designer's mental model of the problem environment. This study provides many observations of breakdowns and design behaviors not reported in previous studies and necessary prior to developing a model of the cognitive activities during software design. This study also provides critical information to guide the design of tools and methodologies to improve the efficiency of software designers.

MOTIVATION AND GOALS

The goal of this study is to identify the breakdowns most often experienced by professional software designers and determine the software tools that would alleviate these breakdowns. This chapter will not describe these tools but will concentrate on describing the breakdowns. Breakdowns have been broadly defined as ineffective design activities, undesirable consequences of these ineffective activities, activities that are difficult to perform because they tax the designers' limited cognitive resources, or causes of these ineffective or difficult design activities. These breakdowns are likely to produce design solutions that are incorrect. Our strategy toward the identification of breakdowns has been to:

- Study designers with real, extensive, and widely varied software design experience.
- Give the designers a more complex and realistic problem than has been given in other studies of software design, yet not so different that our results cannot be easily compared to them (e.g., Jeffries, Turner, Polson, and Atwood (1); Adelson and Soloway (2); Kant and Newell (3)).
- Use the observational technique of thinking aloud protocol rather than controlled experimental manipulations because of the scarcity of previous empirical work on software design. This initial study is exploratory and we have observed many design behaviors and many breakdowns that will provide a foundation for modeling cognitive activities during software design.

Our study differs from other studies of software design by individuals on two main points. First, we are taking a next step in advancing the empirical study of software design by using a more complex and realistic design problem than used in other software design studies. Second, this study is especially oriented toward identifying the breakdowns occurring during software design by professional designers.

DESCRIPTION OF THE METHODOLOGY

Participants

Thinking aloud protocols were collected from 8 professional programmers and system designers. Three experienced designers were selected for a full protocol analysis from these eight professionals. P6 had a Ph.D. in Electrical Engineering with more than 10 years of professional experience, mainly in communication systems and hardware architecture. P8 had a Masters in Software Engineering with 5 years of experience, mainly in real time systems. P3 was a Ph.D. Candidate in Computer Science with 3 years of professional experience, mainly in logic programming. These particular designers were selected because they were considered by their peers to be experienced and competent designers, because of the wide variety of their educational backgrounds and years of experience, because their design solutions were considered the best among the eight designers, and because of the wide variety of their design strategies and solutions. We deliberately choose to analyze the widest spectrum of design behaviors in order to gather a wide variety of breakdowns and design strategies.

Problem Statement

The *lift control problem* is currently a standard problem used in the areas of software specification and software requirements modeling research. The goal is to design the logic to move N lifts between M floors given the constraints expressed in the problem statement. The problem statement is given in the Appendix.

Procedure

Thinking aloud reports were collected from participants who were asked to design the logic for the N-lift problem. They were given two hours to produce a design solution that was in such a form and level of detail that it could be handed off to a competent system programmer to implement. The participants were videotaped and given paper and pencil to work their solution. The notes and diagrams produced by the participants were time-stamped regularly by the experimenter. The transcript of each participant was also time-stamped, and the written notes and diagrams were included in the transcript. The procedure departed from typical verbal protocols in that the experimenter intervened more substantively, often acting as a client and sometimes providing some help when the participants encountered difficulties. There were two reasons for this departure. First, in realistic design situations one or more people are typically available to answer questions or arbitrate issues in the requirements. This communication and negotiation between client and designer is perceived as a critical element in early design. Carroll, Thomas, and Malhotra (4) have provided an analysis of the cyclic nature of these interactions. At least one participant, P6, would frequently want to discuss design issues with the experimenter as this represented his normal mode of designer-client interactions. However, such a veridical feature conflicts with the traditional methods for collecting and analyzing verbal protocols. Second, our objective was to generate as much design behavior as possible in order to observe a broad range of design breakdowns. The participants were selected and the verbal protocols collected by the second author. The videotapes and transcripts were independently analyzed by the first author later.

Protocol Analysis Process

The process of protocol analysis was divided into three major steps:

1. Enumeration of possible cognitive activities that could occur during the session based on previous studies, the problem-solving literature in psychology, and artificial intelligence models of design. The function of these preliminary models is to guide the protocol analysis, though not limit it. New activities or interactions between them are also sought.
2. Segmentation of the protocols into episodes indicating breakdowns or corresponding to cognitive activities during software design.
3. Identification of the relations between the software design activities. Four main types of relations were identified: 1) temporal (e.g., precedence, iteration, interruptions, and resumptions); 2) transition between internal, mental activities and external activities (e.g., from mental to external representation of lifts and floors on paper); 3) transition between activities dealing mainly with the problem domain (e.g., lifts, floors, buttons) and activities dealing mainly with the solution domain (e.g., control structures, data structures); 4) functional composition (e.g., the activity of understanding the requirements was composed of shorter episodes such as disambiguation of the problem statement through mental simulations, the addition of an assumption, or the abstraction of critical statements).

Verbal protocol analysis is essentially an exploratory observational technique particularly suited for research in new domains. The study of cognitive processes during software design is such a domain.

Issues of Validity Generalization

There are three issues that must be addressed in determining the validity of generalizing results from these data to realistic design situations. These issues deal with the task, the sampling of participants, and the external validity of the experimental situation. As stated earlier, the lift problem is a standard exercise in research on software specification techniques. Although it is not as complex a task as, for example, designing a distributed electronic fund transfer system, it is nevertheless a next step in increasing the technical challenge offered by tasks used in empirical studies of design. Thus, as we begin to understand how designers marshal their cognitive resources to solve problems of this complexity, we can move on to tasks of even greater complexity.

The second issue concerns how representative our sample of participants is of the larger population of software designers. There is simply no reliable way to answer this question given the current maturity of the field. That is, there are no population data available against which to compare the variability of our sample. There is no standard type of individual who becomes a software designer. Their educational backgrounds, work experience, job settings, and variability of skills differ radically. Furthermore, there is not even agreement on the relevant variables to measure if we wanted to characterize this population. Another significant problem is that there is no standard job title or description for those who perform software design.

We attempted to get a broad sampling of educational backgrounds, application experiences, and previous working environments in the eight designers selected to participate. Further, we selected three protocols for analysis that represented completely different strategies in attacking the design. We make no claim that these protocols represent the full range of strategies in the larger population of software designers. Rather, we believe that since it is unlikely that a multi-environment population study of software designers will be funded in the foreseeable future, the description of this population must be pieced together from studies like this that describe the problem-solving characteristics of a few designers in great depth.

The third issue concerns the extent to which the conditions under which the data were collected are representative of those under which actual design occurs. Clearly, designing programs of any significance normally takes more than two hours, unless the designer has extensive experience in designing programs of great similarity. Our goal in collecting these data was to gather information on a concentrated problem-solving effort that would provide a broad range of cognitive behaviors and would display an interesting array of breakdowns. We cannot be sure that additional breakdowns would not have been observed had we carried the data collection out over several days or even weeks with a more complex problem. Furthermore, some of the breakdowns may have been exacerbated by the concentrated nature of the two-hour session. However, other studies of software design by individuals have collected verbal protocols over a session of two hours (Jeffries, Turner, Polson, and Atwood (1); Adelson and Soloway (2); Kant and Newell (3)). Therefore, we can at least compare our results to their results legitimately.

Finally, some of the breakdowns and processes we have observed were also reported by Kant and Newell (3) and Adelson and Soloway (2), and more importantly in a study of mechanical engineering design using a ten-hour design session by Ullman, Stauffer, and Dietterich (5). This overlap between some of our findings and findings in other studies performed in other domains and under different conditions supports the validity and generalizability of our new findings.

GENERAL OBSERVATIONS ON DESIGN BEHAVIOR

The three designers adopted very different strategies during design. A brief characterization of their overall strategies follows.

P6 seems to have the most relevant specialized computer science knowledge to solve the N-lift problem - he has **specialized design schemas** relevant to distributed systems. P6 uses these design schemas to **decompose the problem into simpler subproblems.** He opts for a distributed control solution. He then decomposes the problem into two subproblems, communication between each lift and route scheduling by each lift. However, he clearly has better design schemas for the communication subproblem than for the scheduling subproblem. He successively refines his solution for the communication subproblem while he performs much more exploratory design for the scheduling subproblem. By exploratory design, we mean design with many mental simulations of the problem environment and mental simulations of tentative solutions unguided by a plan. Another aspect of his design activities is that they are **issue-driven:** he identifies some critical features his solution should have, such as *reliability and no single point of failure*, and uses them to **control** the selection of alternative solutions for many of the subproblems (e.g., selection of a control structure and selection of a communication scheme between lifts). Moreover, P6 also consciously generates many **simplifying assumptions**, which he evaluates for their plausibility, as a **complexity reduction strategy**. So, P6's process is mainly characterized by the use of specialized design schemas, by being issue-driven, and by the generation of simplifying assumptions.

P8 seems to follow more closely than the other participants a **meta-schema for design**. This meta-schema seems to be derived from software engineering practices, especially the Jackson System Development method (6). P8 explicitly acknowledges the need for **exploring the problem environment** to achieve a good understanding of the requirements before seeking a solution. The problem environment is the set of objects, events, and behaviors in the domain relevant to the computer system being designed (e.g., floors, lifts, buttons, buildings, people waiting, fires). An important part of his design activities is the representation of entities and relations in the problem environment and their mental simulations. However, P8 does not seem to have as relevant specialized design schemas as P6, which may have induced him in exploring the problem environment. Possibly as a consequence of exploring the problem environment, the design process of P8 is partly controlled by recognition of **partial solutions, at different levels of detail or abstraction**, without having previously decomposed the problem into subproblems. We call such design process **serendipitous design**. As another aspect of P8's process, he decomposes the problem into handling the requests coming from floors and handling the requests coming from inside the lifts. He also attempts, within this problem decomposition, to solve initially for one lift and then attempts to expand the solution to N lifts. However, he experiences great difficulty in merging the partial solutions from handling requests from floors and requests from lifts and expanding the solution from 1 lift to N lifts. The decomposition of the problem into requests from floors and requests from lifts, and the reduction of the problem from N lifts to 1 lift does not appear to be based on a specialized design schema. Such a design schema would have provided P8 a plan for a well-motivated decomposition of the problem into subproblems and a merging of the partial solutions. So, P8's design process is characterized by the use of a meta-schema for design, by exploration of the problem environment, by serendipitous design, and by difficulty in merging the partial solutions.

P3's design activities appear the least systematic and the most locally governed. They are the least systematic because P3 does not seem to use a meta-schema for design and he does not seem to use specialized design schemas to guide the decomposition of the problem into subproblems. They are the most locally governed in the sense that he does not exhibit exploration of the problem environment and consideration of alternative solutions to problems. P3 does not, as opposed to P6, consider one or more issues as crucial and select the solution from a set of alternative solutions that best satisfies the issues. His approach seems mostly governed by a **familiar computational paradigm**, logic programming. He produces many cycles of generating a tentative solution, simulating it, debugging it locally, and simulating it again. He has difficulty with mental simulations of the many tentative solutions and with keeping track of the test cases during these simulations. So, P3's design process is characterized by a generate-test-debug strategy and difficulty with mental simulations of tentative solutions.

Likewise, the solutions produced by the designers are quite different. We will discuss mainly the solution architectures and the representation schemes of the solutions.

P6's solution is a communicating ring of independent elevators. He selects distributed control over centralized control. In this scheme, each elevator operates on its own and passes information around the ring to the others, coordinating the schedules of pickups that they had decided on independently. P6's solution is represented as finite state machines. In each elevator there are two communicating finite state machines; one for handling the local processing of the elevator as it decides what stops to make along its route, and the second for communicating with the other elevators independently.

P8 adopts the classic star architecture in which the elevators communicate through a central process. P8 uses abstract data types, data flow diagrams, and pseudocode as representation schemes.

P3 works at developing a global model of system behavior described as a set of logical assertions with initial thoughts of centralized control. P3 represents the behavior of the system by logical assertions written in a Prolog style.

So, experienced designers can exhibit a very wide variety of design strategies, both between and within designers. This variety of design strategies is also accompanied by different types of breakdowns (which will be described in the next section). Finally, design solutions vary widely between designers. These observations highlight the complexity of the design process. These observations also highlight the critical contribution of specialized knowledge to the design process, and as a consequence, the wide individual differences that will be observed between designers' strategies. Finally, these observations indicate that a wide variety of tools and methodologies are needed to best support the variety of design strategies.

SOME OF THE BREAKDOWNS OBSERVED DURING DESIGN

The breakdowns that we are reporting consist of both symptoms and causes of difficulties during the design process. Moreover, these breakdowns are not necessarily independent of each other. We observed two main classes of breakdowns, with a third class being a combination of the other two. The first class consists of **knowledge-related** breakdowns. They are due to 1) lack of specialized knowledge of computational solutions corresponding to characteristics of the application domain, 2) lack of knowledge/experience of the design process itself, or 3) lack of domain knowledge. The second class of breakdowns are due to general **cognitive limitations**. They result from 1) capacity limitations of short-term or working memory, and 2) the unreliable retrieval of relevant information from long-term memory. They are also due to the weakness of our standard tools and methodologies aimed at alleviating cognitive limitations (e.g., checklists). The third class of breakdowns results from a combination of both knowledge deficiencies and cognitive limitations. These latter breakdowns occur because the lack of relevant specialized knowledge induces designers to use weak problem-solving methods, such as generate and test and means-end analysis. Unfortunately, weak methods can be very taxing cognitively and they often translate into poor performance because they require search of a large space of possibilities (Laird, Rosenbloom, and Newell (7)). Moreover, the lack of specialized knowledge is also associated with a lack of cognitive knowledge structures supporting memory for the activities during the design process (e.g., supporting memory for postponed subproblems or memory for test cases).

Knowledge-Related Breakdowns

Lack of Relevant Problem-Specific Design Schemas. The main determinant of performance appears to be the presence or absence of specialized design schemas. Design schemas are mental representations of software design families. Borrowing from a definition given by Rich and Waters (8), a design schema consists of a set of roles embedded in an underlying matrix. The roles of the schema are the parts that vary from one use of the design schema to the next. The matrix of the schema contains both fixed elements of structure (parts that are present in every occurrence) and constraints. Constraints are used both to check that the parts that fill the roles in a particular occurrence are consistent, and also to compute parts to fill empty roles in a partially specified occurrence. These schemas can be instantiated through refinements and specializations to particular instances of software designs. The design schemas embody the knowledge of alternative solutions to classes of problems. Problem-solving using design schemas proceeds through recognition that the requirements may be an instance of a known design schema followed by propagation of constraints from the explicit and implicit requirements and specialization of the design schema. Examples of design schemas and their specializations are given in the work by Lubars and Harandi (9) and Rich and Waters (8). The Inventory Control System design schema can be specialized into the Reservable Inventory Control System schema and the Non-Reservable Inventory Control System schema. A Library Inventory Control System schema is a specialization of the Non-Reservable Inventory Control System schema. In the Library Inventory Control System schema the role Check Out Book (an operation) is a specialization of the role Dispense Inventory specified in the Non-Reservable Inventory Control System schema.

Regarding retrievability, a design schema is composed of a description of the conditions under which its solution is relevant. These conditions contain an abstract representation of critical features in the given problem environment. For example, in the N-lift problem the abstract representation could be in terms of many clients who might make simultaneous requests for service to many servers (lifts) at different times and locations. Such a description could be sufficient to retrieve a design schema appropriate for the N-lift problem. Regarding problem decomposition, a design schema also contains a solution plan to guide the decomposition of the problem into subproblems, each subproblem with its own design schema. The design schema as a cognitive structure also supports the storage and retrieval of intermediate solutions and backtracking if necessary, and as a consequence, reduces working memory load during design and increases the probability that partial solutions and postponed subproblems will be retrieved when needed. The design schema also guides the expansion of a reduced solution or the merging of individual solutions to subproblems into a complete solution.

P6, because of his specialized design schemas for distributed and communication systems, could quickly identify the main design issues (i.e., no single point of failure) and knew alternative solutions to be evaluated (e.g., central vs. distributed solutions for control and communication between lifts). He could also quickly retrieve from memory, for example, known solutions for posting messages and for avoiding a race condition. However, for the subproblem of scheduling service and especially its subproblem of choosing a route, for which he seems to lack design schemas, his design process appeared much more exploratory and accompanied with mental simulations.

The following excerpts from the protocols indicate the use of such schematic knowledge. P6 immediately recognizes that in scheduling N lifts the problem of control arises. His design schema for control represents two alternatives, centralized and distributed, which he immediately retrieves. His knowledge of the alternatives also contains their advantages and disadvantages. He opts for distributed control. He then recognizes the next problem to solve, communication between lifts. He retrieves the possible alternatives and again opts for distributed communication between lifts, where each lift broadcasts which requests it will service to all other lifts. He then recognizes the problem of a race condition and immediately retrieves from his design schemas a solution to the race condition problem, that is, arrange the lift in a ring for sequential polling of the lift requests.

P6- *"I'm going to schedule the elevators. Do we have a central controller? It doesn't say in the problem. We have a central controller or a distributed controller, is that up to me? ... The good news about central control is it's an easier algorithm vs. distributed control. The bad news is that you have a single point of failure... I'll start off by thinking about a distributed control system..."*

P6- *"Let's say all the elevators are sitting down at the bottom floor and there's an up button pressed on floor three. Someone's got to post that request and someone's got to pick it up and mark it that he's responding to it. That implies a centralized place to post the requests and we're back to the single point of failure... Well, you could broadcast a message to all the other elevators that you are servicing number one. Seems like the algorithm is: every elevators look at all the buttons all the time; he sees an up posted on floor number three; ... one of them grabs it and post a message ..."*

P6- *"Now we have to make sure we don't get in a race condition. And we can do that algorithmically usually. You can do some kind of ring system by allowing them to scan in sequence and tell one another when they've got scanned so they don't get in a race."*

P3 applies a familiar computational paradigm, logic programming, but seems to lack relevant specialized design schemas. P3 recognizes at the beginning of the session that the lift problem is not a type of problem he is used to solve: *"... this is different from what I am used to thinking about because we don't just have one lift we can decide algorithmically what to do about ...".* As a consequence, P3 adopts central control for its computational simplicity: *"... Maybe I can assume there's some central processor that can receive signals from all the lifts and decide on things? ... Well, I think it might be easiest to do it that way.".*

Lack of or Poor Meta-Schema for Design. The next main determinant of performance appears to be the presence or absence of a meta-schema of software design. A design meta-schema is a schema about the process of design itself and not about a particular class of problems. The meta-schema is used to **control** the design process. A design meta-schema guides the execution of design activities and resource management. A design meta-schema represents design process goals and their alternatives and guides the amount of effort spent in different activities. For example, a design meta-schema will help answer questions such as:

- How much time and money should be spent on the complete design process?
- How much time and money should be spent on exploring the problem environment?
- How much time and money should be spent exploring alternative solutions for identified subproblems?
- Which subproblem should be attempted to be solved next?
- How many alternative solutions should be considered for the selected subproblem?

P8 has been trained as a software engineer and he seems to be using a meta-schema about design to guide the resources he allocates to various design activities and the amount of exploration done. This meta-schema is based on the design technique developed by Jackson (6). P8 first explores his mental model of the problem environment using various representation techniques to a much greater extent than P6 and P3 before proceeding to define an initial solution. The *problem environment* is a part of the real world, outside of the designed computer system, with which the computer system interacts. It contains the objects, properties, behaviors, and constraints in the world that are relevant to the design of a solution. In our case, the problem environment of a lift system contains such entities as floors, lifts, floor buttons, lift buttons, people, people waiting, requests for lifts, buildings, lift doors, lift panels, the safety of passengers, etc. The designer produces a mental model of the problem environment, possibly incomplete and inconsistent, based on the requirements and the designer's knowledge about the world. The mental model of the problem environment specifies more information than is contained explicitly in the requirements, and will often be more complete than the requirements or may sometimes be inconsistent with the stated requirements. The purpose of exploring the problem environment is to increase the completeness of the requirements and to discover unstated constraints, properties, behaviors, or objects that may generate constraints on the solution.

The following excerpt exemplifies how P8 uses a meta-schema about design to guide how much time he spends on various design activities and the amount of exploration done. About twenty minutes after the beginning of the session, while P8 is still exploring the problem environment, he shifts to a subproblem at a very low level of detail. He starts exploring the subproblems of handling inputs on an interrupt basis and of scheduling the service to lift requests. He then dramatically shifts back to a high level of abstraction. *"But at this point I feel I might be getting ahead of myself, so I want to think about other basic strategies. For instance, usually when I'm doing a design I try to think about things in a data abstraction way or object-oriented way. So now I'm trying to see if I can think about the objects and the system kind of independently."* About 5 minutes later, one can again see from the protocol how P8 seems to apply conscious strategies of resource allocation: *"... I'm sort of working at a high-level now, but I just have the feeling that if I maybe just tried working at a lower level for a second I might get some ideas ... just kind of imagine in my mind how I could actually do this at some deeper [i.e., more concrete, precise] level"*. Again about 14 minutes later, P8 makes clear that he is applying some strategies to allocate resources to different activities during design: *"... I feel I still need to think about the problem. On the other hand, I feel a little bit frustrated because I don't know why things haven't gelled enough yet. And so on the other hand, I'm impatient to sort of have things gelling; but on the other hand, I feel like there's some relationship between lift requests and floor requests that I feel I just haven't really grasped that yet."* P8 recognizes that he should explore the problem in greater detail before adopting a solution.

P6 combines exploration of the problem environment and issue-driven design. P6 does not seem to use as sophisticated a meta-schema about design as P8. Nevertheless, about sixteen minutes after the beginning of the session, where he has already explored cursorily the subproblems of posting lift requests and servicing the requests, his use of a meta-schema based on software engineering practices is revealed by his comment: *"I'm just putting down the criteria which I'm basing this algorithm on, and I want to be sure I get the requirements that I'm trying to satisfy before I get the solution... I do not want to fall in the trap of solutions without requirements."*

We hypothesize that the use of a meta-schema for design is particularly useful if the designer lacks more specialized relevant design schemas. The use of a meta-schema about design helps the designer control the amount of effort spent in different activities during design (e.g., exploration for understanding the problem environment, exploration and evaluation of different solutions).

Poor Prioritization of Issues Leading to Poor Selection from Alternative Solutions. Tong (10) views design as a dialectic between the designer and what is possible. Design can be conceived as the process of producing an optimized artifact given a set of interrelated or independent constraints, explicit or implicit, imposed by the problem, the medium, and the designer (see also Mostow (11)). Examples of constraints provided by each of these sources are:

- the problem
  - a given (perhaps informal) functional specification
  - limitations of the available media (e.g., available hardware and software)
  - implicit and explicit requirements on performance and usage (e.g., cost, power, speed, space)
  - implicit and explicit requirements on the form of the artifact (e.g., maintainability, reliability, reusability, simplicity)
- the design process itself
  - time available
  - allowable costs
  - tools available (e.g., type of workstation, special hardware)
  - team work or individual work
  - organizational procedures
- the designer
  - knowledge of the application domain
  - knowledge of the class of system being design (i.e., specialized design schemas)
  - knowledge or experience of the design process itself (i.e., meta-schema for design)
  - cognitive and motivational attributes.

Very good designers seem to know how to prioritize and balance these constraints on the basis of their domain knowledge, knowledge of the type of system to be designed and developed (i.e., design schemas), and their knowledge of the design process itself (i.e., design meta-schema). Following this prioritization, they allocate their time to the various subproblems according to their relation to these priorities. So, this third breakdown is related to management of resources and to the meta-schema of the design process.

Part of this prioritization process is the evaluation of alternative solutions based on a set of selected criteria as described above. These evaluation criteria are called *issues and their alternatives*. For example, P6's main issue is reliability and no single point of failure. He infers this issue from his knowledge of the problem domain and the class of system he is designing. When dealing with the subproblem of control, and its alternatives as centralized vs. distributed, he evaluates the two alternatives and opts for distributed control because of its perceived greater reliability. He does likewise when considering alternatives for communication schemes between lifts. The following excerpt demonstrates his evaluation of alternative solutions on the basis of the inferred issue of no single point of failure.

P6- *"The good news about central control is it's an easier algorithm vs. distributed control. The bad news is you have a single point of failure... You would rather not have a single point of failure because if, you know if all the elevators go down because it goes down... You would not want everything to go down... So, I'll start off thinking about a distributed control system .... you got to post that request and then someone's got to pick it up and mark that he's responding to it. That set of words implies a centralized place to post the request and we're back to the single point of failure. ... Well, you could broadcast a message to all the other elevators that you are servicing number one. Seems like a simple algorithm ..."*

Breakdowns Due to Cognitive Limitations

Difficulty in considering all the stated or inferred constraints in refining a solution. This breakdown represents a failure to integrate known or assumed constraints in the design solution. These failures occurred even though these constraints were explicitly given in the problem statement and the problem statement was available throughout the session to the designers.

In the example below, P3 knows the constraints that all floors must be serviced equally and that direction of travel must be kept. In his design he decides to keep the elevator going in one direction until all outstanding requests in this direction are satisfied.

P3- *"If there are still requests and those requests are higher than we want to go, then we'll keep going up... If an elevator was going up, it keeps going up until all up requests are satisfied ... that insures that requests will eventually be met, otherwise there could just be oscillating between floor one and floor two."*

Nevertheless, later, he forgets about his solution on these constraints and evaluates improperly his overall solution. P3 seems to believe that requests to go down while the lift is going up are going to be serviced immediately. As a consequence, the lift would not keep direction of travel, violating a problem constraint.

P3- *"well this is interesting now, it brings up the questions of what if an elevator is on its way up to a floor to pick up somebody up there and a person snatches it at the floor below and wants it to go down... it's going to be priority driven and that's nasty..."*

A somewhat related breakdown is to disregard certain relevant aspects of the problem - the "rose-colored glasses" syndrome. In the excerpt below, P3 proposes a non-deterministic solution to allocate floor requests to lifts. He also acknowledges that this may jeopardize the requirement that all floors be given equal priority, thereby violating a given constraint. He nevertheless adopts the non-deterministic solution without any more analysis of its consequences.

P3 - *"Our processor will look to see what elevators are moving up and down. We'll do this non-deterministically. Maybe that's dangerous for this priority (all floors given equal priority) but OK."*

Difficulty in performing complex mental simulations with many steps or with many test cases. Designers find it very difficult to mentally simulate their partial or complete solutions. They find difficult to simulate the interactions between components of the artifact. They also find difficult to simulate the behavior of a component if it extends over many steps. We also observed the multiple simulations of the same test case and the failure to simulate a crucial test case during evaluative simulations, leading to incorrect assessment of the correctness of the solution to a given subproblem and hindering progress on other subproblems. To help mental simulations, designers often resorted to diagrams. However, because they were poor medium to represent changes in location and time, they were not sufficient to prevent the breakdowns. The following excerpts show how designers had difficulty even with the simplest simulations.

P8 - "... it's kind of confusing, there's lifts (requests) and there's floors (requests) and it says "all requests for floors within lifts must be serviced eventually with floors being serviced sequentially (in the direction of travel). Apparently that means ... Let me give a better example ... I'll have to draw a picture."

P3 - "...the way I've written this doesn't capture the continuity of direction. 'Cause this just looks to see some other. We've happened to have reached some floor, this now just picks some other request. Oh, no, that's right, this tries to find a request that's in the same direction."

P8 - "When an interrupt happens it adds a request to my list and the structure of requests are floor request, a lift request, or the emergency button... Let's say the third guy wants to go the fifth floor. Let's say there's a floor request on the. Oh, I missed something here. Floor request has originating floor and direction... Could I borrow that pencil? (to draw a picture)."

The next excerpt shows how the mental simulation of the test cases is at the beginning quite systematic and quickly becomes unsystematic and finally incomplete as other concerns attract the attention of the designer.

P3 - "... Given the fact that somebody in a lift has pushed a 'go to floor' button (that's a floor he wants to go to). First of all, if that lift is at that floor then I can just de-illuminate the button..." Here, he digresses for about one minute. "... On the other hand, if he push a lift button and he's not at the floor he requested, what I'll do is I'll put that into this global base which means that by the deamon watching, the light will go on. And that's all I really have to do other than examine this and decide which way the elevators move. So I'm trying to handle the request right now... So really all I'm doing is filtering out requests that can be handled immediately, but OK, let's go with that for a second.... I'll handle emergencies later." He digresses for about 30 seconds and then changes topic drastically. He abandons the simulations of the other test cases, those requests that cannot be handled immediately. "Ok. Now comes time to build a mechanism which causes all the stuff to change."

Breakdowns Due to Lack of Knowledge and Due to Cognitive Limitations

Difficulty in keeping track and returning to aspects of problems whose solution refinements have been postponed. When focusing on one aspect of the problem and postponing the solution refinement of others, the designer must be able to remember to return to the postponed subproblems. If the designer fails to do so, the partial solutions could be incomplete and could not be merged or expanded into a complete solution. This problem is especially acute if the designer does not have specialized design schemas for the given problem, since its structure acts as an aid for the storage and retrieval of intermediate solutions. However, failing to return to a postponed subproblem is not always detrimental. A designer may uncover a new solution or adopt a new strategy that makes useless returning to a postponed subproblem. Nevertheless, this is different than failing to return to a subproblem because one forgets to look at one's mental notes or external notes or because these mental notes or external notes are insufficient.

In the following excerpt, P8 explicitly mentions an aspect of the problem he plans to return to. He forgets to return to it as he concentrates on the decomposition of the problem into requests from floors and requests from lifts and on merging the partial solutions. Note here that postponing that subproblem is appropriate because it is at a lower level of detail than the other subproblems he is handling. However, the postponed subproblem is crucial for the complete solution.

P8- *"It seems like in my interrupt system I don't just want a way of sequentially handling requests. I'm really going to need to be able to scan all outstanding requests because of the service constraints. I think I'll do that next. Capture these constraints in some way."*

Difficulty in expanding or merging partial solutions into a complete solution. The designers in our study had difficulties expanding their solution, from 1 lift to N lifts, or in merging their partial solutions, handling requests from lifts and handling requests from floors. Kant and Newell (3) also observed that the merging of the individual solutions was very difficult in the convex hull problem. Once acceptable solutions have been reached for some or all of the subproblems, these solutions must be merged together or expanded to compose a solution for the complete problem. This expansion relies on a history of the design process, and general and specialized computer science knowledge. The expansion of partial solutions actually seems difficult for most designers (this was also observed in Kant and Newell (3)). We hypothesize that the expansion of or merging of partial solutions is more difficult than the decomposition of the problem into smaller problems for three reasons:

1. Evaluative simulations for the merged or expanded solutions are more complex, more taxing cognitively than evaluative simulations for the partial solutions to the subproblems. This is because merged or expanded solutions are more complex, they have more solutions components and more interactions between these components than partial or reduced solutions.
2. Certain problem decompositions based on obvious or surface features of the problem environment (e.g., number of lifts - solve for 1 lift and expand to N lifts) may suggest solutions that do not reflect the structure of the original problem and for which no simple solution expansion exists. For example, in the case of the 1-lift problem there are no notions of coordination, communication between lifts, and race condition, which are crucial in the N-lift problem.
3. One view of the progression from design to solution/implementation is of a process of *dispersion*. When a designer breaks the problem into subproblems and refines the solution for each subproblem into more implementation-oriented representations, the implementation-oriented concepts blur the structure the original problem to solve. The solutions to the subproblems are then more difficult to merge because their original correspondence to each other has been altered. This should be more acute for complex problems where the solution of individual subproblems extends over a long period of time.

There is possibly a fourth reason. If a designer does not follow balanced development, the partial solutions will not be at the same level of detail and will be difficult to merge. This could happen for example to P8 who performed serendipitous design. However, it is difficult to precisely define when partial solutions are at the same level of detail and can, as a consequence, be mentally simulated. Therefore, it is difficult from the protocol to identify whether two partial solutions could not be merged because they were not at the same level of detail.

In the following excerpts from P8, each separate segment comes from different times in chronological order in the session and they capture the difficulty of merging the solution for one lift into a solution for N lifts.

"...I'm basically considering what's happening for one lift. I'm imagining that everything happens independently. That's not a good assumption to make. I guess I'm considering this a global list." He then attempts to solve the scheduling of requests and to perform evaluative simulations for N lifts.

"...Well the fact that I have N lifts makes it kind of complicated. So I'll just try to consider the case of one lift, try to simplify it... I'm going to back up now and try to handle this with one lift."

RELATIONS TO OTHER STUDIES AND OTHER OF OUR FINDINGS

We will now relate some of our breakdowns to other of our findings or to other studies. Adelson and Soloway (12) studied expert designers (about eight years of professional experience) in three contexts: 1) designing an unfamiliar artifact in a familiar domain; 2) designing an unfamiliar artifact in an unfamiliar domain; and 3) designing a familiar artifact in a familiar domain. They also studied two novice designers, with less than two years of experience as designers. If one were trying to compare our designers to those of Adelson and Soloway's study, we could tentatively define: 1) P6, an expert designing an unfamiliar artifact in a familiar technical domain; 2) P8, an expert designing an unfamiliar artifact in an unfamiliar technical domain; and 3) P3, an expert/novice designing an unfamiliar artifact in an unfamiliar technical domain.

The lack of specialized design schemas seems the primary breakdown to alleviate. The reasons are both empirical and logical. P6's design solution was considered superior to P8's and P3's. P6 also exhibited a more balanced systematic design process than P8 and P3. P6 appeared to have more relevant specialized design schemas than P8 and P3. These design schemas are provided by his expertize in a relevant technical domain, i.e., communication systems. Design schemas are assumed to represent a plan to decompose a problem into subproblems. As a consequence we believe that design schemas underly balanced development. During balanced development, which was described by Adelson and Soloway (2), each solution component is developed at a similar level of detail to permit mental simulations.

Design schemas are also believed to provide a cognitive structure to help store partial solutions and their evaluations and to help remember which subproblem to focus on next. As a consequence, they are believed to support mental note-taking. Mental note-taking was observed by Adelson and Soloway (2) and described as a mechanism supporting balanced development. As a consequence, a lack of specialized design schemas will worsen another breakdown, the difficulty in keeping track and returning to postponed subproblems. This breakdown was rarely observed in P6 but was very frequent in P3.

The lack of relevant specialized design schemas appears to be associated with another breakdown, difficulty in expanding a reduced solution or merging of partial solutions. A design schema provides a plan for a well-motivated decomposition of the problem into subproblems. The partial solutions from such decompositions can be easily merged together to form a complete solution. When a problem is not decomposed on the basis of a design schema, the partial solutions may be difficult to expand or merge together. P6 had very little difficulty merging his partial solutions, while this was particularly difficult for P8.

Finally, we believe that the use of specialized design schemas frees the designers from reliance on weak problem-solving methods such as generate and test and means-ends analysis. These weak problem-solving methods, especially generate-and-test, can be very taxing cognitively. In fact, P3 had the least relevant specialized design schemas and adopted a "generate-and-test-and-debug" strategy. Not surprisingly, he experienced many difficulties with mental simulations with many steps or many test cases.

The next important breakdown is the lack of meta-schema of the design process which leads to poor allocation of resources and time to the various activities during the design process. We believe that relevant specialized design schemas obviate the need for sophisticated meta-schemas about the design process. Specialized design schemas provide for systematic decomposition of the problem and for solutions to each subproblem. The need to carefully manage resources is less critical in this context. However, when specialized design schemas are lacking, the need to carefully balance exploration of the problem environment, consideration of alternative solutions, and evaluations of selected tentative solutions is critical for the quality of the solution reached. While P8 seemed have less specialized design schemas relevant to the problem than P6, he appeared to have a sophisticated design meta-schema, which was lacking in P3. P8's solution was considered better than P3's. P8's design meta-schema guided him to explore the problem environment before focusing a testing and debugging solutions. We speculate that the exploration of the problem environment induced *serendipitous problem-solving activities*. By serendipitous design, we mean a design process controlled by recognition of **partial solutions, at different levels of detail or abstraction**, without having previously decomposed the problem into subproblems. We hypothesize that serendipity in design arises from a form of data-driven processing as opposed to goal-directed processing, such as described by Anderson (13). This data-driven processing can be triggered by aspects of the problem environment at different levels of detail or abstraction. The concept of serendipity in design is similar to the idea of *opportunistic* problem-solving (Hayes-Roth and Hayes-Roth (14)), though different in some crucial aspects. The main difference is that in serendipitous design the partial solutions are not synergetic, they do not necessarily interact and they do not fulfill more goals than originally anticipated. An important observation to make is that serendipitous design does not follow balanced development. Moreover, P8 did not extensively exhibit mental note-taking. However, we believe that when specialized design schemas are lacking, the presence of a design meta-schema supporting important exploration of the problem environment is advantageous. We speculate that exploration of the problem environment induces serendipitous design, as opposed to balanced development. However, in the absence of specialized design schemas we believe serendipitous design is advantageous. In fact, serendipitous design might be hallmark of an important type of design, designing new innovative software systems. For such systems are not simply modifications of previously well understood systems, they introduce genuinely new ideas. As a consequence, their design cannot rely on computer science knowledge embodied in specialized design schemas. Moreover, because of real-life constraints designers may often face the situation of designing systems outside their areas of expertize, that is, for which they lack specialized design schemas. Finally, a certain amount of exploration of the problem environment is always desirable as it permits uncovering critical missing information in the requirements. In all these cases, we need to develop tools and methodologies which permit designers to benefit as much as possible from serendipitous problem-solving, as opposed to discourage it because it does not follow the prescriptive practices from software engineering.

While this is a preliminary study, it is very encouraging to see that similar design processes and breakdowns have been observed in other very different fields. After the completion of this study, we became aware of the work by Ullman, Stauffer, and Dietterich (5) on the mechanical design process. They collected verbal protocols from four professional engineers working on problems related to their areas of expertize. Our designer P8 performed a great deal of serendipitous problem-solving, probably underlied by his extensive exploration of the problem environment. Ullman, Stauffer, and Dietterich labelled these problem solving activities opportunistic. We believe that the name opportunistic is misleading, as synergy did not appear in the partial solutions reached by the designers. The partial solutions did not satisfy unanticipatedly more goals than they were originally meant to. Interestingly, Adelson and Soloway (12) described some design behaviors which may be related to serendipitous design. The particularly relevant observation is that the **experienced** designer designing a **familiar object** in a **familiar technical domain** departed from balanced development and systematic expansion of his solution when dealing with the aspect of the problem that was unfamiliar to him, the functionality of a particular chip.

Ullman, Stauffer, and Dietterich also observed that not all designers followed balanced development (even though all their designers were experienced). They observed the use of diagrams to prevent breakdowns from difficulty of mental simulations, even though diagrams were only partly successful. They also observed that designers forgets to return to postponed subproblems. They also noticed that designers have a tendency to elaborate mainly one main design idea throughout the design session with few considerations of major changes to the basic design.

So, it appears that experienced designers are aware of the power of exploration of the problem environment in uncovering new important information (i.e., as part of their meta-schema about the design process). They use exploration of the problem environment when dealing with unfamiliar information or when progress toward a solution is insufficient using balanced development. This exploration of the problem environment induces problem-solving that does not follow balanced development but is more appropriately described as serendipitous.

Similarly, Flower and Hayes and their colleagues have observed rapid shifts between levels of abstraction and detail in the planning and writting of documents and the use of design schemas and of meta-schemas (15). Finally, Schoenfeld (16) has observed similar behaviors in mathematical problem solving.

CONCLUSIONS

While the study reported in this chapter is an exploratory study, it provides a wealth of observations that enrich our understanding of the software design process by individuals. Our findings were related to previous studies of the design process by individuals and revealed new behaviors and some important new questions about the design process.

Our observations of designers working on the N-lift problem show that designers use a wide variety of design strategies, both between and within designers, in addition to the top-down refinement approach described in software engineering. We also found that our designers were able to work at different levels of abstraction and detail and not just follow a balanced development strategy. We also observed serendipitous problem-solving, not reported in previous studies of software design by individuals. We also observed a great emphasis on understanding and elaborating the requirements through mental simulations. We have observed a wide variety of breakdowns, also not reported or emphasized in previous studies: 1) lack of specialized design schemas; 2) lack of a meta-schema about the design process leading to poor allocation of resources to the various design activities; 3) poor prioritization of issues leading to poor selection of alternative solutions; 4) difficulty in considering all the stated or inferred constraints in defining a solution; 5) difficulty in keeping track and returning to subproblems whose solution has been postponed; 6) difficulty in performing mental simulations with many steps or test cases; and 7) difficulty in expanding or merging solutions from individual subproblems to form a complete solution.

There was also overlap between our findings and the findings of other studies in varied fields (e.g., mechanical engineering and mathematical problem-solving). This overlap suggests that we are tapping general problem-solving strategies for design problems. This also suggests that the tools we are designing to alleviate the breakdowns have wider applicability than software design. This overlap also increases confidence about the validity of the findings and their generalizability.

For each breakdown, we have recommended software tools or methodologies to alleviate them (Guindon, Krasner, and Curtis (17)). In further studies, we will test the effectiveness of these tools and methodologies. These further studies will be indirect tests of the hypotheses raised in this study. In addition, they will provide empirical results on the influence of software tools on the design process. We will also explore in greater depth the nature of the application-specific design schemas, their role in design performance, their role in the different expertize exhibited by our designers, their relation to the breakdowns we have observed, and how software tools could be designed to alleviate lack of design schemas.

REFERENCES

1. Jeffries, R., Turner, A.A., Polson, P., & Atwood, M.E. (1981). The Processes Involved in Designing Software. In J.R. Anderson (Ed.), *Cognitive Skills and Their Acquisition*. Hillsdale, N.J.: Erlbaum, 225-283.
2. Adelson, B. & Soloway, E. (1985). *A Cognitive Model of Software Design*. Technical Report 342, Department of Computer Science, Yale University.
3. Kant, E. & Newell, A. (1984) Problem Solving Techniques for the Design of Algorithms. *Information Processing and Management*, 28(1), 97-118.
4. Carroll, J.M., Thomas, J.C., & Malhotra, A. (1979). Clinical-Experimental Analysis of Design Problem Solving. *Design Studies*, 1(2), 84-92.
5. Ullman, D.G., Stauffer, L.A., Dietterich, T.G. (1987) Preliminary Results of an Experimental Study of the Mechanical Design Process. Proceedings of the Workshop on the Study of the Design Process. Oakland, California.
6. Jackson, M. (1983). *System Development*. Englewood Cliffs, N.J.: Prenctice Hall.
7. Laird, J., Rosenbloom, P., & Newell, A. (1986). *Universal Subgoaling and Chunking*. Kluwer Academic Publishers.
8. Rich, C., & Waters, R.C. (1986) Toward a Requirements Apprenctice: On the Boundary Between Informal and Formal Specifications. M.I.T. A.I. Memo No. 907.
9. Lubars, M.T., & Harandi, M.T. (1987) *Knowledge-Based Software Design Using Design Schemas."* Proceedings of the Ninth International Conference on Software Engineering, Monterey, California., pp 253-262.
10. Tong, C. (1984). Knowledge-Based Circuit Design. Ph.D. Dissertation, Department of Computer Science. Stanford University.

11. Mostow, J. (1985). Toward Better Models of the Design Process. *AI Magazine*, 44-57.
12. Adelson, B. & Soloway, E. (1985). The Role of Domain Experience in Software Design. *IEEE Transactions on Software Engineering, Vol. 11, No. 11.*
13. Anderson, J.R. (1983). *The Architecture of Cognition.* Cambridge, MA: Harvard University Press.
14. Hayes-Roth, B. & Hayes-Roth, F. (1979). A Cognitive Model of Planning. *Cognitive Science*, 3(4), 275-310.
15. Flower, L., Hayes, J.R., Carey, L., Schriver, K., Stratman, J. (1986). Detection, Diagnosis, and the Strategies of Revision. College Composition and Communication, Vol. 37, No. 1.
16. Schoenfeld, A.H. (1987) *Mathematical Problem Solving.* Academic Press.
17. Guindon, R., Krasner, H., Curtis, B. (1987). A Model of Cognitive Processes in Software Design: An Analysis of Breakdowns in Early Design Activities by Individuals. MCC Technical Report in preparation.

ACKNOWLEDGEMENTS

We wish to thank Glenn Bruns, Jeff Conklin, Michael Evangelist, and Colin Potts for very insightful comments and criticisms on an earlier version of this paper.

APPENDIX

PROBLEM STATEMENT

An N-lift (N-elevator) system is to be installed in a building with M floors. The lifts and the control mechanism are supplied by a manufacturer. The internal mechanisms of these are assumed (given) in this problem.

DESIGN THE LOGIC TO MOVE LIFTS BETWEEN FLOORS IN THE BUILDING ACCORDING TO THE FOLLOWING RULES:

1. Each lift has a set of buttons, 1 button for each floor. These illuminate when pressed and cause the lift to visit the corresponding floor. The illumination is cancelled when the corresponding floor is visited (i.e. stopped at) by the lift.
2. Each floor has 2 buttons (except ground and top), one to request an up-lift and one to request a down-lift. These buttons illuminate when pressed. The buttons are cancelled when a lift visits the floor and is either traveling in the desired direction, or visiting the floor with no requests outstanding.
   In the latter case, if both floor request buttons are illuminated, only 1 should be cancelled. The algorithm used to decide which to service first should minimize the waiting time for both requests.
3. When a lift has no requests to service, it should remain at its final destination with its doors closed and await further requests (or model a "holding" floor).
4. All requests for lifts from floors must be serviced eventually, with all floors given equal priority (can this be proved or demonstrated?).
5. All requests for floors within lifts must be serviced eventually, with floors being serviced sequentially in the direction of travel (can this be proved or demonstrated?).
6. Each lift has an emergency button which, when pressed causes a warning signal to be sent to the site manager. The lift is then deemed "out of service". Each lift has a mechanism to cancel its "out of service" status.

CHAPTER 6

A Methodology for Studying Software Design Teams:
An Investigation of Conflict Behaviors
in the Requirements Definition Phase

Diane B. Walz
University of Texas / MCC
Austin, TX 78712

Joyce J. Elam
Harvard University
Boston, MA 02163

Herb Krasner
Bill Curtis
MCC Software Technology Program
Austin, TX 78759

ABSTRACT

This paper presents a methodology which the authors have developed for the analysis of the processes involved in designing large–scale computer–based systems. This methodology is based upon a characterization of the design process which 1) recognizes the diversity of team members' underlying conceptualizations, 2) emphasizes the transformation of abstract goals into concrete systems, and 3) distinguishes between those breakdowns in the design process which are a part of the design function, and those which are the results of the group process itself (within the design context). Essentially, the methodology traces interaction behaviors within design group meetings and relates them, hierarchically, to the issues under discussion. The paper also presents empirical results and a preliminary evaluation of the methodology from an analysis of the group aspect (specifically, conflict behaviors) within a series of requirements definition meetings from an actual development project.

INTRODUCTION

Large, complex computer systems are generally designed by a group (or groups) of cooperating experts. Thus, an understanding of the processes of programming–in–the–large will include a group as well as an individual dimension. Guinan and Bostrom [1] hypothesize that project productivity can be significantly improved by identifying effective communications patterns within the software design team, and they advocate research which attempts to identify those specific patterns and behaviors which are effective.

Formal methods such as structured analysis and design (Ross and Schoman [2]) have emphasized the need for development of relationships between the design team and the user group. Studies indicate, however, that the use of these techniques does not necessarily result in proper problem definitions or adequate solutions to the users' needs (Guimares [3], Mantei [4]). In a discussion of methodological issues relative to investigations of programming-in-the-large, Soloway [5] emphasizes the lack of process models in this domain and recommends the use of "research methodologies that are appropriate for the state of our understanding."

The goal of the current ongoing research is the development of a process model for collaborative design of complex computer- based systems. For this purpose, a methodology has been developed for analysis of the interactions of a set of actual software design meetings from a development project within MCC. Thus, this methodology is not intended for the testing of specific hypotheses, but rather as a tool for analysis and subsequent theory building.

The purpose of this paper is to describe this methodology, and to demonstrate its use in an illustrative study of the behaviors of software design team members. In the subsequent sections we:

1. briefly describe the process of software design,

2. discuss the current limitations of investigating the group dimension of software design,

3. describe the methodology which we have developed for this purpose, and

4. present the results of an application of this methodology.

THE DESIGN PROCESS

Churchman [6] defines design broadly as a process for prescribing objects and relationships to achieve some intended purpose, noting that the designer must assume or acquire knowledge about the thinking of the set of clients or users of the ultimate system. Simon [7] views the design process as an ill-structured problem, which can be managed by decomposition into a collection of well-structured component problems.

Studies of individual software design activities have concluded that individuals formulate mental models of the design problem and potential solutions. These are evaluated and explored by mental simulation (Jeffries et al [8], Adelson and Soloway [9], Kant and Newell [10]). In a study of the cognitive processes involved in upstream design activities, Guindon et al [11] have shown that breakdowns (the term breakdown stems from the work of Winograd and Flores [12] who derived this notion from Martin Heidegger's contention that objects and properties are not inherent in the world, except under conditions of interruption or anomaly) occur as a result of cognitive limitations and/or lack of knowledge. Included in the knowledge-related breakdowns are the lack of relevant application knowledge and the lack of a schema for the design process.

The context of programming in the large addresses systems which are, by definition, large and complex, involving knowledge across multiple domains and often including numerous, potentially interrelated constraints and assumptions. In such an environment, the breakdowns described above can be considered to be the norm, as they often represent the reasons why a group is assigned to a project. Such systems generally require knowledge which is unavailable from any individual. In this environment, mental simulation, on a global level, represents a gargantuan task for an individual. For these reasons, the analysis and design of complex computer-based systems is often assigned to a team (or teams).

The design of complex computer-based systems is a longitudinal process of interactions involving (at a minimum) both users and designers. While individual design tasks are largely cognitive in nature, the process of designing software when no individual possesses all of the knowledge and/or skills required, also includes a dimension of interactions.

In general, the process of software design involves the transformation of abstract goals and/or requirements into concrete systems. This process involves the designers' attempts to translate the users' initial request into an actual design, often (and ideally) with additional input from the user community. Especially at the earliest stages, the individual team members hold widely differing mental models of the problem and relevant solutions. These models can differ in numerous ways. They can define differing solution spaces, orientations and/or approaches. They can differ in the degree of completeness of the solution, or in the context of the representation.

These differences are the result of a complex set of interrelated individual differences among team members, including (but not limited to) effort expended, application knowledge, and individual skills and abilities. Individuals may also apply different overall approaches to the design process itself. Strategies for decomposing the problem may also differ.

The team members move toward creation of a design product through both individual efforts and an interactive process which results in gradual shaping, revision, and/or replacement of their mental models. The group process of software design provides explicit relief for certain of the knowledge-related and cognitive breakdowns (described above). A wider base for information sharing, evaluation, simulation, and task organization is provided for those issues to which the group attends. We believe that the space of issues (both resolved and unresolved) addressed by the group impacts the evolution of the team members' mental models toward the shared or compatible models which are necessary for the creation of a software design product.

Additional breakdowns emerge, however, as a result of the group interactions themselves. Group members may be in disagreement about aspects of the problem model, solution model, design approach, goals, sub-goals or goal-paths. A certain amount of this disagreement must be resolved if the group is to effectively produce a design product. If the ultimate design is produced by multiple individuals, enough conflicts must be resolved to achieve compatibility in the individuals' mental models. If the design is, due to steamrolling, a reflection of only one individual's ideas, the "resolution" of conflicts and disagreements within the group is simply the absence of rebellion. Group members may also suffer from difficulties of communication, due to their differing backgrounds, even when no conflict or disagreement exists. And to some extent, these miscommunications can hamper the design process.

We thus characterize the group software design process as one which addresses two classes of breakdowns: those which naturally occur when individuals attempt the design of complex systems, and those which are products of the group interaction itself.

GROUP DYNAMICS

While experimental studies of small group behavior (in general) and small group decision making (in particular) are quite numerous in the literature on group dynamics, there have been no theoretical formulations which can adequately integrate and organize the empirical data. Shaw, [13] cites the complexity of the phenomena, in general, as a reason for the absence of such a theory. Thus, group process and effectiveness may be affected by a complexity of factors. And to the extent that these factors are those that differentiate the domain of software design from the group activities typically studied, the application of the findings of this literature to the group software design process may be inappropriate.

In general, the tasks which have been studied experimentally differ from the task of group software design with respect to several (possibly interrelated) factors:

1 -- the length of time that the individual team member can expect to work together,

2 -- the individual motivations of the team members,

3 -- the composition of the team,

4 -- the level of complexity of the task, and

5 -- the amount of structure of the task.

The individual members of a software design team are working professionals, engaged in a deeply intellectual activity. The composition of the team is often purposefully heterogeneous (relative to the task at hand), including widely differing backgrounds, abilities, knowledge, and functional orientations. The team members generally expect to be working together for the length of the project. For complex systems, this should imply a team effort of considerable duration, measured in months and years. Most studies of group decision making behavior have involved single sessions, after which the subjects did not expect to interact. This represents one aspect where the motivations of actual designers can be considered to be different from the motivations of the participants of controlled studies.

Also, the task of software design represents an individual's job (and thus, their livelihood). The motivations of these individuals should differ significantly from those of the subjects in the problem solving experiments discussed above. The design of large computer-based systems is also a more complex task than those which have been studied in controlled, single-session experiments. And the task is relatively unstructured, in that there is seldom one right solution, solution strategy or enumerable solution set.

Because these factors can be important determinants of group behavior and performance in the design of computer systems, it is difficult to generalize the findings of the empirical literature on group dynamics to the environment of group software design.

A METHODOLOGY FOR THE STUDY OF GROUP DESIGN

Because no formal theories currently exist to describe the underlying processes involved in the group design of complex computer-based systems, controlled studies which test hypotheses about individual factors are not appropriate. Todd and Benbasat [14] recommend the use of process tracing techniques, particularly protocol analysis (Ericsson and Simon [15]), for situations where the researcher is interested in generating hypotheses and/or studying process as well as performance. Soloway [5] offers similar advice for studies of programming-in- the-large, which he contends is still in the stage of theory formation. The methodology described here for the study of group software design is based upon a system of process tracing for interaction analysis.

As originally developed by Bales [16] interaction process analysis is a process tracing technique which is used to understand the ongoing stream of interaction during a group meeting. For interaction analysis, a group meeting is divided into acts. Usually, an act corresponds to an uninterrupted statement (or group of statements) made by one individual. However, if an individual discusses more than one issue or context in an uninterrupted group of statements, then the statements are classified as more than one act. The individual acts are classified according to a predefined coding scheme which represents, hopefully, a mutually exclusive list of behaviors.

The coding scheme should be tailored to the domain under consideration -- in this case, the design of complex computer software by teams. That is, the coding scheme represents an a priori hypothesis of what is important in the interacting activities of the group being studied. The interaction process coding scheme developed by the authors (Table 1) is based upon the characterization of the group software design task as a process where individuals with a diversity of mental models interact to produce a design product.

Interactions are thus classified as one of three general types:

1) The portrayal of one's own internal representation, or mental model, of some problem, topic, or issue,

2) The attempt to create bridges of understanding between other group members, and

3) The management of the meeting and of the project.

Each of these general types encompasses a set of specific interaction behaviors. Also, when actions are classified, an identifier of the actor is also recorded with the interaction behavior, since we expect the roles and the relationships of the collaborating individuals to affect the group process.

Because the notion of movement between levels of abstraction is fundamental to the design process in the context of the issues addressed by the group, the methodology includes the creation of a hierarchical issue chart for a meeting, or series of meetings. The nodes of the chart represent the issues addressed by the group, with a hierarchy (general--specific) superimposed (see Figure 1). Lower level nodes represent sub-classes of the relevant parent node.

TABLE 1. INTERACTION PROCESS CODING SCHEME

I. Portrayal of an individual's mental model.
   A. Opinion: an individual's expressed opinion.
      1. offered without explanation.
      2. offered with explanation.
   B. Clarification: a statement for clarifying one's opinion.
   C. Modification: a statement which modifies a previously stated position.
   D. Agreement: a statement which expresses support.
      1. offered without explanation.
      2. offered with explanation.
   E. Conflict: a statement which expresses disagreement.
      1. offered without explanation.
      2. offered with explanation.

II. Processes for "Bridging" mental models.
   A. Asks: a statement which requests information.
   B. Interprets: a statement which describes the mental models of others in the group.
      1. Relative to the entire group.
      2. Relative to some subset of the group.

III. Management.
   A. Calls for resolution on an issue.
   B. Seeks postponement of discussion on an issue.
   C. Set agenda.
   D. Assign tasks.
   E. Set deadlines.

The issue under discussion is recorded with the interaction process data so that changes in the level of abstraction of the disagreements can be tracked. Specifically, this should provide information on the manner in which the group moves through multiple levels of abstraction, and offers the potential for identifying behavior patterns which can facilitate or hinder this effort.

For example, the statement "No, I think interaction with the customer is valid." (expressing disagreement with a suggestion for communication with the customer group) is classified as conflict with explanation at a higher level of abstraction. The speaker is expressing disagreement on the grounds of a higher principle: that personal interaction with the customer is valued. Conversely, a statement such as "I think your approach implies an amount of messages that becomes computationally infeasible very quickly, even ignoring the memory considerations." represents a decrease in level of abstraction, as the speaker is using a physical implication of an overall strategy to evaluate the strategy.

Because of the complexity of the methodology, live meetings are not analyzed. The meetings are videotaped and the videotapes are transcribed. The observer is instructed to view the videotape of a meeting at least once before applying the methodology on the transcript of that meeting.

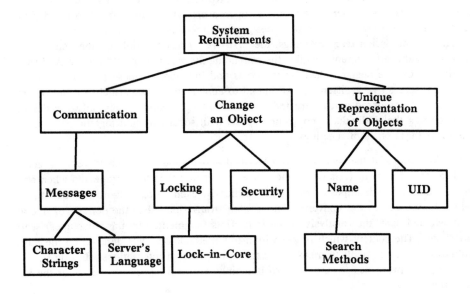

Figure 1. An Abbreviated Example of An Issue Chart

DATA

The Software Technology Program at MCC is involved in a directed research program aimed at improving both the productivity of the software development process and the quality of the ultimate product. The Design Process group is attempting to develop models of the design process as a basis for creation of an environment for the design of large computer-based systems. The developing models are based (at least in part) on empirical evidence from actual development activities. An experimental plan for the observation of an actual development project (an object based server) was formulated at MCC, where the data was collected. The goals of this plan, ex ante, were:

1. development of a methodology for large-scale observational studies of the software design process, and
2. formulation of preliminary observational data on an actual development project into a preliminary model of team design.

All of the team meetings relative to the object server project were videotaped. This represented a total of 43 meetings, covering a time span of about four months. The sessions tended to be about two hours in length. All of the participants in the project were experienced software designers and/or researchers. The project's goal was the development and exploration of an object base server. The software design team was formed for the project and, in most cases, the individuals had not previously worked with one another. Only formal team meetings were recorded. Individual design activities and informal discussions were not included in the data collection.

Of the 43 meetings videotaped, the first nine involved only users. The purpose of these meetings was to identify and agree upon a project for assignment to the design team. The remaining sessions were design team meetings, with some user representation. Of the design team meetings, the first five focused mainly on the determination of system requirements, while the remaining 29 meetings primarily involved the production of the design. Because the goals and functions of these three types of meetings were so very different, we intend to analyze them separately so that our results can be compared and contrasted. And we intend to study group software design by analyzing the individual and group aspects both separately and together, across the these three types of meetings.

Some limitations of the methodology described above should be considered. In general, a loss of content (relative to the "live" interactions) is to be expected when observers analyze videotapes of meetings. Similarly, even more content may be missed when the videotapes are converted into written transcripts. For the domain of interactions studied here, the analysis of the transcripts (augmented by the videotapes) seems adequate. The content which is lost within this methodology will tend to be the more subtle (and thus difficult to measure) aspects of personal interactions. In this study of group software design, the concern is mainly with task-specific aspects of the interactions.

The reliability of the methodology across various observers has not yet been assessed. Variation between observers may occur in the categorization of individual acts, the identification of issues, and the determination of the relative levels of abstraction across issues. Also, because of the need to track issues and relate them to a hierarchy, observers may require, ex ante, a significant level of knowledge about design (and design strategies) as well as knowledge about relevant technical and application areas.

USE OF THE METHODOLOGY: AN ILLUSTRATIVE CASE

The purpose of this study is to examine the group aspect of software design. Ideally, the group process is itself a remedy for some of the breakdowns which are observed at the individual level. Yet the group process itself produces breakdowns of conflicting mental models and miscommunications between group members. Specifically, this study addresses those breakdowns which are inherent in the group process itself. We examine these breakdowns within the context of the requirements determination phase of an actual design project.

The five meetings which focused on requirements determination involved the designers' attempts to acquire knowledge from the users about the system being requested.

Instances of disagreement or miscommunication between group members represent breakdowns (within the software design process) when they "interrupt" other actions (e.g., description, questioning, etc.). Instances of these breakdowns occur only in the presence of explicit statements reflecting conflict or disagreement. For the purpose of analyzing the breakdowns inherent in group software design, the current study involves the examination of those acts which are classified as conflict behaviors according to the interaction process coding scheme described in Table 1. This coding scheme contains two classifications of conflict behaviors: those which are offered with some substantiating explanation and those which are not.

Conflict behavior and interpersonal disagreement are considered to be normal products of group interaction, and are neither intrinsically good nor bad. Studies of groups engaged in solving complex planning problems have observed tendencies to avoid uncertainty and smooth over conflict (Brodwin and Bourgeous [17]). Such groups have also been found to retain invalid assumptions that reduce solution quality when thorough testing and critiques of these assumptions were not explicitly made (Janis [18], Mitroff [19]). Other studies have shown that conflict behavior increases the quality of group decision making by stimulating critical thinking, increasing group involvement, and widening the search for alternatives (Fisher [20]). These results imply that "a certain amount" of interpersonal disagreement is beneficial for group problem solving. Further investigation of the role of conflict behaviors (and the factors which affect these behaviors) will provide important input to the development of a process model of group design of computer–based systems.

Measures.
The five meetings of the design team which were classified as the requirements definition phase form the basis for the analysis reported in this paper. See Appendix A for a brief synopsis of each meeting. Both users and designers were represented in these meetings, in varying numbers.

Transcripts of each of the five meetings were divided into acts. The individual acts were then classified according to the IPA coding scheme described above in order to identify the conflict behaviors. An act is classified as conflict behavior (according to the coding scheme displayed in Table 1) if it represents a challenge to or a disagreement with a previous statement. For example, an initial statement may be challenged on its own merits, or its underlying assumptions or critical elements may be disputed. Similarly, a statement which questions the relevance of a previous statement to the problem at hand is also classified as a conflict action.

A conflict act may or may not involve the offering of an explanation for the disagreement. Substantiation is defined broadly as any explanation offered for an individual's disagreement. Thus, statements such as "No, that's not true." and "I disagree." are considered to offer no substantiation. Statements such as "No, that's not what I said." and "Not if sockets are a requirement!" are classified as offering substantiation. For the conflict behaviors identified here, the relationship of the explanation (if any) to the source of the disagreement on the issue chart was recorded as either a higher, a lower, or the same level of abstraction. Also, the roles (user/designer) of the individuals involved in the acts classified as conflict (the individual who expresses disagreement and the speaker of the statement which was the source of the disagreement) were recorded.

The following measures were recorded:

Frequency:
o the percentage of acts in a meeting which are identified as conflict acts.
Roles:
o the percentage of conflict acts which represented a user disagreeing with a statement made by another user,
o the percentage of conflict acts which represented a user disagreeing with a statement made by an designer,
o the percentage of conflict acts which represented an designer disagreeing with a statement made by another designer,
o the percentage of conflict acts which represented an designer disagreeing with a statement made by a user,

Substantiation:
o the percentage of conflict acts which represented statements offered with some substantiation.
Changes in level of abstraction:
o the percentage of the substantiated conflict acts which represented: a) an increase, b) a decrease, and c) no change in the level of abstraction of the original statement.

The percentages in the 'Roles' category described above which would have obtained if the participants in the conflict acts had been chosen randomly were computed for comparison to the actuals. For the set of identified conflict acts, the probability that an individual of role type 'x' expresses disagreement with an individual of differing role type 'y' (x \= y) is:

$Prob(x,y) = N_x/N * N_y/(N-1)$,
  where x = designer, user
    y = designer, user
    N_i = number of individuals of role type 'i' in attendance at the meeting,
    N = total number in attendance at the meeting.

The probability that an individual of role type 'x' expresses disagreement with an individual of the same role type is:

$Prob(x,x) = N_x/N * (N_x-1)/(N-1)$,
  where x = designer, user
    N_x = number of individuals of role type 'x' in attendance at the meeting,
    N = total number in attendance at the meeting.

For each meeting, a Pearson Chi-square statistic will be computed to test whether the frequencies actually observed within the 'Roles' categories are the same as these expected frequencies.

Results.
The measures described above for each of the five meetings are presented in Table 2,

along with descriptive information concerning the number of participants in each meeting and the length of the meeting in minutes.

The overall frequency of conflict behavior was fairly constant across the five meetings. The relatively lower frequency found within the last meeting can be explained by the fact that a new designer had been assigned to the project and considerable time was spent providing background and general information for this person. Conflict behaviors, on average, represented about 13% (14.5% if meeting 5 is excluded) of the group interactions. This represents an overall average rate of about three conflict actions every four minutes, which is considerable.

For the first and second meetings, the results of the Pearson Chi-square test (See Table 2) imply that the distribution of the conflict interactions between users and designers is not different from that which would have occurred if the participants had spoken randomly. For the third and fourth meetings, however, we must reject the hypothesis that the distribution of conflict interactions between users and designers is the same as that which would have been expected randomly. The percentage of conflict actions which involved users is greater in all categories. For example, the percentages of conflict interactions which involved users disagreeing with users were 25 and 24% for meetings three and four (respectively), as compared to an expected probability of .04. While the fifth meeting's percentages appear to correspond more closely to the expected random distribution than do those of meetings three and four, the hypothesis that the frequencies observed are the same as those expected cannot be rejected. Again, these results for meeting five may have been affected by the fact that a new designer was present who required briefing throughout the session.

The process dimension measurements reveal that, for the most part, team members offered substantiation when they expressed disagreement with a previous statement. For the first, second and fifth meetings the explanations offered were more likely (73%, on average) to be based on issues at the same conceptual level or higher. For the third and fourth meetings, an average of 75% of the explanations offered were at the same conceptual level or lower.

A major difference between the first and second pairs of meetings is the number of users in attendance. For the first and second meetings, only one user was present. For these meetings, the designers dominated the conflict interactions with discussions between themselves as they attempted to interpret the initial specification document from the users. For the third and fourth meetings, two users were present and most of the conflict interactions involved one or both users. The third and fourth meetings were also somewhat different in their structure, as the descriptions in appendix A reveal. Within these sessions, the designers questioned the users from a prepared list.

CONCLUSIONS AND OBSERVATIONS

For the design group studied here, while a considerable amount of conflict behavior was observed, it did not appear to be dysfunctional. The conflict that we observed was mild -- nonaggressive and nonpersonal -- and was generally offered with substantiation. It is possible that we are seeing in this team the same smoothing over of conflict that was seen in planning groups in other studies. In general, we found little

TABLE 2. DESCRIPTIVE MEASURES AND RESULTS

MEETING NUMBER:	1	2	3	4	5
Elapsed time (minutes)	115	90	80	103	120
Number in attendance	5	6	7	7	7
Number of users	1	1	2	2	1
Total no. of acts	592	537	394	694	753
No. of conflict acts	86	74	48	116	58
Frequency					
Conflict acts (% of total)	15%	14%	12%	17%	8%
Roles					
Designer with designer	60%	66%	10%	13%	47%
	(.6)	(.67)	(.48)	(.48)	(.71)
User with user	NA	NA	25%	24%	NA
	--	--	(.04)	(.04)	--
Designer with user	14%	11%	33%	32%	24%
	(.2)	(.17)	(.24)	(.24)	(.14)
User with Designer	26%	23%	31%	36%	29%
	(.2)	(.17)	(.24)	(.24)	(.14)
Chi–square	2.94	3.15	66.17*	143.85*	19.41*
Substantiation.					
% substantiated	93%	86%	94%	80%	83%
Level of abstraction.					
% substantiated at a:					
higher	30%	40%	20%	31%	27%
lower	16%	30%	47%	42%	35%
the same	54%	34%	33%	27%	38%
level of abstraction					

* indicates significance at a = .001

(Numbers in parentheses denote expected random probabilities.)

evidence of conflict resolution in the meetings, and observed a tendency for conflict over specific issues to reemerge in later meetings. This implies that proper management of and attention to unresolved issues may hasten the process of requirements definition. This finding is consistent with another study (Curtis et al, [21]) which asserts that the number of issues raised and the proportion remaining unsolved may be the most valuable leading indicator available to management about a system's progress.

The empirical results described above reveal significant differences in the group interactions among the meetings. Essentially, meetings three and four were found to differ from the other meetings with respect to: the distribution of conflict interactions between users and designers, and the level of abstraction with which the disagreement was substantiated. These meetings differed from the other three on two major dimensions: they had more than one user in attendance, and a list of questions (prepared in advance by the designers) was used as an agenda throughout the meetings.

The extent to which these results are due to the group composition, presence of an agenda, or both is not clear from the current study. And further research is needed to develop any rigorously normative implications. We may speculate that the user group should not be thought of as one homogeneous group with the same goals and assumptions -- even when a single requirements specification document has been created. Adequate representation from the user community on the design team may require input from more than one user, specifically within the requirements definition phase.

We may also speculate that an agenda of prepared questions (usually requesting the filling of individuals' knowledge gaps) can greatly facilitate the transfer of information between and among group members. This implies that the formalization of one aspect of the breakdowns which occur on an individual level may enhance the group process of software design.

These results also suggest that additional work should study the manner in which the group addresses the various levels of abstraction within the design process. The data point out fairly strongly that the design team does tend to move up and down what we have dubbed "a conceptual ladder" in providing substantiations for their disagreements. An understanding of the communication patterns involved in moving up and down this "conceptual ladder" should provide insights for developers of computer support for software design teams.

One insight gained from the characterization of design and empirical results in this study is that an environment of group software design should not be a conflict-free environment, but a conflict-managed environment. Conflict is seen as a normal part of the group process, and is considered to serve as an identifier of the breakdowns which occur when groups meet to design software. Thus, one goal of a software design task should not be the minimization of conflict, but the identification (or surfacing) and subsequent resolution of conflict.

The methods appropriate for the surfacing, management and resolution of conflict should vary, depending upon the nature of the conflict and its underlying basis. The relative changes in the level of abstraction of the discussions may provide signals as to the underlying basis of the conflict. Specifically, these results imply that (at least) two different strategies may be appropriate: one strategy which relates to higher level concepts and principles, and another which relies upon more concrete implications and examples. Further study which investigates these differences and their relationship to the changes in the levels of abstraction of the discussion should prove valuable.

The current study also provides an arena for ex post evaluation of the empirical methodology proposed here. While the reliability of the methodology has not yet been appraised formally, the authors themselves found that the classification process was not a difficult one. One exception was the characterization of changes in levels of abstraction. To relieve this, the category of "same" level of abstraction was introduced at an early stage in the analysis, which seemed to ease the burden of classifying issues according to hierarchical level. For two of the five meetings, the acts were classified by a second observer. The classifications for "conflict" were in agreement with those of the first observer 74 and 75% of the time. Both observers felt that viewing the videotapes prior to their coding was beneficial.

Both observers also agreed that technical knowledge about computing and knowledge about the design function in general were essential in the categorization of issues and their relevant hierarchies. This knowledge was also considered valuable, although not as critical in the classification of individual acts according to the interaction process coding scheme.

The methodology seems to be a reasonable tool for identifying the breakdowns which occur as a result of the group process: disagreements and miscommunications. If group members address but do not resolve strategically relevant breakdowns, an inferior design should result. A limitation of the methodology for understanding with an end toward improving the group software design process exists to the extent that potential breakdowns are unstated by group members.

Generalizations of the results of this study must be tempered by the fact that only one project was studied, and this project involved only one team (as opposed to a multiple–team project). Also, no formal design methodology was imposed upon the team. We feel, however, that the results do represent a valuable preliminary attempt at developing an understanding of the early aspects of the design of complex computer systems. As such, they represent a platform for future research.

APPENDIX A--DESCRIPTIONS OF MEETINGS

Meeting #1

This meeting represented the first formal design meeting of the project. Four designers (a designated project leader and three team members) met with one customer. The overall purpose of the meeting was to brief the designers on the nature of the system being requested. Prior to this meeting, a specification document (written by one member of the user group and read, but not criticized or amended by the other users) was distributed to the design team members. The designers had read this spec and had dome some thinking about it prior to the meeting. This document became the focus for much of the ensuing discussion, as the group made their first attempts at understanding, clarifying, and specifying the system requirements. As this discussion progressed, the designers agreed that they would each go off and create a list of questions. The team agreed to meet again after these lists were completed in order to integrate them into a single list which would then be sent to the users.

Meeting #2

This meeting represented the second formal design meeting of the project. Five designers (a designated project leader and four team members) met with one customer (user). All of the individuals from the previous meeting were in attendance. An additional member of the design team was also included. The overall purpose of the meeting was to discuss the questions on the lists which the project team members had compiled since the last meeting. There was a good deal of discussion generated by these questions, both about project requirements and methods for communicating with the users about these issues. One of the designers volunteered to collect the lists and integrate them into one list for submission to the customer group.

Meeting #3

This meeting represented the third formal design meeting of the project. The five designers (the same individuals from the last meeting) met with a set of customers (users). The user in attendance at the two previous meetings was present for most of this meeting, from the beginning. Of the other two users in attendance, one was present for the entire meeting and one was present for a short time. At no time during the meeting, however, were more than two users present. Prior to this meeting, the users had received the composite list of questions from the designers. The overall purpose of the meeting was to discuss the specific questions on the list. Only the first two questions (out of 29) were considered during this meeting. A follow-up meeting was scheduled for the following day to address the remaining questions.

Meeting #4

This meeting represented the fourth formal design meeting of the project. The five designers met with two customers (users). Both users had been in attendance at the previous meeting. One of the users left the meeting after about 30 minutes. The user who had attended all of the previous three meetings was not present. The purpose of the meeting was to address the 27 questions (out of 29) which had not been answered in the previous session. One of the designers (not the project leader) presented the questions to the group and documented the users' responses on the question sheet. All 27 of the questions were addressed.

Meeting #5

This meeting represented the fifth formal design meeting of the project. Six designers (the five designers from the previous meetings, plus a new addition to the project) met with one user (the individual who had attended the first three meetings). The members discussed the merits of a particular language for the system, and discussed some database tools. These discussions lead to general discussions of requirements. Also, since a designer was present who was new to the project, considerable time was spent in briefing this individual and explaining various facets of the project to him. The team agreed to do more general research and to begin looking into specific problems.

REFERENCES

1. Guinan, P. and Bostrom, R. (1986). Development of Computer-Based Information Systems: A Communication Framework. *Data Base*, 17(3), 3-16.

2. Ross, D. and Schoman, K. (1977). Structural Analysis for Requirements Definition. *IEEE Transactions on Software Engineering*, 3(1), 6-15.

3. Guimares, T. (1981). Understanding Implementation Failure. *Journal of Systems Management*, 31(3), 12-17.

4. Mantei, M. (1981). The Effect of Programming Team Structure of Programming Tasks. *Communications of the Association for Computing Machinery*, 24(3), 106-113.

5. Soloway, E. (1986). What to Do Next: Meeting the Challenge of Programming-in-the-Large. In E. Soloway and S. Iyengar, (eds.), *Empirical Studies of Programmers*, (pp.263-268). Norwood, NJ: Ablex.

6.   Churchman, C. (1971). *The Design of Inquiring Systems*, New York, NY: Basic Books.

7.   Simon, H. (1975). The Structure of Ill–structured Problems. *Artificial Intelligence*, 4, 181–201.

8.   Jeffries, R., Turner, A., Polson, P., and Atwood, M. (1981). The Processes Involved in Designing Software. In J. Anderson (ed.), *Cognitive Skills and Their Acquisition*, (pp. 255–283). Hillsdale, NJ: Erlbaum.

9.   Adelson, B. & Soloway, E. (1985). The Role of Domain Experience in Software Design. *IEEE Transactions on Software Engineering*, 11(11), 1351–1360.

10. Kant, E., and Newell, A. (1984). Problem Solving Techniques for the Design of Algorithms. *Information Processing & Management*, 20(1–2), 97–118.

11. Guindon, R., Krasner, H., and Curtis,B. (1987). Cognitive Processes in Early, Upstream Design: Differences in Strategies among Experienced Designers. *Proceedings of the 2d workshop on Empirical Studies of Programmers*. Norwood, NJ: Ablex. forthcoming.

12. Winograd, T. and Flores, F. (1986). *Understanding Computers and Cognition*. Norwood, New Jersey: Ablex.

13. Shaw, M. (1981). *Group Dynamics: The Psychology of Small Group Behavior*. New York, NY: McGraw–Hill.

14. Todd, P., and Benbasat, I. (1986). Process Tracing Methods in IS Research: Exploring the Black Box. Working Paper No. 1140, University of British Columbia, Faculty of Commerce and Business Administration.

15. Ericsson, K. and Simon, H. (1984). *Protocol Analysis*. Cambridge, MA: The MIT Press.

16. Bales, R. (1950). *Interaction Process Analysis: A Method for the Study of Small Groups*. Cambridge, MA: Addison–Wesley.

17. Brodwin, D., and Bourgeous, L. (1984). Five Steps to Strategic Action. In G. Carroll and D. Vogel (eds.), *Strategy and Organization: A West Coast Perspective*, (pp. 167–181). Boston, MA: Pitman.

18. Janis, I. (1972). *Victims of Groupthink: Psychological Studies of Foreign Policy Decision and Fiascoes*. Boston, MA: Houghton–Mifflin.

19. Mitroff, I. (1982). Dialectic Squared: A Fundamental Difference in Perception of the Meanings of Some Key Concepts in Social Science. *Decision Sciences*, 13, (222–224).

20. Fisher, B. (1974). *Small Group Decision Making.* New York, NY: McGraw–Hill.

21. Curtis, B., Krasner, H., Shen, V., and Iscoe, N. (1987). On Building Software Process Models under the Lamppost. *Proceedings of the 9th International Conference on Software Engineering*, 96–103.

CHAPTER 7

Comprehension Strategies in Programming

Nancy Pennington
Center for Decision Research
Graduate School of Business
University of Chicago
1101 E. 58th Street
Chicago, IL 60637

ABSTRACT

This report focuses on differences in comprehension strategies between programmers who attain high and low levels of program comprehension. Comprehension data and program summaries are presented for 40 professional programmers who studied and modified a moderate length program. Illustrations from detailed think-aloud protocol analyses are presented for selected subjects who displayed distinctive comprehension strategies. The results show that programmers attaining high levels of comprehension tend to think about both the program world and the domain world to which the program applies while studying the program. We call this a cross-referencing strategy and contrast it with strategies in which programmers focus on program objects and events or on domain objects and events, but not both.

INTRODUCTION

The ability to understand programs written by others is an important component of a programmer's skill. Program comprehension underlies performance on programming tasks such as debugging [6] and modification [10]. The extraordinary individual differences in programmers' performance on these tasks, even among professionals of many years experience [17], suggest that research on effective comprehension strategies may provide information that can be used to improve programmer performance, education, design technologies and programming environments. Equally important, the study of program comprehension processes can add to the ongoing development of cognitive theories of programming skill, and more generally of expert skill.

In a previous paper [13], we reported research relevant to the question of what kinds of information programmers had available after studying program texts, that they could use to respond to comprehension questions (see also [5, 12], for discussions of information in programs). In particular, we examined comprehension of the following categories of program information:

Operations. We defined operations as the actions the program performs at the level of the source code, for example reading a record, assigning a value to a variable, comparing the value of two variables. In our research, comprehension questions about operations asked whether or not specific actions occurred in a program. For example, "Is VAR1 set to zero?", "Is the value of VAR1 compared to the value of VAR2?"

Control Flow. Control flow relations reflect the execution sequence of a program, the order in which actions will occur. Comprehension questions about control flow asked about the temporal ordering of program actions. For example, "Is VAR1 incremented after FILE1 is read?", "When VAR1 and VAR2 are found to be equal, is an error message written out?"

Data Flow. Data flow relations reflect the series of transformations that data objects (variables, files) undergo from their initial states to the final program outputs. Comprehension questions about data flow asked about the dependencies between variables. For example, "Will the value of VAR1 affect the value of VAR2?"

State. State relations concern the connections between execution of an action and the state of all aspects of the program that are necessarily true at that point in time. Comprehension questions about program states asked about preconditions for program actions. For example, "When ACTION1 is reached, will VAR1 have a particular known value?"

Function. Functional relations concern the main goals of the program and the hierarchy of subgoals necessary to achieve the goal. Comprehension questions about program function asked about the purpose of the program and the role of program procedures in accomplishing that purpose. For example, "Is the sum of VAR1s accumulated in order to compute an average?", "Does this program update a file so that it contains current area information?"

When programmers studied short program texts for limited amounts of time [13], we found that they made the fewest errors on questions about operations and control flow, more errors on questions about data flow, and the most errors on questions about function and state relations. In comparing the programmers with the highest overall comprehension scores (first quartile, Q1) with the programmers with the lowest overall comprehension scores (fourth quartile, Q4), we found that the biggest difference in performance occurred on function questions (see Figure 1A). From these results, and from patterns of recognition memory accuracy and response times [13], we proposed that comprehension of program control flow and procedures precedes understanding of program functions. We also suggested that additional time and/or changing task goals resulted in a change in the dominant memory representation from procedural to functional [13].

We have also proposed the outline of a model, interpreting these comprehension patterns in terms of current theories of text comprehension developed by van Dijk and Kintsch [2, 8, 14, 16]. In this work, van Dijk and Kintsch suggest that two distinct but cross-referenced representations of a text are constructed during comprehension. The first representation, the textbase, includes a hierarchy of representations consisting of a surface memory of the text, a microstructure of interrelations among text propositions, and a macrostructure that organizes the text representation. The second representation, the situation model is a mental model [4, 7] of what the text is about referentially. Using a program text from our present research as an example, in which the program keeps track of engineers' wiring specifications for the design of an industrial plant: the textbase is concerned with searches, merges, computations, and so forth; and the situation model is about cables that take up space, determining the size of a particular cable, computing the total size of the cables allocated to a particular space, comparing the cable allocation to the size of the space, etc. It is plausible that the functional relations between program procedures are more comprehensible in terms of the real world objects. Thus the textbase macrostructure may be dominated by procedural relations that largely reflect how programs in traditional languages are structured while the functional hierarchy is developed in terms of a situation model with reference to real world objects and states. Van Dijk and Kintsch [2] also suggest that the construction of the situation model depends on construction of the textbase in the sense that the textbase defines the actions and events that need explaining.

To recapitulate, the background for the current report is a model of computer program comprehension in which two representations are constructed: a representation that highlights procedural program relations in the language of programs, that we will refer to as the program model (corresponding to a textbase), and a representation that highlights functional relations between program parts that is expressed in the language of the domain world objects, that we will refer to as the domain model (corresponding to a situation model). Effective comprehension also requires that the two (mental) representations be cross-referenced in a way that connects program parts to domain functions. Our evidence to date suggests that the program model is constructed prior to the domain model.

Given this background, the present research addresses the question of how programmers who attain different levels of program comprehension (whose comprehension profiles are shown in Figure 1A) differ in terms of their comprehension strategies and the resulting mental representations of the program text. Can we find the distinguishing characteristics of those programmers who show the best comprehension performance in our tasks? The data we examined to answer these questions were derived from analyses of responses to comprehension questions, programmers' program summaries (which provide partial information as to the content of mental representations [15] and preliminary analyses of "think-aloud" protocols collected while programmers studied a program text.

RESEARCH METHOD

Subjects

Forty professional programmers, with a minimum of three years experience, from Chicago businesses and research firms, participated as subjects in the research. These 40 programmers were the top and bottom quartile comprehenders (20 each) from our original "short-text" study (Figure 1A). Half of the programmers were FORTRAN programmers and half were COBOL programmers although language differences did not emerge in this study and this distinction will not be mentioned again. Subjects were paid $50.00 for their participation.

Top quartile comprehenders (Q1 subjects) and bottom quartile comprehenders (Q4 subjects) differed reliably on only two background attributes: Q1 programmers had on average a few more years of programming experience (14.6 years vs. 10.3 years) and had taken fewer programming courses (2.6 courses vs. 4.4 courses). They did not differ in age, educational level or college major, whether or not they had taught programming, or number of programming languages.

Materials

The stimulus program used for this research was a 200-line program currently in production use at a Chicago firm. The program was one of a series of programs that keeps track of and computes specifications for industrial plant designs. Originally written in COBOL, the program includes both file manipulation and computation, and was easily translated into a believable FORTRAN program. The program contained a minimal amount of documentation, as was true of the original production version of the program; this included an introductory set of comments describing the program as one that keeps track of the space allocated for wiring (called cables below) and the wiring assigned to that space during the design of a building. No documentation was included within the COBOL text but the FORTRAN version contained comments that corresponded to information in COBOL paragraph headers. Thus the level of documentation in the two versions was judged to be equivalent with the naturally-occurring exception that variable names were much shorter in FORTRAN.

A modification task was devised that required altering the program to produce an additional output file and an exception list. As with most non-trivial modifications, this task required a relatively complete understanding of the goals of the original program (function), how different variables entered into computations and outputs (data flow), and where in the execution sequence certain transformations occurred (control flow).

A list of 40 comprehension questions was constructed that included questions about control flow, data flow, function, and program states. The forty questions were divided into two matching lists of twenty questions.

Procedure

Subjects participated in a single experimental session lasting approximately 2.5 hours at the University of Chicago, Northwestern University, or their place of business. All instructions were presented on the display monitor of an IBM PC. The first part of the session consisted of general task instructions and detailed instructions concerning the method of displaying and altering the program text, including practice in manipulating a sample program listing using these features.

Programmers were instructed that they were to make a modification to a program normally maintained by another programmer. However, the "other programmer" was going on vacation and the modification was urgent. The subject's task was to become familiar with the program and to make the changes to it. Furthermore, the hypothetical other programmer had left the program with the subject to study and would return in 45 minutes to explain the modification task. Thus, in the study phase programmers studied the 200-line program for 45 minutes. Half of the subjects were instructed to think aloud while they studied and the remaining half were allowed to study silently.

The program text was presented on the computer display and subjects could scroll forward or backward, jump to another place in the program, split the screen into halves and scroll either half. Subjects were also allowed to take notes or draw diagrams while studying the program. Most of the programmers were familiar with studying programs on a terminal but for those who were not, the split screen feature served the purpose of keeping a finger in a listing and jumping ahead in the listing. The program controlling the experiment kept track of the programmer's study sequence by recording which program line was in the center of the display screen.

After the 45 minute study period, programmers were asked to type in a summary of the program, then to respond to the first list of 20 comprehension questions and to explain their responses. After a short break, the modification task was presented to the programmer and a time limit of 30 minutes was specified. Subjects were told that they should begin actual modifications at any point when they felt ready. If necessary, the full 30 minutes could be spent continuing to learn about the program. However, all programmers had at least begun to make modifications by the end of the period and many had completed their changes. During the 30 minute modification phase, the think-aloud subjects were again asked to think aloud while they worked and the silent subjects were permitted to work silently. The session concluded with a second request to summarize the program and then to respond to the second list of 20 comprehension questions. The procedure for these tasks was the same as before. The controlling program recorded all responses, explanations, and times to respond.

ANALYSES AND RESULTS

Comprehension Questions

Results from comprehension questions after the study phase and after the modification phase are shown in Figures 1B and 1C. After the 45 minute study phase, comprehension results were similar to those obtained after the study of short texts: control flow and data flow questions elicited more correct responses than function and state questions (see Figure 1B), $F(3,96) = 11.64$, $p < .001$. However, after the modification phase, this pattern shifted so that function and data flow comprehension performance improved over that on control flow and state questions (see Figure 1C), $F(3,96) = 14.85$, $p < .001$. Comprehension patterns were similar for Q1 and Q4 comprehenders although Q1 comprehenders showed uniformly better comprehension after both study and modification phases, $F(1,32) = 15.75$, $p < .001$ (assignment to comprehension level was based on scores from the first study).

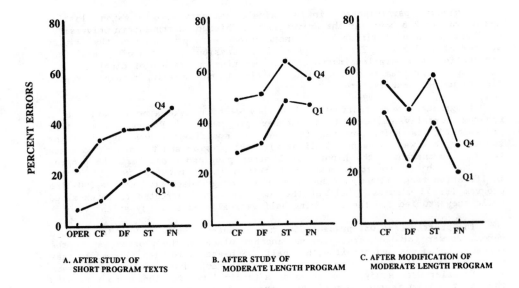

A. AFTER STUDY OF
SHORT PROGRAM TEXTS

B. AFTER STUDY OF
MODERATE LENGTH PROGRAM

C. AFTER MODIFICATION OF
MODERATE LENGTH PROGRAM

Figure 1. Comprehension errors as a function of information category (operations, control flow, data flow, state, function) and comprehension quartile (Q1, Q4) after three comprehension tasks.

These comprehension results supply part of the basis for our dual representation hypothesis, that programmers construct a model of the program based on procedural relations and a model of the domain that is based on functional relations. We will now present analyses of program summaries and illustrations from selected protocols to provide a more detailed picture of the differences between the best and worst comprehenders. These program summary analyses and protocol analyses are based on data collected during and after the 45 minute study phase.

Program Summaries

Program summaries were analyzed by classifying each statement according to the type of program relation to which it referred and according to the level of detail specified in the statement. The first classification is referred to as the <u>type</u> of summary statement in terms of information categories; types included <u>procedural</u>, <u>data flow</u>, and <u>function</u> statements. These distinctions are best illustrated by the following excerpts from summaries. Procedural statements include statements of process, ordering, and conditional program actions. For example, the summary of S109 consisted of mostly procedural statements,

> "...after this, the program will read in the cable file, comparing against the previous point of cable file, then on equal condition compares against the internal table...if found, will read the tray-area-point file for matching point-area. In this read if found, will create a type-point-index record. If not found, will read another cable record..."

Data flow statements also include statements about data structures. S415 wrote a summary that contains references to many data flow relations,

> "The tray-point file and the tray-area file are combined to create a tray-area-point file in phase one of the program. Phase two tables information from the type-code file in working storage. The parameter file, cables file, and the tray-area-point file are then used to create a temporary-exceed-index file and a point-index file..."

S057 wrote a summary that contains many function statements,

> "...the program is computing area for cable accesses throughout a building. The amount of area per hole is first determined and then a table for cables and diameters is loaded. Next a cable file is read to accumulate the sum of the cables' diameters going through each hole..."

The examples above also differ in the <u>level of detail</u> contained in the summaries, the second dimension on which we classified summary statements. Four levels of detail were specified for coding: (a) <u>detailed</u> statements contained references to specific program operations and variables; (b) <u>program</u> level statements referred to a program's procedural blocks such as a search routine or to files as a whole; (c) <u>domain</u> level statements referred to real world objects such as cables and buildings; and (d) <u>vague</u> statements did not have specific referents. These categories were chosen because they reflect distinctions we are making between the <u>program</u> model (detail, program level statements) and the <u>domain</u> model (domain, vague level statements) representations.

The excerpts presented above were also chosen because they differ in the predominant level of detail. S109's procedural summary is most detailed; S415's data flow statements are at a program (file) level; and S057's function statements are at a domain level. An example of a vague statement is, "this program reads and writes a lot of files." However most summaries contained a mixture of statement types and levels and can be summarized in terms of general trends across subjects and comparisons can be made between comprehension quartiles.

In terms of statement <u>type</u>, the majority (57%) of programmers' summary statements were classified as procedural, 30% were data flow/data structure statements, and 13% were function statements, $F(2,64) = 29.31$, $p < .001$. This pattern did not differ by quartile, by language, or by talk-aloud condition. In terms of the <u>level of detail</u>, classifying the same set of summary statements in a second way, the predominant level was the program/file level accounting for 38% of the statements, 18% of the statements were detailed, 23% were specified at the domain level, and 21% were vague, $F(3,96) = 10.47$, $p < .001$. This pattern across level of detail differed for upper and lower quartile subjects, $F(3,96) = 4.65$, $p < .01$, with lower quartile comprehenders' summaries containing relatively more statements at a detailed level (20% Q4 versus 16% Q1) and more statements at a vague level (30% Q4 versus 14% Q1). A final observation concerns a relation between summary statement type and level. A majority of program summary statements about program function were expressed in the language of real-world objects (cables, space, crowding, etc.) rather than in the language of programs. The majority of procedural summary statements were expressed in terms of program objects (files, computations, searching, etc.) rather than in the domain language, $F(6,222) = 12.90$, $p < .001$.

To investigate the Q1 versus Q4 differences further, summaries were sorted into three "summary strategy" groups according to the proportion of statements at different levels of detail. The first group (n = 9 subjects) were those programmers whose summaries included predominantly (>80%) statements at the level of program operations and program procedures (Figure 2A) and we called these __program__ level summaries. The second group (n = 20 subjects) showed a more even distribution over operation, program, and domain levels (Figure 2B) and we called these __cross-referenced__ summaries. The third group (n = 11 subjects) wrote summaries that included high proportions of domain or vague statements (Figure 2C) and we called these __domain__ summaries. These three groups reflect our early distinction between program and domain models. The idea is that program summaries refer predominantly to the program model, domain summaries to the domain model and cross-referenced summaries to both. Statistical analyses support the observation that the three groups differ in level profiles as shown in Figure 2, $F(6,111) = 7.97$, $p < .001$ (strategy by level interaction).

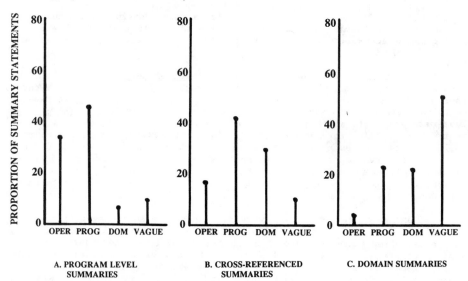

Figure 2. Distribution of summary statement levels (operations, program, domain, vague) by summary strategy.

Having divided the subjects by summary strategy according to references to program or domain model, we now ask how this corresponds to comprehension level (Q1, Q4), to types of inferences (procedural, data flow, function), and to accuracy of summary statements. These correspondences are shown in Table 1. As might be expected from the fact that Q4 comprehenders showed more detail and vague statement levels in their summaries, the three strategy groups were highly related to comprehension quartile as shown in Table 1A. High comprehension (Q1) programmers almost uniformly use a cross-referencing summary strategy that combines statements about the domain world with statements about the program world. In contrast, low comprehension (Q4) programmers tend to produce either a program level summary or a domain summary. In terms of inference types and accuracy (Table 1B), program level summarizers generated low rates of reference to domain objects (8%) and a low proportion of function statements (9%). However, when a domain statement or a function inference was made, the probability that it was in error is extremely high (55% errors for domain statements, 39% errors for function inferences), especially when compared to the error base rate for this group (14%). The domain summaries show a higher error rate overall (26%) and also show higher than base rate conditional probabilities of error for domain (37%) and function (36%) statements. However, the domain group attempts more function statements (18%), in keeping with our observation that function statements are expressed in terms of domain objects. The cross-referenced summaries have an overall error rate of 12%, and 13% of all statements are function statements. However, in contrast to the other groups, the conditional probability of error for function statements is no higher than the base rate (10%) and is lower for domain statement errors (6%).

Table 1

Correspondence Between Program Summarization Strategy,
Comprehension Quartile (A) and Summary Features (B)

| | Summarization Strategy | | |
	Program	Cross-Referenced	Domain
A. Comprehension Quartile			
number of Q1 subjects	2	16	2
number of Q4 subjects	7	4	9
B. Summary Features			
% function statements	8.5	13.3	17.6
% domain statements	7.7	30.3	21.8
% overall error rate	13.6	11.6	25.6
% function error rate	38.5	10.3	35.7
% domain error rate	54.6	6.3	36.8

Discussion. Program summaries cannot be considered to be a complete map of subjects' mental representations of programs. However, to construct a summary, the programmer must retrieve information from one or more memory representations and we therefore assume that the summary reflects at least some properties of the mental representations [15]. Our view is that abstract knowledge of program text structures plays the initial organizing role in memory for programs, and that control flow or procedural relations dominate the macrostructure memory representation (program model). In later stages of program comprehension, under appropriate task conditions, a second representation is created that reflects the functional structure of the program and is expressed in the language of the real world domain to which the program is applied (domain model).

Interpreting our findings in terms of this view, we propose that summary statements at the domain and vague level are derived from the domain model and that summary statements at the operations and program level are derived from the program model. This is expressed in Figure 3 by dividing our summary statement levels into two parts, corresponding to program model and domain model representations. Figure 3 shows the relative concentrations of summary statements by type (information category) and level (operation, program, domain, vague) for the three strategy groups of programmers. Distinguishing features of top comprehenders summaries include coordination of levels of representation (program and domain), a procedural orientation for program level statements and a functional orientation for domain level statements, and low error rates across all categories. In contrast, poorer comprehenders express their summaries in terms of either the program model or the domain model <u>but not both</u>. This is accompanied by very high error rates for connections to the domain world and function inferences.

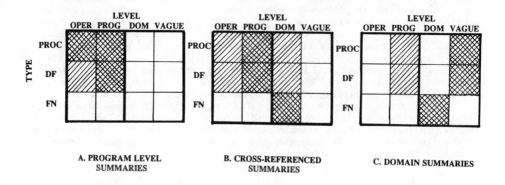

A. PROGRAM LEVEL SUMMARIES

B. CROSS-REFERENCED SUMMARIES

C. DOMAIN SUMMARIES

Figure 3. Schematic summary profiles for each summary strategy group.
▧ = three highest entry cells; ▨ = other cells > 7%; ☐ = cells < 7%.

In the following section, we examine three example comprehension think-aloud protocols to explore features of comprehension strategies that result in cross-referenced representations for Q1 programmers and singular (domain or program but not both) representations for Q4 programmers.

Protocol Analyses

In this section we present protocol analyses for three subjects, one from each of the summary strategy groups (program level, cross-referenced, and domain) selected because they used comprehension strategies that were typical of each summary group. Protocols reflect the record of thoughts reported during the 45-minute <u>study</u> phase of the study, prior to learning what modification was required. We should note that this experimental requirement, to study the program without knowing what modification was to be made, constrained the comprehension strategies available to the programmers. Littman et al. [10] noted that programmers differ in their preferences for <u>systematic</u> or <u>as-needed</u> comprehension strategies when performing a modification task. The use of an <u>as-needed</u> strategy requires knowing some specifics of a maintenance task in order to decide what "is needed," and is therefore unlikely to occur in the present experimental task. However, in defense of our method, it is quite common for a programmer, assigned a program for maintenance, to be given a period for familiarization prior to discussing the "bug list" or the "enhancement list." Most of our programmers accepted our scenario as realistic although 2 of them said that they would have liked to start guided by the modification requirements (i.e., indicating a preference for the <u>as-needed</u> strategy had they been given a choice).

Protocols were analyzed by segmenting them into propositions, each constituting a task assertion or programmer behavior, and then propositions were aggregated into episodes, a set of task assertions and behaviors driven by a common goal [3, 11]. At the level of propositions, each assertion was identified in terms of actual behavior such as read, scan, pose question, offer hypothesis, note information (either paraphrasing text, inferring with certainty, or retrieving knowledge), making an external note, or commenting on intentions. In keeping with our emphasis on different types (process, control flow, data flow, data structure, function) and levels (operation, program procedure, domain) of information, we also annotated propositions as to type and level. For example, a programmer might note a data flow relation at the operation (variable) level, or hypothesize a function relation at the domain level. For this report, we do not offer analyses of the protocols at this detailed level. Rather, we are interested in the incidence and time course of the episodic units identified from sequences of these lower level task assertions.

Identifying episodes involved identifying particular task assertion sequences and making inferences about what the programmer was doing. The episode types we have identified include: plan identification, anomaly spotting, simulation, connection, exploration, and evaluation. We were impressed by difference in the occurrence of connection episodes in our three subjects' strategies.

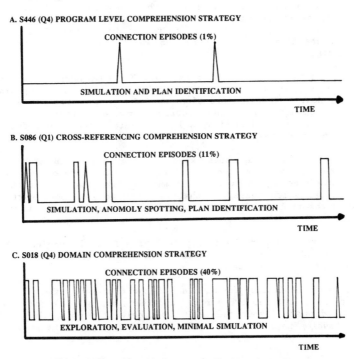

Figure 4. Connection episodes over the 45 minute time course of comprehension for three subjects.

Connection episodes involve a trigger event followed by the formation of a hypothesis (conjecture in the terms of Letovsky [9]) about the domain world. The trigger event can be simple, such as reading a line of program text or noting a program action, or, it can be more complex, for example, a plan identification episode or simulation episode. We call these hypotheses about the domain world connection episodes because they are the means by which a programmer constructs the domain model and connects it to the program text (examples are provided below). In Figure 4 we show the time trace of connection episodes over the 45 minute protocol for three subjects: S446, a low comprehension (Q4) subject who produced a program level summary (Figure 4A); S086, a high comprehension (Q1) subject who produced a cross-referenced summary (Figure 4B); and S018, a low comprehension (Q4) subject who produced a domain level summary.

Program level comprehension strategy. The comprehension strategy of S446 (Figure 4A) is characterized by the almost complete absence of connection episodes during comprehension. Not surprisingly, this comprehension strategy resulted in a program level summary and this subject shows relatively poor overall comprehension. This subject's strategy consists mostly of simulation episodes with weak plan identification. A typical excerpt from S446 is,

> "...we're going to write out a file/ with points that's the same as the first one/ and then we're going to define a new area as the square of the width/ and write that out/ and then we're going to read in another point-one and point-two/ and then we're going to go back to 100 which I think are those tests/...right./...(later) we're matching files here./

What is interesting is that the programmer does not go on to determine why it is that the program needs to match files. This requires coordination across procedures and in principle could be done at the program level. However, we believe there is something about connection to the domain that facilitates the process of understanding why procedures do what they do. This programmer misses this crucial explanatory connection.

Cross-referencing comprehension strategy. The comprehension strategy of S086 (Figure 4B) is characterized by the regular but infrequent appearance of connection episodes. These connection episodes are triggered by fairly extensive simulation and plan identification. In the following excerpts, we show plan identification, followed by a later related connection, followed by simulation. S086 showed very high overall comprehension levels.

> "...ok, it's setting up some kind of previous pointer here./ Normally that's something I would use in publishing a report where I wanted to break on a part number or something like that./ So setting up the initial value there/ so that we could do like some sort of break when the numbers change. It probably has nothing to do with that though..."

> "...ok, they're trying to evidently collect all of the cables going through that point/ and get their accumulated areas and so on/ something along those lines..."

> "...So it's accumulating the squares of the diameters/ and writing out something to the temporary file/ and then looping back up/ after doing a read on the input file./ Ok, so there it's doing the read/ prior to testing to see if the cable point differs from the previous point..."

S086 does not stop with the identification of a control break pattern. He goes on to explain why "the program wants" to do a control break on the cable point. His hypothesis is expressed in domain terms in the second excerpt. He then verifies his hypothesis by extensive simulation of the procedure. In Figure 4B, we can see that there are five clusters of connection episodes. The program consists of an introduction (comments, variable declarations, and file descriptions) and four main procedures (each with subparts). These connection episodes occur for each and serve a vital role in connecting procedures.

Domain comprehension strategy. The comprehension strategy of S018 (Figure 4C) is flooded with connection episodes. S018 showed low overall comprehension and follows the course of hypothesizing about the domain world on minimal triggers. That is, reading a variable name is sufficient to generate an entire fantasy about the real world objects, as in the following excerpt.

"...(reading) NUMBER OF SEGMENTS/ It's obviously got to be for the various cables./ Maybe it's a multiple segment cable/ so they just split it up/ and use the number of short segments with various connectors in different parts of the building./ Those number of segments would tell them how many little pieces of cable they've got/ but...(continues)"

In S018's protocol, almost anything in the program leads to a speculation about the domain world. More important however, the speculations are accumulated and rarely verified by figuring out if what the program does is consistent with the vision of the domain world.

   Discussion. These initial analyses of three representative protocols from groups showing different summary types and comprehension levels are suggestive, although firm proof awaits additional analyses and further research. These analyses suggest that a distinguishing feature of top comprehenders is the use of a cross-referencing strategy that alternates between systematic study of the program, translation to domain terms, and verification in program terms. In contrast poorer comprehenders use a singular strategy, either concentrating on the program world or the domain world exclusively, but not connecting the two. Connections between the two are either absent or wildly speculative and never verified. These strategies produce program summaries reflecting the singular or cross-referenced representation of the program that is constructed as a result. The program level comprehender understands what the program does but not why. The domain level understander has vague and erroneous ideas about why, but not much idea of what happens in the program. The cross-referencer has the beginnings of two cross-referenced representations, one a procedural model of the program and the other a functionally based model of the domain.

GENERAL DISCUSSION

   Our general conclusion that construction of a domain model, and especially one connected to program parts, is essential to good comprehension is consistent with recent work on the role of domain knowledge in design [1]. In design, it has been suggested that "where the domain is unfamiliar, a global model of the design was not formed...the ability to form a global model is tied in with familiarity with the domain of the object being designed. [1, p. 1357]" In our research, comprehension was strongly related to subjects' strategies in constructing a model of the domain.

   Other research has proposed that programmers construct a mental model of the program, both in program design and in comprehension (e.g., [1, 9, 10]. This raises the question of which one of the two representations we propose is "the" mental model and more generally the question of what precisely is a mental model. We propose that under some definitions both qualify as mental models and therefore that the terminology that we have adopted, distinguishing between a model more closely tied to the text and a model of the domain to which it refers, is more precise (see also [14, 16] for discussion of this issue). In other definitions, the mental model is presumed to be a layered network that includes a goal hierarchy as well as program implementation features (see [9]). In this case, our proposed representations would be considered, together, part of a mental model. This conception is closer to our own, but leaves open the question of the more general usage of the term, for example whether mental models are distinguished from other forms of representation by certain features, such as being "runnable."

   The essential message of this research is that to understand skilled intellectual performance we have to study cognitive representation of the stimulus. Furthermore, we must be prepared for a multiplicity of mental representations, even within one head. In the case of programming, as in other tasks involving language comprehension, we must identify at least two mental representations, a model of the program text and a model of the domain to which it refers, in order to understand the behavior of experts.

We conclude with two limitations of the present research. Performance on our modification task will refine our designation of programmers as good or poor comprehenders. The ability of programmers to answer our comprehension questions is a limited indicator of success at more goal directed programming tasks. Data from the modification task are being analyzed and we leave as an open question whether or not, as we would predict, comprehension levels, summary strategies, and program comprehension strategies will be strongly associated with success in modifying a program.

The stimulus program we used was only moderately complex. Therefore, the present observations are only suggestive of avenues to pursue in understanding processing strategies in environments that are more complex by an order of magnitude. As has been pointed out [10], it is difficult to understand how simulation, for example, could be used as a main comprehension strategy for a 100 page program. It is plausible, however, that a domain model, or models of subparts of the domain will play a critical role in understanding complex programs.

ACKNOWLEDGEMENTS

This research was sponsored by the Personnel and Training Research Programs, Psychological Sciences Division, Office of Naval Research, under Contract N00014-82-K-0759, Contract Authority Identification Number 667-503.

REFERENCES

[1] Adelson, B., & Soloway, E. (1985). The role of domain experience in software design. IEEE Transactions on Software Engineering, SE-11, 1351-1360.

[2] van Dijk, T. A. & Kintsch, W. (1983). Strategies of discourse comprehension. New York: Academic Press.

[3] Eriksson, K. A., & Simon, H. A. (1984). Protocol analysis: Verbal reports as data. Cambridge, MA: Mit Press.

[4] Gentner, D., & Stevens, A. L. (1983). Mental models. Hillsdale, NJ: Erlbaum.

[5] Green, T. R. G. (1980). Programming as a cognitive activity. In H. T. Smith and T. R. G. Green (Eds.), Human interaction with computers. New York: Academic Press.

[6] Gugerty, L., & Olson, G. M. (1986). Comprehension differences in debugging by skilled and novice programmers. In E. Soloway & S. Iyengar (Eds.), Empirical studies of programmers. Norwood, NJ: Ablex.

[7] Johnson-Laird, P. N. (1983). Mental models. Cambridge, MA: Harvard University Press.

[8] Kintsch, W. (1986). Learning from text. Cognition and Instruction, 3, 87-108.

[9] Letovsky, S. (1986). Cognitive processes in program comprehension. In

E. Soloway & S. Iyengar (Eds.), Empirical studies of programmers. Norwood, NJ: Ablex.

[10] Littman, D. C., Pinto, J., Letovsky, S., & Soloway, E. (1986). Mental models and software maintenance. In E. Soloway & S. Iyengar (Eds.), Empirical studies of programmers. Norwood, NJ: Ablex.

[11] Newell, A. & Simon, H. A. (1972). Human problem solving. New York: Prentice-Hall.

[12] Pennington, N. (1985). Cognitive components of expertise in computer programming: A review of the literature. Psychological Documents, 15, No. 2702.

[13] Pennington, N. (1987). Stimulus structures and mental representations in expert comprehension of computer programs. Cognitive Psychology, 19, 295-341.

[14] Perrig, W., & Kintsch, W. (1985). Propositional and situational representations of text. Journal of Memory and Language, 24, 503-518.

[15] Rumelhart, D. E. (1977). Understanding and summarizing brief stories. In D. Laberge & S. J. Samuels (Eds.), Basic processes in reading: Perceptions and comprehension. Hillsdale, NJ: Erlbaum.

[16] Schmalhofer, F., & Glavanov, D. (1986). Three components of understanding a programmer's manual: Verbatim, propositional, and situational representations. Journal of Memory and Language, 25, 279-294.

[17] Vosburgh, J., Curtis, B., Wolverton, R., Albert, B., Malec, H., Hoben, S., & Liu, Y. (1984). Productivity factors and programming environments. In Proceedings of the 7th International Conference on Software Engineering. Washington, DC: IEEE Computer Society.

CHAPTER 8

Graphical vs. Textual Representation:
An Empirical Study of Novices' Program Comprehension

Nancy Cunniff
Robert P. Taylor
Center for Intelligent Tools in Education
Teachers College
Columbia University

ABSTRACT

This paper reports a study which demonstrates that certain fundamental aspects of computer programs are comprehended more quickly and more accurately when represented graphically than when represented in textual form. It is one in a series of reports on an on-going investigation into the influence of graphical representation on program comprehension and debugging being undertaken at Teachers College. It assumes that program comprehension is both definable and measurable and that the aspects of comprehension measured in this study are important components of novices' programming skill. This particular study involved 23 novice programmers who had learned to program in two languages, one graphically and the other textually represented. It investigated the speed and accuracy with which the subjects responded to comprehension questions about eight short program segments, each represented during the experimental session in both forms. The findings indicate that, for the comprehension measures considered, almost all of the subjects comprehended the graphically represented program segments both more rapidly and more accurately than their textually represented equivalents.

INTRODUCTION

One picture is worth 10,000 words.

-ancient Chinese proverb

Because we believe this intuition is in some measure correct, graphical representation of programming has been integral to the teaching of programming at Teachers College for more than 10 years. Because we also believe it essential that every student learn more than one language, introductory programming courses normally require students to work in two languages, one graphical and one textual. Despite some interesting studies focusing on various graphical techniques (Blaiwes (1); Kammann (2); Shneiderman, Mayer, McKay & Heller (3); Brooke & Duncan (4); Scanlan (5); Sheppard, Kruesi & Bailey(6)), there is little *conclusive* empirical research either to support or to disprove the intuition that graphical representation is superior to text. Thus, our particular approach to teaching programming has led quite naturally to development of a research program investigating whether one representation may be better than another (Cunniff, Taylor & Black (7); Cunniff, Taylor & Taylor (8); Cunniff (9)). Is one representation better only for certain stages of learning, only for certain aspects of programming, or only for certain learners? These are the primary questions in which we have become interested. So, as we teach, our classes serve as a lab for some of the research we conduct to help us answer or at least better formulate the questions.

In this paper we report some findings of a study of program comprehension of novice programmers. The study investigated the speed and accuracy with which the subjects could answer questions about short program segments. This paper proceeds with a description of the study, presents and discusses the results, and suggests some appropriate conclusions. The findings of this study very clearly support the contention that, so far as comprehension of certain levels of programming detail are concerned, graphical representation is superior to textual representation.

DESCRIPTION OF THE STUDY

The major research hypothesis for the study was that comprehension of programs coded in a graphically represented language (FPL) would be faster and more accurate than comprehension of the same programs coded in a traditional, textual language (Pascal). In addition, we postulated several sub-hypotheses, focusing on specific aspects of the investigation:

1. Certain types of questions will be answered more rapidly and more accurately for programs written in FPL than in Pascal.
2. Certain types of program segments will be more rapidly and more accurately comprehended in FPL than in Pascal.
3. Subjects with high visual aptitude will have more rapid and more accurate comprehension of the graphically encoded program segments.

Comprehension was selected as the focus of the study because it is a vital aspect of programming practice (Embly (10); Shneiderman (11); Brooks (12)) and because certain aspects of it are readily measurable. Comprehension plays a role in nearly all aspects of programming activity. Various approaches to evaluating comprehension have been used in earlier studies (Gould (13); Shneiderman (14); Hall & Zweben (15)). This study concentrates on simple recognition of programming details and deductions based on such recognition. It does so because we presupposed that a program is a representation of actions the programmer wants the computer to take and that comprehending a program involves recognizing which actions are represented, how many times each is represented, and how many times each will be executed during a single execution of the program or segment under consideration. Additionally, particularly for novice programmers, a good deal of time is spent trying to comprehend small, "screen-size" segments of code, trying to get hold of the details, putting together "pieces to rebuild the meanings of the program" (Pennington (16), p.8).

Based on this approach, we measured a subject's comprehension of a displayed program segment by how quickly and how accurately he or she answered questions requiring such recognition and deduction. The questions required the subject to :

1. recognize and count particular types of constructs/details within a segment;

2. determine values of specific variables;

3. deduce the number of times a given construct within a segment would be executed during a single execution of the entire segment.

FPL: A Graphical Representation of Programming

The graphically represented programming language that we used in the study is FPL (*First Programming Language*). FPL is under development at Teachers College, Columbia University where we have been using it for several years to teach programming to novices. For a complete description of the language and its online implementation on IBM-PC computers, see Taylor (17) and Taylor, Cunniff & Uchiyama (18). In FPL, all programming constructs and concepts are represented using icons and spatial arrangement in place of the reserved words and sequential presentation characteristic of text-based programming languages. Each of the eleven FPL icons represents a specific programming action; eight ultimately include programmer inserted text, the variables and constants of the program. Through this unique representation, FPL provides a visual map of the program that directly emphasizes its logical structure. Functionally, FPL is equivalent to Pascal, FORTRAN, COBOL, and other languages in the classical tradition. As illustration, Figure 1 presents a brief program rendered in both FPL and Pascal.

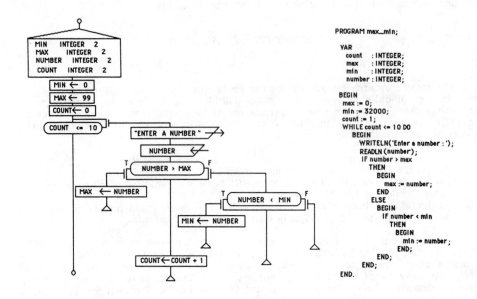

Figure 1

FPL Program with Pascal Translation

Pascal: A Textual Representation of Programming

Pascal, a well-structured language designed for student use, is the textually represented language taught in our introductory courses and used in the study. Pascal programs are entirely represented by the words and the other textual symbols included in the language's syntax. However, as with other textual languages, Pascal as conventionally written also routinely includes some non-textual, or spatial clues. Because this study revolved around spatial representation in FPL, it is worth noting how spatial representation is embedded in a textual language too, even though far less strongly. It is important to know how it might or might not confound the interpretation of results.

The principal means of spatial representation in Pascal (and all other textual languages) is, of course, indentation. The consistent use of indentation has been shown to improve comprehension (Kesler et al. (19); Miera, Musselman, Navarro & Shneiderman (20)). In their discussion of Elements of Style for programmers, Kernighan and Plauger (21) emphasize the importance of indentation:

> The single most important formatting convention that you can follow is to indent your programs properly, so the indentation conveys the structure of the program to the reader at a glance. (p. 146)

Certain aspects of Pascal's syntax are also almost certainly used by readers as visual clues: the order of words (*e. g.*, filename first inside a **READ** or **WRITE**); the semicolon as terminator of complete statements; parentheses and brackets. Probably the most obvious visual aspect of Pascal is the use of a combination of indentation and the **BEGIN-END** bracketting of a section of code. The occurrence of a **BEGIN** cues the reader to find the matching **END** and to analyze the sectioned-off code as a unit. Given the cuing role of **BEGIN-END** pairs, we think that when reading a program, those words are not really *read* but just *taken in* as visual/spatial clues to highlight the structure of the program, making it more accessible.

Subjects

There were 23 participants. All were American born, originating from 12 states; ten were female and 13 male, with an average age of 37. All but one were involved in education as teachers, administrators or school support personnel. All of the subjects were novice programmers and were completing an introductory programming course in which FPL and Pascal were taught in tandem. Reasonable mastery of both languages was ensured by requiring examinations, class assignments and programming projects to be completed in both languages. Participation in the experiment was a requirement of the course.

Materials

Aptitude Tests. Two screening tests from the *Kit of Factor-Referenced Cognitive Tests* (Ekstrom, French & Harman (22)) were administered to all subjects to provide information on their visual and verbal aptitude. *The Paper Folding Test* (VZ-2) measured visual aptitude, and the *The Advanced Vocabulary Test II* (V-5) provided a measure of verbal aptitude. High raw scores on these tests were indicators of high aptitude in the traits measured. Subjects were ranked according to their scores, and *high* and *low* aptitude were identified by the relationship of individual scores to the group mean score.

Program Segments and Comprehension Questions. Reflecting programming tasks familiar to the subjects, eight different program segments were designed. Each was logically correct and complete, and each was coded twice, once in Pascal and once in FPL. Thus, there were eight *pairs* of segments, or sixteen individual segments in all. Though the FPL and Pascal members of each pair were *logically* identical, their variable names and contextual details were distinctly different, to mask the repetition and minimize training effects. Figure 2 shows one representative pair of segments.

It should be emphasized that each pair of FPL and Pascal program segments used were identical in structure. The counterpart datanames and literals involved in each pair were also approximately the same length to avoid problems of one program segment having more "reading" that the other. The focal point of the study, then, is directly related to the idea that the same information (content) can be represented in multiple ways, and that some representations are easier or faster or more accurately comprehended than are others.

The two representations of programming used in this study were "informationally equivalent" (Larkin & Simon (23)), thus allowing comparison of the comprehension speed for "reading" graphical *versus* textual representations even though one of those representations had "more" words. For the FPL programs, the subjects had to "read" the graphic representation, deciphering the meaning of the program based on the visual representation and the spatial layout. When "reading" Pascal programs, the subjects had to "read" the words and to derive all program information from the words along with whatever weak spatial cuing indentation, position and key words provide. The key here is that although the Pascal programs had more "words" in the strict sense of the term, both representations contained identical information. Thus, the critical issue at hand is whether there was any difference in the "reading" and processing times for the alternative representations.

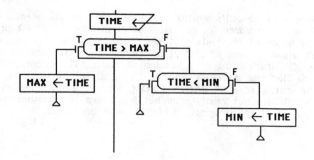

```
READLN(score);
IF score < lowest
  THEN
    BEGIN
      lowest := score;
    END
  ELSE
    BEGIN
      IF score > highest
        THEN
          BEGIN
            highest := score
          END
        ELSE
          BEGIN
          END;
    END;
```

Figure 2

Sample Pair of Program Segments

To test the comprehension of a program's micro-structure (Atwood and Ramsey (24)), one comprehension question based on each of the following categories was asked about each segment (three questions in all):

- TYPE I: *recognition* of specific simple structures
- TYPE II: recognition of *flow of control* and *Input/Output*
- TYPE III: *evaluation* of flow of control, output, or variable values

With respect to the FPL and Pascal members of any one pair of segments, the questions were identical. In all cases, the questions could be answered from the current display; none required a larger context. The vocabulary of the questions was carefully selected based on terms with which the subjects were familiar.

We collected two types of data for each of the questions, as measures of comprehension. We recorded the *reaction time* between the appearance of a question on the display (stimulus) and the subject's answer *via* a keypress (response). These times were recorded in milliseconds but, for ease of presentation and discussion, the times were transformed to seconds for this analysis. The second measure of comprehension was *accuracy of response*. Each response was captured and recorded, and later coded as correct or incorrect.

Procedure

Using an online reaction time system, every subject viewed all program segments and answered the three questions posed about each. There were detailed online instructions which included a review of terms, illustrated with FPL and Pascal examples. Subjects were advised that, if necessary, they should ask for clarification of terms while they were reading the instructions. These instructions also advised the subject to respond *as quickly and accurately* as possible to individual questions.

The sixteen segments were then presented one at a time, in random order, to each subject. The segment details appeared in the top 20 lines of a 24 line display and the three questions, also in random order, appeared one after another within the remaining four-line area. Each answer required a single keypress as answer. Correct or incorrect, the response caused a new question to replace the old, or, when the last question had been asked, caused the entire screen to be cleared. Since the new segment did not appear until requested *via* an additional keypress, subjects controlled their rate of progress between segments.

Design

The analysis of the data was based on the two dependent variables, reaction time and accuracy. We will present some descriptions of the data which combine all reaction times and/or responses by language (FPL or Pascal) or by question type (I, II and III) to provide an *overall* picture of the data. However, the main analysis of both reaction time and accuracy is within-subjects, comparing a single subject's reaction time and accuracy to a question about an FPL segment with his/her reaction time and accuracy to *the same question* about *the same segment* coded in Pascal.

Each subject answered three questions for each of the eight program segments in each of the two languages. Therefore, 24 data *pairs* for each of the dependent variables were collected for each subject. A 3x8 repeated measures analysis of variance was applied to the pairs of reaction time data (3 questions x 8 program segments). Accuracy was initially analyzed by cross-tabulating paired responses and then by examining categories of incorrect responses.

RESULTS

Reaction Time

An initial observation of the reaction time data, examined *overall* averages for the two languages across all other variables. Table 1 presents the means and standard deviations, indicating that *overall*, comprehension was more rapid for the graphically represented FPL than for textually represented Pascal.

Table 1

Means and Standard Deviations for Reaction Time by Language

	FPL	Pascal
Mean	12.92	17.60
SD	3.94	5.10

All but two of the 23 subjects had faster *overall* reaction times for the FPL segments than for the Pascal, indicating that the ratio observed in Table 1 are generally representative of individual results. Figure 3 graphs each subject's average reaction time for FPL and Pascal.

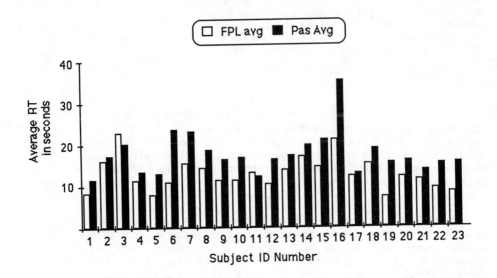

Figure 3

Average FPL and Pascal Reaction Times for Each Subject

To reflect the repeated measures nature of the experiment, twenty four *difference scores* were computed for each subject, calculated by subtracting the FPL reaction time from its corresponding Pascal reaction time for each pair of responses. We constructed a null hypothesis stating that there was no difference between FPL and Pascal reaction times for paired reaction times. If the null hypothesis were true, then the difference between the paired reaction times should be zero. A 3x8 repeated measures ANOVA was performed on the difference scores. Table 2 presents the ANOVA summary table.

Table 2

Summary Table: 3 X 8 Analysis of Variance for Reaction Time Data

Source	Sum of Squares	DF	Mean Square	F	Tail Prob.
MEAN	12123.4	1	12123.4	34.83	0.000*
Error	7657.2	22	348.1		
QUESTION	1190.1	2	595.1	4.02	0.025*
Error	6521.3	44	148.2		
PROGRAM	2179.2	7	311.3	1.63	0.131
Error	29389.8	154	190.8		
QxP	7374.3	14	526.7	2.39	0.003
Error	67775.2	308	220.0		

n = 23

The overall difference between the two languages, as indicated by the *grand mean* in the first line of the ANOVA table, was significantly different from zero ($F_{1,22}$ = 34.83, $p < .000$). Since the analysis of variance was performed on the *difference scores*, calculated by subtracting the FPL reaction times from Pascal reaction times, the significant *grand mean* indicates that we should reexamine the actual means in Table 1. The mean FPL reaction time is approximately five seconds smaller than the mean Pascal reaction time, thus, based on the significance in the ANOVA, we can conclude that FPL reaction times were significantly faster than Pascal times. This suggests that graphically represented programs are more rapidly comprehended than their textually represented counterparts.

The results also indicate that the main effect of question type was significant ($F_{2,44}$ = 4.02, $p < .05$), suggesting that the significance observed in reaction times between FPL and Pascal was partly a function of the different types of questions. Figure 4 graphs this difference, illustrating the difference in the reaction time for different question types for both FPL and Pascal. The largest difference between languages is observed for questions of Type III. This result was not surprising, since the questions in that group required the subjects to perform such comprehension tasks as evaluation of input and determination of output.

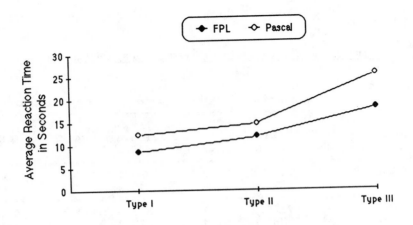

Figure 4

Reaction Time Averages for FPL and Pascal by Question Type

Finally, the findings also indicate that, although reaction times for different program segments did not differ significantly from one another ($F_{7,154}$ = 1.63, $p > .05$), there was a significant interaction between program segment and question type ($F_{14,308}$ = 2.39, $p < .01$).

The results strongly support the hypothesis that there is a difference in comprehension times between FPL and Pascal, and further, that this difference is in a direction clearly indicating that the graphically represented FPL program segments are comprehended more rapidly than their textually represented Pascal counterparts. Thus the null hypothesis of no difference between representational forms of programming (as embodied in FPL and Pascal) was rejected. The research hypothesis suggesting a difference in speed of response for different question types was also supported, although the hypothesis of a difference in reaction time for different program segments was not supported.

Accuracy

The analysis of accuracy was also based on 24 pairs of responses (3 questions for each of the 8 segments). Each pair consisted of a response to a question about the FPL version of the segment and a response to the *same question* about the corresponding Pascal segment. Because the questions were deliberately designed so that they would be answered correctly, we were not surprised that of the total of 1104 responses (FPL and Pascal combined), 91% were correct. Despite the relatively small number of incorrect responses, we proceeded with a detailed examination of the data anyhow, hoping to observe some patterns with respect accuracy. We first performed a cross tabulation on the paired responses. Table 3 shows the results of the cross-tabulation, categorizing each of the 552 pairs as either:

- correct in both languages
- incorrect in both languages
- correct in FPL and incorrect in Pascal
- incorrect in FPL and correct in Pascal

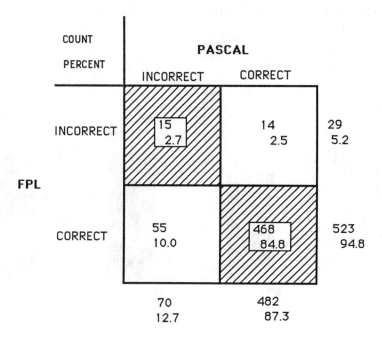

COUNT
PERCENT

PASCAL

	INCORRECT	CORRECT	
FPL INCORRECT	15 2.7	14 2.5	29 5.2
FPL CORRECT	55 10.0	468 84.8	523 94.8
	70 12.7	482 87.3	

Table 3

Cross Tabulation of Accuracy for Question Pairs

As can be seen in Table 3, there were 15 cases in which a subject responded incorrectly to *both* the FPL and the Pascal versions of a specific question. These cases were excluded from further analysis because they could not serve to inform us about differences in comprehension between the two languages. The 468 pairs in which both responses were correct were also excluded from the analysis. Consequently, we focused attention on those pairs of responses with *mixed accuracy*, that is, those pairs which consisted of a correct response in one language and incorrect response in the other. There were 69 pairs of responses in the two cells of the cross tabulation representing mixed accuracy, which means, of course, that there were 69 incorrect answers. Of those incorrect responses, 55 (79.7%) were incorrect responses to questions about Pascal segments while only 14 (20.3%) were incorrect responses to FPL segments. Although the total number of incorrect responses is only a small percentage of the data, the large discrepancy between the number of incorrect responses to questions about FPL and Pascal segments suggested that the language of the program segment affected accuracy, and that responses to questions about the graphically represented FPL segments were more often correct than were responses to the same questions about Pascal segments.

As can be seen in Figure 5, there was a clear difference in the number of incorrect responses between FPL and Pascal for all three types of questions. However, notice that the incorrect answers to the Pascal segments were quite evenly distributed across the three types of questions; the same is not true of FPL. Thus, we decided to attempt an alternative categorization of incorrect responses, classifying questions by programming constructs. Table 4 summarizes incorrect responses according to this classification.

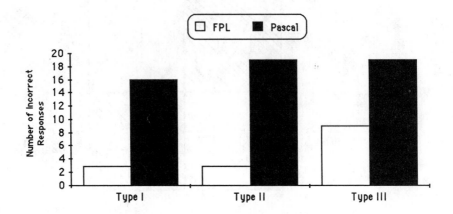

Figure 5

Number of Incorrect Responses by Question Type

Table 4

Incorrect Responses Classified by Programming Construct

QUESTION AREA	FPL	Pascal	TOTAL	
EITHERs (IF/THEN/ELSE)	8	27	35	50.7%
INPUT/OUTPUT	3	16	19	27.5%
WHILEs	1	6	7	10.2%
Assignments	2	6	8	11.6%
TOTAL	14	55	69	

As can be seen from this classification, questions about flow of control aspects of a program segment (number of EITHERs, IF/THEN/ELSE, how many would be executed, value of a specific variable after the execution of a series of nested statements, etc.) were the source of the greatest number of errors in both languages; due to the greater number of total errors, this trend was more noticeable for Pascal. Questions about input and output also were the source of a large percentage of the errors.

Correlation of Aptitude and Comprehension

We hypothesized that high visual aptitude would speed up comprehension of graphically represented segments, so we looked for an *inverse correlation* between visual aptitude and reaction times (*e.g.*, as aptitude scores increase, reaction times decrease). Table 5 summarizes the results of the correlation of aptitude and performance. An examination of the relationships indicates the identical moderate inverse correlation ($r = -.35$) between visual aptitude and *overall* reaction time (combining all reaction times, FPL and Pascal) and between visual aptitude and *FPL* reaction time. A low inverse relationship was also observed between visual aptitude and Pascal reaction times ($r = -.29$).

Table 5

Pearson's Product-Moment Correlation between Aptitude and Comprehension Speed and Accuracy

	FPL RT	PAS RT	FPL Accuracy	PASCAL Accuracy
VISUAL Aptitude	-.35	-.29	.52	.26
VERBAL Aptitude	.19	.28	.08	-.17

A positive correlation between accuracy and aptitude indicates that as aptitude scores increase, accuracy increases. The results show a moderate correlation between visual aptitude and accuracy, both overall ($r = .40$) and especially on the FPL questions ($r= .52$) See Figure 6 for an illustration of this relationship. No relationship between verbal aptitude (as measured by the screening test we chose) and accuracy was detected.

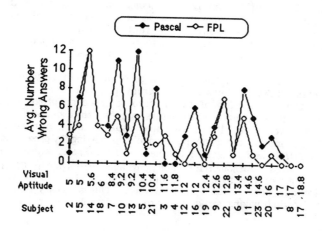

Figure 6

Correlation between Visual Aptitude and FPL and Pascal Accuracy

DISCUSSION

The findings of this study suggest that, for almost all subjects, for the type of comprehension questions asked and for the type and length of program segments presented, FPL's graphical representation of programming is comprehended both more rapidly and more accurately than the traditional textual representation as embodied by Pascal. The findings also suggest that high visual aptitude correlates with more rapid and more accurate comprehension of programs no matter which representation is used.

Comprehension and Reaction Time

The clear positive finding of this study is that with respect to those aspects of comprehension being studied here, novice programmers comprehend short program segments faster when those segments are graphically represented than when they are represented in a traditional, textual language. We hypothesized that this would be the case, but the findings supported the hypotheses much more strongly than anticipated, suggesting that for almost all subjects, a graphical representation speeds up comprehension. We expected that for program segments with fairly complex flow of control (*i.e.*, with nested compound structures), the advantage of graphical representation would be greater than for less complex segments. As it turns out, however, this study revealed no significant differences across program segments, even when some of those segments were more complex than others. It may be that the screen size used (24 lines) limited the range of length and complexity of the program segments so severely as to mask noticeable performance differences along this dimension. We will therefore examine this further in a subsequent study, using far more extensive segment displays, so that a greater range of complexity and length differences can be presented to subjects.

Comprehension Accuracy

In the design of the experiment, we decided that the major focus should be on reaction time, and thus we deliberately wrote comprehension questions that we thought the subjects would be able to answer. In so doing, we certainly constrained the conclusions we could make about the effect of graphical representation on comprehension accuracy. However, even the relatively small number of incorrect responses formed a pattern clear enough to warrant analysis.

After noting that a substantial percentage of incorrect responses (70.7% of *all* incorrect responses; 79.7% of the *Mixed Accuracy* responses) were to questions about Pascal programs, the examination of those response based on programming constructs proved to be quite interesting. The results suggest that certain features of the graphical representation of FPL make some aspects of programming easier to comprehend. In particular, the concept of decision making in programming, embodied in FPL as the *EITHER*, and in Pascal as the *IF-THEN-ELSE*, was the source of the largest number of errors. Although for each language, errors about *EITHER*s reflected the same *percentage* of the total, it is quite obvious that there were far fewer overall errors for questions about FPL programs. This suggests that comprehension questions, about decision making structures, are considerably easier for novices in FPL.

We suspect this is so because of the spatial layout characterizing the FPL icon for decision making, since it places the alternatives in sharp horizontal juxtaposition. By comparison, the Pascal representation tends to mask visually the alternative structure through a vertical, sequential layout of the text. The horizontal design of the FPL *EITHER* more clearly delineates the idea of choice, and the spatial arrangement separates the options more radically. These findings certainly confirm the results of our studies of bugs in novices' FPL and Pascal programs (Cunniff *et al.* (7); Cunniff *et al.* (8)). They suggested that the spatial layout of FPL helps novices avoid introducing some bugs that are quite commonly found in Pascal program written by novices. It seems that FPL's graphical/spatial representation may help programmers *see* what the alternatives are, thus avoiding certain logical flaws.

Another trend observed in the data on accuracy of response was that there was a considerably greater number of errors for Pascal than for FPL on questions about *input and output*. We included these questions because we suspected that the presence of the *arrow* and the unique file icon in FPL input and output representation would result in faster, more accurate comprehension. This seems to be the case, again implying that graphic representation aids understanding and results in more accurate comprehension.

Comprehension and Aptitude

We also investigated whether subjects' visual and verbal aptitude affected performance on one or the other representations of programming. We hypothesized that more visually apt subjects would do better with a graphical representation of programming, and the findings confirmed this. However, the findings suggest more, namely that, *regardless of subjects' visual aptitude*, the graphical representation of programming was comprehended more rapidly. Additionally, we found there was a high correlation between visual aptitude and subject performance on the Pascal segment comprehension.

The results indicate a relationship between the aspect of visual aptitude measured by the *Paper Folding Test* and performance on the comprehension tasks, including performance on Pascal segments. This seems to confirm the importance of the spatial cuing that has been included *via* indentation and key words in Pascal and that, even in otherwise "textual" representation of Pascal programs, the visual/spatial component inherent in the location and format of the text is used by the reader as an aid to comprehension. Consequently, the comprehension of those subjects with high scores in visual aptitude was improved by virtue of the match between their aptitude and the inherently spatial aspect of the task.

While the visual aptitude measure did produce some interesting correlations, the verbal measure chosen did not. It is possible that the aspect of verbal aptitude measured by the *Advanced Vocabulary Test* is not particularly strongly related to programming comprehension. Further research should explore this question, possible using multiple measures of verbal aptitudes.

SOME SPECULATION

Larkin and Simon (25) suggested that "when two representations are informationally equivalent, their computational efficiency depends on the information-processing operators that act on them" (p. 65). The program segments used in this experiment were completely "informationally equivalent," that is, FPL and Pascal versions represented identical programming sequences. Thus, the focus of the experiment was to measure the computational efficiency of the two representations. One major difference between FPL and Pascal is that in FPL programs the action domain, or flow of control information is explicitly represented *graphically and spatially*. Even though the same information in Pascal is highlighted by means of indentation and BEGIN-END bracketting, this is a less noticeable, less graphically distinct representation that FPL's. As Larkin and Simon explain:

The fundamental difference between our diagrammatic and sentential representations is that the diagrammatic representation preserves explicitly the information about the topological and geometric relations among the components of the problem, while the sentential representation does not. (p. 66)

It has been proven that pictures are remembered better than words (see Anderson (25) for a summary of this research); thus it is possible that the representation of programming concepts as rendered in FPL is more memorable than is the textual representation of Pascal. Santa (26) reports a study of memory for geometric figures *versus* words, and found that objects such as geometric figures tend to be stored and remembered according to the spatial position in which they were presented while words tend to be stored according to linear order. This suggests that certain often-used programming segments (*i. e.*, "stereotypical solutions to problems" (Soloway (27)) might be remembered more easily in their FPL representation than in their Pascal representation. So memory of graphic symbols may be a factor in student performance here.

There is empirical evidence that when concrete and diagrammatic elaborations are provided for abstract material, that material is comprehended and remembered better (Egan & Schwartz (28); Larkin & Simon (23); Mayer (29)). In studies such as Mayer's, the elaborations were, in a sense, imposed on top of the material to be learned: the graphic or diagrammatic representations were not integral to the material being learned. In FPL, since the graphical representation is integral to the language, one would expect the known benefits of diagrammatic representations to be even more powerful. The graphical representation provides ready-made images for the learner; those images do not have to be constructed or meshed with the actual representation. By contrast, with textual languages, if a learner wants or needs an image, he or she must do the constructing and create a mental link between the actual and the imagistic representation, thus requiring some mental transformation during the comprehension process.

Such evidence gives credence to the suggestion that the FPL's graphical representation results in the creation of mental images and also probably supports the development of multiply linked representations. Because images are also associated with verbal labels, the names of the icons and the verbal functional labels provide access to the image *and* the verbal or propositional knowledge about programming. During the experiment, when an FPL program was viewed, the graphical representation likely caused an image to be recalled. At the same time, the textual questions caused access to memory about programming via yet another mental connection -- that formed originally by the verbal/textual aspect of programming. Thus, the way the experiment was constructed may have encouraged multiple connections to be activated resulting in the rapid reaction time. By contrast, the textual representation of both the program and the question for Pascal segments may have slowed recall by activating only the verbal connections for memory.

In short, it is plausible that when learning programming, the subjects involved in this study were encouraged by the graphical representation of FPL to build a mental image of certain programming structures. When trying to answer comprehension questions about a program, the subjects had to draw upon memory to determine what those structures looked like, and the mental image of the structure was recalled and then identified significantly more rapidly for the graphically represented programs than for the textually represented program.

CONCLUSIONS

The findings of this study clearly indicate that, at least for short program segments, graphical representation of programs improves novices' comprehension by two specific measures: *time and accuracy*. In this study, the relatively high comprehension accuracy with respect to both languages involved confirms subject facility with both, minimizing the possibility that results were due largely to subjects actually being more knowledgeable in the graphical language. At the same time, the case for graphical representation is strengthened by the pattern observed in the relatively few errors; when errors occurred, they were much more likely to occur in comprehending the textual representation. We believe these findings are of particular import to those involved in teaching novices to program as well as to those involved in the design of materials and languages for teaching programming.

Despite these findings, we think research in this area has hardly begun. For example, this study raises many questions that need further investigation. It deals with novices. Would the same comprehension results appear if the subjects were experienced programmers? This study deals with looking at the "trees" of programming. Would similar advantages accrue to graphical representation of programming's "forests"? Does the finding that visual aptitude correlates with comprehending Pascal imply that even textual representation of programming has always included a spatial element, namely that indentation and keywording are really a weak form of graphical representation? Which components of programming ought to be graphically represented and which should remain textually represented? Is program type really independent from the other issues we investigated, or would more distinct types bring out the differences our study failed to find?

Thus we have taken a few short steps toward verifying that, *A picture is worth 10,000 words* but it is evident that there is a long way to go. Perhaps we can only safely say at this point that :

One picture is worth a lot of indented keywords.

REFERENCES

1. Blaiwes, A. S. (1974). Formats for presenting procedural instructions. *Journal of Applied Psychology*, **59**. 683-686.

2. Kammann, R. (1975). The comprehensibility of printed instructions and the flowchart alternative. *Human Factors*, **17**, 183-191.

3. Shneiderman, B., Mayer, R., McKay, D. & Heller, P. (1977). Experimental investigations of the utility of detailed flowcharts in programming. *Communications of the ACM*, **20**, 373-381.

4. Brooke, J. B. & Duncan, K. D. (1980). An experimental study of flowcharts as an aid to identification of procedural faults. *Ergonomics*, **23**, 387-399.

5. Scanlan, D. (1987). Data-structures students may prefer to learn algorithms using graphical methods. *SIGCSE Bulletin*, **19**, 302-307.

6. Sheppard, S. B., Kruesi, E., & Bailey, J. W. (1982). An empirical study of software documentation formats. *Proccedings: Human Factors in Computer Systems*, 121-124.

7. Cunniff, N., Taylor, R. P., and Black, J. B. (1986). Does programming language affect the types of conceptual bugs in novices' programs? A comparison of FPL and Pascal. *Human Factors in Computer Systems: Proceedings of CHI'86*, 175-182.

8. Cunniff, N., Taylor, R. P., and Taylor, S. (1987). The effect of programming language on the conceptual bugs in novices' programs: A comparison of FPL and Pascal. In B. W. Hamill, R. C. Jernigan & J.C. Boudreaux, (Eds.), *The Role of Language in Problem Solving II*, Amsterdam: North-Holland Publishers. p. 391-407.

9. Cunniff, N. *Graphical vs. textual representation: A study of novices' comprehension of computer programs*. New York: Teachers College, Columbia University. Dissertation in preparation.

10. Embly, D. W. (1978). Empirical and formal language design applied to a uniform control structure. *International Journal of Man-Machine Studies*. **10**, 197-216.

11. Shneiderman, B. (1977). Measuring computer program quality and comprehension. *International Journal of Man-Machine Studies*, **9**, 465-478.

12. Brooks, R. (1983). Toward a theory of the comprehension of computer programs. *International Journal of Man-Machine Studies*, **18**, 543-554.

13. Gould, J. D. (1975). Some psychological evidence on how people debug computer programs. *International Journal of Man-Machine Studies*, **7**, 151-182.

14. Shneiderman, B. (1980). *Software Psychology*. Cambridge, MA: Winthrop Publishers, Inc.

15. Hall, W. E. & Zweben, S. H. (1986). Cloze procedure and software comprehensibility measurement. *IEEE Transactions on Software Engineering*, SE-12, 608-623.

16. Pennington, N. (1985). Stimulus structures and mental representations in expert comprehension of computer programs. *University of Chicago: Center for Decision Research*.

17. Taylor, R. P. (1982). *Programming primer*. Reading, MA: Addison-Wesley.

18. Taylor, R. P., Cunniff, N. & Uchiyama, M. (1986). Learning, research and the graphical representation of programming. *Proceedings of the Fall Joint Computing Conference, 1986*, 56-63.

19. Kesler, T. E., Uram, R. B., Magareh-Abed, F., Fritzsche, A., Amport, C. & Dunsmore, H. E. (1984). The Effect of indentation on program comprehension. *International Journal of Man-Machine Studies*, 21, 415-428.

20. Miara, R. J., Musselman, J. A., Navarro, J. A., & Shneiderman, B. (1983). Program indentation and comprehensibility. *Communications of the ACM*, 26, 861 - 867.

21. Kernighan, B. W., & Paulger, P. J. (1978). *The Elements of Programming Style.* New York: McGraw-Hill.

22. Ekstrom, R. B., French, J. W,, & Harman, H. H. (1976). *Manual for Kit of Factor-Referenced Cognitive Tests.* Princeton, NJ: Educational Testing Services.

23. Larkin, J. H., & Simon, H. A. (1987). Why a diagram is (sometimes) worth ten thousand words. *Cognitive Science*, 11, 65-99.

24. Atwood, M. E., & Ramsey, H. R. (1978). *Cognitive Structures on the Comprehension and Memory of Computer Programs: An Investigation of Computer Program Debugging.* (Tech. Rep. TR-78-A21). Alexandria, VA: U.S. Army Research Institute.

25. Anderson, J. R. (1980). *Cognitive Psychology and Its Implications.* New York: W. H. Freeman.

26. Santa, J. L. (1977). Spatial transformations of words and pictures. *Journal of Experimental Psychology: Human Learning and Memory*, 3, 418-427.

27. Soloway, E. (1986). Learning to program = learning to construct mechanisms and explanations. *Communications of the ACM*, 29, 850-858.

28. Egan, D. E., & Schwartz, B. J. (1979). Chunking in recall of symbolic drawings. *Memory and Cognition*, 7, 149-158.

29. Mayer, R. E. (1975). Some conditions of meaningful learning for computer programming: Advance organizers and subject control. *Journal of Educational Psychology*, 143-150.

CHAPTER 9

Parsing and Gnisrap*: A Model of Device Use

T. R. G. Green
R. K. E. Bellamy
Applied Psychology Unit
15 Chaucer Road
Cambridge CB2 2EF, UK

J. M. Parker
STC Technology Ltd.
Copthall House
Nelson Place
Newcastle-under-Lyme ST5 1EZ, UK

ABSTRACT

This paper introduces a model of coding which highlights features of the device, task, interaction medium and user knowledge that are important in determining the ease of use of a programming support environment. The model has been implemented in Prolog and applied to the domain of expert coding; where it is used to explain results from an observational study of expert coding behavior. Although the model is still at an early stage of development, it clearly shows the need to build device languages and support environments which complement each other, in the light of users' tasks and knowledge structures. Methods for achieving this aim are discussed.

INTRODUCTION

To understand how to build support tools for programming environments it is necessary to understand what programmers do. It is also necessary to understand what programmers do if one is to understand how to design programming languages that are easy to read and write. Most design efforts are based on folk theories of programming, and more generally of cognition at large, which accounts for some of the poor designs that are to be found. In this paper we offer a simplified model of one aspect of programming, namely coding, which is the aspect where the influence of poor cognitive ergonomics in the support environment and in the language design will make itself most felt. In support of this model we offer some detailed observational studies of the coding process which we interpret with respect to the model.

The research topic is an instance of the dominant scenario of HCI research today, in which an applications program (in our case, a text editor) is used to create and manipulate an information-rich structure in some externally-defined domain (in our case, a program). However, most HCI research either concentrates on the user, e.g. by constructing models of user performance, or else concentrates on factors related to the domain of application. The research we report here is unusual in aiming to model how the user's behavior is determined by the *relationship between the two halves*. Only in this way can a support environment be designed that properly complements a given programming language.

We shall follow recent fashion Payne (17) and refer to the "device language", in which the user gives commands to the editor or its equivalent; and to the "task language", meaning the rules that describe the target domain. For example when writing a computer program using a text editor such as EMACS; the programming language is the task language and the commands used to manipulate the editor are the device language. We shall also refer to the "interaction medium", e.g. pen and paper; VDU, because that too helps to determine the user's behavior.

---

*pronounced 'nice rap'

Phenomena to be Modelled

Our purpose is not to refute earlier models but to extend them, and thereby to help find out why programmers behave the way they do. Figure 1 shows one sample from a number of detailed records of highly experienced programmers (not college students, but professionals) writing programs for very simple problems. Because such a problem as 'reverse an array in place' is trivial for such programmers, problem-solving activity is minimized, and the program can perhaps be generated in strict left-to-right order ('linear generation'). When the program is not generated in strict linear order, the departures indicate problems in task and device languages or their relationship. Typically, gaps are left to be filled later. Our records (to be described in full elsewhere) indicate, not surprisingly, that the pattern of gaps-to-be-filled is fairly consistent within particular combinations of task and device language, but is different for different task languages (i.e. programming languages). At the time of writing we have not investigated the effects of different editing environments.

```
1       10 Restore
2       20 Dim data%(9)
6        :  Dim Reversed%(9)
3       30 For I% = 0 To 9:  Read data%(I%):
7       Reversed
9       %
8       (9-I%) = data%(I%):
4       Print; data%(I%); " ":  Next
5       40
10      Print:  For I% = 0 TO 9:
        Print; Reversed%(I%);" ":  Next
11      50 Data 1,2,3,4,5,6,7,8,9,0
```

Figure 1: A typical Basic protocol for the "reverse array in place" problem. The arrows indicate the jumps and the leftmost numbers the order of writing.

(Note on Figure 1. There are some difficulties in using a static medium to describe temporal phenomena; for ease of reference we have introduced a column of line numbers on the left-hand side which record the order in which fragments were written by the programmer. Do not confuse these numbers, introduced by the authors for reference, with the Basic-line-numbers.)

Departures from linear generation are significant. They increase mental workload, they risk omissions and oversights, and they can demand (depending on the editor) many extra keystrokes and mental operations which are solely within the device language, not the task language. A particularly striking example is reported by Whitefield (22), in the context of CAD, where experienced users of CAD tools were observed spending up to 10 consecutive minutes just operating the device, not making progress with the externally-defined task. Similar examples probably come to the mind of any reader who has used editing tools. Our first aim is to model the causes of these problems, so that they can be better understood, anticipated and cured.

A second phenomenon to be modelled should be equally familiar. What user of the Unix *ed* line editor has not experienced the difficulty of reading an editing script containing such lines as this?

$$\mathbf{s/\backslash\backslash\backslash/\backslash./.\backslash\backslash\backslash//}$$

("Change the pattern \\/. to .\\/".) Yet *ed* commands can easily be generated in linear order. The difficulties they raise are difficulties not of generation but of comprehension, and in particular of 'perceptual parsing' (Payne et al., 16). Similar difficulties apply to programming languages, and it is widely assumed that some programming languages are harder to read than others. Unfortunately, although the work of McKeithen et al. (13) has shown that the ability to perceive structure in program text is one of the distinguishing features of the expert, there has been no detailed work on the processes involved, in the tradition of the psycholinguistic investigation of natural language parsing.

Despite the lack of detailed knowledge, it is obvious that when programmers adopt non-linear code generation they are forced to read and comprehend earlier parts of the code before they can successfully insert subsequent parts. The model discussed in the following section presents the view that the coding process, except for certain special cases, inevitably leads to non-linear generation, and that the re-comprehending of partial text is therefore inextricably part of the coding process. The programmer's strategy will be partly determined by the difficulty in re-comprehending the text: if the programming language is particularly hard to read, non-linearities will be resisted.

Of course, when non-linearities are unlikely to occur the difficulty of reading the program does not affect the programmer, because there is no need to re-comprehend a partial text. Hence the notorious difficulty of understanding *ed* commands appears not be a problem (at least during interactive working).

Some attention to the problem of linear generation has already been paid by Brooks (3) who reports on a prolonged study of a single subject writing simple programs in a single programming language (Fortran). Brooks developed a production system model of the coding process which he claimed generated lines of code in an order very similar to the observed order. He proposed that programming knowledge was plan-based and viewed "code generation as being accomplished by a large body of independent coding rules" (p. 749). In another seminal paper, Brooks (4) proposes a model of the comprehension of programs. Although the bulk of this paper treats the process of 'mapping' between 'domains', a topic which lies outside the scope of the present paper, it introduces the important idea of 'beacons' which can give strong indications for the existence of particular plans, whether hypothesized or not, and in this way can combine elements of top-down and bottom-up comprehension (p. 548).

Our model continues this approach but extends his treatment in three ways. First, it introduces the 'Parsing-Gnisrap' cycle, in which code is alternately output and ingested. Second, and as a corollary, it emphasizes the importance of the 'external memory', the fragment of code already generated (referred to only briefly by Brooks (3), p. 745); and third, we show how some language features facilitate the Parsing component of the cycle, while other features facilitate the 'Gnisrap'.

OVERVIEW OF THE PARSING-GNISRAP MODEL

The Parsing-Gnisrap model is a model of *coding*, rather than of programming; it starts at the stage when the programmer has already solved the main problems of how to write the program, and wishes to turn these into code. The model describes two fundamental psychological processes. The programming text is mentally elaborated from a skeletal plan, and when working memory is full part of the text is output to the VDU (or some other external medium, such as paper). When the programmer needs to recover the details of parts of the text that have been externally stored, the text must be read and comprehended, to recover the details of the former mental structure.

The model contains an architecture, determining how knowledge is to be represented and used, and of course a specific knowledge component for a particular programming language and a particular editing medium, represented at a coarse level of granularity. By changing the specific knowledge, different behavior is generated from the same architecture. Most of the model has been realised in Prolog, using a frame representation of knowledge (Figure 2), and currently it is able to generate code for simple problems in Pascal and Basic; knowledge of other languages will be added. However, the model does *not* contain any representation of the semantics of the programming language. Semantic knowledge is required for solving a problem but not for coding the solution in a specified language.

(Our model can also be viewed more generally, as a *planning* model, describing how to build structures in the task domain by performing actions in the device domain.)

Following the work of Rist (19), we suppose that the output of the problem-solving stage is a skeletal plan of how to write the program, which in our experienced programmers will be evoked by forwards-chaining from the problem statement (cf. Larkin's (12) model of expertise in physics). The skeletal plan is a list of 'programming schemas' which have to be coded and assembled so that they operate correctly. Each schema is represented by a frame. The frame is built around Rist's concept of the 'focal line': what our model contributes is a description of how the programmer instantiates the focal line in a working program. A frame (see Figure 2) states the code, its purpose, the role of the components within the code, the preconditions for using the schema, and the postconditions of using it.

For a very simple program, the skeletal plan consists only of a single 'focal line'. Even the more complex problems for which we took records only require two or three 'focal lines' in the representation we used. To elaborate the skeletal plan into a working program, its code is fleshed out, and other schemas may be invoked by both backward and forward chaining: the skeleton invokes a schema which requires a precondition, and so a schema must be found whose postcondition satisfies that precondition, this process continues until the parsed input matches the skeletal plan. The 'ideal' programmer, blessed with an infinite working memory, could build the whole program up like this.

```
frame([(name, iteration),
       (parent, activity),
       (code, [for, Var1, ':=', Var2, to, Var3, do, gap, ';']),
       (purpose, generator(Var2, Var3)),
       (stop, Var3),
       (start, Var2),
       (controlled_var, Var1),
       (precondition, [variable_declaration(Var1),
             variable_declaration(Var2), variable_declaration(Var3)]),
       (postcondition, [Var1, has, taken, values, Var2, to, Var3])
       ]).
```

Figure 2: A frame describing iteration, taken from the representation of
programming knowledge for a Pascal expert.

What is new in our model is that it also postulates that programmers, having a severely limited internal working memory, make use of the external medium (e.g. the VDU screen) as a temporary store or as a dump when overload threatens them. Rather than build up the whole program internally and then output it to the editor from start to finish, they output fragments as they are completed, or incomplete fragments if working memory becomes overloaded. In our model, code fragments that have been output to the external system are simply deleted from internal memory — a simplifying assumption. When subsequently the programmer needs to refer to the fragment, it will need to be parsed. Parsing aims to recreate the original plan structure, in which the roles of each component were marked.

The parser component of our model relies on a simple psychological assumption which has been used to model parsing of English sentences (Bever, 1). Knowledge of syntax is stored as 'discontinuous templates', such as N... V (noun phrase .... verb phrase). According to Bever's account, when the parser identifies a noun phrase which is not preceded by a subordinate clause marker such as 'although', it tentatively assumes that that is the subject, seeks the first verb phrase it can find, and assumes that that is the main verb. While this strategy does not give a complete account of human parsing of natural language, it accounts for a substantial proportion of the findings. When applied to our languages, it successfully separates the code fragment

$$k := 1; \text{ for } j := 1 \text{ to } n \text{ do } k := k * j;$$

into the following two portions and identifies the plan constructs:

$$k := 1 \text{ (;)} \dots\dots\ k := k * j \qquad \text{accumulator}$$
$$\text{for } j := 1 \text{ to } n \text{ do } \dots\dots \text{ (;)} \qquad \text{generator}$$

Thus, our model describes two fundamental psychological processes, inverses of each other. An external structure (the program code) is created from the internal structure of purposes and requirements, and inversely, the internal structure is recreated when necessary from the external structure. Since the second process is more usually known as 'parsing' we have dubbed the first process, its inverse, as *gnisrap*, the reverse of parsing, and our model is therefore termed the parsing-gnisrap model.

This model is not a serially staged model. Instead, processes can be driven by need, by availability, or by agenda-list: the programmer outputs code to external memory when a fragment is ready *or* when the limitations of memory make it necessary. Similarly, material that has been output to external memory is parsed when the construction of a plan demands information no longer in internal memory, *or* when an agenda-list contains a note that unfilled gaps remain in the external memory.

Figure 3 displays output from the current version of the model, for the 'reverse an array in place' problem in Basic (This is one of the problems used in our empirical study described below.) The skeletal plan from which the code is generated is: read array; write array; reverse array; and write the reversed array. Working memory is set to six items.

First chunk output from memory

```
Read a(i)
For i = 1 to 10 :  gap :  Next
Dim a(10)
Print ; a(i)
For i = 1 to 10 :  gap :  Next
b(10 - i) = a(i)
For i = 1 to 10 :  gap :  Next
```

Second chunk output from memory

```
Dim b(10)
Print ; b(i)
For i = 1 to 10 :  gap :  Next
```

Figure 3: Output from the model. (NB: The model does not as yet support the interleaving of plans, thus the chunks are not ordered.)

Determinants of Strategy

The behavior of the model (and thus our explanation of "why programmers behave the way they do") depends on characteristics of the device language, the task language, the interaction medium, and the knowledge representation. We draw on a more extensive, but as yet incomplete, analysis of 'dimensions of notations', in which the authors and others are attempting to create an operationalizable terminology describing attributes of interaction. (See Green, 8; Gilmore, 6; Green, Bellamy and Gilmore, 9) In this analysis, terms that are important for the present purpose are 'access window', 'role-expressiveness', and 'viscosity'. These terms are explained below.

Access Window

True linear generation is only required, as an absolute necessity, in rather special situations, such as dictating a program blindfold. Try doing that: which programming language would you prefer? Informal observation shows that problems with declaring variables, balancing parenthesis, etc. become truly important in such a task. In contrast, when the medium of interaction is paper and pencil, an overlooked parenthesis or an undeclared variable can be readily inserted. Another advantage of paper is that it allows access to the course of development of the program (Figure 4). Paper is a medium with a wide 'access window' — one can get at any part of the expression being built — while in dictation the access window is limited to a single point. In between those two limiting cases lie word processors, interactive graphics devices, and most other methods of interaction in HCI. The user must do a certain amount of work to access any point except the current cursor location.

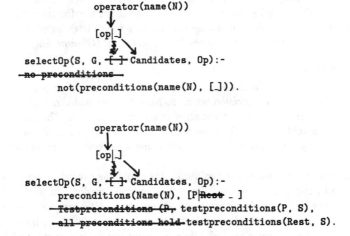

Figure 4: An example of code being developed on paper.

The width of the access window is an attribute of the interaction medium, not of the task language; algebra or Pascal can be handwritten or dictated, and the language remains the same but the interaction medium varies. However, the *importance* of window size depends on the task language. It is important to have a wide window when writing algebra or Pascal because they have many right-to-left constraints (see below). Some other notations, such as reverse polish or Basic, have fewer constraints of this sort.

Viscosity

Some languages are resistant to local change; we call them viscous. Viscosity can be found at both the task level and the device level. At the task level, it is harder to insert a new section into a Pascal program than into the equivalent Basic program (although in Pascal the extra effort may be worthwhile, producing a better-structured resulting program); similarly, using a conventional word processor, say WordStar or MacWrite, inserting a new diagram into a paper may be difficult because all subsequent diagrams must be renumbered. This 'external' viscosity can be lowered by using a knowledgeable editor, such as Scribe or Perfect Writer, which uses soft numbering.

At the device level, some editors require more effort to achieve a given action. Indeed, users can spend very significant proportions of their time simply 'driving' viscous editing devices — performing actions relating solely to the management of the interaction dialogue rather than furthering their external goal. The observations of Whitefield (22), mentioned above, indicate that existing CAD tools do not reduce viscosity enough. The notion of a 'viscous' device has something in common with Moran's ETIT analysis of the complexity of mapping between external and internal device tasks (Moran, 14).

Role-Expressiveness

Because of the limitations of working memory, users spend much of their time consulting the existing structure to remind themselves of what they were doing and how they were doing it. In a 'role-expressive' language, the programmer can readily perceive the purpose, or role, of each program statement. This is the parsing cycle of our model; it has previously been referred to as 'de-programming' by Sime, Green and Guest (20). Linearly generated structures, such as *ed* commands are not necessarily role-expressive — indeed, although linear generability and role expressiveness are both desirable, they may be somewhat opposed, because linearly generable notations contain rather few indications of what is going to happen next, nor any similar organizational clues, yet such indications are a powerful aid to readers. In order for users to understand a program structure, they must induce the fundamental structural elements and the role of each element in the overall structure. High-lighting the different structures is one way to make a notation more 'role-expressive' (Gilmore and Green, 7).

Right-to-left Constraints

A common reason for departing from linear code generation is that the programmer needs to make a decision before the information on which to base it is available. A typical example is the need to declare program variables at the start of a Pascal program. The user can at best make a guess at the variables that will be needed and usually has to amend the guess in the light of the finished program. Similar 'right-to-left' constraints occur in other programming languages.

A good development environment will minimize the problems caused by right-to-left constraints. Paper and pencil, for instance, offers an interaction medium in which every part of the target structure (program) is within reach at any time. Alternatively, the device language (the editor) could be altered: the development environment for the language B is able to infer all the variable declarations needed, while the language Basic dispenses with variable declarations altogether. (NB: these decisions involve various trade-offs — we are not necessarily recommending any particular choice as best overall. In particular, the Basic language exposes users to problems of mistyped variable names. In return for that risk, they do not have to worry about declarations.)

Knowledge Representation

The pattern of user activity is not solely determined by the the formal structure of the task language. It is also affected by the structure of the user's knowledge of how to perform external tasks. In the domain of programming, especially Pascal programming, there has been research (Soloway and Ehrlich, 21) suggesting that experienced programmers have 'plans' or 'methods' which are fragments of code, possibly discontinuous, with knowledge about the role or purpose of each component of the plan. Many of these 'plans' comprise a major part and a necessary but minor part, which may be less salient: for example, Pascal summation plans require a minor part, namely an initialization which simply sets an identifier to zero, and Prolog list processing plans require a base case which simply defines the treatment of the empty list. These minor and possibly less salient parts of plans are sometimes left out by programmers during the first pass, either intentionally or by mistake, and are inserted later. On the other hand, it is extremely rare to see the minor part included in the first pass and the major part omitted. This asymmetry suggests to us that the effect is caused by asymmetry in the knowledge structure: the major part is 'focal' to the plan, but the minor part is invoked only as a precondition required by the major part.

EMPIRICAL SUPPORT

A fundamental assumption of our model is that programs are linearly generated where possible, following a 'natural' development path which can under some conditions conflict with the text order. This is demonstrated by Hoc (10) who shows that where the text order of statements varied from the order of execution, programmers tended to develop algorithms in order of execution, even though this requires more work at the device level. Note, however, that this work was done with a procedural language: equivalent results from a more declarative language are not at present available. Also, Hoc's study used problems hard enough to require problem-solving rather than coding. We report here on a study comparing coding behavior in different programming languages.

Fourteen expert programmers were subjects in this study, using the languages of their expertise, which were Basic (N = 5), Pascal (N = 4), and Prolog (N = 5). These three languages were chosen to exemplify some important differences in language design. Pascal and Basic are imperative, assignment-based languages, while Prolog is nearer to logic programming; Prolog and Basic have lower degrees of right-to-left constraint than Pascal; Pascal is more role-expressive, we believe, than Prolog or Basic; plan structures in Pascal and Basic are easily identified, but are more conjectural in Prolog.

Subjects solved three simple problems. The first was to reverse an array in place (Basic and Pascal) or reverse a list (Prolog). The second was based on the 'traffic counting' problem (Ratcliff and Siddiqui, 18); the problem here is to analyze a data file from a survey in which each passing vehicle generated one signal and each elapsed time interval a different signal. Our programmers had to write a program to count the vehicles, the length of the survey period, and the longest time without a vehicle. The third problem was to consult a timetable of Cambridge-London trains and find the last train to arrive at or before a stated time. These problems were all easy by professional standards — indeed, we assumed they would be trivial. In retrospect, it was clear that they demanded more problem-solving than we expected, so that our results were not purely coding behavior, as we had hoped.

The programmers used the screen editor Microsoft Word on a Macintosh, and their actions were recorded using the Journal desk accessory. They were not allowed to use paper for drafting but could make notes on-screen if so desired. After the experiment, subjects were asked to fill out a questionnaire, the analysis of which will be reported elsewhere.

Code Is Not Generated Linearly

Our principal interest was in the distribution of non-linearities in generating code, as illustrated in Figure 1. The questions we wished to address were:

1. is code generated linearly?

2. are there differences between languages?

3. do non-linearities occur at the points we expected?

A non-linearity in code generation was indicated when an editing action (insertion or deletion) was followed by moving the cursor to another location and performing another editing action. We called this a *jump*. (NB: although goto statements are sometimes called jumps, we are using the term solely to refer to discontinuities in the generation of text.) Note that moving the cursor to inspect code elsewhere, without altering the code, was not counted. Figure 1 illustrates two points where the programmer made backward jumps, to amend previously-written code, and also a forward jump (line 8) where a backward jump to line 7 was followed by amending code lying between that point and the end of currently-existing text, which at that moment was at line 6. Jumps to refer to or to alter on-screen notes, which were often placed at the head of the text, were not counted.

There are several ways to score non-linearities, but of the metrics we examined the most conservative (i.e. the one that minimized between-group differences) was to count only those jumps which went backwards from the end of the program to some earlier point. No further jumps were scored, whatever the programmer did, until new material had been added at the end of the program. In this way a sequence of jumps though the program to change related items woulds be score as a single jump.

The absolute number of backward jumps is not an unbiassed metric of differences between languages, since it may be affected by the length of the program (longer programs giving more opportunity). This would not be a problem if programs were on average much the same length, but we found that Pascal programs were substantially longer than others and that Prolog programs were shortest. There are two questions of interest: whether a Pascal programmer will make more jumps than a Basic or Prolog programmer solving the same problem, and whether the density of 'jumps per inch' differs between languages. We therefore analyzed both the absolute number of backward jumps per group and also, as an estimator of 'jump density', the weighted value obtained by scoring each jump as the reciprocal of the number of words in the final program. (Nor, of course, is the number of 'words', as defined by lexical analysis, an ideal metric; for instance it treats commas, which are very frequent in Prolog, on the same terms as argument names. The ideal would be to estimate the number of psychologically significant lexemes.)

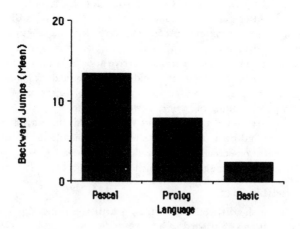

Figure 5: Mean number of backward jumps for each language.

The main finding is that backward jumps occurred in all languages: this answers question (1) above. They were commonest in Pascal (Figure 5); inspection showed that the between-group differences were not caused by, say, a single atypical Pascaleer. Statistical comparisons, using the distribution-free Kruskal-Wallis test, showed that the differences in Figure 5 were highly significant (p < 0.01). When the scores were weighted to correct for program length the differences between groups were still statistically significant (p < 0.02). Mann-Whitney paired comparisons were made using both metrics, absolute and weighted. Using absolute jumps, the Prolog group jumped significantly more than the Basic group (p = 0.008) but the Pascal and Prolog groups did not differ significantly (p = 0.095), whereas using the weighted metric the Prolog and Basic groups did not differ significantly while this time the Pascal and Prolog groups differed significantly at p < 0.008. In answer to question (2), therefore, it appears that a programmer working in Pascal or Prolog will probably make many more jumps than a programmer working on the same problem in Basic, and that this difference is due to a greater density of jumps within the program as well as to the greater length of programs; but the comparison of Prolog and Basic suggests that any difference in density between them may depend critically on the precise definition of the metric, and whether commas, for instance, are included in the estimate of program length.

As regards the location of jumps, question (3) above, our expectation was that non-salient fragments of plans would frequently be omitted. We examined this in rather crude fashion by looking for points where the programmer had made a backward jump to insert initializations for summations (N := 0 statements) in Pascal and Basic. The nearest equivalent type of Prolog statement seems to be the base case, so we counted jumps to insert base cases. Such jumps were much more frequent in Pascal than in Basic, and hardly occurred at all in Prolog. This question deserves much deeper analysis than can be given here.

Strategy Depends on Language

Pascal and Basic programmers produced essentially similar programs for a given problem. Prolog programs varied much more, especially for the second and third problems. Compared to the other groups there appeared to be a greater variety of programming styles within the Prolog group, from the pure logic programmer to a style looking suspiciously like straight hacking.

Although Pascal programmers produced programs with similar structures to the Basic programmers, their behavior showed importance differences. They frequently used a stepwise-refinement approach, whereas Basic programmers more often generated code almost linearly from beginning to end (as in Figure 1). Pascal programmers also made far more on-screen notes than the other groups (Figure 6): it is not clear whether that was a side-effect of the design of the Pascal language, or a consequence of their stepwise-refinement approach. Finally, the stepwise-refinement strategy, and the greater length of the programs, meant that Pascal programmers were traversing their programs far more often than in the other groups, and we observed that if syntactic errors were noticed they tended to be adjusted at the time, suspending completion of the current goal.

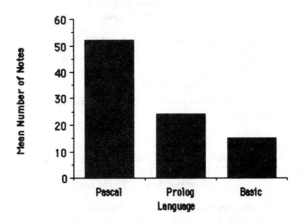

Figure 6: Mean number of notes for each language.

If Pascal and Basic programmers generated the same plans, why did their strategies differ? We suggest several possible reasons. First, Pascal procedures offer better facilities for this approach than Basic subroutines. Second, the Pascal teaching tradition has always emphasized this method. Third, Pascal is more viscous (harder to change) than Basic, and an approach which minimizes interleaving is to be preferred. Finally, Basic is less role-expressive than Pascal, so Basic programmers have to generate their code linearly, since once generated they will have trouble understanding it.

Plan Structures Depend on Language

Although this experiment was not particularly intended to study the knowledge structures used by our programmers, we were gratified to discover that non-linearities could be used to identify what appeared to be programming plans. Frequently the programmer generated code for one plan and then jumped back to insert additional code for a second, interleaved, plan. The programming plans observed in this experiment, for Basic and Pascal groups, are consistent with the type described by Rist (19), deriving in turn from the work of Soloway and others. Figure 7 illustrates a Basic program which appears to be built to a plan structure; different typefaces indicate different plans. We are not aware of any previous demonstration of plan structures in Basic, and indeed an experiment on program comprehension by Gilmore and Green (7) found no evidence for the use of plans by Basic programmers. Gilmore and Green's interpretation is that Basic is not 'role-expressive' — i.e. it is harder to perceive plan structures in the written code — but this would not gainsay the use of plans when writing programs, rather than reading them.

```
10 Restore
20 Dim data%(9)
   : Dim Reversed%(9)
30 For I% - 0 to 9: Read data%(I%)
   Reversed%(9 - I%): Print; data%(I%); " ": Next
40
   Print: For I% = 0 To 9: Print Reversed%(I%);" ": Next
50 Data 1,2,3,4,5,6,7,8,9,0
```

Figure 7: A Basic program for problem 1. Fonts indicate the plan structures: bold denotes input into an array and italic denotes the reversal and printing of the array. The code shown in bold was generated first, then the code shown in italics was inserted.

Prolog plans can be characterized as the linking of variables across the program functions, with interleaved plans demanding extra variables. Figure 8 shows a typical example of plans within Prolog. A plan is often generated either with markers for variables to be decided later, or with variables missing from the function. When a second plan is interleaved, the markers are overwritten with the correct variable name or structure and it may be necessary to add variables to the existing structure.

```
analyze ([ ],0,0,0,0)
analyze ([1|T],0,P,L,N) if analyze (T,Pa,P,L0,N0) and L=L0+1 and N=N0+1
analyze ([2|T],Pa,P,L,N) if analyze (T,Pb,P0,L0,N) and Pa=Pb +1
                 and longest (Pa,Pb,P) and L=L0+1
```

Figure 8: A Prolog program for problem 2. Fonts indicate typical plan structures: bold indicates the base case, for both 'increment' and 'filter' plans; italic indicates an 'increment' plan; plain a 'filter' plan; and underline shows where variable names were changed. The code was generated in precisely that order — the code shown in bold generated first, etc — except for one unimportant deviation; in the 'base' case, the two italic zeros were inserted before, not after, the bold face zeros.

A characteristic of Prolog, not directly observable, but indicated by our data, is the importance of variable names. Salient variable names are almost the only method of making a

Prolog program 'role-expressive' and thereby revealing the plan structures. There are very few alternative cues to the purpose of a piece of Prolog code — for instance it is impossible to know if a variable is to be used for input or output at any one time in the execution of a Prolog program. The importance of variable names is not captured by our model, and exactly how to achieve this is not clear at the current time.

Summary of Observations

- all programmers, in all languages, showed significant non-linearities in generation, as expected;

- most jumps were made in Pascal, least in Basic, due both to different program lengths and to a lesser extent to differing jump densities;

- since significantly more jumps (absolute metric) were made in Prolog than in Basic, the differences are not solely due to the greater syntactic tightness of Pascal over Basic;

- Pascal and Basic programmers used similar plan structures but displayed different strategies, stepwise refinement and top-to-bottom working respectively;

- Pascal programmers used on-screen notes much more extensively than others;

- Prolog plan structures appeared to be built around the interlinking of variables, and the variable names were the only means of cueing them.

Assessment of the Model

We have not attempted to construct a complete theory of programming, but to develop a model which highlights those features of the environment that substantially affect the coding process. To what degree do our empirical observations support that model?

In the first place, we were not prepared for the discovery that Pascal programmers used stepwise refinement on such simple programs. Since our present model makes no provision for hierarchical planning it is not capable of performing stepwise refinement. Also, its present knowledge structures are too fragmented; Rist (19) points out that recently-used programming plans are available as a single unit. Not surprisingly, many of our programmers started with the plans that were directly invoked by the problem givens, in accord with results of Ratcliff and Siddiqui (18), and here again the model is over-simplified, making no attempt to represent the process of mapping problem givens onto plan structures.

Despite these limitations, the model was clearly successful in showing that the generation of code (the 'gnisrap') is fitful and sporadic, and that the degree of fitfulness depends on the design of the programming language.

Turning to the parsing, our model does not yet offer a metric for role-expressiveness, but it does at least highlight its relevance. Parsing in programming is an area needing more research. Our parser corresponds fairly closely to 'gap-and-filler', one of the several candidate models of linguistic parsing vying for supremacy (Fodor, 5). At present, however, it is purely symbol-driven; a more accurate version should incorporate 'beacons' and should show the effect of perceptual cues such as indenting, which have been shown to greatly affect program comprehension (Gilmore, 6). More empirical research is urgently needed on this topic, comparing the comprehension of many different types of language. We are particularly interested in the effects of support environments which provide syntactic templates invoked by single keys: we predict that while they simplify the gnisrap they make the parsing, if anything, slightly harder, since the programmer has still less idea what the roles (or even the boundaries) of the templates are. Devices by which role-expressiveness can be increased should be investigated.

Certain important inferential steps in parsing are not included in our model as yet. In particular, Sime et al. (20), discussing the comprehension of Basic-style conditionals, mention number and type of mental operations required, for which we have at present no analogue.

IMPLICATIONS

The major implications of our model concern the building of programming languages and support environments that complement each other, in the light of users' tasks and knowledge structures. Even though our model contains no mental representation of program semantics, it correctly predicts that programmers — even highly experienced ones — will depart from linear generation in certain ways. We doubt whether the designers of either Pascal, Basic or Prolog paid attention to this aspect. An effective development environment should, amongst other features, find a solution to that problem.

The most familiar means to support program coding is the structure-based editor. Almost all the structure-based editors known to the authors are designed for imperative languages and are built around the syntax of the language. (Lisp, being protean by nature, offers some alternatives.) If our model is correct, these editors have taken the wrong approach.

Instead, editors should be designed to promote linear generation of code by identifying those characteristics of the programming language that inhibit it. For instance research on the effects of programming environments is reported by Hoc (11) using a tool designed to reduce left-to-right constraints. Despite its good intentions, this tool requires users to specify high-level aspects of the program in detail too early. Hoc concludes that linear generation requires a system where the user can make use of intermediate representations and can have easy access to all parts and levels of the developing structure, and which (in our terms) has very low viscosity. Universe (Parker, 15) is another tool, designed to assist Pascal programmers by allowing them to work directly in plan terms; a limited empirical investigation suggested that the technique was extremely promising.

Comparable tools for Basic or Prolog have yet to be devised, as far as we know. In these languages, if our model is correct, the problem of parsing is more severe than in Pascal. It is intriguing to speculate on how the linkages of Prolog variables, which give trouble to our parser and to humans as well, could be highlighted.

Another solution is to introduce an *intermediate task language*. We found that some programmers invented and used an intermediate language, which relaxed some of the constraints of real programming languages. This seems to happen most often in the Pascal group. Our model is not capable of *inventing* an intermediate language, of course, but is capable of assessing the effect of an intermediate language, and it seems clear from present data that intermediate languages reduce the mental workload as assessed by the model.

Intermediate languages are well-known in the Pascal literature. Stepwise refinement solves the linear generation problem by using an intermediate high-level language and by postponing the use of the VDU until the program is fully developed on paper, a medium with a wide access window. Bonar and Cunningham (2) have developed 'Bridge' an intermediate language teaching system of great interest. Structure-based editors (another form of intermediate language) have been developed for Pascal-like languages, but generally these take little account of the user's knowledge representation, so they are built around the syntax of the task language rather than the user's plan structures. In consequence they are sometimes unsuccessful.

An alternative solution would be to change the task language itself — i.e. the programming language: it is too late to change Prolog or Pascal, but future languages could be devised with the user's cognitive architecture more firmly in mind. The Parsing-Gnisrap model suggests that a number of language features will determine usability (although in practice there are numerous other considerations that affect programming language design, besides these). According to the model, during the 'Gnisrap' component of the cycle linear generation will be inhibited when:

- the language is diffuse, so that working memory is filled too soon;

- the language contains right-to-left constraints;

- the user's plan structures contain non-salient fragments which can be forgotten, and which are not prompted by the syntax

- the method of composing two or more plans within one program requires interleaving of syntactic fragments, whether statements (Pascal, Basic) or variables (Prolog).

Identifying features that inhibit the Parsing component is more speculative, but strong candidates are:

- the existence of interleaved plan structures;

- absence of strong 'beacons' to suggest which plan structures are present;

- lack of perceptual cues indicating the program's internal structure.

We do not believe that the user's needs are likely to be fully met by considering the programming language on its own. The features which make Pascal easier to parse into plan structures may well be the very features that inhibit the linear generation of Pascal, and vice versa with Basic. Creating a system in which users can generate code linearly, and thereby reduce wasted effort, yet can subsequently parse the code with fluency is an aim which will require the design of the language and of the support environment to be undertaken together.

ACKNOWLEDGEMENTS

We would like to thank Praxis of Bath for their participation in this research.

REFERENCES

1 Bever, T.G. (1970). 'The cognitive basis for linguistic structures'. In J. Hayes (Ed.) *Cognition and the Development of Language*. New York: Wiley.

2 Bonar, J. G. and Cunningham, R. (in press) 'Bridge: an intelligent tutor for thinking about programming'. To appear in J. Self (Ed.) *Intelligent Computer-Aided Instruction*. Chapman and Hall.

3 Brooks, R. (1977) 'Towards a theory of the cognitive process in computer programming'. *Int. Journal of Man-Machine Studies, vol.9*, 737–753.

4 Brooks, R. (1983) 'Towards a theory of the comprehension of computer programs'. *Int. Journal of Man-Machine Studies, vol. 18*, 543–555.

5 Fodor, J. D. (1985) 'Deterministic parsing and subjacency'. In *Language and Cognitive Processes, vol.1*, 3–42.

6 Gilmore, D. J. (1987). *The perceptual cueing of the structure of computer programs*. PhD. Thesis. University of Sheffield.

7 Gilmore, D. J. and Green, T.R.G. (1987) 'Are "programming plans" psychologically real — outside Pascal?'. Proceedings of INTERACT '87.

8 Green, T. R. G. (1985). 'The design and use of programming languages'. In J. K. Skwirzynski (Ed) *The challenge of advanced computing technology to system design methods*. Springer: NATO ASI Series.

9 Green, T. R. G., Bellamy, R. K. E. and Gilmore, D. J. (In preparation.) 'Psychological dimensions of interaction languages'.

10 Hoc, J-M. (1981). 'Planning and direction of problem solving in structured programming: an empirical comparison between two methods'. *Int Journal of Man-Machine Studies, vol.15*, 363–383.

11 Hoc, J-M. (In press). 'Assessment of computer aids in designing programs'. To appear in T.R.G. Green, J-M. Hoc, G. C. van der Veer, and D. Murray (eds.) *Working with Computers: Theory versus Outcome*. Academic Press, London.

12 Larkin, J. H. (1981). 'Enriching formal knowledge: a model for learning to solve problems in physics'. In J. R. Anderson (ed) *Cognitive Skills and Their Acquisition.* Lawrence Erlbaum Associates, Hillsdale, N.J.

13 McKeithen, K.B., Reitman, J.S., Rueter, H.H., and Hirtle, S.C. (1981). 'Knowledge organization and skill differences in computer programmers.' *Cognitive Psychology, vol. 13* 307–325.

14 Moran, T.P. (1983). 'Getting into a system: external-internal task mapping analysis'. *Proceedings of the ACM SIGCHI conference on Human-Computer Interaction,* Boston, M.A., pp.45–49.

15 Parker, J. and Hendley, B. (1987). ' The Universe program development environment'. Proceedings of INTERACT '87.

16 Payne, S.J., Sime, M.E., and Green, T.R.G. (1984) 'Perceptual cueing in a simple command language'. *Int. Journal of Man-Machine Studies, vol. 21,* 19–29.

17 Payne, S. (In press) 'Using models of users' knowledge to analyze" learnability'. In J. B. Long and A.D. Whitefield (Eds) *Cognitive Ergonomics and Human-Computer Interaction.*

18 Ratcliff, B, and Siddiqui, J.I.A. (1985) 'An empirical investigation into problem decomposition strategies used in program design'. *Int. Journal of Man-Machine Studies, vol. 22,* 77–90.

19 Rist, R. S. (1986) 'Plans in programming: definition, demonstration and development'. In E. Soloway and S. Iyengar (Eds) *Empirical Studies of Programmers.* Ablex.

20 Sime, M. E., Green, T. R. G. and Guest, D. J.(1977) 'Scope marking in computer conditionals — a psychological evaluation'. *Int Journal of Man-Machine studies, vol.9,* 107–118.

21 Soloway, E. and Ehrlich, K. (1984) 'Empirical studies of programming knowledge'. *IEEE Transactions on Software Engineering, vol.5,* 595–609.

22 Whitefield, A.D. (1985). *Constructing and applying a model of the user for computer system development: the case for computer aided design.* PhD. Thesis. University College, London.

CHAPTER 10

Improving Children's Debugging Skills

Sharon McCoy Carver
Sally Clarke Risinger
Department of Psychology
Carnegie-Mellon University
Pittsburgh, PA 15213

ABSTRACT

Expert programmers use a wide variety of high-level problem-solving skills to deal effectively with diverse programming tasks. The hope that children might develop some of these high-level skills has inspired many parents and educators to advocate the inclusion of computer programming, usually Logo, in the school curriculum. Despite the intuitive appeal of this campaign and the vote of confidence many school districts have given in the form of computer equipment, researchers have found strikingly little evidence that children are developing any general problem-solving skills from their programming experiences. Our thesis is that children *can* indeed develop such skills if educators specify the skill components and teach them explicitly. Carver and Klahr (1) specified the components of debugging skill in the form of a computer simulation model, and Carver (2) designed a debugging curriculum to teach the specific components directly. We gave this explicit debugging instruction to 18 sixth graders in the context of a 25 hour Logo list-processing course over a four month period while 17 of their classmates were in study hall. After instruction, the Logo students' debugging speed and efficiency improved because they learned to narrow their search for bugs. We also found that the children who acquired effective debugging skills in the Logo course improved more on transfer tasks involving debugging written instructions than students who did not take the Logo course. We suggest that using a detailed model of a problem-solving skill as the basis for explicit instruction could be an effective methodology for fostering other high-level programming skills such as problem decomposition, procedurality, or planning.

INTRODUCTION

The growing body of literature on expert programming continually emphasizes the vast number of complex skills it involves and the difficulty of acquiring those skills. Yet well-intentioned educators are continually surprised to find that students do not develop these high-level problem-solving skills spontaneously when they are given exposure to programming environments such as Logo. We suggest that students do not acquire high-level skills in programming contexts because those skills are never taught directly and, further, that those skills are never taught because educators do not have a full understanding of what they entail.

Over the past several years, we have been studying ways to improve debugging skills in programming contexts to such an extent that children can apply them generally, even in non-programming domains. Carver and Klahr (1) developed a computer simulation model of debugging skill as the basis for a debugging curriculum that Carver (2) included in a Logo graphics and list-processing course. Students in Carver's course both *acquired* effective debugging skills and successfully *transferred* them to debugging situations in domains other than programming. The goal of the research presented here was to replicate and further explore the effects of this model-based curriculum on children's debugging skills with particular emphasis on tracing individual learning paths.

First we present a brief introduction to list-processing commands in the context of an example program. We then provide a general description of the Carver and Klahr debugging model with example simulations to contrast good and poor debugging strategies. We conclude that section by describing our applications of the model to detailed evaluation of students' debugging skills and to curriculum design. Next, we describe a study designed to monitor the effect of the explicit debugging curriculum in the context of a Logo list-processing course taught to 35 sixth graders. Then, we discuss our assessments of individual children's acquisition and transfer of effective debugging skills. Finally, we conclude with a discussion of the importance of task analysis and curriculum design for fostering generalizable high-level skills.

BASIC LOGO LIST-PROCESSING

Logo, though best known for its turtle graphics features, retains many of the powerful list-processing capabilities of its parent language, LISP. To make our examples comprehensible, we introduce here some basic principles and commands of *Apple Logo* list-processing. In general, commands and numerical inputs require no punctuation, inputs that are single words require a double quote before them, inputs that are lists require brackets around them, and variable names must be preceded by a colon. The PRINT command expects one argument, which it prints on the screen followed by a carriage return. If more than one argument is given, the entire PRINT statement must be enclosed in parentheses. The MAKE command expects two arguments: a word, which will become a global variable name, followed by the value to be assigned to the variable. If the value is READWORD or READLIST, Logo will wait for either a word or a list to be entered from the keyboard and use that as the value of the global variable. Finally, the IF command begins a conditional statement with three arguments: the condition to be tested, a list of commands to follow if the condition is true, and a list of commands to follow if the condition is false. The most frequent conditional tests are for equality (EQUALP, with two arguments) and membership (MEMBERP, with two arguments, the second of which must be a list).

In Table 1, we show a simple example. The procedure LIVING prints the question "DO YOU LIKE LIVING IN PENNSYLVANIA?" and sets the global variable called LIVING to a word entered by the user. If the value of the variable equals YES, then the procedure WHERE is called to ask where the user lives; otherwise, the procedure WORKING is called to ask whether the user likes working in Pennsylvania, and so forth.

Table 1: A simple Logo list-processing program.

```
TO LIVING
  PRINT [DO YOU LIKE LIVING IN PENNSYLVANIA?]
  MAKE "LIVING READWORD
  IF EQUALP :LIVING "YES [WHERE] [WORKING]
END
TO WHERE
  PRINT [WHERE DO YOU LIVE?]
  MAKE "WHERE READLIST
  (PRINT :WHERE [IS A NICE PLACE TO LIVE.])
END
TO WORKING
  PRINT [TOO BAD, DO YOU LIKE WORKING HERE?]
  MAKE "WORKING READWORD
  IF EQUALP :WORKING "YES [JOB] [PRINT [I DON'T EITHER.]]
END
TO JOB
  PRINT [WHAT IS YOUR JOB?]
  MAKE "JOB READLIST
  (PRINT :JOB [IS AN INTERESTING JOB.])
END
```

A COGNITIVE MODEL OF DEBUGGING SKILLS

The debugging instruction, learning assessments, and transfer assessments discussed in this paper were based on a detailed task analysis of Logo debugging skills (1). The analysis was intended to capture, in the form of a concrete model, the decision processes, knowledge, and sub-skills necessary for efficient debugging of Logo graphics and list-processing programs with one or more semantic and/or syntactic bugs.

Carver and Klahr (1) distinguish between the *discrepancy* and the *bug*.

The former refers to the difference between the program plan and the program output. The latter refers to the erroneous component of the program that caused the discrepancy. The goal of the debugging process is to detect and correct the discrepancy-causing bug given knowledge about the program plan (the desired outcome), the buggy program, the output that the buggy program produces, and the Logo language. Table 2 shows a buggy version of the JOB procedure from the example program described above. The goal was to print the statement "TV REPAIR IS AN INTERESTING JOB.," but the actual outcome was "JOB IS AN INTERESTING JOB." The discrepancy between the goal and the program output is that the variable name was printed instead of its value. The bug that caused the discrepancy is the quote before **JOB** in the last line of the JOB procedure. The quote designates **JOB** as a word rather than a variable name (which requires a colon).

Table 2: A buggy version of the program in Table 1.

```
Buggy Code

   TO JOB
     PRINT [WHAT IS YOUR JOB?]
     MAKE "JOB READLIST
     (PRINT "JOB [IS AN INTERESTING JOB.])
   END

Buggy Output

   ?living
   DO YOU LIKE LIVING IN PENNSYLVANIA?
   no
   TOO BAD, DO YOU LIKE WORKING HERE?
   yes
   WHAT IS YOUR JOB?
   tv  repair
   JOB IS AN INTERESTING JOB.
   ?
```

Carver and Klahr (1) specified their task analysis of debugging skill and demonstrated its sufficiency for debugging Logo programs by implementing it as a computer simulation model in GRAPES, a goal-restricted production system (3). The GRAPES model consists of a set of 84 rules, called productions, that specify the actions to be taken if certain conditions exist. The productions test for conditions, including the goal the model is trying to achieve and the information currently available in working memory (the set of known facts). A production is selected and executed only when the appropriate conditions exist. Thus, the current state of the environment (current goals and knowledge) determines which actions will be performed. Possible actions include updating or adding to both working memory and goal memory.

In the following sections, we will describe three essential components of the model: goals, which represent steps in the debugging process, heuristics, which represent general and specific search strategies used for efficient debugging, and operators, which represent sub-skills that are essential, but not central, to the debugging process (e.g., editing skills). The descriptions will be followed by demonstrations of how these components work together to debug faulty Logo list-processing programs.

Goals Direct the Solution

The debugging model's goal structure is shown in Figure 1. The system has a set of productions for each goal to represent the different responses a debugger might make to the same goal in different situations. The "situations" are represented by the current contents of the system's working memory.

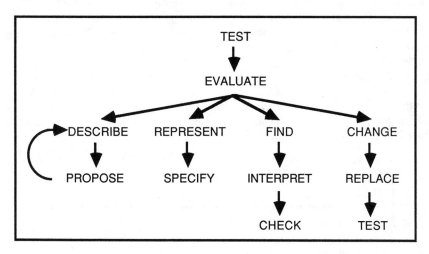

Figure 1: Goal structure of the debugging model.

Productions that check for *test* goals run the program or a subprocedure. Those that test for *evaluate* goals compare the program plan with the program output. If the plan and output do not match perfectly, then four subgoals are established to identify the likely bug, represent the program, locate the bug, and correct the bug. The *describe* and *propose* goals satisfy productions that describe the discrepancy between the program plan and the program's buggy output and those that propose possible bugs and ways to discriminate among them. Productions requiring *represent* and *specify* goals look for information about the program structure and the bug's likely location within that structure. Then, productions that test for a *find* goal begin to search for the bug in the code. The efficiency of this search process depends on the outcome of the bug identification and program-representation processes. At best, the model searches for a perfectly specified bug (both the buggy command and its arguments are specified) in a highly constrained set of possible bug locations. At worst, the model must perform a step-by-step examination of the program (*interpret* each command and *check* its effect) because it has no knowledge of the bug's identity and no clues about its location. Then, the *change* and *replace* goals fire productions that identify the appropriate correction and change the program listing accordingly. Finally, the *test* goal is reset to rerun the program. This re-evalutation is slightly different from the initial test in that the model knows a change has just been made. It first determines whether the correction fixed the original problem. If the correction worked, the model will determine whether there are any more bugs to fix; otherwise, it will debug the correction before proceeding.

Heuristics Narrow the Search

The system has two sets of debugging heuristics to narrow the search for the bug: one set for identifying the bug type (found in *describe* and *propose* productions) and one set for identifying the location of the bug in the program (found in *represent* and *specify* productions). Heuristics for identifying the bug correspond to the mappings between observed discrepancies and potential bugs. Examples are listed in Table 3. The heuristics may suggest that several types of bugs could have caused a particular type of discrepancy. They may either seek further information to distinguish among alternatives or may simply suggest scanning for either possibility. In the example case described above, the model would suggest looking for a variable name that has a quote instead of a colon or a variable name that has been enclosed in brackets (see line one of Table 3).

Table 3: Sample discrepancy-bug mappings for Logo list-processing.

DISCREPANCY	BUGGY COMPONENT
Print variable	Punctuation
(it printed 'score' instead of the number)	Quoted variable or variable in brackets
Not matching	Nesting
(I put the right answer and it marked it wrong)	READLIST/WORD or EQUALP vs. MEMBERP
Wrong value	Variable name
(it printed the number instead of the place)	Wrong variable name

Heuristics for locating the bug involve knowledge of program structure types. For example, if the program is identified as having subprocedure structure, the model will ask for information about which subprocedure is likely to contain the error and will confine its search to that subprocedure (unless no bug can be located there). If no subprocedure clue is available, the model will seek other structural clues, such as location within an IF statement or location after a particular command. For example, if the user can identify a correct command that was executed before the bug occurred, the model will use that command as a marker and begin its search after that command.

Operators Process Information and Produce Behavior

According to our task analysis, the debugging process uses two types of operators or sub-skills, to process available information and take specific actions. Some of these operators correspond to inspection of the buggy output and/or the plan (MATCHing the program plan and the output to determine whether a discrepancy exists, CONTRASTing the two outcomes to describe the discrepancy, EXAMINing the buggy portion of the output, INTERPRETing the effect of particular Logo commands, and GENERATing the Logo commands to create a particular effect). Others correspond to maneuvering in the Logo environment (RUNning the program, ENTERing the editor, SKIPping to a particular location, READing a command, DELETing a command, and INSERTing a command). The former set of operators are not executed automatically by the model; rather, when they should be executed, the model prints a prompt to the screen requesting information that the operators should produce. The researcher can simulate debuggers with different levels of skill by varying the amount and accuracy of information entered in response to these prompts.

Modeling Different Levels of Skill

This section contrasts two debugging simulations for the example program shown in Table 2. First, we simulate a situation in which the debugger is knowledgeable, so we provide information about both the discrepancy and the program structure in response to the model's prompts (Table 4). The information we entered follows the --> symbol on the right-hand side of the table. First, we identify a list-processing problem without an error message and then classify the discrepancy type as *printvariable* since the variable named JOB was printed instead of its value TV REPAIR. The model responds that the bug causing that discrepancy is likely to be incorrect punctuation, and it asks for the name of the variable. Next the model requests information about the likely location of the bug. We respond that the program LIVING has subprocedures and that the bug is likely to be in the subprocedure JOB. Since the model then has knowledge about both the likely identity and the likely location of the bug, it locates the bug immediately without having to prompt us to *interpret* or *check* the outcomes of any commands. The model then asks for the necessary fix, makes the specified change, and suggests retesting the subprocedure JOB and then the main procedure LIVING. Since the fix was correct and no other bugs exist, the debugging episode is complete.

Table 4: Trace of the model simulating an efficient debugger.

```
Run the program LIVING.                                      -->ok
Did the outcome match the plan [yes or no]?                  -->no

What type of discrepancy is there [graphics or lists]?       -->lists
Did you get an error message [yes or no]?                    -->no
What is the discrepancy between the plan and outcome?
 [printvariable, wrongvalue, notmatching, extent,
  extrapart, wrongpart, missingpart, or ?]                   -->printvariable

The variable has probably been quoted or put in brackets.
Use a colon when printing variables.
What is the name of the variable?                            -->JOB
Look for PRINT "JOB or PRINT [ ... :JOB ...].

Does the LIVING program have subprograms [yes or no]?        -->yes
Is the bug in a subprogram [yes or no]?                      -->yes
Which subpart is wrong?                                      -->JOB

The bug is "JOB in JOB.

How should the fix be made?
 [change, delete, or insert]                                 -->change
What should "JOB have been?                                  -->:JOB

Run the program JOB.                                         -->ok
Did the correction fix the problem?                          -->yes
Run the program LIVING.                                      -->ok
Did the outcome match the plan [yes or no]?                  -->yes
```

Figure 2 shows the goal tree generated during this high-information simulation. Each number represents one sub-goal; the information content of the trace is included next to the corresponding sub-goal number. In contrast, Figure 3 shows the goal tree generated during a low-information simulation in which we responded to the model's prompts with question marks, providing no clues about either the bug's identity or location. In this case, the model begins in the main procedure and prompts us to *interpret* and *check* the effect of each command, in order of execution. Each time a subprocedure call is encountered, the model prompts for information about the likely location of the bug. None is entered, so the model continues its serial search until we identify "JOB as the bug.

The contrasts between the model's behavior in the high- and low-information situations are striking: the former required only 16 sub-goals, while the latter required 68. The high-information simulation represents the ideal case in which the bug is completely specified and its location is known, so the model's goals and heuristics can be used efficiently to narrow the search for the bug. In the low-information situation, little use is made of the *describe, propose, represent,* and *specify* goals so none of the heuristics for narrowing the debugger's search are used and debugging proceeds by brute force, one command at a time. Most of the extra subgoals are the result of this serial search. For the purpose of the low-information simulation, we assumed that the INTERPRET operator correctly identified the bug. If this had not been the case (i.e., if we had identified some other command as the bug), the difference between the two traces would have been even more striking because repeated debugging cycles would have been necessary, both to undo the erroneous fix and to make the correct one.

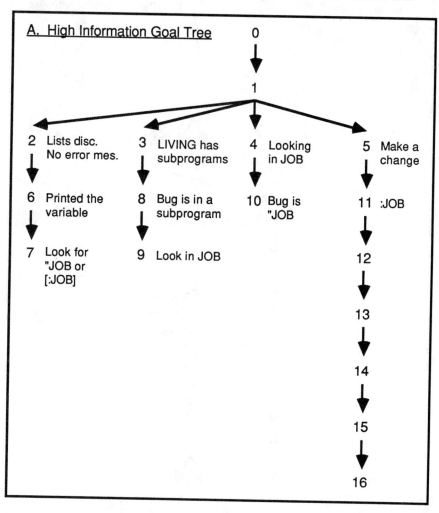

Figure 2: Simulated goal tree for an efficient debugger.

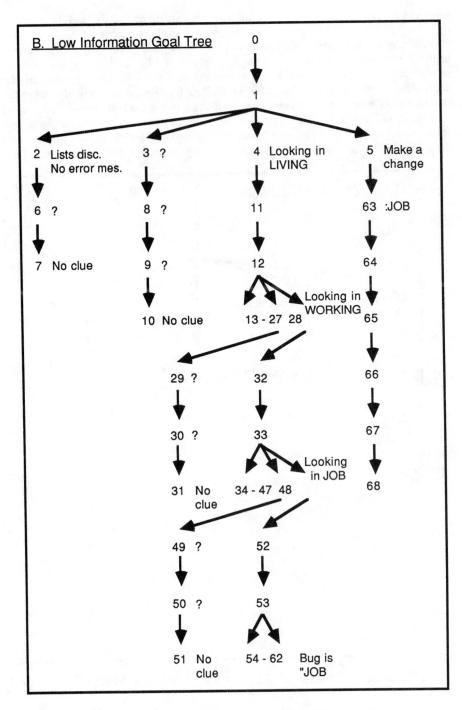

Figure 3: Simulated goal tree for an inefficient debugger.

Applications of the Model

We used our skill level simulations as standards for measuring the debugging skills students acquired, by discovery, from Logo experience. We have evidence from two pilot studies that good debugging skills are not learned spontaneously. Carver and Klahr (1) established that nine 2nd and 3rd grade students given 24 hours of structured Logo graphics experience did not learn the central components of the model. In collaboration with Seymour Papert's research group at MIT, Carver also studied whether 5th grade students given extensive unstructured Logo experience (roughly 200 hours) acquire effective debugging skills. Subjects in both studies were unable to gather effective clues about the identity and location of the bug; therefore, they relied heavily on serial search. Furthermore, their serial search was ineffective because their weak INTERPRET operator caused frequent errors. Similar difficulties with debugging have also been demonstrated among Logo teachers (4) and adult novice programmers (5, 6, 7, 8, and 9).

In addition to using the model to characterize student difficulties, Carver (2) used the debugging model as the basis for designing curriculum to teach components of debugging skill explicitly. The "cognitive objective," in Greeno's terms (10), of the debugging curriculum was for students to acquire the same goal structure as the model, especially the initial phases where clues to the bug's identity and the program structure are gathered to narrow the search for the bug. With only slight rewording of the goal structure shown in Figure 1, Carver produced a step-by-step debugging procedure to teach the students. To highlight the similarity between the model and the instruction, Figure 4 shows the debugging procedure students are taught in terms of the flow diagram of the GRAPES model. Carver's curriculum also includes specific heuristics the model uses to map discrepancies onto likely bugs and to focus search on particular parts of the program. Since all of the possible discrepancy-bug mappings can not be taught, students are directed to keep records of the problems (what went wrong) and causes (likely bugs) they encountered.

The curriculum is designed for students with 6 - 8 hours of programming experience. By this time, students have experienced the difficulty of debugging, so they are well able to understand the usefulness of the skills being taught. After the step-by-step debugging procedure is introduced, the students use the debugging steps to correct the bugs in purposely buggy programs (written by the experimenters) as well as in their own and other students' programs. Only one half-hour lesson is devoted explicitly to debugging; throughout the rest of the course, however, students are frequently prodded to use the debugging procedures and challenged to find new clues.

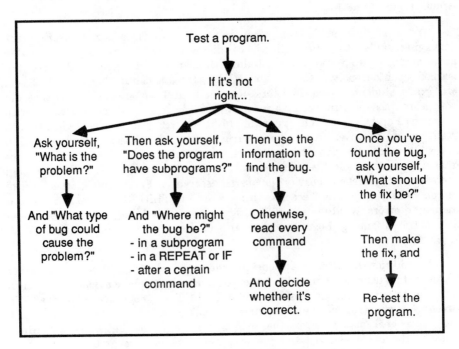

Figure 4: Step-by-step debugging procedure.

METHOD

Our thesis is that after explicit debugging instruction students will develop effective debugging strategies in the Logo context and transfer them to non-programming contexts. Carver (2) provided evidence that 3rd - 6th grade students who were taught debugging skills in the context of a 25 hour Logo graphics course were better at debugging in a subsequent list-processing course than classmates who took list-processing first, and vice versa. The students also demonstrated better debugging strategies, took less time, and were more accurate on transfer tests of debugging in non-programming contexts after debugging instruction than before.

The improvements students demonstrated in both graphics and list-processing are evidence that learning did take place. However, it is not possible to trace the within-course improvement because Carver used a between-subjects design and did not counterbalance tests within each course. Also, because the students in Carver's study worked on the debugging tests in pairs, it was not possible to trace each individual's acquisition and subsequent transfer of debugging skills. Finally, Carver did not include a control group that did not receive Logo experience between transfer test sets, so the improvement on the transfer tests could be a practice effect.

For the current study, we implemented a list-processing course in a private girls' school; all 35 of the school's sixth graders participated in our study. This study includes a within-subjects design with individually administered tests. We also used isomorphic tests that could be counterbalanced with test time so that individual improvements could be monitored more precisely. In addition, half of the students in our sample took the Logo course during the first semester while the rest, the control group, were in study hall. Those in study hall took list-processing during the second semester. This section includes descriptions of our basic design and our assessment techniques.

Design

The design of our study is depicted in Figure 5. We randomly assigned half of the students to the computer condition (Group A) and half to the control condition (Group B). The girls in the computer condition attended a Logo list-processing class for the first semester (about 30 classes). The girls in the control condition took the computer classes during the second term. In this paper, we discuss the results of the first half of this design (data from the second half are still being analyzed).

Learning design. In order to specify precisely which skills students acquired and had available for transfer to the non-programming tasks, debugging skill development was evaluated two times during the list-processing course, once shortly after the debugging instruction and once near the end of the course. At each test time, each student was given one class period to write a program according to one of two isomorphic program descriptions (A or B in Figure 5). During a subsequent class period, the student was asked to fix a program written (according to the same description) and bugged (with one of two isomorphic sets of bugs) by the experimenters. The student was given the buggy programs online and asked to fix all the bugs. The student was allowed to work until the program ran correctly or one class period had elapsed, whichever came first. At the second test time, each student used the other program description and was asked to fix a program with the other set of bugs.

The programs used for the debugging test were well-structured, i.e., they used subprocedures and other Logo substructures, such as conditional statements, appropriately. (The example program shown in Tables 1 and 2 is part of one test.) In addition, two sets of eight bugs were created and counterbalanced with the two test times and the two isomorphic programs. Each set included 3 syntactic bugs, which stop the program, and 5 semantic bugs, which cause faulty output. The sets of bugs were isomorphic in the sense that they caused similar discrepancies at the same point in the program output. We used bugs that commonly occur in novice Logo programs, but we did not base our selection on an underlying theory of bug generation (cf., 7 and 11). The bug sets were constructed so that the discrepancy caused by one bug would not obscure the discrepancy caused by another bug. The only other criterion for bug selection was that there be a variety of discrepancy types in each program (non-matching, wrong variable, printed variable, etc., as in Table 3).

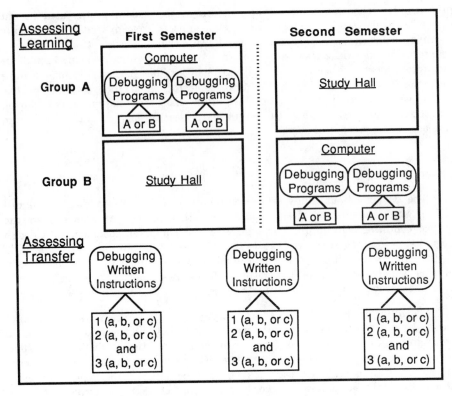

Figure 5: Design of the study.

Transfer design. The goal of the transfer assessments is to discover which of the knowledge and skills available for transfer are actually applied in new instances. Debugging skills in a non-computer context were assessed at the beginning of the year, in the middle of the year (after half of the girls had been given explicit debugging instruction in the Logo context), and at the end of the year. At each test time, students took three types of tests (1, 2, and 3 in Figure 5), all of which involved debugging a written set of instructions about how to achieve a well-specified goal (arranging something, distributing something, or traveling somewhere). Three versions of each type of transfer test were used so that they could be counterbalanced with test time (a, b, or c in Figure 5).

Our debugging model provided specific guidelines for the transfer task design and the predicted transfer effects. The transfer tasks were designed to contain the same types of information as are available in the Logo debugging situation:

1. The transfer task cover stories specified that the instructions had been executed perfectly but that the desired outcome had not been achieved because one of the directions was incorrect. This situation mimics program debugging, where the execution of commands is perfect but the commands are wrong.

2. Information about the desired and actual output was provided before the buggy instructions could be viewed, just as discrepancy information is available from test runs in debugging situations. From this tabular or pictorial information, subjects could gather clues about the identity of the bug and its probable location just as they could in the program debugging situation.

3. The lists of instructions were structured in ways similar to Logo, primarily like subprocedures. This structuring was accomplished by the addition of headings between sections of instructions to label their purpose. Subjects could use the headings to determine which sections of the instructions were likely to contain the bug, just as they could use the subprocedure names to guide their search for program bugs.

The following example will illustrate the differences we expect in students' performance before and after they have acquired effective debugging skills. The differences parallel the contrast we made earlier between the model's brute-force (low information) and selective (high information) search strategies. Figure 6 shows the plan and outcome for the buggy furniture arranging directions listed in Table 5. Before viewing the discrepancy information, students read the following cover story.

Mrs. Fisher was moving into a new house with the help of two movers. She asked them to arrange the furniture in her house and gave them a list of directions to follow. The movers followed the instructions perfectly, but there was one problem with the directions so the furniture was not arranged correctly.

The next page shows the way Mrs. Fisher wanted the furniture to look and the way it looked after the movers arranged it. Use these pictures to help you find the problem with Mrs. Fisher's directions. Then fix the directions so the movers could arrange the furniture correctly.

Students who have acquired a focused search strategy should compare the two floor plans to gather clues about the bug's identity and location. Here, possible clues include a misplaced *table* between *two chairs* in the *living room*. Students who have gathered such clues might scan the instructions for one describing the placement of a table, might scan for a phrase about a table between chairs, might ignore the dining room directions and focus only on the living room ones, or some combination of the above. In contrast, students who have not gathered such clues must rely on the tedious brute-force strategy. They would read each line and check the picture to make sure it was correct until the buggy instruction was located. Students using either strategy could successfully locate and correct the bug; what differs is the efficiency of the search process.

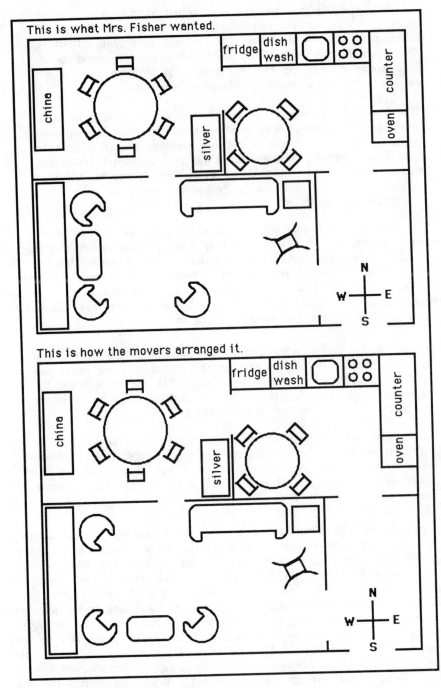

Figure 6: Discrepancy information from a sample transfer test.

Table 5: Buggy directions from a sample transfer test.

Here are the directions Mrs. Fisher gave to the movers.

To arrange the dining room,
  Center the china cabinet on the west wall.
  Place the silver cabinet in the south-east corner.
  Put the table in the center of the room.
  Arrange the 6 chairs around the table evenly.
To arrange the living room,
  Place the cabinets against the west wall.
  Place one chair in front of each end of the cabinets.
  Place the square table in the north-east corner.
  Put the sofa on the north wall, next to the square table.
  Place another chair on the south wall, across from the sofa.
  Put the coffee table between the two chairs.
  Put the rocker on the east wall, next to the square table.
To arrange the kitchen,
  Put the refrigerator in the north-west corner.
  Put the dishwasher to the right of the refrigerator.
  Put the sink to the right of the dishwasher.
  Put the stove to the right of the sink.
  Place the counter next to the stove and along the east wall.
  Put the oven along the east wall, next to the counter.
  Place the table in the south-west corner of the room.
  Arrange the 4 chairs around the table evenly.

Change or add one thing to fix Mrs. Fisher's directions.

Data collection

The primary goal of assessing skill acquisition and transfer is to understand the cognitive processes involved. Several methods were used to ensure collection of data that would facilitate this understanding. The students' behavior was videotaped to get a detailed record of the intermediate steps in their solution processes. They worked on all tests individually and were asked to "read and think aloud" while they worked so that the goals, strategies, and knowledge influencing their solutions could also be recorded (12).

RESULTS

In this section, we provide evidence that after just one explicit lesson in debugging our students began to acquire effective debugging skills in the Logo list-processing context. They also demonstrated better debugging strategies on transfer tests given after their Logo course than they did prior to the course and than control subjects did at either test time. Finally, we discuss individual patterns of learning and transfer to show that the students who learn skills better in the Logo course are also better able to transfer those skills.

Learning Debugging Skills in a Logo Context

The goal of the debugging analysis was to document which debugging skills students were able to acquire from our direct instruction and apply to novel debugging situations, i.e., our tests. Evidence of effective debugging skills was derived from students' verbalizations during debugging and from their actual debugging behavior (the time they took, the code they searched, the changes they made, etc.). To gather this evidence, we transcribed the videotaped debugging tests directly in terms of the model's goal structure. Each statement or action was categorized by goal type. Then protocols were divided into cycles based on the *test* goal; a new cycle began each time the subject tested a procedure.

Based on our debugging model, we expected that students who develop focused search strategies should become quicker and more efficient debuggers. Developing debugging skill should result in decreased debugging time because our example simulations demonstrate that greater knowledge input results in narrower search for the bug (fewer goals). Also, developing accuracy in debugging should result in fewer debugging cycles needed to locate and correct bugs (i.e., greater efficiency), because giving the model accurate information allows it to locate and correct the bug all in one cycle (from the initial goal to test the program to the final retest goal). In addition to these performance measures, we expected that students using focused search would mention more clues about bug location and bug identity before they began their search than would other students. Also, they should also search only parts of code related to the bug and edit only commands similar to the bug. The following sections describe the results relevant to these predictions. Since there were no differences between program type or bug set, all results are collapsed across these variables.

Speed and efficiency. We expected that the time required to correct each bug would decrease if students' strategies shifted from brute-force to focused search. In fact, the average time students spent for each bug they fixed decreased from 9 minutes 36 seconds per bug on the first debugging test to 4 minutes 43 seconds on the second, $F(1,33) = 13.00$, $p < .001$. As debugging skill improves, students should also take fewer cycles to fix each bug. Students' debugging efficiency did improve by more than 1 cycle per bug from the first to the second debugging test, from a mean of 3.02 to a mean of 1.60 cycles per bug, $F(1,33) = 8.81$, $p < .01$. By the end of the course, students' efficiency scores were near the perfect score of 1 cycle per bug.

Clue gathering. The goal structure of efficient debugging stresses the value of seeking clues to narrow the search for bugs. As students' understanding of that goal structure and their knowledge of discrepancy-bug mappings and location clues increases, they should make more comments about the bug's likely identity and/or location *before* suggesting a command as the bug. Students made few comments overall, but we did find that students mentioned more location clues on the second test than on the first. The proportion of cycles on which students commented about the structure of the program before beginning to search increased from only 19% on the first test to 34% on the second test, F (1,32) = 7.79, p < .01. Though the verbal protocols provided little evidence for effective debugging, students' actual search behavior dramatically demonstrates their increasingly narrow search.

<u>Search behavior.</u> Increasingly focused search should cause a decrease in erroneous search, i.e., the number of correct subprocedures the students erroneously edit and the number of correct commands they identify as the bug (false alarms). The number of subprocedures students examined per bug fixed decreased from 4.42 on the first test to 2.26 on the second test, F (1,32) = 10.68, p < .01. Part of this decrease can be attributed to a decrease in the number of correct subprocedures students erroneously edited (1.13 per bug fixed on the first test and .46 per bug fixed on the second, F (1,32) = 5.09, p < .05). Increased attention to the structure of the program may also contribute to the decrease since students may need to look into correct subprocedures less often to find information about flow of control. In addition the number of correct commands that were mis-identified as the bug and then actually changed decreased significantly from a mean of 7.29 on the first test to a mean of 2.41 on the second, F (1,32) = 16.14, p < .001.

<u>Conclusions.</u> In summary, after one debugging lesson, students began to develop effective debugging strategies. They took less time and fewer cycles to fix each bug on the second debugging test than on the first. Their search is restricted to a smaller portion of the program and to a more specific type of bug. Also, they were more likely to mention accurate clues about the bug's location on the second test. These results demonstrate that students, given explicit debugging instruction, had begun to use focused search in the Logo context.

Transferring Debugging Skills to a New Domain

The research described thus far demonstrates that students can learn high-level debugging skills when the component skills are appropriately specified and taught explicitly. We must now determine whether these skills are general enough to transfer beyond the programming domain. In this study, we compared students' performance on *non-computer* debugging tasks before and after their debugging instruction in the Logo context. As with the learning assessments, verbal and behavioral protocols, transcribed from videotapes of the test sessions, were our primary source of data. Our goal was to determine whether students who learn the importance of seeking clues to narrow their search in the Logo context can transfer this practice to the new task.

Our model's concrete goal structure and knowledge is the basis for our specific predictions for transfer effects, including both the choice of tasks where debugging skills would be useful (as described above) and the particular improvements we expect (or do not expect). Again, since search strategies are central to our model, we expected the difference between subjects who have acquired effective debugging skills and those who have not to be in the search process, rather than in the outcome of that process. Therefore, the primary measure in our transfer analysis is a qualitative assessment of the subjects' search strategies.

From the transcripts, we first classified each student's strategy for *reading* each set of buggy instructions. Three qualitatively different strategies were possible:

1. Focused search (F). The student selectively focuses only on the appropriate subsection of the instructions and/or on the part near the bug or referring to the bug.

2. Self-terminating brute-force search (S). The student reads and simulates every instruction until the bug is located and then disregards the rest.

3. Brute-force search (B). The student reads and simulates every instruction.

We also classified each subject's strategy for *simulating* the buggy directions, i.e., actually interpreting the effect of a direction by referring back to the discrepancy information. For simulating, the subject may use any of the three strategies listed above or may simulate no instructions at all (N for no strategy). We expected that more subjects would use focused search strategies for reading and simulating directions after having acquired debugging skills in the Logo context than before. Subjects in the control (study hall) condition were, therefore, not expected to improve.

We also predicted that the accuracy of fixes would improve as a result of more focused search. Students should process fewer lines so the number of false alarms should decrease, causing their overall accuracy to increase. Once again, the control group was not expected to improve. On the other hand, we did not predict differential improvement on measures of skills that we did not model, teach, or test. These non-debugging skills include reading skills (such as comprehension or speed), math skills (useful for correcting buggy distribution directions), or map skills (useful for correcting buggy travel directions).

Search behavior. As we predicted, differential improvement did occur between the computer and control groups in terms of their actual search process. Both experimenters categorized each subject's strategies on each test, with an inter-rater reliability of 86%. Figures 7a and b show the percentage of strategy usage for the two groups on the pre- and mid-tests. Each subject debugged three sets of buggy directions at each test time so the total number of strategy scores equals three times the number of subjects.

The upper left cell in Figure 7a shows that the brute-force reading/no simulating strategy (column B, row N) was used 44% of the time. This cell represents the worst strategy combination (read exhaustively and never seek discrepancy information), whereas the bottom right cell (focused reading/focused simulating) represents the best strategy combination. Therefore, the expected shift for the computer group was from the top left cells to the bottom right cells. Analysis of the column and row marginals in Figure 7a reveals that students in the computer group shifted toward more focused strategies for both reading and simulating (χ^2 (2) = 9.83, p<.01 for reading and χ^2 (3) = 14.42, p<.01 for simulating). Comparable analysis for the control group data shown in Figure 7b shows no such shift.

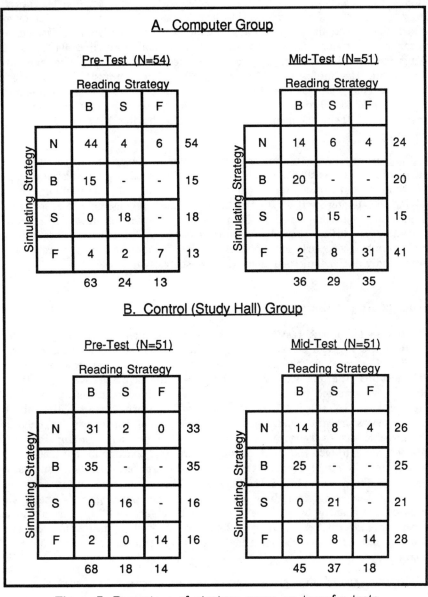

Figure 7: Percentage of strategy usage on transfer tests.

Accuracy. Since the computer group did demonstrate better search strategies, we also expected them to make fewer false alarms and, therefore, more accurate corrections. The proportion of computer students who accurately debugged the instructions increased from 33% on the pre-test to 55% on the mid-test. In contrast, the accuracy rate of the study hall group remained constant (41% and 39%).

Checking fixes. The transfer tasks provided no opportunity to re-run the directions after making a change, as we taught students to do for computer debugging; however, some students attempted to mentally re-simulate the effect of the change to test its correctness. After program debugging experience, students in the computer group more frequently checked the directions *after* making a change. On the pre-test, students in the computer group read a total of 109 lines and simulated 94 lines after making fixes. The number of lines they checked by reading and simulating increased on the mid-test to 157 and 160. The number of lines checked after a fix changed little for the control group (136 to 143 for reading and 119 to 133 for simulating). The computer students were able to transfer the re-test part of their debugging strategy despite having to tailor it to a new situation.

Conclusions. To summarize, after explicit debugging instruction, based on a detailed task analysis, students acquired focused search strategies in the Logo context and transferred them successfully to non-programming contexts involving debugging written instructions. Their increasingly focused search and modified re-testing resulted in a greater accuracy of fixes. Students in the control condition showed no improvement. The following sections will provide further support for this claim by demonstrating the relationship between individual acquisition and transfer scores.

Tracing Individual Learning and Transfer Patterns.

Because all of the testing in this study was done individually, we could go beyond the aggregate results to test whether the subjects whose debugging skills improve most in the Logo context are also the ones whose strategies shift most on the transfer test. In order to facilitate such correlational analysis, we converted our strategy classifications for the transfer tests into a numerical score, N=0, B=1, S=2, and F=3. Since each subject gets two strategy scores (reading and simulating) for each of three tests at each test time, possible scores range from 0 to 18. We are not arguing that these strategies are, in fact, equidistant on a strategy continuum but rather that this scoring will simply reflect the strategy differences. In fact, analyses of variance on these quantitative strategy data show the same pattern as the x^2 analyses of the categorical data showed. The computer group's mean score increased significantly from a mean of 7.00 to a mean of 11.06 from the pre-test to the mid-test, $F (1,32) = 9.28$, $p < .01$. The means for the study hall group did not increase significantly (7.76 on the pre-test and 9.35 on the mid-test).

For the experimental group, the correlation between students' changes in strategy scores from the pre-test to the mid-test and their changes in debugging efficiency from test 1 to test 2 during the Logo course was .52 (p < .05). All students either improved on both measures or failed to improve on both; there were no students who improved in Logo debugging but performed worse on the transfer task or vice versa. Similarly, the correlation between students' change in strategy scores relative to their decrease in debugging time per bug fixed was .58 (p < .05). For the control group, the change in strategy scores from the pre-test to the mid-test clustered around zero; in other words, with no Logo experience there was no change in Logo debugging efficiency and no change in transfer test search strategy.

We found a similar lack of transfer due to a lack of learning in one of our pilot studies. We gave one set of transfer tests to the fifteen students who had 200 hours of unstructured Logo experience and to fifteen of their school-mates who were not in the Logo project. Students in both groups rarely used focused search strategies. The percentage of focused reading and simulating strategies (column F, row F) was only 7% for the Logo group and 2% for the non-Logo group. Thus, with or without Logo experience, students who did not receive debugging instruction did not demonstrate effective debugging skills in programming or non-programming contexts. In contrast, we demonstrated that those who do receive debugging instruction *can learn* high-level debugging skills from Logo programming experience and *can generalize* these skills to non-programming contexts.

DISCUSSION

The underlying assumption of our research is that teaching and learning computer programming is valuable, despite past difficulty demonstrating just that. Soloway (13) said quite explicitly that programming is a good domain for teaching high-level synthesis skills such as testing boundary conditions, simulation, and problem simplification. The pivotal point in his claim, though, is the *teaching* and not the *domain* itself. The goal of our research program has been to provide evidence that potential for yielding significant cognitive consequences for students lies in explicit instruction, rather than in Logo itself. Our specific goals were to determine whether children can learn efficient debugging skills in a computer programming context if the component skills are specified precisely and taught directly and, then, whether the skills are generally transferable once they have been learned.

We specified a model of effective debugging skill that emphasized the importance of gathering clues about a bug's identity and location for focusing one's search for bugs in program code. We then included one debugging lesson, derived directly from our debugging model, in an otherwise conventional Logo course and assessed students' learning and transfer of debugging skills. In this context, we found that students did learn to debug effectively and that they could transfer their debugging skills to non-programming contexts. Students demonstrated better debugging strategies and were more accurate on transfer tests after debugging instruction than before. Students who did not receive debugging instruction in the Logo context did not improve on the transfer tests. In addition, among the computer students, there was a positive correlation between the amount of improvement in Logo debugging and the amount of strategy shift on the transfer tests.

There is a striking contrast between these positive results and the largely negative results from previous studies of the transferability of high-level problem-solving skills from computer programming experience (14, 15, 16, and 17). The key to our students' acquisition and transfer of debugging skills was our careful task analysis of debugging skill components and our explicit debugging instruction. Preliminary reports from Clements (18) and Perkins (19) also emphasize the importance of precise instruction regarding strategies, particularly at the meta-level. We suggest `.at the use of precise cognitive models of skill components, similar to the one we described for debugging, could be used as the basis for more effectively designing instruction to foster other high-level problem-solving skills in programming as well as non-programming domains.

ACKNOWLEDGEMENTS

This research was supported by a grant jointly funded by the Program for Applications of Advanced Technology and the Program for Research in Teaching and Learning at the National Science Foundation (MDR-8554464). We thank Carolanne Fisher and the E.S.P. reviewers for helpful comments on earlier drafts of this chapter and the students, teachers, and administrators of the Ellis School in Pittsburgh, PA for their cooperation and participation in this project.

REFERENCES

1. Carver, S.M. & Klahr, D. (1986). Assessing children's Logo debugging skills with a formal model. *Journal of Educational Computing Research, 2*(4), 487-525.
2. Carver, S.M. (1986). *LOGO debugging skills: Analysis, instruction, and assessment.* PhD Dissertation, Department of Psychology, Carnegie-Mellon University.
3. Sauers, R. & Farrell, R. (1982). *GRAPES User's Manual.* Department of Psychology, Carnegie-Mellon University.
4. Jenkins, E.A., Jr. (1986). *An analysis of expert debugging of LOGO programs.* Working Paper, Department of Psychology, Carnegie-Mellon University.
5. Gould, J.D. (1975). Some psychological evidence on how people debug computer programs. *International Journal of Man-Machine Studies, 7,* 151-182.
6. Jeffries, R. (1982). A comparison of the debugging behavior of expert and novice programmers. In *Proceedings of the American Educational Research Association.* New York, NY: AERA, March 1982.

7. Katz, I.R., & Anderson, J.R. (1986). *An exploratory study of novice programmers' bugs and debugging behavior.* Poster presented at the First Workshop on Empirical Studies of Programmers. Washington, D.C., June 1986.

8. Gugerty, L. & Olson, G.M. (1986). Comprehension differences in debugging by skilled and novice programmers. In E. Soloway & S. Iyengar (Eds.), *Empirical Studies of Programmers* (pp. 13-27). Norwood, New Jersey: Ablex Publishing Corporation.

9. Kessler, C.M. & Anderson, J.R. (1986). A model of novice debugging in LISP. In E. Soloway & S. Iyengar (Eds.), *Empirical Studies of Programmers* (pp. 198-212). Norwood, New Jersey: Ablex Publishing Corporation.

10. Greeno, J.G. (1976). Cognitive objectives of instruction: Theory of knowledge for solving problems and answering questions. In D. Klahr (Ed.), *Cognition and Instruction* (pp. 123-159). Hillsdale, N.J.: Lawrence Erlbaum Associates.

11. Spohrer, J.C. & Soloway, E. (1986). Analyzing the high frequency bugs in novice programs. In E. Soloway & S. Iyengar (Eds.), *Empirical Studies of Programmers* (pp. 230-251). Norwood, New Jersey: Ablex Publishing Corporation.

12. Ericsson, K.A. & Simon, H.A. (1984). *Protocol analysis: Verbal reports as data.* Cambridge, MA: The MIT Press.

13. Soloway, E. (1987). Invited address on the topic of why children should learn to program. In *Proceedings of the Third International Conference on Artificial Intelligence and Education.* Pittsburgh, PA: AIED, May 1987.

14. Pea, R.D. (1983). Logo programming and problem solving. In *Proceedings of the American Educational Research Association Conference.* Montreal, Canada: AERA, April 1983.

15. Garlick, S. (1984). *Computer programming and cognitive outcomes: A classroom evaluation of Logo.* Honors Thesis, The Flinders University of South Australia.

16. McGilly, C.A., Poulin-Dubois, D., & Shultz, T.R. (1984). *The effect of learning LOGO on children's problem-solving skills.* Working Paper, Department of Psychology, McGill University.

17. Mohamed, M.A. (1985). *The effects of learning LOGO computer language upon the higher cognitive processes and the analytic/global cognitive styles of elementary school students.* PhD Dissertation, School of Education, University of Pittsburgh.

18. Clements, D. (1987). Componential employments and development in LOGO programming environments. In *Proceedings of the Society for Research in Child Development Conference.* Baltimore, MD: SRCD, April 1987.

19. Perkins, D. (1987). Instructional Strategies for Problems of Novice Programmers. In *Proceedings of the American Educational Research Association Conference.* Washington, D.C.: AERA, April 1987.

CHAPTER 11

An Analysis of the On-Line Debugging Process

Murthi Nanja
Curtis R. Cook
Department of Computer Science
Oregon State University
Corvallis, OR 97331

ABSTRACT

This paper reports the results of a protocol study that compared the debugging process of expert, intermediate, and novice student programmers. Subjects used a microcomputer to debug a Pascal program with three semantic and three logic errors. The following performance differences were identified:

(1) Experts employed a comprehension approach in which they first attempted to understand the program and then used this knowledge for finding the bugs. Intermediates and novices employed an isolation approach in which they immediately attempted to identify candidate bug locations by searching the output for clues, recalling similar bugs, and testing program states.

(2) Experts corrected multiple errors before verifying the corrections while intermediates and novices corrected and verified single errors. Intermediates and novices corrected the semantic errors first and then the logic errors while experts corrected both semantic and logic errors at the same time.

(3) Experts were the fastest and most successful in correcting all of the errors, modified fewer statements, and did not introduce more errors. Most of the novices did not correct all of the errors, made very extensive modifications and introduced many new errors. Most intermediates corrected all of the errors but they made considerable modifications and introduced several new errors.

INTRODUCTION

Debugging, the location and correction of the errors in a computer program, is one of the most common computer programming tasks. Yet surprisingly little is known about the debugging process other than experienced programmers debug more effectively.

Almost all debugging studies have concentrated on performance differences between expert and novice programmers. They have shown that experts make fewer errors and locate and correct bugs faster than novices [6]. Several studies have also shown considerable difference in debugging speed even among experts [1,2]. Novices frequently add additional bugs during debugging while experts rarely do [3]. Expert programmers are less dependent upon debugging aids such as line numbers in error messages and make better use of whatever debugging aids are available [1]. Debugging tools such as on-line debuggers are used infrequently [1].

Typically in these studies the subject task was to locate or locate and correct a single error seeded in the program and the performance measures were whether the error was correctly identified and fixed and the time to do so. Since only the correctness and time were recorded, these studies provided almost no information about the debugging process - what debugging strategies were used and how, when, or where they were applied.

However, three recent protocol analysis studies [3,4,5] investigated differences in the debugging process of expert and novice programmers. In a verbal protocol analysis of 16 professional programmers Vessey [5] found that "chunking ability" was a better measure of debugging expertise than years of programming experience. Vessey classified the 16 programmers, into two groups of eight novices and eight experts, on the basis of their chunking ability. Each programmer was asked to debug a COBOL program containing a single error. She found that experts took less time to find and correct the bug, stated fewer hypotheses about the bug, and made fewer mistakes. Experts attempted to gain a high-level understanding of the program and how it functions, with the goal of placing the error in context. They "allow the program structure to unfold, place the clues in the context of that structure, and conceptualize the error in terms of the program structure". Novices, on the other hand, appeared more anxious to find the error and more committed to their error hypothesis which led them into a depth-first search for the error. Without a model of the program's function and structure, novices frequently changed program reference positions and took longer to confirm or reject error corrections. Hence Vessey concluded that while both groups used essentially the same basic debugging methods, the experts were more effective in their application of specific techniques.

Jeffries [4] reported findings from an informal study of the debugging behavior of six experts and four novices. Her experts were graduate students in computer science, while the novices had just finished their first programming course. Each subject debugged two short Pascal programs, each containing a number of bugs. Subjects worked with a printed listing of the program and printed output from several test runs. Experts found more of the bugs and found them faster. Expert programmers read the program in the order in which it would be executed, main program first, then procedures called by the main program, then the procedures called by these procedures, etc. This apparently allowed them to form a hierarchical understanding of the program. They understood the program at many levels - from overall understanding of what the program does to the role of individual statements. In contrast, novices read the program sequentially from beginning to end like a piece of prose. Because of the structure of Pascal, the result was a bottom-up reading of the program. Hence they recognized only the simplest, low-level patterns, such as incrementing a counter, and they had difficulty judging which parts of the program were relevant and which were irrelevant to the bug they were searching for. As a result, they spent too much time simulating some parts of the program and not enough time on others. In tracking down a bug with several possible causes, the experts were better at switching between hypotheses as evidence accumulated while novices focused on only one hypotheses at a time. Because of the small number of subjects she tested, no statistical evaluation of her findings was reported.

Gugerty and Olson [3] conducted two experiments to investigate expert-novice differences in debugging. They asked expert and novice student programmers to find and correct a single error in a program using on-line debugging. Subjects in the first experiment debugged a LOGO program while subjects in the second experiment debugged a Pascal program. From the protocol data, they found that experts and novices employed the same debugging strategy and they hypothesized that experts were faster and more successful because of their superior program comprehension abilities. They also found that novices frequently added bugs to the program while trying to find the original one.

In this paper we present the results of a preliminary protocol study that compared the debugging process of novice, intermediate and expert student programmers. The subjects were presented listings of a defective program with six errors, input data file and desired output, and the program on a floppy diskette and were asked to correct the defective program on an Apple Macintosh computer. In addition, subjects were asked to think-out-loud during each program edit session. All subjects had previous experience with the MacPascal programming environment on a Macintosh computer.

We attempted to simulate a real environment as much as possible. The program used in the Vessey [5] and Gugerty and Olson [3] studies contained only a single error. Our program contained multiple errors. In Jeffries [4] study the subjects were given a program listing, sample runs of "experimenter selected test cases", and if specifically requested, runs from an interactive debugging system. Our subjects were free to use the on-line debugger or any other debugging aid and to run the program as often as they liked.

SUBJECTS

The subjects in this experiment were six novices, six intermediates, and six expert Pascal programmers, all volunteers. The novices were just finishing their second term of an introductory Pascal programming course at Oregon State University. The intermediates were finishing their third term of a junior level data structure sequence at Oregon State University. The expert group was composed of graduate students in computer science at Oregon State University. All experts were very experienced student programmers and, in addition, they had either taught introductory Pascal programming courses or served as a consultant for students enrolled in Pascal programming courses at Oregon State University.

MATERIALS

The program to be debugged was a 73-line Pascal program that read in 19 integer values from a file, sorted them in ascending order using a bubble sort, and searched for five key values in the sorted list using a binary search routine. All subjects were familiar with the binary search routine and the bubble sorting algorithm used in the program. The program was implemented as two procedures (ReadData and BubbleSort) and one function (BinarySearch). These three subprograms were called by the main program in that order. It was written in a structured fashion with indenting and meaningful names, contained three lines of comments describing the program, but had no in-line comments.

There were six errors -- three semantic errors and three logic errors -- in the program. Programs with semantic errors (e.g. undefined variables, array bounds, division by zero) compile correctly, but when executed terminate abnormally with an error message and no other output. Programs with logic errors have no compilation and/or semantic errors, but when executed terminate normally with incorrect results. Each procedure and function contained one semantic error and one logic error. The three types of semantic errors were (i) attempt to read past end-of-file mark in the ReadData procedure (ii) an index exceeding array bounds in the BubbleSort procedure, and (iii) incompatibility between data types in the BinarySearch function. These errors were selected because they are errors commonly made by students. For the three semantic errors, the MacPascal interpreter displayed the following three error messages along with an index pointing to the line number of the statement where the error occurred:

- An attempt has been made to access data beyond the end of a file or string.
- The value of a variable or sub-expression is out of range for its intended use.
- An incompatibility between types has been found.

The three classes of logic errors selected were:

- off-by-one error -- the number of iterations through a loop is counted incorrectly in the ReadData procedure.
- assignment statement error -- a variable is assigned an incorrect value in the BubbleSort procedure.
- predicate error -- an incorrect conditional expression in the BinarySearch function.

The listing of the defective program, with six errors, is shown in Appendix A. Each of these errors could be corrected by modifying only one statement. Correct versions of these statements are shown in the defective program listing as in-line comments.

PROCEDURES

Subjects performed the debugging task individually. They were given a printed listing of the defective table lookup program and a printed copy of input data file, both of which were also available to them on a floppy diskette. They were also given a copy of the correct output (see Appendix A). Subjects were not told how many or what type of errors the program contained and that each of these errors could be repaired by changing only one statement. Subjects were informed that they could debug the program at their own pace and use any debugging techniques or on-line aids.

During the debugging session, an experimenter recorded what program objects the subjects were examining and asked what activities they were performing. For the purpose of this study, we considered the following program objects: program segments (i.e. global comments and declarations, main program, ReadData procedure, BubbleSort procedure, and BinarySearch function), listing of input data file, printed copy of expected output, listing of program, Pascal program window, error message window, program output (text) window, and observe window. Activities performed by subjects were categorized as follows:

- examine listing of input data
- examine listing of expected output
- examine program segment (in program listing or on screen)
- examine error window
- examine program output window
- examine observe window
- hand simulate program segment (in program listing)
- enter input data
- compare expected output and actual output
- use on-line debugging tool
- run program
- modify program segment

After program modification(s) and before they ran the program subjects were asked to state their hypotheses. In addition, whenever subjects encountered a semantic error they were asked to explain the meaning of that error. The subject's debugging process was recorded as an episode outline representing his/her activities on program objects. As an example, part of the episode outline of subject N2 is given in Appendix B.

RESULTS

Most subjects began their debugging session by studying the program. Table 1 shows that even though experts spent more time in their initial reading of the program, their debugging time was considerably less. Experts spent an average of 4.83 minutes reading the program prior to testing their first hypothesis whereas intermediates and novices spent an average of 1.5 and 1.0 minutes, respectively, in their initial reading of the program. Half of the novices and intermediates immediately ran the program without doing any initial program reading.

Experts, intermediates, and novices also differed in the order in which they read the program. Experts read the program in the order in which it would be executed - main program, ReadData procedure, BubbleSort procedure, and BinarySearch function. Most novices and intermediates read the program from beginning to end like a piece of prose. This supports similar findings of Jeffries [5] that experts first attempt to gain a high level understanding of the program and how it functions while novices use a bottom-up approach to understand the program.

All the experts successfully located and corrected all six bugs, two of the intermediates failed on the logical error in the BinarySearch function, and only two novices found all the errors. All novices introduced at least one new error while five intermediates and three experts introduced errors. Table 1 shows that novices introduced an average of 4.83 new errors (NEI) during debugging, and intermediates introduced an average of 2.33 new errors, most of which were not immediately corrected. The six errors introduced by experts were immediately corrected.

The number of debugging statements (NDWS) in Table 1 is the number of write statements inserted in various program segments to keep track of certain variables at particular locations in the program. Novices and intermediates inserted many more debugging write statements than experts. They generated considerable output because they inserted write statements inside loops to print an entire array or traced the values of variables not involved in an error. Experts inserted far fewer debug write statements, usually at end of procedures, but often used on-line debugging tools to trace variables. However, none of the novices and intermediates used on-line debugging tools. They often hand simulated the execution of one or more of the procedures in the program making notes about the values of the variables at various stages of the program. No expert explicitly hand executed the program. We also see from Table 1 that novices made three times as many and intermediates twice as many program runs (TNR) as experts.

Experts made far fewer references to the source program than novices and intermediates. Table 2 shows the total and percent of different program segments that subjects referenced during debugging. Overall, novices and intermediates referred to program segments more often than experts (total = 241 for novices, total = 199 for intermediates, and total = 103 for experts).

Experts, intermediates, and novices differed in both the order and the way in which they corrected errors. Novices (except N5) and intermediates corrected only one error at a time while experts corrected groups of errors before verifying the corrections. As shown in Table 3, the first group of errors corrected by subject E1 were semantic error 2 and logical errors 1 and 2, then semantic error 3 and logical error 3 in the second group, and finally semantic error 1. Four novices who did not find all the errors failed to to find at least three errors. These four novices (except N3) found only the semantic errors. With few exceptions, intermediates corrected the three semantic errors first and then the three logical errors. Note that subjects I2 and I6 did not correct the logical error in the BinarySearch function. The groups of errors corrected at the same time by experts included both semantic and logical errors and often involved several procedures and a function. The groups of multiple errors corrected ranged from two to five. Also the experts made error corrections in one minute or less bursts.

The general single error correction strategy for novices and intermediates was to repeatedly perform the three steps: (1) Form hypothesis about a bug; (2) Modify one or more program statements to test the hypothesis: and (3) Run the program to see the effect of the changes. When the modified statements introduced additional errors, four novices and three intermediates did not immediately restore the program to the previous state. The experts error correction strategy had basically the same three steps. However, their program editing was more extensive and for multiple error correction they ran the program to verify the corrections after making all the corrections. The three experts who introduced errors immediately removed them by undoing the previous modification.

There was a considerable differences in total debugging time between the three classes of subjects. The novices, intermediates, and experts averaged 56.0, 36.55, 19.8 minutes respectively (Table 1). Novices took as long to find the semantic error as the experts took to find all the errors. Most novices spent over half their debugging time working on logical errors.

Table 1 shows that novices modified over twice as many statements as intermediates (mean = 23.16 for novices, and mean = 10.33 for intermediates) while experts only modified an average of 8.83 statements. Each error could be repaired by changing only one statement as shown in Appendix A. Experts changed a single statement to repair almost all errors. In several instances novices almost totally rewrote the function or procedure. Over half of the intermediates substantially revised some functions and procedures. This seems to imply that the novices, and intermediates to a lesser degree, are familiar with the functions such as bubble sort and binary search, but they know how to perform these functions in only one particular way. As examples, versions of the ReadData procedure and BinarySearch function constructed by novices are given in Figures 1a and 1b. All reflect extensive modifications to the original procedure or function.

DISCUSSION

The results of this study provide some insight into the differences between novice, intermediate, and expert programmers and the role of experience. Like previous debugging studies we found that experts located and corrected the errors faster and did not introduce new errors. From the protocol data we collected we can begin to see the reasons for these performance differences.

The debugging strategy used is the major difference between the experts and the novices and intermediates. There appear to be two general debugging strategies: comprehension and isolation. The experts used a comprehension strategy in which they first gained an overall understanding of the programs and how it functions and then used this knowledge to locate and correct errors. Novices and intermediates seemed to first attempt a comprehension strategy, and then shift to the isolation strategy in which they focused entirely on one error at a time.

Perhaps the strongest support of the experts' comprehension strategy was their ability to correct multiple errors at the same time. They corrected both semantic and logic errors at the same time. Often these errors were in different procedures. Our protocol data showed that the experts made these multiple error corrections in one minute or less bursts. This type of burst activity suggests that the experts in their search for the cause of a particular error were able to recognize and correct other errors they encounted. It would seem impossible to do this without a good overall comprehension of the program because it involves recognizing an error in the context of the entire program. The experts also appeared quite confident of their corrections. They did not stop and verify each correction, but instead waited until all corrections were made before running the program to verify them.

The data for both the semantic and logic errors indicates that the novices and intermediates initially attempted to use a comprehension strategy and then switched to an isolation strategy. They first tried for an overall understanding of the program, but failed because they adopted a bottom-up-approach in which they read the program statements in their physical order. From this bottom-up approach they were only able to gain low level understanding of parts of the program. This is in marked contrast to the experts who read the program in the order it would be executed and hence were able to gain an overall understanding. The novice and intermediate programmers' lack of success may explain why they spent less time on their initial study of the program than experts.

After their initial reading, the novices and intermediates quickly plunged into experimenting with the program. Since the program contained semantic errors, their experimenting resulted in a semantic error message and a pointer to the statement where the error occurred. The error message and pointer to the statement were ready-made for a shift to an isolation strategy. Since most intermediate and novices found all the semantic errors first, it suggests that they successfully applied the error message and statement pointer information in an isolation strategy to find all the semantic errors. However, the logic errors were harder to find using the isolation strategy because the only information available was the discrepancies between the actual output and the correct output. There was no specific information about the type of the error or where it occurred. This lack of specific error information seems the most probable explanation for why the four novices, who could not find all the errors, altogether could find only one logic error but only failed to find two semantic errors. This suggests that novices need explicit information, such as semantic error messages, about errors in order to repair them. They seemed unable to determine which procedure or function contained the logic errors. Many spent a long time attempting to correct the logic error in the BinarySearch function, but could not verify the correction because of the errors in the ReadData and BubbleSort procedures.

The isolation strategy adopted by the novices and intermediates seems to explain why they systematically located, corrected, and verified a single error at a time starting with the semantic errors. The protocol data showed that when novices and intermediates searched for the cause of a semantic error they generally confined their search to one procedure or function and frequently passed over a logic error in the same procedure. They seemed to be looking for the cause of one particular error and were oblivious to other errors. This is similar to Vessey's [5] finding that novices use a depth-first debugging approach concentrating on one error at a time.

Vessey [5] concluded that experts and novices use the same overall debugging strategy -- comprehension. However, all her subjects were professional programmers. Our results suggest that experts use a comprehension strategy while intermediates and novices use an isolation strategy. We believe that some of our intermediates and novices probably briefly attempted a comprehension strategy before switching to an isolation strategy. Vessey's results may have been influenced by the fact that her subjects' task was a paper and pencil exercise.

Our data showed that experts studied a program twice as long as intermediates and novices before making a modification. This is inconsistent with Gugerty and Olson's [3] finding that novices spent more time than experts. We believe that the type of errors in the programs account for much, if not all, of this difference. Our program contained both semantic and logic errors while the Gugerty and Olson program contained a single logic error. Our subjects received an error message and a pointer to the statement where the error occurred when they ran the program. Hence many of our subjects attempted to correct this error first. The only information about the logic error in the Gugerty and Olson study was the discrepancy between the actual program output and the correct output. Hence the subjects spent the time studying the program listing and program statement of purpose, and using a note pad to hand simulate execution of the program in order to find the cause of the logic error. Another difference was the MacPascal environment was familiar to our subjects while the Gugerty and Olson subjects only had a 25 minute training session to become familiar with the Turbo Pascal environment. This may also explain why their subjects did not use on-line debugging tools and ours did.

In all previous debugging studies the subjects made very little use of on-line debugging aids. In our study only the experts made use of on-line debugging aids to trace variables. However, our novices and intermediates inserted debugging write statements. Many of these were placed inside loops. From the considerable output they generated, it seemed clear that they only had a general idea about the error. The few of our experts who inserted debugging write statements seemed to have a good idea about the error as they placed the debugging write statements at the beginning and end of subprograms and hence generated only a small and useful quantity of output. This appears to demonstrate the value of debugging experience and practice.

CONCLUSIONS

This research provided some understanding of the on-line debugging process of student programmers. Program comprehension was a major difference between the three classes of student programmers. Experts gained the best understanding of the program because they read the program in the order in which it would be executed - main program, read data procedure, sort procedure, and binary search function. On the other hand many intermediates and most novices read the program from beginning to end like a piece of prose. Hence the experts were able to employ a comprehension approach to debugging while intermediates and novices employed an isolation approach. The comprehension approach seems to explain why the experts were faster and more successful in correcting all six errors and why they often corrected multiple errors. The isolation approach seems to explain why intermediates and novices were slower and corrected single errors. Lack of overall understanding of the program and no explicit error messages seems to explain why novices had so much trouble correcting the logic errors.

Each error could be corrected by changing a single statement. Experts changed a single statement to correct almost all errors and they immediately corrected the few new errors they introduced. Novices made very extensive modifications to the program and compounded their problems by introducing many new errors. Intermediates successfully corrected most of the errors, but they were more like novices in their program modifications and introduction of new errors.

This study raises many interesting questions for future investigations of debugging.

1. We classified our subjects' debugging strategies as either comprehension or isolation. There does not seem to be a taxonomy of debugging strategies.

2. Our intermediates and novices seemed to briefly attempt a comprehension approach before switching to an isolation approach. Additional studies should investigate when programmers use a particular debugging strategy and how often they switch to a different approach.

3. Our grouping of subjects into three classes, experts, intermediates, and novices was based almost entirely on computer programming courses taken. Although it was good, it was not perfect. For example subject I1 performed more like an expert and subject N5 more like an intermediate. Also subjects I2 and I6 were more like novices and E6 more like an intermediate. What is a good set of criteria for classifying subject experience other than year in school or number of computer programming courses taken? Vessey [5] used programmer chunking ability to classify subjects.

4. What is the depth and level of subject program understanding after the initial program study? at the time of the first modification? at the end of the debugging session?

5. How much of an aid to program understanding was breaking the program into small procedures and functions? Would subject performance be different if the program were monolithic?

REFERENCES

[1] Gould, J.D. (1975). Some psychological evidence on how people debug computer programs. *International Journal of Man-Machine Studies*, 7, pp. 151-182.

[2] Gould, J.D., and Drongowski, P. (1974). An exploratory study of computer program debugging. *Human Factors*, 16, pp. 258-277.

[3] Gugerty, L., and Olson, G.M. (1986). Comprehension differences in debugging by skilled and novice programmers. *Empirical Studies of Programmers*, Soloway, E., and Iyengar, S. (Eds.). Ablex, Inc., Norwood, New Jersey, pp. 13-27.

[4] Jeffries, R.A. (1982). Comparison of debugging behavior of novice and expert programmers. Paper presented at the AERA Annual Meeting.

[5] Vessey, I. (1985). Expertise in debugging computer program: A process analysis. *International Journal of Man-Machine Studies*, Vol. 23, pp. 459-494.

[6] Youngs, E. (1974). Human errors in programming. *International Journal of Man-Machine Studies*, 6, pp. 361-376.

Table 1. Debugging Performance Data

Subjects	IPRT	TFM	TNSM	TNR	NEI	NENC	TDT	NDWS
Novices								
N1	1	4	14	11	2	3	67	2
N2	0	3	30	26	10	0	66	5
N3	0	3	32	24	7	4	55	2
N4	3	5	18	17	3	3	55	3
N5	2	3	18	7	1	0	35	1
N6	0	6	27	21	6	3	58	4
Mean	1.0	4.0	23.16	17.66	4.83	2.16	56.0	2.83
Intermediates								
I1	3	4	7	9	0	0	17	1
I2	0	5	12	16	5	1	52	3
I3	2	4	8	12	1	0	38	4
I4	4	4	10	10	2	0	32	3
I5	0	3	12	15	3	0	31	3
I6	0	3	13	17	3	1	49	0
Mean	1.5	3.83	10.33	13.16	2.33	0.33	36.5	2.33
Experts								
E1	2	7	7	4	0	0	14	0
E2	8	11	6	2	0	0	12	0
E3	7	8	10	7	2	0	23	1
E4	5	8	8	5	1	0	20	1
E5	7	13	7	4	0	0	17	1
E6	0	3	15	14	3	0	33	2
Mean	4.83	8.33	8.83	6.0	1.0	0	19.83	0.83

Legend:

IPRT   ----   Initial program reading time (in minutes)

TFM   ----   Time to first modification (in minutes)

TNSM   ----   Total number of statements modified

TNR   ----   Total number of runs

NEI   ----   Number of new semantic errors introduced

NENC   ----   Number of errors not corrected

TDT   ----   Total debugging time (in minutes)

NDWS   ----   Number of debug write statements

Table 2. Frequency of Program Segment References

Subjects	global declaration and comments	main program	Read Data procedure	Bubble Sort procedure	Binary Search function	Total number of references
Novices						
Total	14	45	66	51	65	241
Percent	6%	19%	27%	21%	27%	
Intermediates						
Total	21	29	31	53	64	199
Percent	11%	15%	16%	27%	32%	
Experts						
Total	16	21	27	13	26	103
Percent	16%	20%	26%	13%	25%	

Table 3. Bug Correction Order

Subjects	Sem1	Sem2	Sem3	Log1	Log2	Log3
Novices						
N1	1	2	3	*	*	*
N2	1	2	3	6	5	4
N3	1	2	*	*	*	*
N4	1	2	*	3	*	*
N5	3	1	4	5	1	2
N6	1	2	3	*	*	*
Intermediates						
I1	1	3	4	2	5	6
I2	1	2	3	5	4	*
I3	1	2	4	6	3	5
I4	2	3	5	6	1	4
I5	1	2	3	6	5	4
I6	1	2	4	5	3	*
Experts						
E1	3	1	2	1	1	2
E2	2	1	1	1	1	1
E3	2	1	3	4	1	4
E4	1	2	3	1	2	3
E5	2	1	1	2	1	1
E6	1	2	3	4	4	5

* did not correct error

Legend:

Sem1	----	Semantic error in ReadData procedure
Sem2	----	Semantic error in BubbleSort procedure
Sem3	----	Semantic error in BinarySearch function
Log1	----	Logic error in ReadData procedure
Log2	----	Logic error in BubbleSort procedure
Log3	----	Logic error in BinarySearch function

```
procedure ReadData (var infile : text; var a : arraytype;
                    var count : integer);
var
   index : integer;
begin
   for index := 1 to size do
      a[index] := 0;
   index := 1;
   while not eof(infile) do
      begin
         while not eoln(infile) do
            begin
               read(infile, a[index]);
               write(a[index]);
               index := index + 1;
            end;
         readln(infile);
      end;
   count := index;
end;
```

Figure 1a. Subject N4's Correct Version of ReadData procedure

```
function BinarySearch (a : arraytype; key, count : integer) : integer;
var
   low, high, middle : integer;
begin
   low := 1;
   high := count + 1;
   middle := trunc((low+high) / 2);
   while (low <> high) and (a[middle] <> key) do
      begin
         if key < a[middle] then
            high := middle
         else
            low := middle + 1;
         middle := trunc((low+high) / 2);
      end;
   if key = a[middle] then
      BinarySearch := middle
   else
      BinarySearch := 0;
end;
```

Figure 1b. Subject N5's Correct Version of BinarySearch Function

```
{*********************************************************************}
{            The purpose of this program is to read in a set of       }
{            integer values, sort them in ascending order, and        }
{            then search for certain key values in the sorted list.    }
{*********************************************************************}

program TableLookup (input, output);
   const
      size = 1000;
      numkey = 5;
   type
      arraytype = array[1..size] of integer;
   var
      t : arraytype;
      i, count, key : integer;
      infile : text;


   procedure ReadData (var a : arraytype; var count : integer);
   var
      index : integer;
   begin
      index := 1;
      while not eof(infile) do
         begin
            read(infile, a[index]);      {  readln(infile, a[index]);  }
            index := index + 1;
         end;
      count := index;      {  count := index - 1;  }
   end;


   procedure BubbleSort (var a : arraytype; count : integer);
   var
      i, j, temp ; integer;
   begin
      for i := 1 to count - 1 do
         for j := 0 to count - 1 do      {  for j := 1 to count - 1 do  }
            if a[j] > a[j + 1] then
               begin
                  temp := a[j];      {  temp := a[j + 1];  }
                  a[j + 1] := a[j];
                  a[j] := temp;
               end;
   end;
```

```pascal
function BinarySearch (a : arraytype; key, count : integer) : integer;
var
   low, high, middle : integer;
begin
   low := 1;
   high := count;
   while low <> high do
      begin
         middle := (low + high) / 2;      {middle := (low + high) div 2;   }
         if key >= a[middle] then      {  if key <= a[middle] then   }
            high := middle
         else
            low := middle + 1;
      end;
   if key = a[low] then
      BinarySearch := low
   else
      BinarySearch := 0;
end;



begin
   showtext;
   reset(infile, 'debug.protocol:data);
   ReadData(t, count);
   BubbleSort(t, count);
   for i := 1 to numkey do
      begin
         write('key = ');
         readln(key);
         writeln('key = ', key, ' value = ', BinarySearch(t, key, count));
      end;
end.
```

Expected Output

key = 4567	value = 19
key = 0	value = 3
key = -5	value = 2
key = 234	value = 0
key = 77	value = 8

APPENDIX B

Partial Episode Outline of Subject N2

Time | Activity

2:40   run program
interpreter displays semantic error in ReadData procedure
examine semantic error message
experimenter collects verbal protocol to identify subject's speculation of semantic error
examine ReadData procedure
examine BubbleSort procedure
examine BinarySearch function
examine main program
examine ReadData procedure
examine main program
examine global declaration
hand-execute ReadData procedure

2:43   insert **var infile:text** as formal parameter in ReadData procedure header line
modify **ReadData(t,count)** to **ReadData(t,count,infile)** in main program
experimenter collects verbal protocol to identify subject's hypothesis
run program
interpreter displays semantic error in ReadData procedure
examine semantic error message
experimenter collects verbal protocol to identify subject's speculation of semantic error
examine main program
examine ReadData procedure
examine main program
examine ReadData procedure
examine main program
examine ReadData procedure

2:46   insert **writeln(index)** after **read(infile,a[index])** in ReadData procedure
experimenter collects verbal protocol to identify subject's hypothesis
run program
program displays values of index
interpreter displays semantic error in ReadData procedure
examine values of index
examine semantic error message
experimenter collects verbal protocol to identify subject's speculation of semantic error
examine input data listing

2:48   delete **writeln(index)** in ReadData procedure
examine ReadData procedure
hand-execute ReadData procedure
modify **read(infile,a[index])** to **readln(infile,a[index])**
experimenter collects verbal protocol to identify subject's hypothesis
run program
interpreter displays semantic error in BubbleSort procedure
examine semantic error message
experimenter collects verbal protocol to identify subject's speculation of semantic error
examine BubbleSort procedure
examine main program
examine BubbleSort procedure

2:50   modify **if a[j] > a[j+1] then** to **if a[j] > a[j-1] then**
....
....
....

CHAPTER 12

Change-Episodes in Coding:
When and How Do Programmers Change Their Code?

Wayne D. Gray
Army Research Institute
5001 Eisenhower Ave.
Alexandria, VA 22333

John R. Anderson
Psychology Department
Carnegie-Mellon University
Pittsburgh, PA 15213

ABSTRACT

Any change in a programmer's code or intentions while coding constitutes a change-episode. Change-episodes include error detection and correction (including false positives) as well as stylistic, strategic, and tactical changes. In this study we examine change-episodes to determine what they can add to the study of the cognition of programming. We argue that change-episodes occur most often for constructs that allow the most variability (with variability defined by the language, the task, and the programmer's history). We predict and find that those constructs that are involved in the most change-episodes are those for which much planning is needed during coding. Similarly, we discuss two ways in which a goal can be changed in a change-episode. One involves relatively minor editing of a goal's subgoals, suggesting that much planning is local to the current goal. The other entails major transformations in the goal's structure. Finally, we find that change-episodes are initiated in one of three very distinct circumstances: as an interrupt to coding, a tag-along to another change-episode, or a byproduct of symbolic execution. Our findings support the distinction between inherent and planning subgoals (2, 3) and the distinction between progressive and evaluative problem-solving activities (6).

INTRODUCTION

Although making changes and catching errors while coding seems a ubiquitous part of our own programming behavior we have never seen the topic referred to, let alone treated in a systematic way. It occurred to us that such changes without external feedback represent key junctures in the process of coding. At these junctures existing plans are modified, scrapped, or fixed, and new plans are developed. If these junctures could be studied systematically they might provide a wealth of information about the cognitive processes involved in coding.

In this paper we examine the changes that programmers make while writing, but before testing, their code. We present the analysis techniques that were developed to probe the nature of these junctures, or *change-episodes*. The results of this analysis help illuminate the nature of programming as a complex cognitive skill.

In the next section we define change-episodes, provide a perspective on coding as a problem-solving activity, and propose hypotheses in the context of a tripartite analysis of change-episodes. This discussion is followed by the details of this empirical study. We then present the data and conclude by summarizing the findings, assessing their implications for understanding programming in particular and problem-solving in general.

CHANGES WHILE CODING

A change-episode occurs when either the programmer alters code that is already on the screen or modifies plans that have been articulated (based on the verbal protocol). There are three parts to a change-episode: the change-goal, the noticing event, and the fix. The *change-goal* is the goal that the programmer later decides to change. Are all goals equally likely candidates for change or can we identify systematic differences between those that are and those that are not change-goals? The *noticing event* is the first indication that the programmer wants to change the goal-structure of his/her solution. Do noticing events occur at random or at particular times or places during coding? The *fix* is the goal-structure after it has been changed. Are there as many types of changes as there are change-episodes or can most changes be placed in one of a small number of change categories?

The next section presents our theoretical perspective on coding. Then for each part of the change-episode, that is, the change-goal, noticing event, and fix, we present hypotheses that arise from this theoretical perspective and discuss how we count, measure, or otherwise quantify each part.

Coding as Problem Solving

We view coding as a type of problem-solving activity and problem solving as involving search in a problem space (1). The initial state for our programmers is defined by the problem statement in conjunction with the knowledge and skills that the programmers bring to the experiment. The problem statement defines as the goal state a LISP function that will search a hierarchy to determine if =*person1* has as a descendent =*person2*. It also provides certain design specifications and constraints, such as, the search must be depth-first and self-terminating, iteration must be used (not recursion), and so on. (See the THE STUDY section for more details.)

The knowledge and skills that our programmers possess (advanced novice LISPers) determine what parts of the code involve problem solving and what parts simply entail the retrieval of information from long-term memory.

The goal-structure of the problem solution can (and will) be presented hierarchically. However, because a superordinate goal is retrieved effortlessly from long-term memory does not mean that its subordinates also exist in long-term memory. For example, in coding the function, most of our programmers retrieve a subgoal-template for coding the let/loop body of the function (a let/loop construction is specified in the problem statement) from long-term memory:

right-paren predicate-let variable-declaration loop-body left-paren

We view each part of this template as a separate subgoal. Solutions to the first two subgoals "(" and "let" are available in long-term memory and are immediately typed. The third subgoal, the variable-declaration, constitutes a subproblem that has its own subgoals, some of which require lookup in long-term memory and others which require problem solving. The types of problem-solving activity varies between subgoals. For example labeling the variable may require finding an appropriately mnemonic name whereas deciding upon an initial value for the variable may require determining the best data-type (atom or list) based upon how the variable later is used. Similar considerations surround the coding of the loop-body subgoal.

The above subgoal-template lists only *inherent goals*. A complete goal-structure hierarchy would include all inherent goals as well as all *planning goals* used in coding the function. The distinction between inherent goals and planning goals was made by Anderson, Farrell, and Sauers (2, 3). The important feature of inherent goals is that, in achieving them, one achieves part of the original task. On the other hand, planning goals produce results that are used to guide solution of the original problem but the results themselves are not part of the final solution. For example, if the programmer decides that the variable will initially have the value of the first parameter, s/he still must decide the data-type for the variable, whether to make it an atom or a list. Making that decision requires determining how the variable will be used in the function. The goals associated with this determination are clear-cut examples of planning goals in that they are used to guide the solution to the problem but are not part of the final solution. In contrast the goal of initializing is part of the final solution and is therefore an inherent goal. (Note that, as in the above example, an inherent goal can have both planning and inherent subgoals but, strictly speaking, planning goals can have only planning subgoals.)

As experience in dealing with a particular goal and its subgoals is gained, planning goals drop out of the goal-structure hierarchy and the goal-structure that remains increasingly mirrors that of LISP (as represented in the subgoal-template shown above). This evolution of knowledge structures is explained by the ACT* process of knowledge compilation (4, 5).

Following Allwood (6) we distinguish between two types of problem solving (and therefore, coding) activities: progressive and evaluative. Progressive activities work directly towards the goal state of the problem. Evaluative activities evaluate some already executed part of the problem solution. By this dichotomy, coding and planning what to code are progressive activities while checking and changing code (that is, change-episodes) are evaluative activities. However, while Allwood saw evaluative activities as merely affirming the correctness of the solution or flagging it as erroneous, we view them as also involved in issues of programming style and elegance. Hence, rather than talking as Allwood does about *error detection and correction* we prefer to talk about change-episodes. This difference in terminology arises because we study programming while Allwood studied statistics problems, a domain that is much less tolerant of individual choice. In our definition, error detection and correction is a subcategory of change-episodes.

Historically most accounts of problem-solving have emphasized progressive activities and tended to ignore evaluative activities. The study of programming has followed this trend. Even those areas that may be thought to involve evaluative activities, such as debugging or software maintenance and revision, really deal with the progressive side of problem solving. For example, debugging activities that involve working from a given symptom (initial state) to a working program (goal state) are progressive activities. Questions as to how programmers evaluate their progress while debugging and when they decide to test the code, that is, activities that involve the problem solver evaluating his/her problem solving efforts, are usually not addressed.

Change-Goals

A change-goal is the problem-solving goal that a programmer either sets or completes and, at a later time, changes; it is the goal that is the target of the change-episode.

Hypotheses

We predict that the probability of a goal being the target of a change-episode will be correlated with the amount of planning involved in its execution. Hence, an analysis of change-episodes will identify many of the places where planning occurs.

Rationale. Based upon the analysis in the preceding section, we expect goals to have a lot of planning subgoals if either (a) the goal is not yet well learned and has not been subjected to knowledge compilation, or (b) if there are so many variations as to how the goal can be used that it is unlikely that a specific rule for the required variation has yet been compiled. In the first case, poorly learned goals can easily be coded wrong and become the target of an error detection type of change-episode. In the second case, choosing the correct instantiation of a goal may depend upon having a fairly complete idea of how the rest of the function will be coded. To the extent that the exact plan depends upon the instantiation of a number of different highly variable goals, we would expect the exact instantiation of any one variable goal to affect the programmer's plan and through that plan, to affect the specifications of other goals (both coded and not yet coded).

In the present study, our programmers' instructional and programming histories were known. Therefore a first estimate of the relative ratio of inherent to planning subgoals in a particular goal was based upon a task analysis of LISP plus knowledge of this history. Analyzing change-episodes to identify which goals were the most frequent and least frequent change-goals was expected to provide a second, and converging, estimate of the amount of planning required to execute a given goal. If so, it would provide additional support for the distinction between inherent and planning goals and the role of knowledge compilation. Additionally, if this measure could be validated it could then be applied to situations in which the programmer's history was not well known. This would provide a tool for identifying weaknesses in computer language curricula as well as a means of predicting likely places for bugs and problems in code comprehension.

The next section provides a detailed exposition of the syntax and semantics of the LISP goal-structure hierarchies upon which much of our analysis rests. Since our hypotheses and conclusions are independent of these hierarchies, readers can skip this section and still be able to appreciate our main findings and follow our conclusions regarding change-episodes in coding.

What are Change-Goals?

A change-goal is identified as a goal-structure in a goal-structure hierarchy. The goal-structure for a given change-goal consists of a node#, a goal-label, and a subgoal-template. In this section we discuss the parts of the goal-structure and how they are derived. In a later section we will discuss how a given goal-structure is identified as *the* change-goal for a change-episode.

As an example, consider the following piece of code whose goal-structure is shown in Figure 1:

```
(cond  ((null queue) (return nil))
       ((equal (car queue) ancestor) (return t))
)
```

This is a two clause, LISP conditional (hence the **cond**) that occurs inside the loop in an iterative let/loop construct. The first clause tests whether the list contained by variable **queue** is null (that is, empty) and if so, exits the loop and returns **nil**. The second clause tests whether the first item in queue is **equal** to the target **ancestor**, if so it exits the loop and returns the value **t** for true.

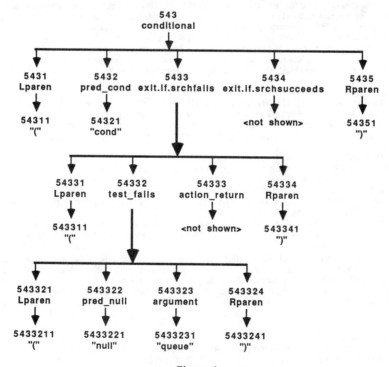

Figure 1
Goal-Structure Hierarchy

The node#, *543*, (see Figure 1) uniquely places the goal-structure in the goal-structure hierarchy. The goal-label, *conditional*, contains semantic information regarding the purpose of the goal. The subgoal-template, *Lparen pred_cond exit.if.searchfails, exit.if.searchsucceeds, Rparen*, contains both semantic information regarding the nature of the subnodes, and syntactic information regarding their left-right order in the goal. Note that each slot in the subgoal-template is itself a goal-label that has a subgoal-template. Hence the goal-structure for a given goal comprises two levels in the hierarchy: the goal and its immediate subgoals.

The goal-structure hierarchy distinguishes between higher goals and leaf goals. The leaf goals in Figure 1 are the terminal nodes of the goal-structure to which they are attached. They are what actually gets typed. For example, node# *54321*, goal-label: *cond* is what gets typed as the predicate, or operator, for its superordinate (node# *5432*, goal-label: *pred_cond*). Leaf goals do not have subgoal-templates; they are the keystrokes that get executed. Higher goals are all of the non-terminal nodes in the hierarchy; they are cognitive constructs.

We can further define higher goals by distinguishing between two types: penultimate goals and higher-order goals. Penultimate goals have one subgoal which is always a leaf. For example:

> Node#: *5432*
> Goal-label: *pred_cond*
> Subgoal-template: *"cond"*

In contrast, a completed higher-order goal always has more than one subgoal none of which are leaf goals. In Figure 1 five higher-order goals are shown: Node# *543*, goal-label: *conditional*; node# *5433*, goal-label: *exit.if.searchfails*; node# *5434*, goal-label: *exit.if.searchsucceeds*; node# *54332*, goal-label: *test_fails*, and node# *54333*, goal-label: *action_return*.

There are two points to emphasize regarding goal-structures and the goal-structure hierarchy. First, the hierarchy captures inherent goals only, not planning goals. When planning goals are stripped away, what remains, the inherent goals, closely mirrors the structure of LISP.

Second, our estimation of what goals are compiled and what are not is built into the semantics of the hierarchy. For higher-order and penultimate goals, all labels other than *predicate* or *argument* reflect estimations of the compiled knowledge that our programmers have acquired. For example, in Figure 1 the first conditional clause, node# *5433*, is actually the first argument of the predicate **cond**. If our programmers had had no or very little experience with conditionals, we would have given this node the label *argument* with the prediction that its subgoal-template would contain a large number of planning subgoals. If our programmers had been introduced to conditionals and had used them enough to have learned their structure, then we would have labeled this node (node# *5433*) *clause1*. Such a label would presume that our programmers knew that a conditional clause required a left-paren, a test part, an action part, and a right-paren; quite a few planning subgoals would be required to turn *clause1* into an exit test. Instead of calling this node *argument* or *clause1*, we have labeled it *exit.if.searchfails*. This label reflects the knowledge and skill that our advanced novice programmers had in using a conditional clause to exit a loop when a guard variable became null. As shown in Figure 1, we believe that our programmers had a subgoal-template for this goal that consisted of a left-paren, a standardization of a clause test (labeled *test_fails*), a standardization of a clause action (labeled *action_return*), and a right-paren. In this case we believe that knowledge compiled at the *exit.if.searchfails* goal largely dictates the type of subgoals (as reflected in the subgoal-labels) and the syntax of the subgoals. Hence, the subgoal-template for *exit.if.searchfails* should have very few planning subgoals.

The Fix

The *fix* is the goal-structure after it has been changed. Comparing the goal-structure before the change-episode to the goal-structure after the change-episode enables us to pinpoint the change-goal and, in so doing, to determine the relationship and distance between the change-goal and the noticing event. Additionally, comparing the before and after goal-structures provides information as to *how* the goal changed; this is the main topic of this section.

Issues & Hypotheses

There are two issues. First, are there as many types of changes as there are change-episodes or can most changes be placed in one of a small number of change categories? For this issue we did not start with a hypothesis but with the hope that most types of fixes could be classified into one of a small number of categories. As discussed in the next section (How are Fixes Identified?), in encoding the fix types we were able to induce two categories that accounted for the vast majority of change-episodes.

Second, what can the type of changes tell us about the role of planning in coding? For this issue our perspective on coding as problem solving led us to hypothesize that most changes would be limited to minor alterations of the change-goal's subgoal-template.[1]

Examples of minor changes would be inserting missing subgoals or transposing the order of subgoals already coded. More major changes would involve the deletion or addition of entire subgoal levels, as when a missing intermediate level goal is inserted between its already partially coded superordinate and its completely coded subordinates. If most planning involves planning subgoals directly attached to the goal being coded then we would expect that most changes would involve modifications to the current goal and would therefore be relatively minor. In contrast, if the

---

[1]Note that minor changes to the subgoal-template could reflect major additions or deletions of lines of code. For example, the **conditional** shown in Figure 1 has two clauses. If the programmer had decided to delete the second clause (node# *5434*; goal-label: *exit.if.searchsucceeds*) this would have been a substantial deletion of code but only a minor change to the **conditional**'s subgoal-template.

planning subgoals encountered while coding had little to do with the currently active goal then changes might involve modifications to distant cousins or siblings, or involve major deletions or additions of intermediate level goal-structures.

How are Fixes Identified?[2]

Our meta-rule is to compare the before and after goal-structure hierarchy to locate the change-goal as the highest goal that changes. For each change-episode we derived two goal-structure hierarchies (such as shown in Figures 1 and 2). The first was the goal-structure hierarchy at the time that the noticing event occurred (discussed in more detail in the Noticing Event section). The second was the goal-structure hierarchy after the fix had been made. By comparing the before and after goal-structure hierarchies, two rules were induced.

Rule A: **Change in subgoal-template.** In locating the change-goal, the single most important rule is to find the goal whose subgoal-template changes. There are four basic changes to the subgoal-template: replacements, transpositions, insertions, or deletions. Replacements and transpositions are prototypical of two different kinds of changes. Transpositions signal a syntactic change in the subgoal-template, while replacements involve the semantics of subgoal-labels. Deletions and insertions involve both types of change.

Changes identified by Rule A are relatively minor changes that are local to the goal. As such, Rule A suggests the operation of planning subgoals located at the level of the change-goal's subgoal-template. In the course of coding a function in a general depth-first, left-to-right fashion (3), the programmers sometimes encounter a planning subgoal that causes them to transpose, replace, insert, or delete a sibling subgoal (where both subgoals share the same superordinate).

Rule B: **A goal-label by any other subgoal-template.** The identifying characteristic of a goal is its label, not its subgoal-template. As an example, consider the case in which a penultimate goal is changed to a higher-order goal. In Figure 2 we have diagrammed a portion of both the before and after goal-structure hierarchy for the body of a local variable update: **(cons (expand (car storer)) storer).**

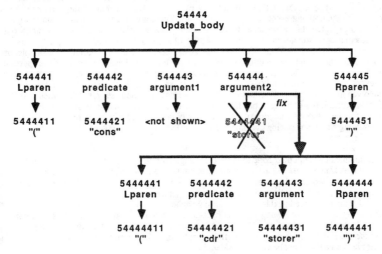

Figure 2
Goal-Structure Hierarchy for Body of a Local Variable Update

In this case the predicate, **cons,** will take whatever is returned by argument1, **(expand (car storer)),** and add it to the front of argument2, **storer.** Later the programmer changes her mind and decides that she wants to add whatever argument1 returns to what is left of the list **storer** after the first item is removed, **(cdr storer).** From the point of view of node# *54444,* goal-label: *Update_body,* nothing has changed. The subgoal-template is still:

Lparen predicate argument1 argument2 Rparen.

In contrast, for node# *544444,* goal-label: *argument2,* much has changed. Where before it was a penultimate goal with a subgoal-template of *storer,* now it is a higher-order goal with a subgoal-template:

Lparen predicate argument Rparen.

Despite these drastic changes, the goal has not changed. It is still *argument2* for the *Update_body* goal. However, the goal-structure has been transformed (see Figure 2). There is now an intermediate goal between *argument2* and *storer.*

---

[2]A detailed understanding of this section is not needed to follow our conclusions regarding change-episodes. Readers may want to skim this section now, refering back as needed.

Noticing Events

A noticing event signals the beginning of a change-episode. It is the first indication that the programmer wants to change the goal-structure of his/her solution. Noticing events are indicated by either keystrokes or verbal protocol. For example, if the programmer decides to interrupt his/her coding to change something that was coded three lines above, the noticing event might be indicated by the use of the *upline* command. Verbal indications might be something as simple as an *oops* followed by revision, or may include a complete statement of the change-goal.

How are Noticing Events Classified?

Noticing events are classified by the activity in which they occur. Our analysis yields four categories: interrupts, tag-alongs, symbolic execution, and miscellaneous.

Interrupts are interruptions in the progressive activity of coding. To count as an interrupt, a noticing event has to occur shortly after some keyboard event with no intervening activity. For a *tag-along* classification, the noticing event has to occur during another change-episode (an evaluative activity).

Symbolic execution (7) is really a category of programmer activity not just a type of change-episode. By symbolic execution, Kant and Newell refer to that programming activity in which the programmer is symbolically (or mentally) executing the program (or a portion of the program) with either general symbols or specific values as inputs. As a category of noticing events, we use symbolic execution to apply to those change-episodes that are initiated during symbolic execution (in contrast to interrupts and tag-alongs). The final category, *miscellaneous*, includes noticing events that occur when the programmer is straightening up the screen (prettyprinting), reading the text, or whatever.

Hypotheses & Rationale

Are change-episodes begun as an abrupt interruption to the progressive activity of coding or are they a more natural outcome of an activity such as symbolic execution that was begun for some other reason? Do change-goals differ for change-episodes initiated by different types of noticing events? Is there a relationship between the activity that immediately precedes the noticing event and the change-goal? These are the three broad questions regarding noticing events that we had expected this study to address. In some cases we had hypotheses based upon our theoretical perspective; in other cases we did not and were unable to think of any theory that would make predictions.

First, while we would have been surprised if all change-episodes were noticed during, for example, interrupts and none were noticed during symbolic execution, we did not have any hypotheses regarding the proportion of change-episodes in each noticing event category. Second, we had expected (as discussed above under **Change-Goals**) that for each noticing event category the probability of a goal being the target of a change-episode would vary with the amount of planning involved in its execution. Within this constraint we had no hypotheses regarding whether different change-goals had different probabilities of being noticed, for example, by an interrupt versus by symbolic execution.

It was only for the interrupt category of noticing events that we had a specific hypothesis regarding what the programmer was doing when the noticing event occurred. This hypothesis is discussed next.

Issues for Interrupts.

When programmers interrupt their code to initiate a change-episode, what is the relationship between the goal that they interrupt and the change-goal? To ask the same question from a different perspective -- if a given change-goal is noticed with an interrupt, when is that interrupt most likely to occur? In the context of the goal-structure hierarchy, will the interrupted goal be a superordinate, subordinate, sibling, uncle, or so on, of the change-goal?

We predict that the interrupted goal is more likely to be either the change-goal itself or a subordinate of the change-goal than either a superordinate or sibling. This is because the programmer will only maintain a representation of a piece of code while it is being worked on. Thus, if the interrupted goal is subordinate to the change-goal, the change-goal will be in the state of being worked on. On the other hand, if the interrupted goal is a sibling or parent of the change-goal, the change-goal will not be under consideration.

Pinpointing the Interrupted Goal.[3] For each change-episode, we derived a goal-structure hierarchy of the programmer's code at the instant that the noticing event occurred. Because of our hypothesis concerning the relation between the interrupted goal and the change-goal, we were interested in (1) whether the interrupted goal was a leaf, penultimate, or higher-order goal, and (2) its relationship to the change-goal. In the preceding section, The Fix, we discussed how we pinpointed the change-goal. Here we discuss the criteria used to pinpoint the interrupted goal.

Consider, as an example, the change-episode (discussed earlier) whose before and after goal-structure hierarchies are diagrammed in Figure 2. The interrupted goal would be a leaf goal if the noticing event occurred during the typing of **storer** (node# *5444441*). To be precise, if the programmer had either partially typed **storer**, for example, **sto** or had just finished typing the final **r**, then the noticing event would be said to have interrupted a leaf goal that was the *child* of the change-goal *argument2* (node# *544444*). In contrast, if the noticing event occurred after the programmer typed **storer** *plus* a space (**storer_**) then the interrupted goal would be the penultimate goal *argument2* (node# *544444*) and the interrupted goal would be the change-goal itself (*self*).

Finally, if the programmer had completed the *update_body* goal (node# *54444*) by typing the closing right parenthesis (node# *544445*) and (perhaps) a space but had not yet started the next goal, then the interrupted goal would be the higher-order goal *update_body* goal (node# *54444*) and the interrupted goal would be the *parent* of the change-goal. (Note that in our analysis scheme, parentheses play the role of delimiting the beginning and end of higher-order goals.)

---

[3]Those not interested in methodological details may wish to skip this section.

Summary

Any change in a programmer's code or intentions constitutes a change-episode. Change-episodes include error detection and correction (including false positives) as well as stylistic, strategic, and tactical changes. In this study we examine change-episodes from the general perspective of coding as problem solving and from the more specific perspective offered by Anderson et al.'s (2, 3) theory of inherent and planning goals and Allwood's (6) distinction between progressive and evaluative problem-solving activity.

We argued that change-episodes occur most often for constructs that allow the most variability (with variability defined by the language, the task, and the programmer's history). Therefore we predicted that the more planning a goal needs during coding, the more likely it is to be the target of a change-episode. Similarly, we discussed two ways in which a goal-structure can be fixed. One way, Rule A, involves relatively minor editing of the subgoal-template, the other, Rule B, entails major transformations in the goal-structure. Finally, we proposed that change-episodes may be initiated (the noticing event) by interrupts to coding, as tag-alongs to other change-episodes, or during symbolic monitoring. We predicted that for interrupts, the interrupted goal was more likely to be either the change-goal itself or a subordinate, than a superordinate or sibling.

THE STUDY

The tripartite analysis of change-episodes and the techniques for analyzing the goal-structure hierarchy were based upon the analysis of ten advanced-novice LISP programmers writing one LISP function. Because data for the current study was collected in the course of a larger, non-related study, five of the programmers received special training prior to coding the function. Consequently, although the analyses developed were based upon an examination of data from all ten programmers, only protocols from the five programmers in the control group were encoded. These are reported below.

Programmers (their prior experience)

The five programmers were paid volunteers from the introductory LISP course offered by the Psychology Department at Carnegie-Mellon University. None of the five had any prior experience with LISP; all had had some programming experience ranging from a failed PASCAL course to self-rated expertise in PASCAL and BASIC. All programmers were in the 12th to 13th week of the 15-week course and all had completed the eleven modules offered on the LISP Tutor (8).

The Function

The function that the programmers coded was similar to those they would find in the *Search Techniques* chapter of their textbook (9). The specifications for the function were fairly complete. The programmers were told to write an iterative function, using the let/loop construction, and not to make any recursive function calls. The function was to take two parameters and perform a depth-first search of a tree, returning t if the second parameter was a descendent of the first, and returning nil otherwise. Additionally, they were told to use an expansion function, called *expand*, that takes a node in the tree and returns a list of all of its immediate descendents. Finally, they were told to create a local variable to store nodes returned by the expansion function until they could be individually checked. The experimenters' code for this problem is given below:

```
(defun descendent (ancestor progeny)
  (let ((queue (expand ancestor)))
  (loop
    (cond ((null queue)(return nil))
          ((equal (car queue) progeny)(return t)))
    (setq queue (append (expand (car queue))(cdr queue)))
    )))
```

Procedures

Programmers were run individually. Upon arriving for a session they were given an overview and asked about their programming background. They then practiced talking aloud while solving mental arithmetic and anagram problems (10).

Programmers next read an abridged version of the search chapter from their textbook (9). They were then given a description of the problem along with a sample tree diagram and told to talk aloud as they read. After they indicated they understood the problem, they were asked to list the nodes from the tree diagram in the order in which they would be visited. This task provided a check to see if they understood what a depth-first search entailed. None of the programmers had any difficulties with this task.

Programmers then talked aloud as they coded the problem on a computer terminal using a version of the EMACS (11) editor. All programmers were familiar with EMACS, though some occasionally tried to use commands that were not implemented in our version. Programmers worked on the problem until they were satisfied that it was complete. While coding, programmers were free to consult their textbook or the experimenter regarding any LISP questions they might have. (The experimenter did not tell the programmers how to code the function, but did, when asked, provide *textbook* answers to how a particular function worked or the syntax of a particular construction.) Programmers were also free to consult the problem description and diagram. The experimenter prompted the programmers to talk aloud as needed.

Data Collected and Protocol Transcriptions

Both keystroke and videotape data were collected. The keystroke data was time-stamped at the one second level. The videotape was time-stamped to the millisec although in practice all times were rounded to the nearest second.

The video camera was focused on the screen. This permitted us to correlate what programmers were typing and seeing with what they were saying. It also greatly facilitated the interweaving of the time-stamped keystroke data with the verbal protocol.

RESULTS

Overall

As Table 1 indicates, there were large differences among our programmers in time to code the function. Time in minutes ranged from 52.60 to 7.92 with a mean of 20.83. Likewise the number of change-episodes per programmer varied from 8 to 37. Looking at the relationship between the number of minutes to code the function and the number of change-episodes yields an average of one change-episode every 1.01min. To examine the distribution of change-episodes throughout the coding period, we divided each programmer's coding time into ten equal intervals. The distribution of change-episodes by interval did not differ from what would be expected by chance (χ^2 [9, n=105] = 9.56). (Note that .05 is the level of significance for all statistics reported in this article and all tests reported are two-tail.) Change-episodes occur both frequently and evenly while the programmer is coding.

Table 2 shows the type of change-goal by programmer. There were large differences overall and between programmers in the distribution of type of change-goal. Overall 27% of the changes involved leaf goals, 14% penultimate goals, and 59% higher-order goals. These differences contrast with the proportion of leaf, penultimate, and higher-order goals in the experimenters' solution shown above. There are 156 goals in the experimenters' solution: 44% (68) leaf goals, 44% (68) penultimate goals, and 13% (20) higher-order goals. A χ^2 test indicates that the number of changes for a goal type is not proportional to the number of goals of that type in the experimenters' solution (χ^2 [2, n=105] = 202.63). This difference in found versus expected is also significant when parentheses are excluded from the count of leaf and penultimate goals (χ^2 [2, n=105] = 60.35). For both tests, the proportion of change-episodes involving higher-order goals is much greater than would be expected by chance. Concomitantly, the proportion of change-episodes involving leaf and penultimate goals is less than expected.

Table 1

Time to code and number of change-episodes by programmer

Programmer	Time(min)	Change-Episode	Changes per Min
MK05	52.60	37	.70
NS03	16.43	14	.85
WB12	16.23	33	2.03
AP02	10.98	13	1.18
MK02	7.92	8	1.01
Mean	20.83	21	1.01

Table 2

Frequency of change-goal type by programmer
(with percentages in parentheses).

Programmer	Leaf Goal	Penultimate Goal	Higher-order Goal	Total
MK05	9 (24)	3 (8)	25 (68)	37 (100)
NS03	7 (50)	5 (36)	2 (14)	14 (100)
WB12	6 (18)	4 (12)	23 (70)	33 (100)
AP02	4 (31)	3 (23)	6 (46)	13 (100)
MK02	2 (25)	0 (0)	6 (75)	8 (100)
Sum	28 (27)	15 (14)	62 (59)	105

Detailed Analyses

Which Goals are the Change-Goals?

Rules A and B were used to identify the change-goal for each of the 105 change-episodes. Since the goal for leaf goals was always the word being typed, the goal-label was more or less unique to a particular programmer coding a particular function. Because of this we did not tabulate changes in leaf goals. In contrast, since goal-labels for penultimate goals and higher-order goals were common across programmers, it made sense to ask which of these goals changed the most and the least often.

Penultimate goals. We counted 15 types of penultimate goals represented in our 5 programmers' final code. Since there were only 15 change-episodes involving penultimate goals (see Table 2), we reduced the penultimate change-goals to two categories: predicates (any LISP operator or function name) and arguments. In their final code our programmers had 86 predicates and 75 arguments. One change-episode involved a predicate (with 8 expected by chance) while the other 14 involved arguments (7 expected by chance). This difference is significant (χ^2 [1, $n=15$)]= 13.10).

As judged by our task analysis of LISP and our programmers' LISP histories, the predicates were more standardized (and therefore had fewer associated planning goals) than the arguments. To support this assertion we looked in the programmers' final code for the labels that each had given to the same penultimate goal. For predicates there were ten cases where, if a penultimate goal was used, it was given the same label by all programmers (for 5/10 cases the label was explicitly mentioned in the problem statement). In contrast, for arguments, there were only three cases where the same label was used for the same penultimate goal (and 3/3 of these labels were explicitly mentioned in the problem statement).

This difference in specification of penultimate predicates and arguments is directly represented in the goal-structure hierarchy analyses. For example, in Figure 1, node# *5432*, goal-label: *pred_cond* is a penultimate goal whose subgoal-template consists of the leaf goal *cond*. The leaf goal is completely determined by the penultimate goal-label. In contrast, the penultimate goal at node# *543323*, goal-label: *argument* does not demand that its subgoal-template be *queue*; presumably there are planning subgoals associated with this node that help select the label. This lack of specificity at the subgoal level exists despite the fact that the higher-order goal *test_fails* (node# *54332*) is standardized to take exactly one argument that must occupy the third slot in its subgoal-template. Therefore the analysis of penultimate goals involved in change-episodes supports the notion that the more standardized a goal is (that is, the fewer planning subgoals associated with it), the less likely it is to be involved in change-episodes.

Higher-order goals. For higher-order goals we looked at the found versus expected frequencies of being involved in a change-episode for 15 higher-order goals that appeared at least four times in the programmers' final code. A χ^2 was significant (χ^2 [14, $n= 61$] = 118.42); hence, compared to what would be expected by chance, some higher-order goals were more likely and others less likely to be involved in change-episodes. (Note that as for the χ^2 reported above, this χ^2 was weighted by how often a particular goal appeared in the final code for all five programmers.)

Let's take a closer look at one high, one average, and one low probability higher-order change-goal. First is the high. The goal *conditional* was involved in 16 change-episodes with all five subjects contributing at least one episode. All except one of these change-episodes entailed either the deletion (6), insertion (3), transposition (3), or replacement (3) of conditional clauses. From our perspective, this is delightful. The conditional statement is an example of a LISP construct that has a semi-fixed internal structure. All conditionals have a *Lparen*, a *pred_cond*, one or more clauses, and a *Rparen* (see Figure 1). Within this rigid structure the number, type, and order of clauses can vary and it was these attributes that were involved in the 15 change-episodes. (For example, in the experimenters' solution to the problem, shown above, we used one conditional which included two conditional clauses. In contrast, none of our programmers coded their conditional(s) as we did. Two used two conditionals with two or three clauses per conditional. Two used one conditional with three clauses. And one used one conditional with the same two clauses we used, but in a different order. Although some are inelegant, none of these approaches are wrong.)

Because of the variability in how it can be used in LISP, the goal-structure for the conditional cannot contain just inherent goals, but must contain a large proportion of planning goals. The presence of planning goals is reflected by the frequency with which the conditional is involved in change-episodes.[4]

The conditional contrasts nicely with its main component, the **conditional clause** which was involved in an average (expected) number of change-episodes. As far as our programmers knew, all conditional clauses, regardless of their standardization, were composed of exactly four elements: **Lparen test action Rparen** (see Figure 1, node# *5433*). Presumably, fewer planning subgoals are attached as subgoals for conditional clauses than for conditionals.

An even better contrast is to compare the conditional with two standardized subgoals for the test component of a conditional clause: **test_fails** (see Figure 1) and **test_succeed**. The subgoal-template for test_fails consists of exactly four elements in an exactly specified order: **Lparen pred_null argument Rparen**. The subgoal-template for test_succeed consists of exactly five elements in an exactly specified order: **Lparen pred_found argument1 argument2 Rparen**. (Note whereas **pred_null** exactly specifies its subgoal-template, **null**, for our programmers **pred_found** could take one of a limited number of functions.) Test_fails and test_found occurred ten times in our programmers' final code; however, neither was ever involved in a change-episode.

Summary. The analysis of which goals are most likely to be change-goals corresponds well with our expectations about which goals have the highest ratio of planning to inherent subgoals. This finding holds for both penultimate and higher-order goals.

---

[4]This is not to say that more specific versions of **conditional** would never emerge. For example, with lots of practice in using the let/loop construction in coding search functions our programmers would probably develop a standardization of **conditional**, *conditional_search.exits*.

How are Change-Goals Fixed?

As discussed earlier, the information contributed by the *fix* plays a large role in deciding which goal is the change-goal. Our two rules are *Rule A*, *changes in subgoal-template*, and *Rule B*, *a goal-label by any other subgoal-template*.

Table 3 summarizes which rule was used to identify the change-goal for each of our three goal types. (Because one change-episode was begun but never *fixed*, the sums add up to 104 change-episodes rather than 105.) For 94 out of 104 change-episodes the change-goal was identified using Rule A. This predominance of Rule A identifications holds for each goal type. For leaf goals it is true by definition. Leaf change-episodes are limited to typographical errors. Any correction that left the name the same would be an insertion, deletion, transposition or replacement. Any change in name would not be considered a leaf goal change. However, for both penultimate goals and higher-order goals Rule B can apply but usually does not. Fourteen out of 15 penultimate goals and 53 out of 62 higher-order goals are identified by Rule A.

Table 3
Rule used to identify change-goal for each type of goal.

	Leaf Goals	Penultimate Goals	Higher-order Goals	Totals
Rule A	27	14	53	94
Rule B	0	1	9	10
Totals	27	15	62	104

Rule A is the primary way of locating the change-goal. In these cases the fixed-goal is basically the change-goal with one or more of its subgoals replaced, deleted, transposed, or inserted. For example, correcting a misspelled word, or changing the order of two clauses in a **conditional** both result in the fixed-goal being essentially the same as the change-goal.

For Rule B, while the goal-label remains the same an entire subordinate level is either inserted or deleted. When a level is inserted then the fixed-goal is the parent (+1) of the change-goal. For example, earlier (see Figure 2) we discussed the case in which the programmer changed the argument from a list **storer** to the list with the first element removed **(cdr storer)**. In this case the argument went from a penultimate goal (node# *544444*) with subgoal-template *storer* to a higher-order goal with subgoal-template: *Lparen predicate argument Rparen*. One subgoal of this new subgoal-template, *argument* (node# *5444443*) had as its subgoal-template *storer*. If the fix had gone the other way, from **(car storer)** to **storer**, then the fixed-goal would have been the child (-1) of the change-goal.

For the 10 change-episodes that required Rule B, a closer analysis revealed that the cases in which the fixed-goal was the parent (superordinate) of the change-goal were qualitatively different from the cases in which the fixed-goal was a child (subordinate) of the change-goal. Deletion of a subordinate level was the case for three of the 10 Rule B change-episodes. In two of these, previously correct code was changed into an obvious (to us anyway) error. In the third, an obvious error was corrected.

The situation for the seven *parent* change-episodes was very different. In all seven cases, correct code existed that represented one subgoal in an otherwise missing super. During the change-episode the rest of the super was built up around the one subgoal. An example was the goal for updating the local variable. The subgoal-template for the update was: *Lparen pred_setq var_name update_body Rparen*. In a parent change-episode the change-goal, *variable_update*, was initially coded as just the *update_body*. During the change-episode the mistake was noticed and the rest of the subgoals for *variable_update* were added.

These are examples of the local goal-structure being *transformed* rather than *unpacked*. (Such transformations have been noticed during debugging by Katz and Anderson [12].) Our interpretation is that these represent relatively uncompiled, unstandardized, goal-structures in which the left-to-right order information is overshadowed by the planning subgoals. Hence depth-first coding of certain subgoals occurs before the coding of more leftward subgoals. The planning goals result in a different order of coding than the hierarchical structure of LISP would dictate, but probably eases the working memory load in that a key part of the goal is coded and the rest can be built around it.

Summary. Our hope for a small number of fix categories was fulfilled. All 104 fixed change-episodes could be placed into one of two fix categories. Perhaps more astonishing was that 90% (94/104) of the fixes were accounted for by just one category, Rule A. Rule A accounts for minor changes (additions, deletions, insertions, or replacements) in the fixed goal's subgoal-template. These findings support the hypothesis that most planning occurs at planning subgoals that are directly attached to the change-goal's subgoal-template.

When are Changes Made? A Taxonomy of Noticing Events.

What is the programmer doing immediately before s/he decides, or *notices*, that something already coded needs to be changed? The protocols suggest that most of these noticing events (102/105) occur either as an interruption to coding (53), during or immediately after another change-episode (a tag-along) (24), or as an outcome of symbolic execution (25). While we intended these categories to be exhaustive, it is interesting that the majority of change-episodes occur as interrupts and not as the result of the more deliberate processes involved in symbolic execution. (These data increase the importance of determining whether interrupts occur randomly during coding or whether there exists a systematic relationship between the goal that was interrupted and the goal that was changed.)

We looked to see if the three goal types were equally likely to be noticed during the three main types of noticing events. First we compared the expected versus found distribution for leaf goals versus all higher goals (higher-order plus penultimate goals). The χ^2 was significant ($\chi^2[2, n=28] = 9.59$) indicating that leaf goals were more likely to be noticed by interrupts (22 cases found versus 14 expected) than during tag-alongs (5 found, 7 expected) or symbolic monitoring (1 found, 7 expected). There were no significant differences in the found versus expected distribution for penultimate versus higher-order goals.

Table 4
Distance & relationship of the interrupted goal to leaf, penultimate, or higher-order change-goal.

Distance	Relation	Change-Goal Type			Totals
		Leaf Goal	Penultimate Goal	Higher-Order Goal	
+3	uncle	---	---	1	1
+3	nephew	---	---	1	1
+2	grandparent	---	---	1	1
+2	brother	---	---	---	0
+1	parent	---	---	---	0
0	self	22	1	7	30
-1	child	/////	3	6	9
-2	grandchild	/////	/////	8	8
-3	greatgrchild	/////	/////	3	3
	Totals	22	4	27	53

Interrupts: Stopping coding to make changes. In support of our hypothesis, the data show that the interrupted goal was more likely to be either the change-goal itself or a subordinate of the change-goal than a superordinate or sibling (that is, at the time of the noticing event the programmers were coding part of the structure that they ended up changing). These data are shown in Table 4 where negative numbers indicate the number of subordinate links from the interrupted goal to the change-goal and positive numbers indicate the number of superordinate links. For example, from Figure 1, if typing *null* (node# *5433221*) was interrupted to change *test_fails* (node# *54332*), the interrupted goal would be a grandchild (-2 links distance) of the change-goal. In contrast, if the *conditional* goal (node# *543*) was interrupted to change *test_fails* (node# *54332*) the interrupted goal would be a grandparent (+2 links distance) of the change-goal. Note that regardless of the direction of the super- or sub-ordinate relationship, most of the interrupted goals were very close to the change-goals; that is, there were very few links between the two. Of the 53 interrupts 30 occurred at distance 0, 9 at distance 1, 9 at 2, 5 at 3, and none at a distance greater than 3 links from the change-goal.

Table 4 indicates that a piece of code was changed only immediately after it was coded (Table 4, distance: 0, relationship: self) or while one of its subgoals was being coded (Table 4, distance: -1 to -3, relationship: child, grandchild, or greatgrandchild). Programmers seldom interrupted their coding to change an already completed goal. This was true despite the drastically restricted range of descendents for leaf and penultimate goals. For example, while the penultimate goals lack grandchildren, and so on, they do have a parent, grandparent, possibly brothers, uncles, and more.

This finding is both very interesting and disappointing for the human intellect. There must be a close proximity between the change-goal and the current activity for change to occur. Programmers will seldom interrupt their coding to change an already completed portion of code. When coding is interrupted to make a change it is either immediately after the code was completed (self) or, if before completion, during work on one of its subgoals. Changes made to completed code result from symbolic execution (discussed below).

Changes initiated by interrupts appear to be part of the planning process. Programmers apparently begin work on a goal before it is completely planned. The early work may serve to help programmers remember the goal-structure of the plan (2) without implying a commitment to particular details. As programmers begin to implement subgoals of the plan, implications are realized that cause the higher-order goal to be revised. Once the details of a plan are worked out in code and the programmer moves on either to finishing work on a superordinate or to working on a sibling goal, spontaneous interrupts seldom result in code revisions.

Tag-alongs: The change-episode as noticing event. Twenty-five change-episodes were initiated during another change-episode. Of these 16 involved the same change-goal as the immediately preceding change-episode with no other events intervening. Five of these 16 involved the repeated misspelling and correcting of the word (leaf goal) that was the change-goal in the prior change-episode. Five involved the programmer either renaming a parameter or variable, or apparently slipping and first typing (or saying) one argument name, then another, and so on (penultimate goals). The other 6 involved problems that two of our programmers had in deciding how many parentheses were required in a variable declaration statement when a single variable is being initialized (a higher-order goal). Examination of the textbook (9) revealed that out of 27 examples of such a statement, 3 different methods were used with no method dominant. We conclude that our programmers' methods of initializing variables were in an intermediate stage of compilation in which they knew that different methods existed but did not know when to apply one rather than another.

Each of the other 9 tag-alongs was noticed during another change-episode but involved a different change-goal. Within this group no patterns were noticed.

Symbolic execution. In 24 change-episodes there was clear evidence that the programmers had been symbolically executing their code immediately prior to *noticing* the need to change a previously coded (or stated) goal. In all cases the evidence for symbolic execution came directly from the verbal protocols.

Almost by definition, there should be a longer interval between the noticing event and the immediately prior keystroke for symbolic execution than for either interrupts or tag-alongs. In the three categories, the mean time in seconds between last keystroke and noticing event was 52.5 (symbolic execution), 2.2 (interrupts), and 4.0 (tag-alongs). An ANOVA (unweighted for unequal numbers of entries) finds these differences significant (F [2, 99] = 41.48). Orthogonal comparisons show that all of this difference is due to the symbolic execution versus rest comparison (F [1, 99] = 82.89) and none due to the interrupt versus tag-along (F < 1).

Summary. Change-episodes are initiated by noticing events that occur either as an interruption to coding, as a tag-along to another change-episode, or as an outcome of symbolic execution. Interrupts occur at close proximity to the change-goal and either immediately after the change-goal was completed (self) or during work on one of its subgoals. Changes made to completed goals when other goals intervene between completion and change are the result of symbolic execution.

SUMMARY & CONCLUSIONS

Change-episodes, a prominent feature of our programmers' behavior (averaging one per min), seem to represent key junctures in the process of coding. As such they cannot be ignored by theories of coding. Here we summarize our major findings and discuss possible directions and applications of our work on change-episodes.

Importance of Change-Episodes to the Cognition of Programming

Overall the most important finding was the systematicity in which goals were change-goals, when the need for a change was noticed, and how the change occurred (the fix). Such systematicity argues for the role and importance of the heretofore ignored issue of evaluative activities (6) in programming. In addition, the particular pattern of findings supports the distinction between inherent and planning goals (3) and the placement of planning goals at the level of the goal-structure for which planning occurs.

For both higher-order and penultimate goals, those least likely to be the target of a change-episode were those which, for a priori reasons, we believed had a low ratio of planning to inherent subgoals (3). Conversely, those most likely to be targeted, such as *code a conditional* were those for which many different (and legal) instantiations exist. It seems reasonable that our programmers required many planning subgoals to code these goals. Our inference is that the more planning involved, the more likely a change-episode will occur.

One of the surprising findings was how easy it was to identify most change-goals by looking for relatively minor changes in a goal's subgoal-template (Rule A). This finding supports the hypothesis that most planning occurs at planning subgoals that are attached directly to the change-goal. The exceptions not captured by this fix category were few. Ten out of 104 change-episodes involved either deleting or inserting an entire hierarchical level (Rule B). For this minority of cases, left-to-right syntactic information seemed lacking and programmers performed a depth-first expansion of rightward subgoals before coding the more leftward ones. The change-episode transformed the goal-structure rather than just rearranging or editing it (see also [12]).

Another surprise was that most (102/105) change-episodes occurred in one of three very distinct circumstances: as an interrupt to coding, as a tag-along to another change-episode, or as a byproduct of symbolic execution. Out of 53 interrupts, 50 occurred either right after the change-goal had been coded or after work on a direct descendent of the change-goal. We characterized this finding as disappointing for the human intellect. There must be a close proximity between the change-goal and the current activity for change to occur. Programmers almost never interrupt their coding to change an already completed portion of code. Changes made to completed code are the result of symbolic execution.

Goals which are unstandardized, either because they have been recently acquired or because of the many different ways in which they can be used, contain a high ratio of planning to inherent subgoals. These high ratio goals are most likely to be the target of change-episodes. Change-episodes are a type of evaluative activity that takes the programmer away from the progressive activity of coding. Understanding the role of such evaluative activities in programming, how they are used and how they are acquired, is a necessary but neglected aspect of the study of programming.

In conclusion, we believe that the issue of change-episodes in coding is a good problem to work on. It is good because change-episodes are very common in coding and seem to represent key junctures in the coding process. Understanding the cognitive processes involved in change-episodes has direct relevance to any theory of coding, implications for debugging, comprehending, and designing programs, as well as for progressive and evaluative activities in other cognitive tasks.

REFERENCES

1. Newell, A. (1980). Reasoning, problem-solving, and decision processes: The problem space as a fundamental category. In R. Nickerson (Ed.), **Attention and performance VIII.** Hillsdale, NJ: Erlbaum.
2. Anderson, J. R., Farrell, R., & Sauers, R. (1982). **Learning to plan in LISP** (Tech. Rep. No. ONR-82-2). Pittsburgh, PA: Carnegie-Mellon University.
3. Anderson, J. R., Farrell, R., & Sauers, R. (1984). Learning to program in LISP. **Cognitive Science, 8,** 87-129.
4. Anderson, J. R. (1982). Acquisition of cognitive skill. **Psychological Review, 89,** 369-406.
5. Anderson, J. R. (1983). **The architecture of cognition.** Cambridge, MA: Harvard University Press.
6. Allwood, C. M. (1984). Error detection processes in statistical problem solving. **Cognitive Science, 8,** 413-437.

7.   Kant, E., & Newell, A. (1984). Problem solving techniques for the design of algorithms. **Information Processing & Management, 20,** 97-118.
8.   Anderson, J. R., & Reiser, B. J. (1985, April). The LISP tutor. **Byte,** pp.159-175.
9.   Anderson, J. R., Corbett, A. T., & Reiser, B. J. (1987). **Essential LISP.** Reading, MA: Addison-Wesley Publishing Company, Inc.
10.   Ericsson, K. A., & Simon, H. A. (1985). **Protocol analysis: Verbal reports as data.** Cambridge, MA: MIT Press.
11.   Gosling, J. (1981). **Unix EMACS user manual.** Pittsburgh, PA: CMU Computer Science Department.
12.   Katz, I. R., & Anderson, J. R. (1986). **An exploratory study of novice programmers' bugs and debugging behavior.** Presented at the First Annual Empirical Studies of Programmers Conference (July). Washington, DC.

AUTHOR NOTES

The research was supported by a Secretary of the Army Science and Engineering Fellowship, a Sloan Foundation Fellowship, and the gracious hospitality of the Psychology Department at Carnegie-Mellon University to the first author. Support for the second author was provided by ONR contract N00014-87-k-0103. Nothing in this paper should be construed as representing official Army policy. Request for reprints should be sent to: Wayne D. Gray, Army Research Institute, PERI-IC, 5001 Eisenhower Ave, Alexandria, VA 22333 or gray@ari-hq1.arpa.

We wish to thank A. Corbett and M. Lewicki for their cooperation and assistance in collecting the protocol data. Also B. John and A. Newell for the use of the Users Studies Laboratory, and L. Reder for space and equipment. Thanks also to F. Conrad, A. Corbett, B. John, I. Katz, and C. Kessler for their comments on an earlier draft. Thanks to H. Simon for advice on encoding verbal protocols and to C. Fisher for assistance in formatting and printing.

CHAPTER 13

Advancing the Study of Programming
With Computer-Aided Protocol Analysis

Carolanne Fisher
Psychology Department
Carnegie-Mellon University
Pittsburgh, PA 15213

ABSTRACT

The study of computer programming in all its complexity requires the use of data gathering and analysis techniques equal to the task. Protocol analysis is ideally suited to both the development and testing of theories in this emerging domain. Protocol analysis is, however, a difficult, time-consuming, and largely ill-defined task that can become formidable if the data set is particularly large or the patterns in it large, complex, or infrequent -- as is the case with computer programming data. To reduce the difficulty and to increase the reliability and objectivity of conducting protocol studies and to extend the range of possible analyses, I have developed a multipurpose computer-aided protocol analysis system. In this paper, I use a set of protocol data gathered from expert programmers developing sizable, real-world programs as a context in which to describe the system and demonstrate the detailed analysis it makes possible.

INTRODUCTION

The computer programmer, like the author, architect, or artist, is a traveler through an ill-charted domain to an uncertain destination. Programming tasks rarely have only one appropriate solution or one correct method of producing that solution. The programmer's problem, therefore, is not only to produce a program to accomplish a specified task, but also to define what a reasonable solution might be and to forge a reasonably efficient path to that solution. Little is known, however, about how programmers accomplish this difficult task; indeed, little is known about how people manage such complex cognitive activities in general. The study of computer programming, then, can both find real and immediate application in the emerging field of computer science and enhance psychological theories of complex cognitive processes.

Like the programmer, the researcher who seeks more than a cursory understanding of the programming process must be concerned with more than just the product of a programmer's efforts. He must trace the route the programmer took to produce the solution, identify the component skills she employed, and specify the knowledge she needed to complete the task. Such a detailed understanding, or model, of the programmer's goals (what is done when), operators (non-decomposable actions), and knowledge, both correct and incorrect, is particularly important for the researcher whose goal is to teach, automate, or optimize programming skills.

As attractive as the investigation of programming is in theory, it is a difficult domain to tackle in practice. Since little is known about the cognitive processes involved in programming, few guidelines exist for their study. Traditional experimental methodologies examine data that provide only sparse and indirect evidence of the cognitive processes involved. For example, patterns of responses on qualitatively different types of problems can be used to *infer* the application of different strategies (1), or reaction time data can be used to *infer* the number or duration of steps in a solution process (2, 3). In contrast, verbal protocol data provide more direct clues in greater density for the researcher to follow, permitting him to form detailed, rigorous models of complex problem solving (4, 5). Furthermore, protocol analysis techniques are so flexible that the researcher can use them to explore domains in which not enough is known to design fruitful traditional experiments. In fact, Soloway (6) suggests that "protocol methodology will, quite naturally and reasonably, become the major source of data in initially studying aspects of programming-in-the-large."

In the next section, I will briefly describe protocol analysis methodology to highlight its reasonable application to the study of programming and other complex domains. I will then describe some difficulties with its application that have hindered its natural development into the primary method of choice. The goal of my research is to develop and test a multipurpose computer system to aid researchers in using protocol analysis to its full potential for developing models of complex problem-solving behavior such as programming. The remainder of this paper, then, will be devoted to introducing this new system and the theory behind it.

Protocol Analysis: A Thumbnail Sketch

The verbalizations of a subject "thinking aloud" while engaged in some cognitive activity primarily reflect the knowledge currently active in working memory. A verbal protocol, therefore, chronicles the ongoing state of a subject's knowledge as she solves a problem. In addition to knowledge, the verbal reports almost always contain explicit evidence for the subject's goals, operators, and evaluative processes (4, 5). These, of course, are the very clues the researcher needs to craft a detailed model of the programmer's processes, including the intermediate processes, in solving a programming problem.

The general methodology for conducting a protocol study consists of three phases. The first phase, gathering and transcribing the protocol, though time-consuming, is, for the most part, non-problematic. The experimenter sets a task for a subject to do, instructs her to "think aloud" as she works, and records her efforts on audio or video tape. The taped session is then transcribed, word for word, in preparation for analysis. In addition to the subject's verbalizations, the transcript usually contains supplementary information such as what the subject was writing or where she was pointing. Usually the verbatim transcript is also divided in to segments, each corresponding to the expression of one distinct thought.

In the second phase, each segment in the protocol is translated, or encoded, into some consistent vocabulary defined by the experimenter. Encoding reduces the variety of expressions for the same idea and eliminates idiosyncratic expressions so that instances of similar processes within a solution or across solutions are easily recognizable. For example, the statement, "Let me see if this printing function works" might be encoded simply as **test print-function** or the statement "ok, check this reading thing out" as **test read-function**. The encoding vocabulary, which must be sufficient to express the contents of the entire protocol, is generally a subset of the vocabulary used by the subject or suggested by the task statement.

If a coarse analysis is desired, the researcher may segment and encode the protocol on the basis of aggregates of behavior rather than on the basis of single statements. For example, in a study of algebra problem solving, if the goal is to detail subjects' algebraic manipulations, each individual arithmetic operation is probably not of interest. Accordingly, instead of chronicling every use of the operators add, subtract, multiply, and divide, a sequence of such operators could be grouped together and encoded with the operator calculate. Or, solution steps may be grouped more globally into units such as collect constants or isolate variables.

In the third phase of protocol analysis, the researcher analyzes the explicit clues contained in the encoded protocol in order to develop a model of the subject's cognitive activities. A process model is a detailed theory of behavior expressing goal structures, operators, conditions for application of operators, component processes, and requisite knowledge. In its most rigorous expression, the model might take the form of a computer program that produces the same behaviors (outputs) as the subject(s) given the same input. In order to develop a process model, the researcher must identify patterns, primarily repetitions of the same or similar behavior occurring under the same or similar circumstances, in the protocol data. Such repetitions make it possible for the researcher to distinguish consistent processes governing the use of operators from idiosyncratic or random processes and to induce with confidence what those processes are and under what circumstances the subject is likely to employ them (7).

In addition, once the process model is complete, the researcher might analyze errors to determine the circumstances under which subjects deviate from the typical pattern of behavior and the point in the process at which they do so. If, instead of developing a new model, he has already developed a theory of behavior and/or computer simulation based on a careful task analysis, the literature, or exploratory research, the researcher may desire to test the validity of his model empirically by comparing it with the new protocol data. Alternatively, the researcher may wish to compare the model developed for one subject with those developed for other subjects to specify the effect of variables, such as level of expertise or the type of problem solved, or to evaluate the range of individual differences.

Problems with Protocol Analysis

The great range of possibilities for encoding and analysis makes protocol methodology a potentially powerful, multipurpose tool for researchers with diverse goals. By providing direct evidence for cognitive processes, protocol analysis can facilitate development of accurate, detailed models in many domains. But there is a catch. Protocol analysis is a difficult, time-consuming, and largely ill-defined task. The problems begin in the encoding phase. Devising an encoding vocabulary is not a trivial matter; it requires some notion of the task environment as well as familiarity with the actual protocols to be encoded. Moreover, once an encoding language is defined and some substantial portion of a protocol encoded according to it, re-coding the protocol if the scheme is modified is tedious and time-consuming. Even more troublesome is the challenge of reliably coding an entire protocol, particularly a long and complex one, according to the defined vocabulary. It is one thing to code the first few statements in a protocol faithfully according to the scheme but quite another to encode statement 1000 as faithfully as statement one.

Problems multiply in the analysis phase because finding patterns in a large data set requires the simultaneous consideration of many statements as opposed to the sequential consideration of single statements required in the encoding phase. If the data set is particularly large or complex, or the patterns in it intricate or infrequent, which is usually the case in programming studies, modeling complex processes may be difficult; verbal patterns representing the processes may be widely spaced in the protocol or may be missing steps (which subjects either skipped or failed to mention).

The lack of a simple way to learn protocol analysis methodology further complicates matters. The technique is generally acquired through apprenticeship, experimentation, and examples. But few researchers have the luxury of a teacher or the time for extensive trial and error. In addition, few publications about protocol analysis exist, and even the most comprehensive text on the subject (5) includes only sketchy instructions on practical protocol analysis techniques. The best and most extensive source of guidance for the novice remains a collection of example analyses provided by Newell and Simon (7) from which the careful reader may extract some general principles of the methodology.

Coping with the Problems

Given the difficulties inherent in protocol analysis and the complexity of the programming domain, it is not surprising that researchers studying computer programming often limit the extent to which they use this valuable methodology. One strategy is to concentrate on one small portion of the total task and examine it in detail. For example, Atwood, Polson, Jeffries, and Ramsey (8) focused only on program planning, while Brooks (9) focused his analysis only on program coding.

Another approach to reducing the difficulty inherent in protocol analysis is to sample only small portions of the total information contained in the protocols, scanning for global characteristics or searching for one particular type of clue to the programmer's processes. For example, Anderson, Farrell, and Sauers (10) gathered extensive protocols of subjects learning Lisp but used only "protocol schematics," their "intuitive characterizations of the essential features of the protocols," in their analysis. In a similar manner, Littman, Pinto, Letovsky, and Soloway (11) used protocols as anecdotal evidence for identifying general strategy types and trends. Adelson and Soloway (12) also focused on the behavior subjects exhibited, not on their verbalizations, and used the verbal portions of protocols simply as anecdotes. In addition, most researchers reduce the difficulty of protocol analysis by limiting the number of subjects they study; for instance, only one of the studies just mentioned included more than five subjects.

Although reducing the unwieldiness of protocol analysis by limiting its scope makes it easier to conduct, it also limits its effectiveness. Snapshots of the programmer's journey may not as accurately describe his route as would a video chronicle. But how can a researcher effectively produce such an active and detailed record of complex behavior? My theses is that a computer-aided protocol analysis system could facilitate these efforts by streamlining the difficult encoding phase and expiditing and extending the range of possible analyses.

Computer-Aided Protocol Analysis

PAW, the Protocol Analyst's Workbench, attempts to reduce the difficulty of conducting protocol analysis by assisting the user with some portions of the protocol analysis process while completely automating others. The system is designed to capitalize on the strengths while minimizing the weaknesses of both humans and computers. While natural language processing remains a difficult problem in artificial intelligence, humans excel at manipulating natural language with seemingly little effort. Therefore, PAW does not encode the raw protocol automatically, but rather guides the user in making the translation, encouraging consistent encapsulation of the original data. While humans are good at natural language processing, they are poor at coping with large amounts of data; limited working memory size and costly long-term memory storage and retrieval operations make recognizing and comparing patterns difficult for people. Yet, to perform data analyses well, especially analyses on data as potentially complex and varied as protocol data, this is precisely what must be done. Fortunately, computers excel at manipulating large amounts of different types of data and at performing a variety of search and match operations. PAW, therefore, embodies a host of analysis routines that are carried out automatically when the user selects them. The work of protocol analysis, then, is divided between the user, who performs the data encoding with help from the system, and the computer, which performs all the analyses.

The PAW system is qualitatively different from the two previous attempts at automated protocol analysis. Waterman and Newell (13, 14) developed Protocol Analysis Systems I and II (PAS-I and PAS-II) that included linguistic and semantic processors to cope with natural language input and generated a problem behavior graph as output. Both PAS systems succeeded in being completely automated only by using one predefined vocabulary and problem space definition (for cryptarithmetic); thus it was useful studying only one domain. Bhaskar and Simon (15) constructed a similarly limited system for studying thermodynamics problem solving, SAPA (Semi-Automated Protocol Analysis). Using its built-in model of thermodynamics problem spaces and strategies, it prompted the user to enter information about subject behavior and produced an encoded protocol. Unlike both of these systems, PAW is a *multipurpose* computer aide. The user constructs the vocabulary of the domain interactively while entering data and determines which analyses she wishes to conduct on it. Thus, the system is useful for a wide variety researchers studying a wide variety of task domains.

In this paper, I will demonstrate the benefits of using such a computerized system to deepen our understanding of expert of programming processes. I have collected

60 hours of video-taped protocol data from six expert programmers, and, without the assistance of a computer-aided protocol analysis system, formulated a general characterization of the processes involved in the task, as well as a list of strategies and knowledge utilized by the subjects (16). I will briefly summarize these findings in the following sections in order to make clear the types of significant clues these typical analyses fail to glean from rich protocol data. In subsequent sections I describe how the PAW system facilitates reliable protocol encoding, demonstrate how PAW has been able to extract additional information from the data thus far, and suggest what further applications might be useful for studying computer programming.

A PROTOCOL STUDY OF EXPERT PROGRAMMERS

Six advanced computer science graduate students at Carnegie-Mellon University were videotaped as they solved two complex programming problems. Subjects were selected from a larger pool of volunteers (all male) on the basis of their programming language preferences. Three of the subjects were recruited to program in Lisp and three to program in C. All received pay for their participation.

Neither of the two problems used, though challenging, required any highly specialized knowledge or techniques that might be beyond the expertise of the subjects; both were fairly realistic data-management problems. One, a program to

Table 1: The key problem used in the programming study.

The Psychology Department has been having difficulty keeping track of who has which keys to access which rooms and by whose authorization. Your job is to write a computer program that will facilitate the record keeping. There are four types of information involved: the key holders, the key numbers, the room(s) they access, and the authorizers. The user should be able to input any one type of information to get all of the information related to it.

So,

Input	Output		
key holder	key1	room(s)1	authorizer1
	key2	room(s)2	authorizer2...
key number	room(s) accessed		
	number remaining		
	holder1	authorizer1	
	holder2	authorizer2...	
room number	keys accessing it		
	holder1	authorizer1	
	holder2	authorizer2...	
authorizer	holder1	key1	room(s)1
		key2	room(s)2
	holder2	key1	room(s)1...

Of course, the user must also be able to add and delete information as people receive and return keys. One complicating factor is that there are three types of keys: masters (which open all rooms), sub-masters (which open more than one room), and individual keys (which open only one room).

Table 2: The index problem used in the programming study.

A book publisher requires a system to produce a page-keyed index. This system will accept as input the source text of a book and produce as output a list of specified index terms and the page numbers on which each index term appears. You are to design a system to produce a page-keyed index. Each book to be indexed is stored in a file. Page numbers will be indicated on a line in the form /*nnn where /* are marker characters used to identify the occurrence of page numbers and nnn is the page number.

The page number will appear after a block of text that comprises the body of the page. Words are delimited by the following characters: space, period, comma, semi-colon, exclamation point, and line-feed. Words at the end of a line may be hyphenated and continued on the following line, but words will not be continued across page boundaries.

A list of terms to be indexed, will be read from a file. The term file contains one term per line, where a term is 1 to 5 words long.

The system should read the source file and term file and find all occurrences of each term to be indexed. The output should contain the index terms listed alphabetically with the page numbers following each term in numerical order.

Error messages and a termination message should be written to the operator's console. Each completed index is to be stored in a file for later listing.

manage the allocation of keys in a university psychology department (see Table 1), was suggested by an actual need in the psychology department at Carnegie-Mellon. The other, a program to produce a page-keyed index for a book (see Table 2), was drawn from Atwood and Jeffries (17) with a few modifications[1].

The subjects participated individually in two 5-hour sessions; all subjects received the key problem during their first session and the index problem during their second session (on a subsequent day). The instructions directed the subject to imagine that the session was simply the first five hours of an unspecified amount of time he would have to work on the problem; he was not expected to finish during the five hours. The subject was instructed to think aloud as he worked and the entire session was video-taped with one camera trained on the subject's computer terminal display and another on a pad of scratch paper he could use for notes and diagrams.

LIMITED ANALYSIS DONE BY HAND

The goal of this study was to develop a detailed model of expert computer programming, including goals, operators, and knowledge as well as the strategies that govern their use. Because of the size and complexity of the protocols gathered, the process model was initially developed from *one* protocol of *one* subject in the following way. Beginning at the point where the subject had read and understood the

---

[1] The original Atwood and Jeffries problem contained references to a card reader and files residing on disk. Because all subjects were writing on a Digital VAX computer running under the UNIX operating system with room to store files on-line, the requirements were changed to state that all data was to be stored in and read from a file.

problem statement, the protocol was divided into episodes, each comprising the statement or the execution of a single goal, and each episode was classified as belonging to one of three distinct categories: DESIGNING THE DATA REPRESENTATIONS, WRITING OPERATIONS, or DEBUGGING. A detailed process model of a typical episode in each category was then developed from *a few* episodes and subsequently refined to make it consistent with the other episodes within that category. Finally, the sufficiency of the model was verified against *samples* from the other subjects and the other problem. In addition to deriving the model of the processes, a list of the strategies and general types of knowledge evident in *samples* from all the protocols was also compiled.

Although the resulting model (see Figure 1) was developed from only a small *portion* of the available data, it appeared to describe all six subjects' behavior well for both problems. The model consists of the processes involved in computer programming as well as the context of the task environment and the programmer's long-term memory. The three phases or cycles of the programming process (REPRESENT DATA, WRITE OPERATIONS, and DEBUG) are depicted in the middle box of Figure 1, each node (e.g. **choose representational method, specify how these data fit**, etc.) signifying one goal or subgoal in the process. The arrows connecting the nodes indicate the possible paths the programmer might take through the process. The process is recursive; any goal or subgoal may return to itself or to the top level goal in its own cycle. (For the sake of simplicity, the arrows representing recursive paths are not drawn.)

In general, the process proceeds as follows. Initially, the programmer specifies the DATA REPRESENTATION and evaluates it with respect to the goodness of the representation itself and, eventually, with respect to the operations that must be performed on it. Completing this evaluation leads to the initial goal in the WRITE OPERATIONS cycle of the model. The programmer specifies the action of the operation (at any level) and then decomposes or composes it with other operations until a programming method is known for solving the sub-problem at its current level of decomposition. The programmer then evaluates the operation just planned or coded; a negative result from any of the three possible evaluation types (evaluation with respect to the operation itself, with respect to other functions or operations, or with respect to the representation) indicates that DEBUGGING is necessary. After identifying and locating a problem, the programmer selects an appropriate fix. If the problem was a simple one, the fix is made and the debug cycle entered again to evaluate the newly modified code. If the problem was a more complex, structural one, then the programmer returns to re-represent the data or re-specify the action of the operations.

The task environment (the top box in Figure 1) includes conditions that affect the programming process, such as the task requirements (as the subject understands them) and the part of the solution he has already completed. Knowledge the programmer brings to the task (outlined at the bottom of Figure 1) also affects the programming process. This knowledge includes a set of programming strategies. Unlike the rigid top-down, breadth-first expansion of programming plans suggested by other researchers (8, 17, 18), my data suggest a more flexible process driven by these strategies in different directions at different times.

While the model characterizes six programmers with very different backgrounds using two very different languages well, it leaves many questions unanswered. The

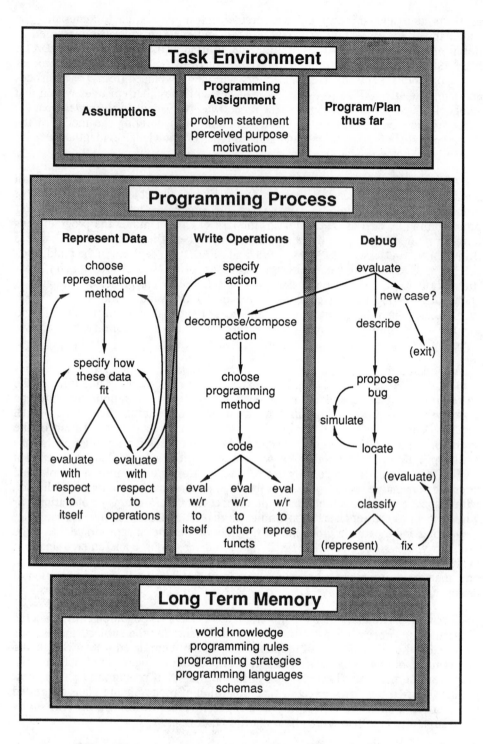

Figure 1: Overview of the programming process in context.

model primarily describes <u>what</u> experts do not <u>how</u> they do it. For example, the model does not specify <u>how</u> a programmer selects a particular programming strategy, nor does it suggest <u>how</u> a programmer chooses a data representation, <u>how</u> he develops a programming method, or <u>how</u> he evaluates his work.

My contention is that a computer-aided protocol analysis system could perform the complex analyses, difficult or impossible for the researcher to conduct by hand, that are necessary to answer questions like these. At the same time, such a system could make the analyses researchers can do by hand easier, faster, and more flexible, as well as more reliable.

PAW: PROTOCOL ANALYST'S WORKBENCH

PAW is being developed in response to two primary problems with using protocol analysis methodology for studying expert programming: 1) encoding the data reliably is difficult because the protocols are usually lengthy and intricate, and 2) the complex analyses necessary to answer the <u>how</u> questions are almost impossible to perform by hand since patterns in the data are usually large, complex, and, as such, elusive. As a consequence, PAW performs two distinct functions: one to guide the user in encoding data reliably and allow the user to modify and update data already entered, and one to perform analyses on the data once they have been encoded. Each of these functions is discussed briefly in the following sections.

Encoding

PAW allows the user both to translate each statement into the appropriate encoding vocabulary and, optionally, to supplement each statement with some additional information. The translation captures what actually occurred in the protocol (what was said or done). At this level, the data are represented as objectively as possible; ideally, reading the translation should be as informative as reading the original. Supplementation, on the other hand, allows the user to categorize statements into different types, such as goals, actions, or comments, or to include any appropriate but not necessarily explicitly stated information from the protocols, such as a time stamp or a note about whether the subject was writing or typing.

The system template for data encoding allows both the translation and supplementation of statements to be captured (see Table 3). For translation purposes (Level 1), the focal point is the action reflected by the statement. Associated with each action is a series of descriptors defined by the user the first time that action is entered. The encoding of a particular statement includes the values the user supplies for each descriptor at Level 1. The unique statement number that precedes the action

Table 3: Data encoding template for a single statement.

			descriptor	descriptor	descriptor...
LEVEL 2:		supplement	value	value	value...
			descriptor	descriptor	descriptor...
LEVEL 1:	num	action	value	value	value...

is automatically generated by the system. For supplementation purposes (Level 2), the focal point is a statement supplement. Supplements also have descriptors defined by the user and values associated with each statement encoded.

The following example illustrates the difference between translation and supplementation of a single protocol statement such as: "Later I think I'll worry about what a room looks like." The words "what a room looks like" and the context (the programmer had just designed data representations for the various objects in the key problem--holders, keys, and authorizers) suggest that this statement is an instance of the REPRESENT DATA phase in the process model. The encoded statement, as represented by PAW, is shown in Table 4. In this case, the subject is considering designing a representation for rooms. The tense of the statement indicates that this action will occur later and "I think" suggests that the action may or may not happen. The statement also could be supplemented with a categorization of the statement. The example statement could be categorized as a goal, reflected by the assertion "I'll." In this case, the goal is postponed since the subject indicates his intent to represent a room but not until "later."

The vocabulary for PAW's two-level data representation is not built into the system. Unlike the PAS (Newell, 1972) and SAPA (Bhaskar and Simon, 1977) systems, PAW is domain independent. That is, it has no knowledge of any actions, supplements, or possible descriptors initially, but rather builds a vocabulary as the user enters data. PAW's open vocabulary allows it to be used *without modification* by researchers with a wide range of research goals studying a wide range of behaviors.

In order to build its vocabulary, the system allows the user to enter action or supplement terms at any time during the encoding process. The new terms are added to its database along with any descriptors the user supplies. Once an action or supplement and its descriptors are in the database, any time that term is subsequently used, the system asks the user to enter values for each of the descriptors associated with it, although the user is never *required* to supply values for any or all of the descriptors. Because the system stores templates associated with each action or supplement, the user is not burdened with the necessity of remembering previous encoding in order to be consistent.

In addition to facilitating the initial encoding of protocol data, PAW's openness allows the user to change any portion of her encoding scheme at any time. For example, not only can new action or supplement terms be added, but more descriptors can be added to any existing term at any time. Furthermore, statements already entered into the database can be modified, moved, or deleted from the

Table 4: Sample encoding of a statement.

| Statement: | "Later I think I'll worry about what a room looks like" |

Encoding:

	<u>status</u>		
goal	postpone		
	<u>what</u>	<u>when</u>	<u>certainty</u>
33 represent	rooms	later	I think

encoded protocol and additional statements can be inserted at any time. Any modifications made in the coding scheme or to the previously entered protocol are retroactive; that is, the portion of the protocol already encoded is updated to be consistent with the new scheme. For example, if the user had been using **test** as an action but decided **evaluate** was a more accurate term, all occurrences of **test** in the protocol already encoded would be changed to **evaluate**. (PAW also allows the user to designate synonymous terms and associates the same list of descriptors with each synonym.) This flexibility allows the user to develop a coding scheme as she codes the data rather than having to specify the entire scheme at the outset. It also allows the user to experiment with different possible encoding schemes that would be too time consuming to do by hand.

Analysis

The goal of the system's data analysis is to uncover patterns in protocol data that reflect cognitive processing, particularly those that might otherwise be obscured by the size or complexity of the data set. Once the data are entered, PAW allows the user to select from a variety of possible analyses. For example, PAW can build general characterizations of _what_ subjects do (a process model), just as I did by hand. PAW, however, uses _all_ the data. In addition, PAW performs analyses designed to help answer the _how_ questions. For example, it can generate a flow model to capture the process the subject used, it can produce a trace of the behavior to illustrate the solution path, it can isolate individual cycles within the process model to suggest why one path was followed rather than another, and it can compare these analyses across data sets. All of these analyses are based on the sequence of actions as they occur in the protocol. Furthermore, PAW allows the user to fine tune the analyses by manipulating the encoded protocol. For example, statements containing particular actions or supplements can be temporarily eliminated from the data set or actions (e.g. **add** and **subtract**) can be temporarily combined into one, more general action (e.g. **calculate**). In the following sections I will illustrate some of PAW's data analyses and describe how PAW dealt with some of the _what_ and _how_ questions encountered in my study of expert programming. I will provide a glimpse of several available analyses in order to demonstrate the way in which PAW facilitates progressively deeper understanding of the complex processes involved in computer programming.

Path analysis. PAW can generate a detailed process model from extensive protocol data in a matter of moments. In addition, unlike the hand-done model development described previously, PAW can model each subject's process independently. Thus, it is possible to compare flow diagrams to determine the overall generality of the process. The following example, based on the expert programming protocols, demonstrates PAW's basic modeling capabilities and the useful comparisons the resulting information facilitates. Figures 2 and 3 show the data representation process diagrams based on PAW's output for two subjects, s1 and s3, both of whom programmed in Lisp.

The primary operators used by each subject are represented in the boxes in Figures 2 and 3. For s3 (Figure 3) these include **read**ing the text of the problem, **paraphras**ing it, **represent**ing a segment of the data, retrieving or modifying knowledge, and finally **evaluat**ing the knowledge or representation choice. These operators are also central to the process model of s1. The additional operators in

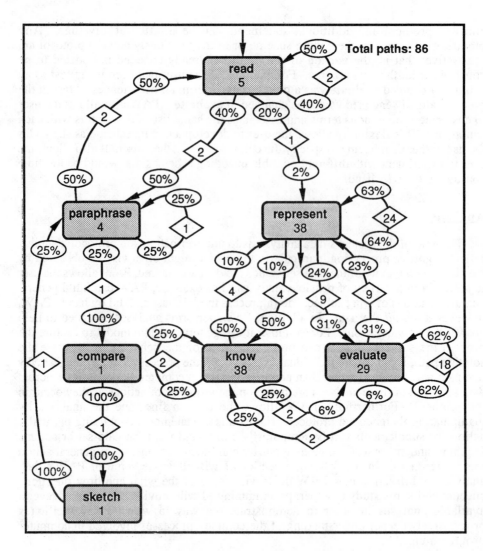

Figure 2: Flow model for s1.

Figure 2, each used only once, are examples of intrusions of <u>operation writing</u> that was continued later in the protocol. In fact, when those additional operators are temporarily removed from the database before building the models, the resulting models are strikingly similar.

Much more detailed comparisons are possible with these flow diagrams than were possible with the hand-crafted model because PAW provides temporal information as well as quantitative information about the absolute and relative number of times each sequence of operators is applied. The arrows in the flow diagrams represent the temporal sequencing of operators. The number in each operator box indicates the number of times it was used (e.g. **represent** 29 in Figure 3), and the numbers in triangles on incoming arrows show how many times an operator followed each other operator (**represent** followed **evaluate** 7 times in Figure 3). Finally, the percentage on either end of each arrow indicates the percent of times one operator led

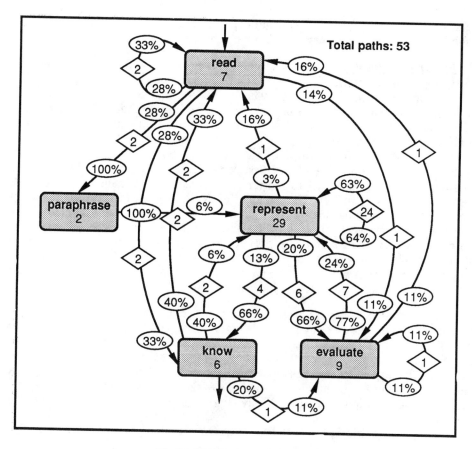

Figure 3: Flow model for s3.

to or followed another operator. For example, **evaluate** led to **represent** 77% of the time (7 of 9) and **represent** followed **evaluate** 24% of the time (7 of 29).

It is possible use this additional information to pinpoint those specific portions of individual models that are almost identical and those that are quite different. First, by following the arrows and the left to right sequence of operators, it becomes apparent that the **read** and **paraphrase** operators were used differently by these two subjects. S1 **read** and **paraphrased** the text before moving to the **represent»know»evaluate** loop and never applied those operators again. The other subject, however, returned to the **read»paraphrase** loop at times during the **represent»know»evaluate** phase of the process as indicated by the paths leading back to **read** from the **represent, know,** and **evaluate** operators.

Both subjects arrived at the final format of their data representation by the end of the cycles represented here (although some small revisions were made as they designed operations and debugged). S3 accomplished the data representation by a more efficient process than did s1, making only 53 traversals of paths compared with s1's 86 traversals. S1 evaluated potential representations more extensively than did s3 (29 versus 9 **evaluate** operator applications including 18 re-evaluations -- 20% of all operator applications), and revised his representation more during the process (38 versus 29 **represent** operator applications). S1 also searched his knowledge base slightly more frequently (8 versus 6 **know** operator applications).

Frequency of paths. While observing the similarities and differences between what subjects do is informative, it is even more informative to compare how they do it. We can begin to address this issue by looking more carefully at the data, comparing individual cycles. Since most of the activity in these protocol samples takes place in the **represent»know»evaluate** cycle, I will provide an example analysis of the cycles beginning with the **represent** node. PAW can display the frequency of all the different paths, or cycles, from any node back to itself. The cycles for **represent** are listed in the first part of Tables 5 and 6 for subjects s1 and s3 along with the frequency of occurrence (for example, s1 made two successive **represent** actions 24 times). The sequence of cycles is shown in the second half of the tables; each entry has the form < cycle number [frequency] >. For example, in Table 5, the sequence begins with 3 instances of cycle 1 (**represent»represent**) followed by 1 instance of cycle 8 (**represent»know»represent**). Further discussion will focus on the simplest and most frequent path types; these include **r e p r e s e n t » r e p r e s e n t , r e p r e s e n t » k n o w » r e p r e s e n t ,** and **represent»evaluate»represent** (printed in bold in Tables 5 and 6).

A fairly consistent pattern emerges from these paths. It is apparent that multiple **r e p r e s e n t » r e p r e s e n t** cycles are often grouped together. Groups of **r e p r e s e n t » r e p r e s e n t** cycles are frequently followed by either **represent»evaluate»represent** or **represent»know»represent** cycles indicating that expansions of data representation goals or plans are either followed by knowledge lookups in memory or evaluations of their appropriateness. This pattern raises several questions, including "Why do **represent»represent** cycles come in

Table 5: Cycle tallies for s1 from node **represent**.

#	freq.	cycle
Cycles from node represent:		
1.	24	**represent -> represent**
2.	4	**represent -> evaluate -> represent**
3.	1	represent -> evaluate -> evaluate -> represent
4.	1	represent -> evaluate -> evaluate -> evaluate -> represent
5.	1	represent -> evaluate -> evaluate -> evaluate -> evaluate -> evaluate -> evaluate -> represent
6.	1	represent -> evaluate -> evaluate -> know -> represent
7.	1	represent -> evaluate -> evaluate -> know -> know -> evaluate -> evaluate -> evaluate -> evaluate -> evaluate -> evaluate -> evaluate -> represent
8.	2	**represent -> know -> represent**
9.	1	represent -> know -> evaluate -> evaluate -> evaluate -> represent
10.	1	represent -> know -> know -> represent

The sequence of cycles is:
1 [3] -> 8 [1] -> 1 [3] -> 8 [1] -> 1 [4] -> 2 [1] -> 1 [11] -> 2 [1] -> 4 [1] -> 1 [1] -> 5 [1] -> 3 [1] -> 1 [1] -> 2 [1] -> 1 [1] -> 10 [1] -> 7 [1] -> 2 [1] -> 6 [1] -> 9 [1]

Table 6: Cycle tallies for s3 from node **represent**.

Cycles from node represent:

#	freq.	cycle
1.	18	**represent -> represent**
2.	4	**represent -> evaluate -> represent**
3.	1	represent -> evaluate -> evaluate -> represent
4.	1	represent -> evaluate -> read -> paraphrase -> represent
5.	2	**represent -> know -> represent**
6.	1	represent -> know -> evaluate -> represent
7.	1	represent -> read -> know -> read -> know -> read -> evaluate -> represent

The sequence of cycles is:
1 [1] -> 7 [1] -> 5 [1] -> 4 [1] -> 1 [6] -> 5 [1] -> 1 [5] -> 2 [1] -> 1 [1]
-> 6 [1] -> 1 [2] -> 2 [1] -> 3 [1] -> 1 [1] -> 2 [1] -> 1 [2] -> 2 [1]

---

groups?" and "What determines whether the subject then seeks knowledge or evaluation?" For the purpose of this description, I present a deeper analysis of the **represent»represent** cycle to answer the first of these questions.

Characterization of paths. PAW can display, almost immediately, every instance of any particular path traversed. Tables 7 and 8 are excerpts from the listing of **represent»represent** paths for s1. Each table displays one instance of multiple consecutive **represent»represent** paths. These groupings embody times when the subject is listing individual items in the projected data representation. These listings are of two types. Table 7 shows an example of *breadth-first* expansion; the subject

Table 7: Example of breadth-first expansion.

	goal	status
		set
		what
12	represent	holder
	goal	status
		set
		what
13	represent	key
	goal	status
		set
		what
13	represent	key
	goal	status
		set
		what
14	represent	room
	goal	status
		set
		what
14	represent	room
	goal	status
		set
		what
15	represent	authorizer

Table 8: Example of depth-first expansion.

plan	recorded	source		
	written	construct		
	what	content		
38 represent	holder	holder/key/rooms/authorizer		
plan	recorded	source		
	written	construct		
	what	content	reason	
39 represent	key	rooms	multiple rooms per key	
plan	recorded	source		
	written	construct		
	what	content	reason	
39 represent	key	rooms	multiple rooms per key	
plan	source			
	restate			
	what	how		
40 represent	key	integer		
plan	source			
	restate			
	what	how		
40 represent	key	integer		
goal	status			
	set			
	what			
41 represent	masters			
goal	status			
	set			
	what			
41 represent	masters			
goal	status			
	set			
	what			
42 represent	submasters			
goal	status			
	set			
	what			
42 represent	submasters			
plan	recorded	source		
	written	construct		
	what	how	content	
43 represent	submasters	list	rooms	

(s1) is simply listing the information that must be included in the data representation for the key problem (holder, key, room, and authorizer). In contrast, the excerpt in Table 8 shows an example of a *depth-first* expansion by the same subject; the subject is refining the data representation for keys by considering all necessary types of key information and their representations (individual keys as integers, and masters and submasters as lists of rooms). By listing and comparing instances of identical paths, it is clear that the subject approaches data representation in both a breadth-first and depth-first manner. Further comparisons across subjects and problems could be done to uncover the conditions under which subjects choose one or the other approach.

To summarize, PAW has been developed to provide researchers with the tools they need to answer difficult questions about complex processes. The system facilitates consistent encoding of protocols and provides automatic analyses that can be tailored to the particular research questions being addressed. PAW generates a process model by calculating the sequence and frequency of actions in whatever portion of the protocol data the researcher selects. Any part of this model can then be analyzed in terms of individual occurrences of particular actions or combinations of actions to reveal patterns in the descriptors or supplemental information. These patterns may, themselves, provoke further questions that can be addressed with the tools PAW provides.

CONCLUSION

In response to researchers' difficulty with both encoding and analyzing complex verbal protocols, PAW has been designed to improve the reliability of encoding by maintaining a user-defined vocabulary and to extend the possible analyses by effectively manipulating large data sets. Because the system is fast and flexible, it allows the user to experiment with different types of encoding and analyses without much cost in terms of time or energy. Being able to delve deeper into the cognitive processes involved in programming has made it possible to begin to specify the conditions under which subjects follow different solution paths. All three phases of the general programming model (REPRESENTING DATA, WRITING OPERATIONS, and DEBUGGING) are currently being analyzed in similar depth and the results compared across subjects, problems, and languages. In addition to being useful in my own studies of programming, PAW is designed to be useful as a general tool for other researchers studying programming and other complex task domains. Furthermore, PAW can be helpful for teaching protocol analysis since it structures the coding process and has many typical analyses built into it. In these ways, PAW and the analyses it facilitates can advance both the study of the complex processes involved in programming and the research technique of protocol analysis.

ACKNOWLEDGEMENTS

This research was supported by a National Science Foundation Graduate Study grant. Many thanks to Herbert Simon and Sharon Carver for helpful comments on earlier drafts of this paper and to Herbert Simon, David Klahr, Kurt VanLehn, and Jill Larkin for their continuing guidance and support.

REFERENCES

1.   Siegler, R. S. (1978). The origins of scientific reasoning. In R. S. Siegler (Ed.), *Children's thinking: What develops?* Hillsdale, N.J.: Erlbaum.

2.   Clark, H. H., and Chase, W. G. (1972). On the process of comparing sentences against pictures. *Cognitive Psychology, 3*, 472-517.

3.   Sternberg, S. (1969). The discovery of processing stages: Extensions of Donders' method. *Acta Psychologica, 30*, 276-315.

4.   Ericsson, K. A. & Simon, H. A. (1980). Verbal reports as data. *Psychological Review, 87, 3*, 215-251.

5.   Ericsson, K. A. & Simon, H. A. (1984). *Protocol analysis.* Cambridge, MA: MIT Press.

6. Soloway, E. (1986). What to do next: Meeting the challenge of programming-in-the-large. In Soloway, E. & Iyengar, S (Eds.), *Empirical studies of programmers*. Norwood, NJ: Ablex.

7. Newell, A. & Simon, H. A. (1972). *Human problem solving*. Englewood Cliffs, N.J.: Prentice-Hall.

8. Atwood, M. E., Polson, P. G., Jeffries, R., & Ramsey, H. R. (1978). *Planning as a process of syntheses*. (Tech. Rep. SAI-78-144-DEN). Science Applications, Inc.

9. Brooks, R. (1977). Towards a theory of the cognitive processes in computer programming. *International Journal of Man-Machine Studies, 9*, 737-751.

10. Anderson, J. R., Farrell, R., & Sauers, R. (1984). Learning to program in LISP. *Cognitive Science, 8*, 87-129.

11. Littman, D. C., Pinto, J., Letovsky, S., & Soloway, E. (1986). Mental models and software maintenance. In Soloway, E. & Iyengar, S (Eds.), *Empirical studies of programmers*. Norwood, NJ: Ablex.

12. Adelson, B., & Soloway, E. (1985). The role of domain experience in software design. *IEEE Transactions on Software Engineering SE-11*, November 1985.

13. Waterman, D. A. & Newell, A. (1971). Protocol analysis as a task for artificial intelligence. *Artificial Intelligence, 2*, 285-318.

14. Waterman, D. A. & Newell, A. (1973). *PAS-II: An interactive task-free version of an automatic protocol analysis system*. Pittsburgh: Department of Computer Science, Carnegie-Mellon University.

15. Bhaskar, R. & Simon, H. A. (1977). Problem solving in semantically rich domains: An example from engineering thermodynamics. Cognitive Science, 1, 193-215.

16. Fisher, C. A. (1986). *How do programmers program: Coping with complexity*. Unpublished manuscript. Carnegie-Mellon University.

17. Atwood, M. E. & Jeffries, R. (1980). *Studies in plan construction I: Analysis of an extended protocol*. (Tech. Rep. SAI-80-028-DEN). Science Applications, Inc.

18. Jeffries, R., Turner, A. A., Polson, P. G., & Atwood, M. E. (1981). The processes involved in designing software. In Anderson, J. R. (Ed.), *Cognitive skills and their acquisition*. Hillsdale, NJ: Erlbaum.

CHAPTER 14

Strategies in Programming Programmable Controllers:
A Field Study on a Professional Programmer

Willemien Visser
Projet de Psychologie Ergonomique pour l'Informatique
Institut National de Recherche en Informatique et en Automatique
Domaine de Voluceau - Rocquencourt
B.P.105 - 78105 Le Chesnay (France)

ABSTRACT

One of the questions raised at the end of the First Workshop on Empirical Programmers (see 17), and which subsequently became the title of a Future Directions paper, was "By the way, did anyone study any real programmers?" (7). Our answer is "Yes." It is our wish in presenting this paper to contribute to the understanding of some aspects of "programming-in-the-large," in particular those concerning the specific strategies that the programmer uses.

A professional programmer constructing a program that was to control an automatic machine tool installation was observed full time for four weeks in his daily work.

In this paper, we chose to focus on the strategies used, under the hypothesis that they differ, at least partially, from those observed to date in most novice, student programmers working on artificial, limited problems.

We observed some strategies already known to be at work in "programming-in-the-small": planning, top-down and bottom-up processing, schema-guided information processing. However, other strategies seem indeed to be characteristic of programming in a work context: the frequent use of example programs, the importance of analogical reasoning, and the search for homogeneity (for comprehension and maintenance reasons). Finally, the opportunistic nature of the activity we observed also seems to be a characteristic of real programming activity.

INTRODUCTION

Most studies on computer programming to date involve an activity:
- performed by more or less experienced novices with little or, more commonly, no professional experience, most often students involved in a learning rather than a work situation;
- starting with a rather simplified, ad hoc problem;
- observed in an experimental setting;
- involving a program from some ten to a few hundred lines at most;
- using a more or less "classical" programming language such as FORTRAN or PASCAL

(see 17, 16).

Specifically, the task and subject characteristics in these studies (novices and/or students working on artificial, limited problems) probably place severe limitations on the validity of the results for "real" programming activity and therefore on their usefulness for the construction of programming aids.

There are some notable exceptions to this characterization (7). Hoc (13) has researched programming by subjects working on quite realistic problems. Valentin (19) studied professional programmers working on management problems in a real work context.

The study we present in this paper deals with:
- an experienced professional programmer,
- solving a real, complex industrial problem (control of a machine tool installation),
- observed during his daily activities, in his real working environment, that is, depending, for example, on information from colleagues (specifications and other information),
- constructing a program of about 1200 instructions (which, due to the type of programming language used, represent many more "lines" (see below Programmable Controller & Programming Language Used)),
- using a kind of programming language that has not yet been studied (a declarative boolean language designed for programmable controllers).

Since our hypothesis was that the aspect of programming behavior most likely to differ in a fairly large, workrelated project was the strategies used, we chose to present these strategies in this first paper on our study.

METHOD

An Observational Study

We conducted full time observations on a professional programmer in a machine tool factory for a period of four weeks. We observed his normal daily activities without intervening in any way, other than to ask him to verbalize as much as possible his thoughts about what he was doing (10, 15).

We collected notes concerning:
- all the programmer's comments and writings;
- the order in which he produced the different documents, and how he gradually built them up;
- the changes he made;
- the information sources consulted;
- events we judged to be indicators of the subject meeting with difficulties.

In addition, we collected all documents produced by the programmer during his work:
- the diagrams and schemas he constructed for himself during analysis and problem solving;
- the different versions of these documents and of the program;
- the rough drafts of (parts of) them.

The Observed Programmer

The observed programmer received two years specialized university training in electronics.

At the time of observation, he had been working for four years as a professional programmer with programmable controllers and the mechanical installations they control.

The Observed Task

The programmer was to construct a program for a programmable controller controlling an automatic machine tool installation, based on the specifications given.

He wrote this program in three main stages. We observed the entire first stage, during which he constructed the first part of the program, which was to control the installation.

Programmable Controller & Programming Language Used

A programmable controller is a computer specialized in controlling industrial processes, in this case a machine tool installation. Greatly simplified, it receives input on the state of the process, mostly from detectors on the installation it controls; the processing of this information (together with internal information) produces output, that is, commands governing installation functions, e.g., shaping operations.

The language used for programming the programmable controller is a declarative boolean language. The most frequently used instructions, called "sequences," control the installation's sequential functioning. They assign logical values to variables.

The logical value results from the evaluation of a logical expression consisting of a boolean combination of bits. The variable which holds the resulting value corresponds to (a) a programmable controller output, that is, a function or a display on the controlled installation or (b) an intermediate variable (see below).

The general semantics of a sequence is the following:
IF the conditions are satisfied
THEN set the result variable to 1
ELSE set the result variable to 0

The following is an example of such an instruction:
(E234 + /E56) B35 = A67
That is, bit A67 will be assigned the value resulting from the evaluation of the following logical expression:
```
(          (the value of bit E234  )
    OR NOT (the value of bit E56   ))
AND the value of bit B35
```

The E bits correspond to the programmable controller's physical inputs and the A bits to its physical outputs. They constitute its basic elements of information. The B bits are derived. They correspond to intermediate variables, that is, combinations of Es and/or As (and/or other intermediate variables).

In the instruction presented above, the bit A67 corresponds, e.g., to the jack for the Advance movement of a cutting tool; E56 to the component detecting the end of this Advance movement; E234 to the detector of the end of its preceding operation; B35 to a combination of conditons that must been satisfied for the operation to occur in mechanical safety.

The program, composed of a series of instructions, is continuously read ("scanned") by the programmable controller. At the end of each scan (< 50 ms), all the E bits and physical output are updated. In other words, the electrical state of each physical input is translated into a logical value for the corresponding E bit, and the logical value of each A bit is translated into an electrical state of the corresponding physical output. Thus, each instruction assigning a value to an A leads, after a maximum of 50 ms, to the activation or inhibition of an operation or display on the installation, according to the logical state of A.

The language can be written in two different ways: in boolean expressions or in relay diagram equations. Programs or program instructions written in one format can be read in the other on the screen of the programming terminal.

Figure 1 presents the relay diagram equation for the example written above in boolean expression.

$$\begin{array}{ccc} & E234 & B35 \\ & /E56 & \end{array} \quad \left(A67\right)$$

Figure 1. Relay diagram equation for the boolean expression
(E234 + /E56) B35 = A67

Parallel instructions or groups of instructions, such as E234 and /E56 here, are said to constitute different instruction "branches." The example we have given shows a very simple kind of instruction. Most instructions are composed of different branches, each one containing from about three to eight bits (see Figure 2).

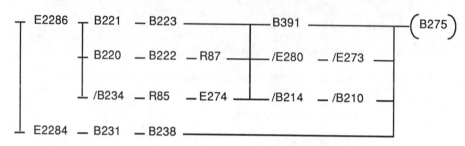

Figure 2. An example of an instruction from the studied program[1]

Comparison of Programmable Controller and "Classical" Programming

Most studies on "classical" programming deal with numerical computations or symbolical data processing resolved in procedural languages (such as Pascal).

The programming of controllers mainly involves defining the activation of physical actions on a controlled process according to the state of this process.

The activation of an action is not defined in a procedural but in a declarative way as a boolean combination of its conditions.

The syntax of the language permits each action to have only one definition in the program, that is, each action may figure only once as the result of a sequence. Most actions however may take place in several states of the process. So this programming amounts to building, for each action, a combination of the different configurations of conditions under which it may occur.

As different actions may share conditions, groups of conditions are gathered into intermediate variables. Many of these variables are themselves combined into other, higher level, intermediate variables (see the example given in figure 2). So, rather than expressing the conditions for an action to occur in terms of (the E bits corresponding to) physical conditions, the programmer combines higher level units whose correspondence to the physical state of the installation is not immediate.

Physical Layout of the Installation Controlled by the Program Written by the Observed Programmer

The installation is composed of four "stations." A central turntable rotates to bring and position the pieces in front of each of them. The pieces are conveyed onto and from the loading-unloading station by a system of conveyors (see Figure 3).

---

[1] R corresponds to a bit similar to B.

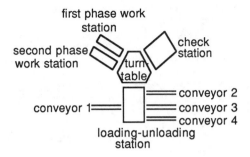

first phase work
station

second phase
work station

check
station

turn
table

conveyor 2
conveyor 3
conveyor 4

conveyor 1

loading-unloading
station

Figure 3. Spatial organization of the machine tool installation

For reasons not relevant here, the second phase work station precedes the first phase work station in the rotational direction of the turntable.

RESULTS

Before presenting the results of the different strategies used by the programmer, we will (a) describe briefly the main specifications documents, so that we can refer to them later, and (b) present some methodological results concerning the verbal protocol method we employed.

Specifications

The programmer received two kinds of specifications:

A program specifying the structure of the program to be written. This "example program" had previously been written by the programmer himself to control an analogous installation. The programmer's manager judged some specific points of this program's structure to be "good" from the point of view of maintenance, and the programmer was to adopt these features.

Five documents specifying the operation and the physical layout of the installation. We will present the three that were most frequently used by the programmer.

The functional representation of the installation (the "Grafcet"). The Grafcet is a process control specification tool. It produces a graphical representation of the sequential progress of the process, showing the alternation of its actions and their enabling conditions. For each function, the graphical illustration is accompanied by documents providing a written description of (a) the safety conditions for each action; (b) the physical starting point of the cycle; (c) the procedure to be followed in the event of a mechanical or process control problem (14).

The physical representation of the installation. The installation and each of its functions are represented in a figurative, schematic form. Each different data and control element is labelled with its mnemonic (e.g., CAOU, "Contrôle Avance Outil," i.e., "Check Advance Tool," next to the electrical detector providing this information).

A document showing programmable controller input and output (the "I/O document"). All electrical data sources on the installation provide input to the programmable controller; the programmable controller's output governs the controlled functions on the installation and its display panels. The I/O document provides the corresponding programmable controller variable for each physical entity in the installation.

Verbalization Problems

When we asked him to verbalize his thoughts before starting our observation, the programmer was quite willing. However, though we repeated our request during observation, <u>the programmer verbalized rather little</u> while writing the program.

In general, as long as he was performing an overt activity (mainly writing), we noticed that he found it very difficult to "think aloud." When we insisted during these periods, his verbalizations consisted of stating (the names of) the elements with which he was currently working: "B67" (Intermediate Variable Bit 67), "Not-E34" (Input Bit 34, connected with the logical operator NOT), or, more rarely, the mnemonics corresponding to the current bits: "AAV" ("Auxiliaire Avance," i.e., "Advance Auxiliary").

In general, he only verbalized his thoughts when he was faced with a problem, when he was not sure what to do, or when he had noticed an error or an omission.

Our hypothesis is that many of the programmer's actions during program construction are automatized (as a consequence of his experience in the field) and that a verbalization other than stating the variables processed would require a "decompilation" of these automatized procedures (2). Encouraging the programmer to verbalize more might lead him to make the knowledge sources underlying these procedures explicit, but such verbalization would not express the real activity the programmer performs in writing his program.

Global Strategy: Organization of the Activity

We have broken the programmer's activities down into three consecutive stages. They are not quantitatively comparable, since the first and the second stages took relatively little time. However, they differ qualitatively, having rather different functions in the total activity.

<u>Studying the specifications</u> (one day). The programmer skims rather rapidly through the documents that give the specifications for the installation. He studies the three documents presented above in some detail, especially the graphical portion of the Grafcet.

<u>Program planning</u> (one hour). The programmer plans his writing along two lines:
- Global breakdown of the task, according to the relative urgency of different parts of the program. While the programmer is writing his program, the installation is being built and tested in the manufacturer's workshop. In order to test installation operation, they need the portion of the program controlling the installation process first. The programmer plans to start with this part. He will then write the part controlling the supply of pieces. Last, he will write the user help portion of the program (a screen with messages about functions that should have been carried out, tools to be changed, etc.).
- Breakdown of the program into programming modules. Referring back to the "example program," the programmer plans the modules for the target program. Only if an example installation function exists in the target installation, its title is copied from the example program. At this stage, only functions existing in the example are planned (although others will appear later during writing).

<u>Program writing</u>. It took the programmer four weeks to write the part of the program controlling the machine tool installation. It contained about 700 instructions (the final program was some 1200 instructions long in all).

Although this third and last stage took a considerable amount of time compared to the others, no qualitatively different stage or sub-stage can be discerned. Program writing was interrupted for (a) functional analysis and problem solving and (b) program checking, but these interruptions were not systematic.

Programming activity organization can be compared to that of the writing (i.e., text composing) activity, as analyzed and modeled by Hayes and Flower (11).

The remainder of this paper presents the strategies used mainly in the last stage.

General Program Construction Strategies

Use of different information sources. The "example program," previously written modules of the target program, and the I/O document were the programmer's most frequently used information sources. A second example program was used for the construction of one target module carrying out a function which had more resemblance with a function on the installation for which this example program was written. The importance of existing modules for the construction of a target program was also shown by the Valentin study (see above) on programmers in a real work situation.

The Grafcet and the physical representation of the installation were seldom used after the first stage of the specifications study.

Inferring installation operation from a representation of its components. Rather than consulting the Grafcet, i.e., the functional representation of the installation, to find out its operation, the programmer often infers it from
- the I/O document

or, to a lesser extent, from
- the physical representation of the installation.

Examples of inference errors. This procedure sometimes leads him to make erroneous inferences.

Example 1. Attributing an erroneous role to a component. The programmer attributes sometimes an erroneous role to components whose correct role is not understood.

Example 2. Attributing an erroneous operation to the installation. At times a function whose components may perform different operations is programmed in a way that does not meet the specifications. For example, on a machine tool, the grip function can be implemented on each separate station or on the installation as a whole. On the current installation, there is only one grip function for both work stations. However, the programmer programs two grip modules, one for each station.

Example 3. Omitting components erroneously judged to be superfluous. When the programmer comes across two series of components that he thinks serve identical functions, he judges one of them to be superfluous and omits it. By doing so, he changes the specified operation.

The example program and the previously written modules played an important role in several other strategies described below.

Following the order and the structure of the example program. To construct the target program, the programmer follows the order of the example program.

The example program has three main parts:
- about ten modules involve General Information retrieval and Command execution (see below);
- about six modules involve each of the installation stations individually, as well as some other functions;
- the last module involves the display.

The first part, the so-called "General Information," includes information concerning the whole installation, rather than just one of its specific functions. It contains the "General" Safety Conditions, Starting Conditions, Commands, and Checks.

An example of a "General" Check is KRUN ("Contrôle Retour Unités," i.e., "Units Return Check"). This variable accumulates individual $KRUN_x$ variables containing information about the position of each of the installation units, i.e., stations. For KRUN to be set to 1, $KRUN_x$ on each station must have been set to 1. Then the central turntable can rotate safely, without damaging the station tools.

The first "General" Command in the program is AATCY ("Auxiliaire Arrêt Cycle," i.e., "Cycle Stop Auxiliary"). This variable is made up of seven parallel branches. If any one of them is set to 1, installation operation stops immediately. The variables composing the branches in question will be defined only later in the program.

Following the order of the example program leads the programmer to adopt a modular top-down strategy at the level of the overall program structure. However, within the modules, he abandons this top-down strategy. At these lower levels, to follow the order of the example program involves adopting a rather bottom-up strategy.

This characterization of the programmer's activity in terms of top-down and bottom-up strategies is only applicable at a very general description level. We noted a great number of deviations from these general lines, some of which will be presented below (see also 20).

Reasoning based on semantic or functional relationships between components. In order to write his program, the programmer makes use of relationships between operations or functions previously written and those that are to be written. The elements involved in such a relationship may be
- (a module of) the example program and (one from) the target program;
- a previously written module of the target program and a module to be written.

Occasionally, this relationship is one of opposition. Very often, the programmer uses a relationship of analogy he feels exists between programs or modules.

Example 1. Opposite functions on the target installation. To write the instructions for the Return of a movement, the programmer often adapts the movement's corresponding Advance instructions (or vice versa).

Example 2. Analogy between the structures of two programs. As we have already noted, the programmer follows the structure of the example program in establishing that of the target program.

Example 3. Analogy between functions of parts of the example and target programs. To determine whether there is an analogous example module for a particular target module, the programmer first decides whether the target installation function that the target module must address sufficiently resembles to an example installation function for a transformation to be worthwhile.

This leads us to distinguish three types of modules in the target program:
- those for which the programmer follows the example module structure down to the instruction component level and for which almost all changes made are at the level of bit and variable numbering (e.g., the "General Information" modules);
- those for which he follows the example module structure down to the level of the instruction's output variables and makes changes in the instruction components, in addition to those mentioned above (e.g., the work and check stations);
- those for which the example program does not offer an analogy and for which he will have to construct the module entirely from the specifications and his knowledge (e.g., the loading-unloading station).

Example 4. Analogy between functions of two parts of the installation. The installation has two work stations, First Phase and Second Phase. Having started with the module of the Second Phase station, the programmer refers back to this module in constructing the First Phase module.

Also, by doing so, he discovers errors in the Second Phase module.

Top-down processing. We have already noted the importance of this strategy. Starting program writing with the general portion and taking advantage of analogical or other relationships between installation operations or local functions were two instances of this strategy. Both require the programmer to use a top-down strategy to analyze the problem of controlling installation operation.

Creation of intermediate variables. By writing "General Information" before the specific parts, the programmer creates and handles variables in which data he has not yet defined are accumulated. Writing, e.g., the instruction defining KRUN before defining the individual $KRUN_x$ variables (see above) requires the programmer to know about the individual functions involved in the installation's general operation.

The programmer is able to adopt this strategy because he has an example program and, perhaps more importantly, because of his expertise in the field of machine tools and machine tool programming.

The use of intermediate variables in which more elementary information is accumulated before it has been processed is frequent.

There are several reasons for this:

- The intermediate variable is used to <u>accumulate pieces of information which are often used together in that specific combination</u> (e.g., the individual station KRUNs we mentioned above, which are made up of several input bits providing information about positions of the stations in question, are each used in about ten instructions).
- The programmer may judge the combination <u>meaningful for him</u> and, he thinks, <u>for future workers on the installation</u>. For example, AAV and ART, the Auxiliaries for Advance and Return, are intermediate variables accumulating along several branches the conditions for the different operation modes (e.g., automatic and manual) of one or more station operations.
- The third reason is pragmatic and involves the <u>capacity of the programming terminal screen</u>. This screen can only display instructions composed of a limited number of bits connected in series or in parallel. Therefore, to keep within this limit, the programmer may have to break up an instruction and construct one or more intermediate variables.

Several reasons are often associated with the construction of an intermediate variable, even though one would be enough.

<u>Economical use of resources</u>. As we noted above, the programmer follows a writing plan inspired by the order of the modules and instructions in the example program. However, he will abandon this order if another is more economical from the point of view of processing available information sources or using his cognitive resources.

Postponing the processing of information not yet available. The programmer skips parts of modules when he needs information from colleagues or other information sources not at hand to construct them. He lists his questions and waits to ask them (or to look up the answers) until he has gathered enough to make it worthwhile to interrupt his writing.

He also skips parts of instructions, often leaving blanks in particular places. This means that he knows the number and type of variables required, which he sometimes even writes above the blank in a comment. (This procedure also reveals top-down processing.)

Information processing guided by the consulted information source. The programmer uses a lot of information from the I/O document. Often, when he looks up which E or A bits correspond to a particular function he is programming, he also retrieves other Es or As mentioned that are close to the one he wants. Taking them into account generally requires interrupting the construction of the current instruction and starting another.

This retrieval of bits other than the one he is looking for can be due to a <u>conscious decision</u> or to a <u>drifting of attention</u>. This last phenomenon sometimes leads the programmer to discover forgotten or unknown variables which he then takes into account.

These and other phenomena contribute to characterizing the programming activity as being guided by circumstances (the information encountered, the processing currently judged to be the least costly, drifting of attention) rather than by a hierarchical plan. Elsewhere (20), we suggested accounting for it in terms of <u>opportunistic planning</u> (12).

Search for homogeneity. Mostly for comprehension and maintenance reasons, the programmer makes the program as homogeneous as possible. He tries to create uniform structures at several levels of the program:

- *Instruction order in the modules.*
  Examples. Process state check instructions precede operation control instructions in the station modules. Advance instructions precede return instructions.
- *Branch order in the instructions.* For instructions controlling operations taking place with different installation configurations, different instruction branches define the conditions for these different operational occurrences.
  Example. The branch defining the automatic mode of an operation precedes its manual mode definition branch.
- *Bit order in instruction branches.* Instructions are scanned continuously (see above <u>Programmable Controller & Programming Language Used</u>). Inspection of an instruction by the programmable controller supervisor is stopped as soon as a bit set to 0 is encountered in a serial connection branch. The programmer takes advantage of this feature of the programmable controller by putting the most "important" conditions at the beginning of this type of branch.
- *Intermediate variable numbering.* Numbering of intermediate variables with counterparts elsewhere in the program is structured.
  Examples. The $KRUN_x$ we described above has analogous numbers on the different stations: B601 on one work station, B701 on the other, and B801 on the check station.
  Some variables nearly always found in a machine tool program are the same from one program to another (in the factory where the programmer is working). Thus, B0, B1, and B2 have the same content in all these programs.

Program changes. The wish to homogenize sometimes leads the programmer to reconsider previousy written instructions. In doing so, he will either
-have the current instruction follow their structure;
or
- copy their structure from the current one.

<u>Schema-guided information processing</u>. Some errors made by the programmer can be explained by the hypothesis that he is using schemata with prototypical values instantiated for particular slots. If he reads the specifications providing other values for these slots, his expectations based on these prototypical values are probably so strong that he does not take the values which are given into account (see also 8). If he writes part of the program without reading the specifications, the schema he instantiates may provide him preferentially with these prototypical values.

Example. In machine tool installations, work operations generally take place during the "Advance" movement of the station. In the target installation however, there is one such operation during "Return." By defining the occurrence of this operation under the same conditions as the others, the programmer modifies the specifications by creating a process in which the operation takes place during "Advance" instead of during "Return" (This error is subsequently corrected by the tester we observed afterwards).

<u>Simulation</u>. Two types of simulation have been observed: <u>simulation of program operation</u> and <u>simulation of installation operation</u>.
The first is sometimes used by the programmer to verify (modules of) the part of the program he has already written. These simulations were among the rare moments the programmer verbalized his thoughts spontaneously. For the most part, he followed one of two basic procedures:
- He attributed hypothetical values to the bits in the logical expressions of the instructions and evaluated the consequences for the output variables.
  Verbalization example: "So, ... if E13 is set to 1 AND NOT-B67 to 1, yes, alright, then A356 fires."

- He evaluated which conditions had to be satisfied for an output variable to be activated.

Verbalization example: "So, for A526 to fire, B80 and AAV have to be set to 1."

He reasoned in terms of numbered bits or, more rarely, mnemonics, as he did when we urged him to verbalize during writing. In other words, for the programmer, there is a direct correspondence between the variable names and variable content. This is probably due in part to the use of numbering rules created by the programmer (see <u>Search for homogeneity</u>).

Simulation of installation operation was mainly used by the programmer when studying the specifications, specifically in order to understand the Grafcet (i.e., the functional representation of the installation).

<u>Jumping ahead of his plan</u>. The programmer sometimes jumps ahead of his program construction plan (i.e., writing modules in the order of the example program). He interrupts the writing of the current instruction and deals with functions he thinks of and is afraid he will forget if he does not handle immediately.

He also thinks ahead to the possible problems the person who will transcribe his program may encounter (see the next paragraph).

<u>Writing style</u>. The programmer writes a paper and pencil version of the program. Another person will enter this program on the programming terminal from where it can be transmitted to the programmable controller.

The programmer writes his program in relay diagrams, judging it easier to read and to evaluate the functioning of the program in this form, especially in the case of parallel branches.

The person entering the program on the terminal uses the boolean format. Although the program can be entered under both formalisms, the relay diagrams require much more typing. Transcribing the paper version of the program from relay to boolean is apparently worth the effort it requires.

The programmer who uses relay diagrams for writing his program creates a mixture of relay and boolean format for some types of instructions. This takes place in instructions in which the elements are arranged in a different order depending on the format (e.g., the "counting instruction"). In this case, the programmer writes down the elements in <u>relay format</u>, but in the <u>order</u> in which they have to be entered in <u>boolean</u>, so that the person entering them at the terminal can follow this order (see Figure 4).

—— C18 —— B82 —— R464 —— M38 —— 0 —— $\left(\text{B86} \right)$

Figure 4. Example of the format used by the programmer to write a counting instruction

The following is the correct relay diagram format representation of this instruction, resulting from entering the elements in the above order (see Figure 5):

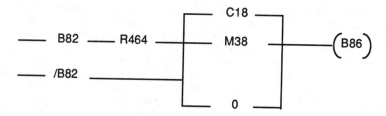

Figure 5. Example of the relay diagram representation for the counting instruction shown above (see Figure 4)

The correct boolean format representation of this instruction is:
C18 . B82 . R464 . M38 . 0 = B86

Thus, the programmer's approach could be interpreted as not only <u>preparing the work</u> of his colleague, but also <u>anticipating the problems</u> this person may encounter.

CONCLUSION

In our introduction, we put forward the hypothesis that the strategies used in "programming-in-the-large" would be different from those that have been observed to date in empirical programming studies which have tended to focus on student programmers working on problems of a somewhat limited nature. Among the strategies we observed, some were the same as those already shown to be at work in other contexts (planning, top-down and bottom-up processing, simulation of the program's execution, schema-guided information processing). This result is encouraging as it may well be hoped that the research conducted on "programming-in-the-small" provides knowledge which is applicable to <u>programming as a whole</u> (16).

However, we did find some hitherto unobserved strategies. Thus, the frequent use of examples and analogy, the search for homogeneity, and an opportunistic organization of the activity.

The frequent use of example programs seems to be characteristic for programming in a work context. The importance of "examples" is not particular to programming. We observed the mechanic who made the specifications for the programmer, drawing the functional representation of the installation. He also used example functional representations (20).

Computer scientists observe from introspection that they seldom create programs <u>ex nihilo</u> and often make use of analogy to debug incorrect programs, modify existing ones, and abstract programming schemata. They even propose to implement analogy as a tool in automatic programming systems (9).

The desire to ensure homogeneity which strongly guided the programmer's activity stemmed from a preoccupation with the future use of the program, and thus, by definition, from a source specific to programming in a real work context.

Another non-trivial result, presented elsewhere in greater detail (20), is the opportunistic nature of the programming activity. This also seems to be a characteristic of real activity as opposed to the hierarchical plan-guided activity mostly observed in problem solving involving artificial, limited problem statements.

The question remains as to whether it is possible to use these results to make generalizations to other programmers and/or programming other problems in other languages?

As with all case-studies conducted on one or two subjects (1, 3, 4), the one presented in this article can of course only lead to a hypothetical model requiring further empirical research in order to test it. But, as Anzai and Simon (3) claim, "[If] one swallow does not make a summer, ... one swallow does prove the existence of swallows. And careful dissection of even one swallow may provide a great deal of reliable information about swallow anatomy" (3, p. 136).

If the possibility of applying our conclusions to other programming contexts is determined by the similarity of languages used and problems resolved, then little case can be made for it. We think however that, to a great extent, the observed strategies do not depend on language or problem characteristics. On this point, we only make a special case for the top-down processing as it was observed, e.g., in the writing of the general portion before the rest of the program and in the construction of intermediate variables before the definition of their components. The possibility of using this strategy in the way the programmer did surely depends, leaving aside the programmer's programming knowledge and experience in the field, on the type of programming language used. This strategy is especially appropriate with languages developed for structured programming.

Two sorts of arguments plead in favor of the plausibility of our conclusions concerning the other strategies being applicable to other programming, or even other problem solving, activities.

Firstly, the duration of our observations allowed us to observe some strategies that were recurrent and general, that is not triggered in only one limited context: the use of examples (programs or parts of programs) as well as analogical reasoning. If the specific examples observed here were particular to machine tools and their control programs, there is nothing in the nature of these strategies that makes them unique to this kind of programming. We have already mentioned the frequent use of examples by professional programmers working in a completely other problem domain, i.e., management (19). Moreover, these programmers used classical, procedural languages (GAP and COBOL).

Secondly, we may support our argument with concurrent results obtained in research on other types of problem solving. In experimental psychological studies, analogical reasoning has been considered, for some ten years (18), as an important mechanism in problem solving (6). In a study conducted on a mechanic making specifications, we observed similar strategies to those used by the programmer (20). Other researchers working on design activity noted that an incremental approach is typical: a designer rarely starts from scratch (5, 11). The opportunistic organization of a problem solving activity has been observed in studies on planification (12).

We are therefore reasonably confident that our conclusions are not simply restricted to programming programmable controllers, even though of course they need other empirical confirmation.

In conclusion, we hope that our results encourage more research on "programming-in-the-large" conducted on professional programmers working on complex problems in a real work context.

REFERENCES

1. Adelson, B. & Soloway, E. (1985). The role of domain experience in software design. IEEE Transactions on Software Engineering, SE-11, 1351-1360.
2. Anderson, J. R. (1986). Knowledge compilation: the general learning mechanism. In R. S. Michalski, J. G. Carbonell & T. M. Mitchell (Eds.), Machine learning. An artificial intelligence approach (Vol. II). Los Altos, Calif.: Morgan Kaufmann Publishers.
3. Anzai, Y., & Simon, H. A. (1979). The theory of learning by doing. Psychological Review, 86, 124-140.
4. Brooks, R. (1977). Towards a theory of the cognitive processes in computer programming. International Journal of Man-Machine Studies, 9, 737-751.
5. Carroll, J. M. & Rosson, M. B. (1985). Usability specifications as a tool in iterative development. In H. Rex Hartson (Ed.), Advances in human-computer interaction (Vol. 1). Norwood, N.J.: Ablex.
6. Cauzinille-Marmèche, E., Mathieu, J., & Weil-Barais, A. (1985). Raisonnement analogique et résolution de problèmes. L'Année Psychologique, 85, 49-72.
7. Curtis, B. (1986). By the way, did anyone study any real programmers? In E. Soloway & S. Iyengar (Eds.), Empirical studies of programmers. Papers presented at the First Workshop on Empirical Studies of Programmers, June 5-6, 1986, Washington, D.C.. Norwood, N.J.: Ablex.
8. Détienne, F. (1986). Program understanding and knowledge organization: the influence of acquired schemata. Preprints of the Proceedings of the Third European Conference on Cognitive Ergonomics, Paris, France, September 15-19, 1986. Rocquencourt: INRIA.
9. Dershowitz, N. (1986). Programming by analogy. In R. S. Michalski, J. G. Carbonell & T. M. Mitchell (Eds.), Machine learning. An artificial intelligence approach (Vol. II). Los Altos, Calif.: Morgan Kaufmann Publishers.
10. Ericsson, K. A., & Simon, H. A. (1984). Protocol analysis. Verbal reports as data. Cambridge, Mass.: MIT Press.
11. Hayes, J. R., & Flower, L. S. (1980). Identifying the organization of writing processes. In L. W. Gregg & E. R. Steinberg (Eds.), Cognitive processes in writing. Hillsdale, N.J.: Erlbaum.
12. Hayes-Roth, B., & Hayes-Roth, F. (1979). A cognitive model of planning. Cognitive Science, 3, 275-310.

13. Hoc, J. M. (in preparation). Towards effective computer aids to planning in computer programming. In T. R. G. Green, J. M. Hoc, D. Murray, & G. C. van der Veer (Eds.), Working with computers: theory versus outcomes. London: Academic Press.
14. Morais, A. (1985). Hierarchical planification in programming. In I. D. Brown, R. Goldsmith, K. Coombes & M. A. Sinclair (Eds.), Ergonomics International 85. Proceedings of the Ninth Congress of the International Ergonomics Association, Bournemouth, England, 2-6 September 1985. London: Taylor & Francis.
15. Newell, A., & Simon, H. A. (1972). Human problem solving. Englewood Cliffs, N.J.: Prentice-Hall.
16. Soloway, E. (1986). What to do next: meeting the challenge of programming-in-the-large. In E. Soloway & S. Iyengar (Eds.), Empirical studies of programmers. Papers presented at the First Workshop on Empirical Studies of Programmers, June 5-6, 1986, Washington, D.C.. Norwood, N.J.: Ablex.
17. Soloway, E. & Iyengar, S. (Eds.) (1986). Empirical studies of programmers. Papers presented at the First Workshop on Empirical Studies of Programmers, June 5-6, 1986, Washington, D.C.. Norwood, N.J.: Ablex.
18. Sternberg, R. J. (1977). Intelligence, information processing, and analogical reasoning. Hillsdale, N.J.: Erlbaum.
19. Valentin, A. (1987). Etude ergonomique exploratoire du poste de travail de l'atelier logiciel Concerto. Observations d'analystes-programmeurs en situations réelles de travail "classiques" (hors atelier) (Rapport de fin de contrat EPHE-CNET). Paris: Laboratoire de Psychologie du Travail de l'EPHE.
20. Visser, W. (1987). Abandon d'un plan hiérarchique dans une activité de conception Giving up a hierarchical plan in a design activity. Actes du colloque scientifique COGNITIVA 87 (Tome 1). Paris: Cesta.

CHAPTER 15

A Cognitive Analysis of a Code Inspection[1]

Stanley Letovsky
Jeannine Pinto
Robin Lampert
Elliot Soloway
Computer Science Department
Yale University
New Haven, CT 06520

ABSTRACT

In this paper we describe a cognitive analysis of a design and code inspection. This formal inspection process, as designed and carried out at IBM, has shown itself to be effective for improving the quality of produced code. Our intent in studying this process was to understand what goes on during a code inspection and why. After analyzing one video-taped, 65 minute inspection in detail, we suggest that the participants in the inspection were attempting to achieve three main goals (clarity, correctness, and consistency), by executing three corresponding behaviors (design reconstruction, mental simulation, document cross-checking). These categories accounted for 89% of the duration of the code inspection. The major overall finding is that, surprisingly, considerable resources (time and personnel) were spent in establishing the relationship between the various software documents, i.e., the requirements, the design, and the code.

1 Introduction

Team reviews of code and other software documents are a proven method of enhancing software quality [14,9,10]. Why are such procedures effective? In order to address this question, we must first understand the inspection process. We know what inspection teams are supposed to

---

[1]This work was supported in part by a grant from IBM. However, the views expressed here are those of the authors.

The software inspection we observed at Houston IBM dealt with actual software used onboard in the space shuttle. However, our comments should not be misconstrued to support the suggestion that this piece of software, or any other piece of IBM developed software, was in any way responsible for the recent Challenger tragedy. The Onboard Shuttle Software System received thorough scrutiny and was judged to be "of the highest quality" by the Presidential Commission studying the tragedy. Moreover, in May 1987, NASA awarded IBM the first Excellence Award for Quality and Productivity for the Onboard Shuttle Software System.

do. The question, then, is what goes on during a code inspection? In an attempt to provide an answer to this question, we observed and video-taped several code inspections. In this paper we present a detailed cognitive analysis of one such code inspection,[2] an inspection of changes to the design and code of a piece of space shuttle software.

The first question that arises in studying inspections is: *how* does one study them? Inspections involve complex situations: social interactions between the individuals in the team, relationships between the teams and the rest of the groups involved, the evolution of the code and the documentation through time. Research into the cognitive processes required in complex situations such as code inspections (e.g., mental processes used in software design and maintanance and group interactions in technical groups) is relatively new and no encompassing theories exist.

In order to conduct a controlled experiment, we must have a theory, however nascent. Since a controlled experiment requires that we pick out a subset of the situation's features and vary them in interesting ways, while holding the rest of the situation constant, we need a theory that expresses the salient features of the activity we are studying and suggests interesting ways in which to vary the situation. Since we do not know yet what the salient aspects of the inspections are, a controlled experiment cannot be used effectively to learn anything about them.

Before we can test any theories, we need to build some. Before we can build some theories, we need to better understand the inspection process as it exists in the real world. In order to gain a better understanding of the inspection process, we employed a protocol-style experimental methodology [8]: we video-taped a number of inspections, and analyzed those protocols. We, as well as others, have successfully employed this methodology in other subject areas, e.g., in program comprehension [11,13], software design [5]. This process allows us to begin gathering information about inspections without the need to form premature theories. However, unlike many other protocol studies, we did not study some artificial situation contrived by the experimenters. Rather, more like a traditional field study, we video-taped regularly scheduled code inspections that followed the guidelines put forth by IBM [3].

Given the variability of the design and code inspections (different groups of people, sections of code, the possibility of difficulties unique to a particular inspection) the danger, in this type of study, is that we have come across or emphasized inspections that are not representative. However, it is our reasoned opinion — and the reasoned opinion of various IBM personnel who have participated in many, many code inspections[3] – that the behaviors we describe and analyze here *are* representative of behaviors found in the design and code inspections of long-lived, life-critical software systems at IBM FSD/Houston. Thus, we feel confident that our analyses do provide an accurate characterization of the essentials of the code inspection process.

Our findings can be summarized as follows: we identified 3 main goals that the code inspection team was attempting to realize: (1) clarity of the design and code documents, (2) correctness of the design and code, and (3) consistency of the code and design documents. Fully 53% of the duration of the inspection[4] was spent on the goals of clarity and consistency

---

[2] We observed and video-taped four different inspections. For this paper we concentrated on describing one of these inspections.

[3] We presented a preliminary report of our findings at a seminar (attended by about 20 people) at IBM FSD/Houston. Attendees were those in the code inspection that is presented here, as well as other technical and managerial personnel; all had participated in design and code inspections. They provided invaluable feedback on our analyses. Moreover, they felt that we did not distort or misrepresent the code inspection process.

[4] Of course, the proportions of time spent trying to realize each of these goals would vary from one inspection to the next.

— goals that are not concerned with the current performance of the code, but with future readers: will the next maintainer down the line be able to understand this design? Associated with each of the goals was one major type of behavior exhibited by members of the code inspection team: (1) in their attempt to achieve clarity, the code inspection team carried out design reconstruction, (2) in their attempt to achieve correctness, they carried out mental simulations of the code, and (3) in their attempt to achieve consistency, they carried out cross-checking of the documents. These three types of goals and behaviors accounted for 89% of the duration of the code inspection.

In what follows, then, we first present background information on the inspection session which we witnessed. Next, we describe our analysis of the code inspection process in some detail. Finally, we close with a few, brief remarks.

2 Overview of the Inspections

The inspections we witnessed were a tiny part of a huge, ongoing software development process that creates and maintains software to control the space shuttle during missions. This process involves several corporations and agencies, many teams of software and engineering professionals, and volumes of documents [7]. In this section we endeavor to provide enough background information on the inspection sessions that we observed in order to allow the reader to understand our data.

2.1 Inspections At IBM

The shuttle's flight software (FSW) controls many of the essential functions of the shuttle during missions. It is "life critical software"; bugs can have fatal consequences. In an effort to provide software of the highest possible quality, IBM has instituted a rigorous and tightly controlled development process, containing numerous checkpoints at which software products are inspected and tested. Team inspections of software take place upon completion of all software stages, including requirements, detailed design (henceforth 'specifications'), code, test plans and test data sets. Changes to all documents[5] are made within a system of written change requests, which must be approved by relevant authorities.

Inspections at IBM follow detailed guidelines, which are set forth in manuals and training sessions. The goal of inspections is to verify the quality of the software documents: requirements should be unambiguous and free of contradictions; specifications and code must be shown to meet both the letter and the intent of the requirements. Checklists of common problems are used in the sessions to help ensure thoroughness.

Members of the inspection team have specific roles assigned to them in the inspection session [2,9]. These roles include a moderator, a reader, the developer (the author of the documents or a close associate), and the requirements analyst responsible for the portion of the requirements affected by the inspection and the independent verification tester are usually present. Other personnel with an interest or expertise in the module being inspected may

---

[5]By *documents* we mean all written material including the code.

also be present; this category usually includes the backup personnel for the members of the inspection team, representatives of customers or subcontractors. Five team members attended the inspection we have analyzed here: the moderator, developer, tester, requirements analyst and peer development programmer. The people involved were all IBM employees with at least a year in their current work and experience with from 40 to over 200 inspections.

Prior to an inspection, members of the inspection team study the documents to be inspected and prepare written "actions" describing any objections or questions they have. For example, a team member might write an "action" identifying a portion of code that is difficult to understand or suggesting that the documentation include mention of a particular flag. These actions are then discussed and resolved during the inspection. Since the stated purpose of the inspections is to find errors — not to spend time working on their solutions — actions initially raised in one session are re-examined in a subsequent inspection in order to verify the satisfactory completion of those action items. During the 65 minute inspection session described in this paper, the team reviewed the specifications and code completely. As they went through the documents, they processed the associated actions: a total of 9 actions raised at previous sessions and 15 actions raised at this session for the first time.

Previous research has found that the inspection process is highly effective at catching errors [9,14], and that inspections catch errors earlier in the development process, thus reducing the cost of correcting them [9,6]. Fagan [9] found "a 23 percent increase in the productivity of the coding operation alone." The quality control procedures used in FSW development have enabled IBM to achieve final error rates of 0.2 errors per 1000 source lines of code [10].

2.2   The Interconnect Sequencer

The flight software contains code to control shuttle functions for a variety of possible situations that occur during shuttle flights. One type of situation is the "mission abort", which occurs if something goes wrong that prevents the shuttle from completing its mission as planned. The module which was inspected in the session was one portion of the abort handling software, the "interconnect sequencer": in the event of an abort it is responsible for controlling the flow of fuel to two sets of small maneuvering jets on the rear of the shuttle. During an abort the shuttle needs to get rid of extra fuel quickly, so the interconnect sequencer sends fuel from the OMS jets to the small RCS[6] jets to be burned off. It does this by sending a sequence of commands to the valves that control the flow of fuel to these jets. There are several different types of abort situations depending on what went wrong, and how much can be done about it. These different situations call for many of the same commands, but the order is different in each. The module is executed during flight every 0.8 seconds.

This module consisted of approximately 1000 lines of HAL/S.[7] It was originally written between 1977 and 1980, prior to the widespread introduction of such software engineering techniques as functional commentary–the documenting of sections of code with their intended function. The maintenance inspection concerned modifications extensive enough to significantly increase the original module size.

---

[6]Orbital Maneuvering System and Reaction Control System, respectively.
[7]HAL/S is a language developed by Intermetrics, Inc. for real-time aerospace programming.

3   Observations

3.1   Categorizing The Protocol Data

We first broke down the activities in the code inspection into episodes, where each episode contained discussion related to a single topic. Then, we categorized these episodes into three basic types. Each episode type can be characterized in terms of the goal being achieved, and the behavior being executed in pursuit of that goal:

EPISODE TYPE I

GOAL – Clarity: Are the code and documents easy to understand?

BEHAVIOR – Design Reconstruction: This category consists of discussion episodes in which the team reconstructed, through conversation, reasoning and collective memory, aspects of the module's design which were not explicitly described in the documentation. Different types of reconstruction were identified, but all are concerned fundamentally with figuring out *what part of the design code achieves what part of the requirements*. We identified 14 episodes of reconstruction, which accounted for approximately 34% of the total duration of the inspection session. Reconstruction appears to be related to the goal of *clarity*: by reconstructing the design themselves, the team could determine, based on their own difficulties, which parts would be hard for future maintainers to reconstruct.

EPISODE TYPE II

GOAL – Correctness: Does the code do what the requirements say it should?

BEHAVIOR – Mental Simulation: We classified as mental simulation those episodes in which the team was tracing out the behavior of the design or code under particular conditions. We identified 9 episodes of simulation, which together accounted for 37% of the inspection. Simulation produces descriptions of the behavior of the code which can then be compared to the desired behavior to determine *correctness*.

EPISODE TYPE III

GOAL – Consistency: Are the code and documents stylistically coherent – do they say the same things the same way in different places?

BEHAVIOR – Cross-Checking of Documents: This category contains episodes in which the team compared parts of one or more documents to ensure that they were in some way consistent with each other. There were 15 episodes in this category, which accounted for a total of 19% of the duration of the inspection session.

Most of the episodes (25 out of 28, 89% of the duration of the inspection) fell into one (or more) of three episode types. In what follows, then, we describe each of the episode types in more detail.

3.2 Episode Type I – Goal: Clarity; Behavior: Design Reconstruction

Before discussing design *reconstruction*, we first need to discuss our perspective on design *construction*. In particular, the objective in design is to translate the requirements into some procedural form. One picks standard methods, which we call *plans*, to realize the goals stated in the requirements. As the design process continues, eventually one instantiates the plans in some programming language. In creating the design, one must make many decisions concerning what plans should be used, and why. These decisions link the requirements to the design in the designer's mind – the requirements are transformed into a design by a series of design decisions. Unfortunately, oftentimes the decisions are not recorded in any way; rather, what is written down is simply the end product of the design process. As a result, the connections between the requirements and the specifications, and the specifications and code, are not made explicit in the documentation.

This missing information can — and does — provide the program maintainer with a grave problem. In order to make a change to the system, the maintainer needs to know more than what is in the code now: s/he needs to know *what* goals the code is attempting to achieve, *how* it achieves them, and *why* that plan for achieving them was chosen. Since this sort of information has not been recorded (or not recorded in an accessible form), the maintainer must reconstruct many of the design decisions, and the rationales behind those decisions, that were made during design process itself. That is to say that in order to be clear on what goals a particularly "tight, convoluted" piece of code is achieving, the maintainer must mentally recreate the linkage between the requirements, the specifications, and the code. As we shall show here, considerable effort is expended during the code inspection to reconstruct the design. We distinguish two types of design information that were reconstructed by the inspection team:

Design Decisions: Design decisions are decisions about how to implement goals in the requirements. These include decisions about what data structures and algorithms to use, and what optimizations to perform.

Design Rationales: A major issue in design is choosing the plans to implement the goals in the requirements. Where more than one plan is applicable, a designer must choose among them on the basis of some *rationale*. These rationales often reflect efficiency concerns such as code size, storage or time efficiency, comprehension concerns, etc.

In short, *design decisions* specify *how* the requirements were implemented, while *design rationales* specify *why* they were implemented that way. In the following sections we describe episodes in which the inspection team reconstructed each of these types of design information.

3.2.1 Reconstructing A Design Decision

In this example, we describe an episode from the inspection session in which a code optimization has obscured the correspondence between the requirements and the design. To understand *how* the design implements the requirements, the inspection team must reconstruct the optimization decision.

The pseudocode in Figure 1 illustrates the situation. In it, several of the cases in a CASE statement needed to perform the same sequence of actions at the end. The programmer therefore factored this sequence out of the cases and put it inside an IF statement after the CASE, which would be executed only when the appropriate cases were executed. Structuring

Actual Implementation

```
Case case_index;
    ...
    Case 3: Some_Case_3 commands; Set case_index to 6;
    Case 4: Some_Case_4 commands; Set case_index to 6;
    Case 5: Some_Case_5 commands; Set case_index to 6;
    Case 6: Some_Case_6 commands;
    ...
End Case;
If case_index = 6
    Then Additional_commands;
```

Alternative Implementation

```
Case case_index;
    ...
    Case 3: Case_3 commands; Additional_commands;
    Case 4: Case_4 commands; Additional_commands;
    Case 5: Case_5 commands; Additional_commands;
    Case 6: Case_6 commands; Additional_commands;
    ...
End Case;
```

Figure 1: Pseudocode of the actual, more space efficient implementation (above) and of an alternative, less confusing implementation (below).

the code this way allowed the *additional commands* to be shared by several of the cases in the case statement. An alternative implementation, which more closely resembles the way the requirements were stated, would have been to include these commands in each of the cases, as illustrated in the lower example in Figure 1. Note that this alternative is less space efficient than the actual implementation.

The presence of this optimization in the code created confusion for the inspection team members. This is illustrated in the following dialogue fragment from the inspection of this piece of code:

Moderator: The implementation of block 190 to 198 is confusing because it's different from the way the requirements are.

Analyst: Let me explain what I was doing there. We've got a case statement of 6 where we do certain processing, then on the bottom, we also have a IF check for case statement 6 where we do more processing. And I guess the reason we do that is because in steps 3, 4 and 5, we, under certain conditions, we set the case index to 6, so that on the same pass that we do those cases 3, 4 and 5 we're also gonna check for case 6 and do the additional processing.

Developer: Because the processing always says, if something's wrong, if a valve fails or something,....

Analyst: ...to terminate.

Developer: Yah. My doing case 6 is the equivalent to going to step 20.

Analyst: What makes it confusing to me is that step 6 in the requirements says to command a sequence of valves -- open or closed, I'm not sure -- and what we're doing by that is we're splitting up, we're doing half those valves in the case statement of 6 and half those valves in the IF statement for the checking of case index equal to 6. I think its a little bit more efficient the way he's done it, but I'm thinking the confusion factor that he's introducing there may not be worth the efficiency that we're saving.

Moderator: OK, so from a maintenance point of view, we might just want to keep it all in.

Analyst: Its tough to trace the requirements back to the design, I think.

An efficiency argument is being made to justify the tricky code in Figure 1: code would have to be duplicated in each of the cases 3, 4 and 5, and this would be space inefficient. The difficulty in understanding the code seems to arise because there is no straightforward match from the requirements to the code. The optimization of sharing subgoals has obscured the correspondence.

The optimization illustrated above took code that (1) performed one conceptual task and (2) was located in one spot (in each of the cases 3, 4, 5), and split it up, and located the parts non-contiguously. The optimized code in Figure 1 is an archetypical case of a *delocalized plan* [13]. In a *de*localized plan, the code for one conceptually unified plan is distributed non-contiguously in a program. Such code is hard to understand; since only fragments of the plan are seen at a time by a reader, the reader makes inferences based only on what is locally apparent — and these inferences are quite error prone. In effect, the program reader may not be able to *predict* that something else in the code is related to what he is currently looking at.

From the verbal protocol, however, it is clear that the code inspectors realize that what has been created is a unwieldly. They know that this piece of code will be changed at some later date, and thus future programmers will pay the price for this optimized code. That is, future programmers will have to go through and reconstruct the relationship between the code and the requirements, and then conjecture why the code was twisted in the way it was. In fact, the difficulty of reconstructing this design decision led the team to consider an alternative design which was less efficient but clearer.

Perceived tradeoffs between efficiency and clarity (or maintainability or comprehensibility) were raised at numerous points in the inspection. Space efficiency is an important issue, since memory on the shuttle's computers is in short supply. However, clarity is also a major concern, and one of the explicit goals of IBM's inspection procedures. At least 5 actions, and approximately half the total inspection time, dealt with how to balance these two concerns.

It is unfortunate that designers are compelled to sacrifice efficiency to achieve clarity, or vice versa. Is there a way to have both? We would have to somehow make the efficient code comprehensible. We note that the developer on the inspection team, who was the person most familiar with code, preferred the more efficient organization: for him, comprehensibility was not a problem, since he had reconstructed the optimization many times. The group was able to understand the optimization as well, given a detailed explanation, but they were not confident that future maintainers would be able to. How could we guarantee that future maintainers could understand it? It seems that the missing knowledge, the knowledge that the team reconstructed, that the programmer already knew, and that the future maintainer might not know, is that the code was derived from the requirements by factoring out certain common steps. This raises an interesting question: what if maintainers had a description of the program which explicitly said, this statement is introduced as a result of sharing common code between steps A,B, and C? It may be that an explicit account of the optimizations (and other types of design decisions) would relieve the burden of reconstruction on the maintainer, thereby allowing the developer to make decisions based purely on performance criteria.

In summary, we have seen that understanding the system can involve inferential reconstruction of design decisions, and that certain kinds of design decisions are hard to reconstruct, reducing the clarity of the correspondence between the code and the requirements. We speculate that delocalization may be one cause of the difficulty, and that more explicit documentation of design decisions may alleviate the problem.

3.2.2 Reconstruction of Design Rationale

In this example, we describe an episode which illustrates the reconstruction of the second type of design information: design rationales. Here the problem is not that it is hard to determine how the requirements are implemented, but rather that it is not clear why they are implemented the way they are. The inspection team must therefore reconstruct the rationale motivating the implementation.

The pseudocode below captures the essential features of the code in question. The code was responsible for controlling a set of "discretes", or fuel valve controller bits. To change the state of a valve, e.g., from open to closed, the corresponding bit must be set to the desired state, and another related bit must be complemented a short time later. We need not go into the reasons for the need to set and then complement a discrete. The key point to note is that the discretes are set only after 1.5 seconds have elapsed, while the discretes are complemented each time through the loop, every .16 seconds.

```
Loop every 0.16 seconds; ...
    Complement discretes;
    If 1.5 sec elapsed;
        THEN set discretes; ...
End loop;
```

When the team inspected this section of code, one of the team members raised a question about why the requirements were implemented in this manner. The following discussion ensued:

Analyst: ...We're setting discretes in this module only every 1.5 seconds. Yet, we're complementing those discretes continuously on every cycle. And the answer I got was that that's the way it was done in the past. *And nobody's really sure why they did it that way.* But I think a better answer is probably it would cost more to put this on the same nesting level as the check for the 1.5 seconds being expired.

Developer: You would have to add a check around all this complementing and say, 'Did these discretes change on this pass?'. And only then will you complement the discretes. And what you have is, instead of executing a lot of code all the time, you execute it every one and a half seconds, but you execute extra code in that one and a half seconds. So it's kind of like you carve off valleys in the processing but you increase the peaks; the peaks increase.

In this example, the plan chosen complements the discretes more often than necessary. The reason the plan is preferred, despite the unnecessary work, is that overall it uses less time than the alternative plan which only complements the discretes when absolutely necessary. The example shows how a particular implementation can sometimes be justified by a complicated argument about efficiency which will not necessarily be obvious to the reader. Understanding *why* a design is the way it is can require that the understander reconstruct these efficiency arguments, since they are not recorded anywhere.

In this section on achieving clarity through design reconstruction, we have seen examples of how the code inspection team expended significant effort in reconstructing a design decision and a design rationale. The code inspection team themselves, as opposed to the software documents, were in large measure the source of the information needed for that reconstruction process. If that needed information were to be captured and then made available in a document, or even better, in a machine interpretable form, we might reasonably expect to see the inspection team expending less effort on the reconstruction process.

3.3 Episode Type II: Goal - Correctness, Behavior - Mental Simulation

The inspection serves as one of several opportunities to check the correctness of changes to the software documents. By *correctness* we mean that the design implements the requirements and the code implements the design – that is, that the plans achieve the goals. Achieving correctness is an explicitly prescribed aim of the inspection process; it appears first in IBM's standard checklist of concerns to be considered during the inspection [4]. How does the inspection team check the correctness of a document? In order to check the correctness of the code, the group mentally simulated it. The group engaged in mental simulation during 37% of the duration of the entire design and code inspection.[8]

We observed two kinds of simulation: code-driven simulation and scenario-driven simulation.

Code-driven Simulation We classified as code-driven simulation episodes in which a team member, following the control flow of the program through its branches, recited the behavior of the code. 33% of the duration of the inspection was spent on code-driven simulation.

Scenario-driven Simulation This group contains episodes in which a team member mentally simulates the code *with a particular scenario* in mind. The inspection team considers how the program will behave under the conditions of that particular situation. 4% of the duration of the inspection was spent on scenario-driven simulation.

In both code-driven and scenario-driven simulation, the inspection team generates the behavior of the code in order to determine whether it behaves correctly according to the letter and intent of the requirements. In the next two sections, we will provide examples of each of these behaviors.

3.3.1   Code-driven Simulation

In the inspection, approximately half of the code inspection took place against the backdrop of an on-going code-driven simulation. Because the changes to the code were extensive, the inspection team simulated the code, case by case. The reader provided a summary of the code, describing its execution-time processes step-by-step, tracing each case and each branch of a conditional through some of its steps. Following along, the other members of the group evaluated the correctness of each case:

```
Analyst: First thing we're doing in case 5 is checking to see that the RCS
    cross-feed valves for manifolds 1, 2 are open and not commfaulted.  If
    that is the case, we then go and check for the manifolds, the RCS tank
    isovalves for manifolds 3, 4 and 5 and check to see if they are closed
    and not commfaulted.  If all the RCS tank isos for 3,4 and 5 are closed
    and not commfaulted, we'll command the RCS cross-feed valves for
    manifolds 3,4 and 5 open.

Moderator: Let me bring up one problem...
```

Following along as the reader summarized the code, the other members of the group evaluated the correctness of each case. In this example, the moderator finds a problem as the analyst

---

[8]Mental simulation occurred only during the inspection of the code in this inspection.

recites the behavior of the code. While at first glance, it would appear here that the analyst is "merely" reading the code, the moderator's response, "let me bring up one problem", suggests that more is going on than just reading. The moderator is comparing the behavior the analyst is describing to the behavior the moderator understands to be prescribed in the requirements. By simulating the code, they could determine whether the code worked and whether its behavior satisfied the requirements.

3.3.2 Scenario-driven Simulation

During the inspection, team members generated two scenarios, arising from previously overlooked values or sequences of values that might arise. In generating these scenarios, the team used specific hypothetical situations or scenarios. In the discussion below, the team considers a specific case, the possibility that the return to normal flag will be true during the first pass of the sequencer. The developer is concerned that the sequencer will not behave correctly under such circumstances.

Developer: I just thought of something. *Is there any processing where we would somehow activate this module, and then do a return to normal on the first pass through?* Is that at all possible?

Analyst: The very first time it's called, can you have a return to normal?

Developer: I didn't see anything to prevent it. I don't know.

Analyst: I don't see anything preventing it. But what's your point? What's the problem that brings up?

Developer: OK, it's just that I initialized the discrete flag to a one, and yet if the return to normal executes first, we're gonna reset these bits on a first pass. We may have to change that initialization.

In this case, the developer had discovered a case, occurring on the boundary of the normal range of data, against which there was no guard. The developer illustrated the import of the case by simulating the behavior of the program when a return to normal condition is the first executed, i.e. "we're gonna reset these bits on a first pass."

How are scenarios discovered? The IBM inspection checklist [1] prompts inspectors to think about some cases (divide by zero, loop termination, indexing). But clearly inspectors go beyond that checklist, identifying boundary cases and sequences of values that have not been identified before. How do they do so? The data available to us is sparse: "I just thought of something." These scenarios are not discovered frequently; in the inspection, we saw only two scenarios generated and considered. Software testing may provide us a fruitful area in which to investigate test case generation. In examinations of testing procedures and the cognitive processes involved in developing test cases, we may find an understanding of the test case generation we see in inspection processes.

3.4 Episode Type III: Goal - Consistency, Behavior - Cross-checking of Documents

Maintaining a consistent and unique terminology was important. Fifteen episodes concerned inconsistencies in the code or documentation. These inconsistencies were not errors; the team's concern with them stems from the goal of keeping the representations principled and predictable in structure. In this sense, all issues of consistency are also sub-goals of the desire for clarity — consistent documents are generally easier to understand. We identified several kinds of consistency concerns: plan choice, terminology, and level of detail, as the examples below illustrate:

- **Consistency of Terminology:** Principled, consistent documents help maintain the clarity of the program. Variations, when programmers assume them to be principled, may be taken to be meaningful. Thus, inconsistent terminology may cause a programmer to assume that different terms refer to different objects. To reduce the chance of such confusion, the inspection team corrected inconsistencies it found, as the remark below illustrates:

  > "There was an action on case 4, instead
  > of saying RCS interconnect valves, we were gonna *say cross-feed just*
  > *for consistency."*

  In this case, the design and code had used the terms "crossfeed" and "interconnect" interchangably to identify a set of valves. So, "just for consistency", the inspection team chose to use only the term "crossfeed" to describe the valves, eliminating any possibility that future programmers would think that "crossfeed" and "interconnect" are different sets of valves.[9] Concern with the consistency of wording even extended to the tenses of verbs. A team member proposed changing verb tenses, from the present to the past tense, to portray a consistent and clear picture of a sequence of events.

- **Consistency of Level of Detail:** The concern for consistency extended to the level of detail at which the requirements, specifications and comments were written. Team members identified and corrected eight instances of inconsistencies in the level of detail, like the example below:

  > "We described all the other flags so I guess we should put the
  > termination flags in too."

  As shown in this example, the group decided to include in the specification mention that a deactivation flag is set to off because they have "got all the other flags so I guess we should put them in too." Omitting mention of the flag could confuse future maintainers since when they see that some flags are explicitly mentioned in the specifications, they might suppose that all pertinent flags are mentioned.

- **Consistency of Plan Choice:** Team members were also concerned that they consistently use the same plan to implement similar goals. The rationale seemed to be that inconsistencies in plan choice may confuse future maintainers. In the following example, a member of the inspection team raises a concern about the inconsistent use of "the mask technique":

  > "I think since we've used the mask technique in other places in
  > this module, we probably should *be consistent and use it throughout."*

  In the example above, the team members chose to use masks when checking a set of valve status bits ("discretes") because they "used the mask technique in other places

---

[9]They chose "crossfeed" rather than "interconnect" because "interconnect" was not used uniquely – it was also used to describe the whole process of pumping OMS fuel to RCS jets.

in this module." Consistency in plan choice was so important to them that they chose to maintain consistency even though they felt the code would be less clear, less 'self-documenting'. To compensate for the lack of clarity in the code, they decided to "just have a lot of documentation showing what discretes are being checked."

Achieving and maintaining the consistency of the documents is complicated by the number of documents used to represent the software. As we analyzed the transcript to relate the discussion to the various documents, one of the first things that struck us was that several actions were repeated at different points in the inspection. This repetition was due to redundancies in the software representations. Aspects of the interconnect sequencer were described in as many as six different places: twice in the specifications, in English and in a flowchart; similarly for the requirements, and finally in the code and the code comments. This observation led us to investigate what kinds of knowledge or information are characteristic of each representational level.

The requirements and specifications each contain both English text and flowcharts, but the two forms are largely redundant. In both documents, the English description of the procedures is organized in the hierarchical pattern typically used in documents, with numbered sections, and subsections. This hierarchical structure roughly mirrors the block structure of the flow diagrams. The English text uses somewhat wordier descriptions, while the diagrams are necessarily terse, but they say essentially the same things. For example, in the text portion of the specification document, a typical paragraph describing a step in the process reads:

```
The RCS crossfeed valves are opened.  Selected OMS crossfeed
valves, Left 'A' and Right 'B', are opened.
```

This corresponds to two consecutive boxes in the flow diagram, which read:

```
1. Issue RCS XFD VLV Open Cmds

2. Issue Selected OMS XFD VLV Open Cmds:  Left A, Right B
```

The requirements and the code also show similar duplication of information with varying degrees of formalization; in the code the two representations take the form of the code and the interspersed English language comments. Redundancy in behavior arises when a change has to be made to a part of the design which is described in more that one place: e.g., in the text and the flowchart. During the inspection session, 6 modifications had to be considered at least twice in a single pass though the documents.

What about differences in information content between levels? Although we find considerable redundancy between levels as well as within them, we also find differences introduced by planning decisions. One major difference between the requirements and the specifications is that the process description has been optimized to allow parts of different scenarios to share structure. Between the specifications and the code, other than the change in representation language, the changes are simpler, involving mainly substitution of complex expressions for things which have concise English descriptions. For example, where the specifications say

```
The RCS crossfeed valves are opened.
```

the code says:

```
C .......CMD RCS CROSSFEED VALVES OPEN
  DO FOR SC = 3 TO 4;
     CGBB_OUT12_HFA_DSCRT3$(SC;3:) =
        CGBB_OUT12_HFA_DSCRT3$(SC;3:) OR HEX'4040';
     CGBB_OUT12_HFA_DSCRT8$(SC;3:) =
        CGBB_OUT12_HFA_DSCRT8$(SC;3:) OR HEX'4030';
     END;
  CGBB_OUT12_HFA_DSCRT8$(3;3:14),
   CGBB_OUT12_HFA_DSCRT3$(4;3:11) = BIN'1';
```

The difference between these two forms may seem substantial, but much of the difference is attributable to formalization rather than change in content. The proper comparison is between the code and a formal representation of the content of the English sentence. We will not present such a representation, since this would require introducing and explaining a formal language. We merely note that such a representation would include definitions for *RCS crossfeed valves* and *opened*. The planning required to convert these definitions to the code involves:

- A mapping from valves to bits, and from actions such as *open* and *close* to assignments of boolean values.

- Some conversions between binary and hex.

- Some local optimizations to consolidate all the bit-settings into a few statements, using a loop and several bitmasks.

Although the construction of such plan compositions can be tedious and error prone when done by text editor, they can often be automated by relatively simple rewrite rules [12].

Many hours might be saved if this redundancy checking could be avoided; however, some advantages may be gained through this repetition. More chances to catch each error are created through viewing each section of the program more than once. Also, different people work best with different representations. Some people prefer working from the code, others from flowcharts, English text or a mixture.

To summarize, we find considerable redundancy amongst the various representations that are used in the development process. If we consider that every part of these documents must be written, inspected and checked for consistency with all the other parts, it is clear that the redundancy of representation is costing IBM many person-hours of work.

4   Conclusions

In this paper we have described a cognitive analysis of a design and code inspection. In particular, we have suggested that the participants in the inspection were attempting to achieve three main goals (clarity, correctness, and consistency), by executing three corresponding behaviors (design reconstruction, mental simulation, document cross-checking). These categories accounted for 89% of the duration of the code inspection. We fully expect that the distribution of time spent within each of these categories may well change from inspection to inspection; moreover, we fully expect to see other goals and behaviors arising at other code inspections. For example, in inspecting code during an earlier stage of development, the code may perhaps be more buggy, and thus we might see debugging type goals and behaviors. In fact, we are currently planning to study other types of inspections in order to develop a more comprehensive description of code inspections. Nonetheless, we feel that the observations made so far — based on a detailed analysis of a representative code inspection, and backed up by analyses of three other inspections — are both illuminating and intriguing: we see that there is a major expenditure of effort in trying to establish the connection between the various software documents. The information needed to establish this connection is not contained explicitly in the documents. Members of the inspection team laboriously draw it out of the available information using the behaviors we described in this paper. Armed with this new found understanding of what information needs to be made available and why, we can now ask the following question, and have some confidence that it can be answered in a positive way: can we make this information more readily available, thus potentially improving the productivity of the code inspection process?

1 Acknowledgements

This project would never have happened if it wasn't for the efforts of a number of people. We would like to explicitly acknowledge their contribution, and publicly thank them: Walter Ellis III, IBM FSD/Bethesda, who has tirelessly supported our research efforts in ways too numerous to count; Barbara Kolkhorst, IBM FSD/Houston, who orchestrated the zillions of arrangements necessary at the Houston end; David White, IBM FSD/Houston, who went way beyond the letter of his assignment and helped us to understand the code being inspected; Tony Macina, IBM FSD/Houston, who put up with some "back east" academics barging in and asking to video-tape "real" work; Mike Fagan, IBM, for his thought-provoking conversations about the inspection process. Last but not least, we would like to thank all those IBM'ers who participated in and reviewed our studies.

References

[1] Onboard shuttle software: design/code inspection checklist. IBM form.

[2] *RSD Development Procedures*. IBM, September 1985. A draft, currently being updated.

[3] *Software Awareness Memo 31*. IBM, September 1983.

[4] Special instructions. From the back side of the IBM "action" form.

[5] B. Adelson and E. Soloway. *A Cognitive Model of Software Design*. 1984. in *The Nature of Expertise*, Chi, M., Glaser, R., Farr, M., Eds.

[6] F. P. Brooks, Jr. *The Mythical Man-Month: Essays on Software Engineering*. Addison-Wesley, Reading, MA, 1975.

[7] P. J. Denning, editor. *Communications of the ACM.* Volume 27, September 1984.

[8] K.A. Ericsson and H.A. Simon. *Protocol Analysis: Verbal Reports As Data.* MIT Press, Cambridge, MA, 1984.

[9] M. E. Fagan. Design and code inspections to reduce errors in program development. *IBM Systems Journal*, 15(3):219–248, 1976.

[10] B. G. Kolkhorst. Space shuttle primary onboard software development: process control and defect cause analysis. Unpublished.

[11] S. Letovsky. Cognitive processes in program comprehension. In *Proceedings of the Conference on Empirical Studies of Programmers*, Washington D.C., June 1986.

[12] S. Letovsky. Program understanding with the lambda calculus. 1987. To appear in the Proceedings of the 10th IJCAI.

[13] S. Letovsky and E. Soloway. Delocalized plans and program comprehension. *IEEE Software*, 3(3), May 1986.

[14] G. J. Myers. A controlled experiment in program testing and code walkthroughs/inspections. *Communications of the ACM*, 21(9):760 – 768, September 1978.

CHAPTER 16

Can Principles of Cognition Lower the Barriers to Programming?[1]

Clayton Lewis
University of Colorado

Gary M. Olson
University of Michigan

Abstract

We analyze the barriers to programming faced by the intelligent, task-oriented non-programmer, such as a working scientist. Part of the analysis is to examine a success story in making programming easier, the spreadsheet. Generalizations about programming extracted from this example are related to principles of cognition. Two general tactics for making programming easier for our target audience are presented: programming by modification, and reform of the primitives of programming languages. Two examples of programming tools that fit this vision are briefly presented, CMU Tutor and NoPumpG.

Introduction

Despite the fact that children can learn some of the basic elements of programming, learning to program a computer in such a way that the skill can make a meaningful contribution to one's work is not an easy task. Most people who use personal computing rely upon application programs, many of them quite powerful, to help them with their work. Nonetheless, there are many whose work could be helped by the adaptive use of a powerful, flexible computational medium. What are the barriers to learning to program? Are there any insights from cognitive psychology that would help in making programming easier? Will programming as we know it persist? If so, in what form?

---

[1]This paper grew out of an informal workshop held at the University of Colorado in July of 1986. The participants in this workshop, in addition to the authors, were Robert Balzer (Information Sciences Institute, University of Southern California), Gerhard Fischer (University of Colorado), Thomas Green (Applied Psychology Unit, Cambridge, England), and Donald Norman (University of California, San Diego). The ideas in this paper represent our attempt to synthesize the ideas contributed by these participants during two days of discussions among the participants.

The Problem

Programming is a complex activity engaged in by many kinds of people for diverse reasons. Accordingly psychological insights could be applicable in many ways. We focus our attention on just one broad issue: How can we make programming accessible to a wider audience? As a point of reference we use the following real-life example.

The case of AC. AC is a research biologist specializing in insect behavior. She has recently collected a large volume of data describing sequences of encounters of butterflies with flowers, in which the species of flower and whether or not the butterfly chose to visit the flower are recorded. Questions of interest in analyzing the data include, "Is a butterfly more likely to visit a flower of a given species if the flower last visited was of that same species?" Because of the need to consider the sequence of data items, and because visits can be separated by varying numbers of other encounters, analyses like these are beyond the scope of the statistical packages available to AC, and beyond the scope of more general tools like spreadsheets. Custom programs to treat such questions are short and easy to write, if one knows how to program. AC has found that she has not been able to develop the needed programming skill within the time she has been willing to invest. She relies on a programmer to assist her, with consequent delay and loss of flexibility.

It's important to specify exactly how the example of AC differs from other programming situations. Above all, AC is a task-oriented programmer. She wants to use programming as a tool to help her with her primary work, which is biology. She understands her problems in biology but at present has a hard time translating her substantive problems into programming constructs. She is not a professional programmer. She does not want to commit large amounts of her time to learning a programming language and programming tricks. She does not want to build complex programs. She wants to write the programs herself, so she does not have to depend upon others, though of course she would be happy to customize or modify existing code if it would save her time and trouble. She is an intermittent programmer, taking on this task when the needs of her primary work require it. Thus, it is annoying if she forgets whatever she learned earlier about programming. Much of her work depends on existing programs, such as statistical packages. Ideally, when she writes customized programs, their outputs would flow smoothly into such existing programs, making her work easier.

Is it possible to create programming languages or tools that would radically decrease the time and effort AC must invest to bend computing power to her needs? Clearly special-purpose tools could be created to support any particular task or tasks, once they are known, but can we give AC the power that programming conveys of dealing with unanticipated tasks? We focus on the case of AC because modern personal computing has put powerful tools into the hands of enormous numbers of people like AC.

What Do We Mean by "Programming"?

In analyzing why programming is difficult and what we could do about it, we must understand what the task is.

The Programming Task. There are several parts to the task of programming. Something which aids one part may not necessarily help another. Indeed, what helps one part may make others more difficult. Though these parts have a rough order to them, in reality they are usually mixed together during the actual writing of a program.

(1) Specification of the Problem. Problems which are to be solved by writing a program require that we explicitly specify the problem and all of the steps needed for its solution. Typically, this forces us to decompose the problem into subproblems, to define what is meant by subproblem completion, and to orchestrate how the achievement of subproblems fits into the overall goal. A variety of formal specification languages have been developed for professional programmers (e.g. GIST: see Balzer, 1985, Swartout, 1983), but these are of little help to the type of programmer we are considering.

(2) Translation into Code. When a problem has been sufficiently specified, it must be represented in the programming language chosen for the task. This can happen either through the generation of raw code or through the modification or incorporation of existing code. Subroutines and other pre-packaged modules are often used.

(3) Testing and Debugging. Code seldom works properly when first written, and the testing and debugging of a program is usually the most time-consuming phase of programming.

(4) Retention and Communication of Program. Whether we wrote the code or we are using code written by someone else, later understanding how it works can be a major chore. The key to the reusability and modifiability of code is to ensure that it can be comprehended.

The Programming Environment. The programming task makes use of both a *programming language* and a set of *programming tools*. Together, these make up the *programming environment*. A particular programming language can be made much easier to use if it is accompanied by a set of useful tools, combined into an environment that has a good user interface. Any discussion of the programming task must take into account this broader picture.

A Success Story: The Spreadsheet

Spreadsheets have extended computing support to a large audience of people who were not formerly computer users. Despite many limitations, spreadsheets have lowered the barriers to some level of programming power for many users. We speculate about the reasons for this success by contrasting a spreadsheet model with a traditional program.

Strengths of Spreadsheets

Familiar, concrete, visible representation. Data values and formulae in a spreadsheet are located in a simple two-dimensional array and are easy to view. Because the spreadsheet uses a familiar representation users may have more the feeling that they are working directly on their task and less that they are using a computer. In traditional programming languages programs and data normally are held in incompatible representations which users may not understand, and complex actions may be required to view them.

Suppressing the inner world. In traditional programming there is an inner world of variables and computation in which processing is done but to which the user has no direct access. Data must be pumped into the inner world from the outer world of the user by special input mechanisms, whose programming is often difficult. Results must be pumped out again by special output programming. Once data have been pumped in they cannot normally be modified by the user but must be reentered and repumped. In the spreadsheet the inner world is managed by the implementation; the illusion is created for the user that data and computations exist in an outer world to which user and system share access (see Draper 1986). Because no pumping is required the user does not have to worry about input or output programming. Because data seemingly stay in the outer world they can be incrementally modified.

Automatic consistency maintenance. In traditional programming the user must specify how and in what order changes in data are to be reflected in results. In the spreadsheet the user specifies the dependencies of quantities on one another and relies on the system to maintain them.

Absence of control model. Flow of control is a difficult concept in traditional programming. The spreadsheet user does not need to be aware of flow of control in normal cases.

Low viscosity. Thomas Green uses "viscosity" to describe the difficulty or ease in changing part of a program without changing other parts. Features like variable declarations and loop constructs which are made up of separated statements raise the viscosity of traditional programming languages. In a spreadsheet changes to a part are not constrained by other parts.

Aggregate operations. The spreadsheet user has direct access to operations like "sum" and "average" which are not normally available in traditional programming languages, but must be built up from more primitive operations and control constructs. We called such constructions "programming games." Programmers learn plans for things like computing sums by accumulation and become fluent with them. For nonprogrammers each case is a difficult problem-solving task.

Immediate feedback. Changes to the spreadsheet model will produce modified output right away, while changes to the program will require reexecution with reentry of data.

Weaknesses of Spreadsheets

While spreadsheets have a number of virtues, they have some limitations that are also informative about the nature of programming.

Difficulty of debugging. Spreadsheets are not easy to debug. The underlying representations are invisible unless made visible, and in most spreadsheet programs only a single cell can be examined at a time. Often the variables in the cell of a spreadsheet are labeled with cell locations rather than mnemonic variable names. On the whole, the representation of spreadsheets makes it difficult to track down errors. Because of these difficulties a number of supplementary software packages have been developed to assist debugging. For example, Spreadsheet Auditor (reviewed in Luhn, 1985) provides a printed representation of all formulae simultaneously in grid format.

Difficulty of redesign. The same features that make a spreadsheet difficult to debug also make it difficult to redesign. It is especially hard to adapt the spreadsheet of another user to one's own task.

No modularity. Spreadsheets are not organized into subroutines or other structured parts. Such modularity is useful in traditional programming, since the parts can often be tested and debugged separately. It also makes it easier to re-use portions of code.

No abstractions. Abstractions in programming allow one to define constructs at a level appropriate to one's task, and then subsequently to treat these as primitives, ignoring their internal detail. This kind of hierarchicalization is a powerful mechanism in programming. A spreadsheet represents an abstraction at a fixed level, and does not allow this powerful mechanism. In fairness, abstraction also has a down side, since it can lead to code that is difficult to understand.

Generality in the Spreadsheet and Beyond

The spreadsheet can be seen as a special-purpose tool, in that its representation maps very well to a range of tasks that would be performed manually using paper spreadsheets. It is possible that a good deal of its success is to be found among people performing just these tasks, for which it was originally intended, and which it supports so directly. But spreadsheet applications are commonly reported that fall well outside this domain, ranging from such near extensions as course grading to quite original uses like the implementation of cellular automata or connectionist models. So it appears that the utility of the spreadsheet does not rest on its fit to a particular prespecified range of tasks. On the other hand, the spreadsheet cannot support AC's requirement for a tool to process long, irregular sequences of data. Traditional programming, with all of its difficulties, offers much greater flexibility.

The flexibility of traditional programming derives from a synthesis model. Complex operations and representations are built up from primitives. The primitives are small and don't do very much, but the success of programming has been ensured by the remarkable fact that primitives can be chosen in such a way that appropriate combinations of them can carry out arbitrary tasks. Programming skill consists of a knowledge of the primitives and the rules of combination, together with a repertoire of higher-level plans for commonly-useful assemblies. Flexibility results from the fact that situations for which the higher-level plans are inappropriate, or must be modified, can be dealt with by descending to the level of the primitives and synthesizing novel forms. This is why abstractions can be so useful.

The synthesis approach to flexibility has a number of drawbacks from a psychological point of view.

(1) Synthesis is inherently hard, because of the large number of possible combinations that must be explored.

(2) Because the primitives are unrelated to the user's task they are difficult to understand.

(3) For the same reason it is hard to see what combination of primitives will produce the correct task-related behavior. (Mastering the primitives, and developing the ability to relate combinations of them to task requirements, are just those difficult and time-consuming jobs AC is unwilling to undertake.)

(4) Synthesis must be carried out with little immediate feedback, because typical subconstructions of primitives don't do anything. When feedback becomes available it is informative only about the behavior of a big assembly rather than about the many little choices that had to be made in putting it together.

(5) Since the fundamental maneuver in programming by synthesis is the replacement of "what is wanted" by "what to do", information about intent is not expressed directly and must be maintained separately, mentally or physically, by the programmer.

(6) As documented by Soloway and his colleagues (Spohrer, Soloway & Pope, 1985) synthesis requires plan merging: constructions must be formed that carry out multiple purposes simultaneously. This is a source of errors.

Besides these complaints about the synthesis approach to flexibility we can offer others that refer specifically to synthesis using the primitives used in traditional languages.

(1) In most languages the synthesis approach results in high viscosity, because the primitives and rules of combination are complex. Thus in many languages one may not be able to change the use of a variable in one place in a program without a coordinated change to its declaration, some place else, and its uses in other places in the program.

(2) The commonly-used primitives enforce the inner world-outer world distinction in which data manipulable by the system cannot be manipulated by the user.

(3) The reliance on sequence as the fundamental mode of combination of primitives requires users to specify much irrelevant information, since order of operation is very often immaterial in accomplishing real task demands.

(4) It takes great care and discipline on the part of the programmer to make sure the code is comprehensible. Code that is difficult to understand can interfere with debugging and with the re-use of program parts. There is a natural tension within the synthesis approach between computational efficiency or elegance and cognitive transparency.

We consider two approaches to overcoming these difficulties: replacing synthesis by modification, and reforming the primitives. Before discussing these in greater detail, we briefly review some of the principles of cognition that are relevant to our discussion. Some of these have already figured in our appreciation of spreadsheets and our critique of current programming methods.

Principles of Cognition that Bear on Programming

Examples and analogies play an important role in understanding. The work of Anderson and colleagues on learning LISP and learning in other domains (Pirolli and Anderson 1985, Anderson 1987) shows that learners rely heavily on examples in building their knowledge. When material is presented both in abstract statements and in illustrative examples learners focus on the examples. When grappling with new material learners often try to adapt examples of earlier material to suit the present situation, modifying the example by analogy. While the basis for the effectiveness of examples, and learners' preference for them, is not fully understood, we can speculate about some of their advantages. First, since an example shows an abstract principle in use, it links the abstract principle to some actual task domain. This may make the principle more accessible. Second, the example provides a check on the correct interpretation of the abstract principle. Abstract terminology is often ambiguous, and an example constrains the possible interpretation of an abstract statement to just those interpretations that account for the example. Third, learners can extend an example by analogy without understanding the example fully: only the parts of the example that must be changed need be understood. Fourth, the learner need not recall those aspects of a solution that already appear in an example. In programming this is especially valuable where difficult to remember points of syntax are concerned: an example program shows directly what a procedure header must look like, for example.

Explanations play an important part in generalizing examples. While examples reduce the amount that must be understood, learners do have to understand the parts of an example that must be modified. In Anderson and Thompson's PUPS model of analogical generalization (1986) the role of parts of examples are explained by specifying what functions they accomplish. Lewis (1986) reviews a number of other approaches to the use of explanations in generalization.

Immediate feedback aids problem-solving. Problem-solving involves a good deal of trial-and-error, the effectiveness of which depends critically on being able to determine whether a move one has tried was a good one or a bad one. Good feedback on the results of one's trial moves is crucial, and delayed feedback not only slows progress but (typically) creates difficulty in determining which of several moves really determined the outcome one sees.

Familiar representations aid control. Norman (1986) and Hollan, Hutchins, and Norman (1986) point out that a person controlling a system confronts two problems of translation, the Gulf of Execution, in which user goals must be translated into actions that the system can perform, and the Gulf of Evaluation, in which results the system actually produces must be interpreted in terms of the user's goals. If the entities with which the system appears to operate are familiar, these translation problems are eased.

Programming by Modification

The relatively easy comprehension and generalization of examples offers an avenue for achieving programming generality without the difficulties of synthesis: new programs would be created by modifying examples rather than from scratch. It is interesting that considering programming from a psychological point of view, and focusing on the needs of nonprofessional programmers, leads to an approach closely related to software reuse, which has been proposed in the software engineering community as a means of reducing the cost of programming by professionals (see papers in Biggerstaff and Perlis 1984.)

Making this idea work requires that we address the following issues.

Providing examples. A library of programs must be provided that includes models for a wide variety of particular applications. Planning a collection of this kind will be difficult. We know from experience with inheritance hierarchies that choosing the right abstractions to support future refinement is hard. It would be desirable if means were available for users to contribute new examples as significant variations are constructed. This entails not only a method of dissemination but also a way of describing examples that are supplied.

Finding examples. The user must have a means of choosing an appropriate starting point for his or her work. This is another hard problem, unsolved for today's complex systems. Descriptions of examples at many levels of abstraction, with system-supported indexing and retrieval, would be needed.

Determining the needed modifications. Figuring out what to change in an example requires knowledge of how the parts of the example contribute to its function, that is, knowledge of the roles of the parts. Thus examples would have to be annotated in such a way as to indicate these roles.

Making the modifications. As suggested by Balzer, we distinguish two cases here. In external modification an example or part of an example is modified by changing its input, output, or both, without affecting its internal functioning. For example, an arithmetic mean operator $m(A)$ can be changed to a geometric mean operator by composing it with log and $antilog : antilog(m(log(A)))$. Note that this can be done without knowledge of the parts of m and how they work. Support for external modification requires a representation in which all inputs and outputs are explicit and interception of all of them is possible.

The same change could be accomplished by <u>internal</u> modification. Suppose *m(A)* is implemented by *divide(sum(A), count(A))* . The geometric mean is obtained by replacing *divide* by *root* and *sum* by *product* : *root(product(A), count(A))* . Support for internal modification requires representation of roles, accomplished in this example by function names, and access to a repertoire of alternative pieces like *root* and *product* .

It is possible that automatic aid could be provided for some internal modifications. Suppose the role of *divide* is given as [*inverse of product*], where *product* is described as [*iterated sum*]. Suppose further that the system has a description of *power* as [*iterated product*], and *root* as [*inverse of power*]. If the user asked the system to replace *sum* by *product* , to obtain the geometric mean, Anderson and Thompson's PUPS (1986) analogical generalizer would produce the correct form automatically, as follows. Examining the role of *divide* it would find *product* , described as [*iterated sum*]. Replacing *sum* by *product* as requested yields [*iterated product*], which is *power* . Replacing *product* by *power* yields [*inverse of power*], which is *root* . The operator *sum* would be replaced directly, and *count* would be unchanged, giving the desired new program.

<u>Locality</u>. Specifying the roles of parts and being able to replace old parts by new will be greatly facilitated if roles are accomplished by connected pieces of the whole. We have noted above that traditional languages contain many violations of this locality principle, such as control constructs that comprise statements in more than one place in a program. The arithmetic mean example above could be handled neatly because *sum* was provided as a simple aggregate operation. If it were represented by a loop, the role specification, and thus the modification, would be harder. In particular, both an initial value (1 instead of 0) and the operator used to accumulate the result (* instead of +) would have to be changed to convert *sum* to *product* .

We can summarize the putative psychological benefits of replacing programming by synthesis with programming by modification by reference to some of the cognitive principles we outlined above.

> (1) Modification starts from an example, which is a good basis for understanding a problem. The example supplies much information that would otherwise have to be recalled. Only those parts of the example that must be modified have to be understood.

> (2) Modification can provide more immediate feedback than synthesis, since the process starts with an example which can be executed, and modifications can be arranged to provide meaningful results from a sequence of intermediate versions.

We believe additional benefit can be gained from the modification paradigm by providing for the <u>retention of the modification history</u> of programs. If an example refers to the form from which it was constructed, and indicates the reasons for the modifications that were made, the task of understanding the example will be simplified. Also, the user would have not only examples of programs but examples of how to modify programs as a guide to his or her own work.

Retaining information about the origin of programs would have other benefits. The user could browse through programs derived from a given one, getting ideas. The system could support modifications of collections of programs that had a common basis. Thus if P' and P" are derived from P the system could assist in making modifications in P' and P" to reflect changes that might be made in P, rather than requiring the user to modify P' and P" individually.

While maintaining derivational relationships among programs may always be a good idea, the more detailed information about the rationale for changes may need to be pruned. At some point it may be that a modified program can more clearly be described from scratch than as a variant of an older program. Means should be provided to support this change of representation, preferably without making the derivation information unavailable.

We believe this vision of programming by modification should mesh with the trend toward greater use of specialized application packages. In contrast to today's implementation techniques, these ideas would make it possible for such specialized tools to be much more flexible than they are now, without changing their appearance, and without forcing the user who has no need for increased flexibility to pay a cognitive price. A spreadsheet user could ask to see the internal structure of a high-level operator and modify it, without disrupting the overall application and without needing the skill that a comparable task would require today. One could envision a common underlying implementation language, supporting role expression and program modification in a standard way across diverse application packages. Users would then have to learn only a single set of modification skills.

Changing the Primitives of Programming Languages

We come to this topic from two directions. First, fleshing out the vision of programming by modification requires us to say something about what the stuff is we are modifying. Second, as mentioned earlier, reform of the stuff of languages, the model of computation on which they are based, could itself lead to a breakthrough in making programming easier. We have not been able to develop a coherent picture from either viewpoint, but we can assemble some ideas.

Avoid programming games. As we mentioned earlier, a hallmark of programming in most (but not all) languages is that operations one thinks of as units must be expressed as sequences of actions. It is instinctive to any programmer to sum a collection of numbers by initializing an accumulator variable to zero, and iterate through the collection adding each one to the accumulator. Even the operation "add this number to the accumulator variable" is expressed in most languages in a way that requires two mentions of the variable. These games are easy, only if you know how to play them. Learning to play them is a big, poorly-motivated nuisance. The stuff of languages should support aggregate operations as routine.

Suppress the inner world. Again, this is a point discussed above. The model of computation should be one in which user and system communicate by sharing a collection of objects, avoiding the tedious specification of input and output operations.

Representational independence. Conventional languages require you to describe what you want by saying how to get it. Languages like PROLOG or GIST (Balzer 1985, Swartout 1983) permit you to describe what you want and arrange for the system to find an implementation (some of the time.) The "how" specification requires you to formulate your problem in terms of one special representation: the objects and operations in the model computer that the language mimics. This formulation requires you to understand not only your problem but also this special representation. Reformed language stuff should permit you to formulate your problem using the objects, relationships, and processes of the problem domain, independently of the inner representation of processes inside the system. Such an approach would be in line with the cognitive principle of using familiar representations that we noted above.

What about the overhead involved in defining the behavior of objects, etc., in a representation-independent scheme? On the one hand, one can argue that this overhead has to be paid in ordinary programming too: you've got to specify how everything works when you define the implementation. But on the other hand, the representation-dependent scheme might have an advantage: it may turn out to be easier to master one computing model, and figure out how to translate object behaviors and relationships into this concrete model, than to figure out how to express object behaviors and relationships in a purely abstract system. Don Norman likes being able to understand what his programs are doing by mentally executing them. He can do this easily (in simple cases) once he has made the investment in mastering the computer model. It is not clear what substitutes for mental execution in a more abstract system.

Informality. A way to lessen the overhead of abstract representations may be to imbed them in an informal, rather than a formal, mode of communication. Some part of the barrier to programming may consist of the cost of formality: the requirement that ideas be expressed in a highly-constrained, one-way communication instead of (as in human-to-human communication) in an interaction that succeeds by iterative convergence rather than by correct initial utterance.

Programming by modification is one approach to supporting this more familiar and possibly easier style of communication. We can modify a program and see what happens without understanding everything about it. If we don't like what it does we can try something else. We are not arguing that this style of work is always appropriate, nor that there are not situations in which the precision and predictability of formal interactions are desirable. But iteration may require significantly less up-front investment in communication than formality.

An important feature of natural communication is the use of defaults, not in the stereotyped form of arbitrary assumed values, but in the form of flexible conventions for eliding and filling in the obvious. Approximating these conventions in an artificial language will be very hard, because of the unbounded inference that seems to underlie them in natural communication. X can use anything he or she can infer about the situation Y is describing describing to help flesh out what Y is actually saying. But this fleshing out could reduce enormously the overhead of describing the behavior and relationships of objects.

The modify-and-try-out cycle in the modification paradigm could be improved by use of the default principle. A given change to a program may produce obvious and unobvious changes to results. A system could attempt to classify the effects of changes and explicitly notify the user of unobvious ones. For example, changing a function in a block-structured language may affect not only the value returned but also the side effects on inherited variables. (Of course it may be profitable to eliminate sources of unexpected effects rather than just warning of them.)

Another feature of natural communication, related to defaults, is tolerance of incompleteness and inconsistency. X may be able to approximate a situation more easily by saying something false about it than by sticking to the strict truth, and can rely on Y to act appropriately when the falsehood is important. Lewis has described "cognitive approximations" which work like this. For example users of a menu system described the function of a particular command as "go back to last screen, sort of." The "sort of" was needed because the command really moved up in a menu hierarchy and there were some obvious cases, but not many, when the result was not the last screen. Despite the efforts of the menu designers and documenters it was easier for users to adopt the approximate, vague description than to master the real facts. And they were able to cope successfully with the cases in which the approximation broke down, simply by falling back to more primitive menu operations to get where they wanted to go.

An artificial partner in informal communication should respond the same way. The user should be able to express behaviors and relationships that are clear and important, and defer dealing with the cases that are not adequately covered. If the system can help, such as by refusing to go into long loops without asking, so much the better.

A hallmark of formal communication is the array of distinctions among things, names of things, names of names, etc. It is remarkable that informal communication succeeds without rigid conventions analogous to the use of quotes or the use of variable names. We suspect that emulating this feature of informal communication, solving the quote problem, will be an important step in the development of artificial language. The QBE language (Zloof, 1977) took a step in this direction, permitting particular objects to be used to stand for any instance of a class, but the user was required to label such uses of examples explicitly. It is possible that heuristics could be devised that would allow a system to detect such uses of examples without requiring explicit marking. For example, in the statement "When I type print Margaret's salary you should show Margaret's salary on the screen," the repetition of "Margaret" and "salary" suggests that they are placeholders that could be replaced by other values. We return to this issue in our discussion of implementation issues, below.

A worry about generality. One of the advantages of the use of procedural models of computation as the stuff of a language is that a great deal is known about the generality of procedural representations. Indeed, there is a clear sense in which almost any procedural model is universal, in that any computation at all could be modelled within it. We have no comparable body of insight into the generality of other ways of describing things. Thus even a very simple computational model will give me some expression of what I want, if I am willing to translate what I want into its terms. But what assurance do I have that a system that allows me to describe what I want in nonprocedural terms will be flexible enough to support my needs?

Don Norman points out that the practical force of formal universality may be much less than this worry acknowledges. You can't get windows and pulldown menus on your Turing machine. You can only get some kind of model of them, which is no good to you at all. What matters is what you can really get, and both procedural and descriptive models will be limited.

Some Technical Notes

Although our explicit intent is to discuss possible advances in language design independent of implementation considerations, it is not surprising that some implementation points must be addressed. Here are some.

Construct, not emit. Older computer technology led naturally to the view that programs are emitted symbol by symbol by programmers. APL's cryptic invented alphabet is an extreme manifestation of the commitment to this technology-imposed approach. Big displays and pointing devices make it easy to think of programming as a construction process guided by the programmer. The program can be built of big pieces that would be hard to emit but are easy to select. The CMU Tutor programming environment is an example of such a philosophy in practice (Sherwood, 1985; Sherwood & Sherwood, 1986). CMU Tutor is a system that allows easy construction of C programs, designed for use by university faculty who want to write instructional software. It allows for easy selection of program parts, for instance, by cutting and pasting from the examples in the on-line documentation.

Visible, manipulable representations. Similarly, technology no longer imposes the "inner world-outer world" distinction discussed above. We can support computational models in which all objects are or can be visible, and can be manipulated and modified by the user. CMU Tutor is again an example of an important step in this direction. Graphic entities can be entered or modified by directly manipulating the drawing, and the relevant code is generated or updated in the program. Multiple fonts and styles are handled by writing them up in a WYSIWYG form and cutting and pasting them directly into the program's write commands.

Inference and constraint satisfaction. Achieving our goals in the area of nonprocedural specification and informal communication place heavy stress on these techniques. How far can we get?

Automated abstraction. This is a possible way to deal with the "quote problem" in some of its manifestations. Consider the problem of controlling the style of headings in a document. Today we have two methods. One is to control the style manually for each heading. To change the style of a particular level of headings requires many separate changes. A second method is to use explicit, planned abstractions. Each heading is labelled to indicate its level. A style is specified for each level, and can be changed for all headings at a level in one operation.

The abstraction system is convenient once it is set up. But can one get its benefits without setting up the abstraction and without having to plan for it? Suppose the system can recognize the style in which a heading is set. Then we can tell the system to modify the style of all headings that are in the same style as a given one. With no preplanning, and no dealing with abstractions, we can change collections of objects in one operation.

Retroactive abstractions like this may be of general value. A constant could be used instead of a variable in specifying an algorithm; changing one occurrence of it could change all. More generally, descriptions could substitute for names in many contexts, as is common in natural, informal communication.

Toward Programming that Fits This Vision

This discussion suggests many directions for exploration in language design, software engineering, and artificial intelligence. It also suggests some priorities in psychological and linguistic research. We need better understanding of learning from examples, the use of analogies, reasoning and communicating with incomplete and inconsistent specifications, informal indicators of abstraction, and generality of description systems.

Of course work is already going forward in many of these areas. As a postscript to this report we want to describe briefly two language development projects which provide concrete illustrations of how some of the ideas we discussed can be reflected in real systems.

Our first example is CMU Tutor (Sherwood 1985; Sherwood & Sherwood, 1986), a language for authoring educational software. The language (and its environment) support programming by modification in two ways. First, its online documentation provides sample programs that can be executed directly from the documentation. Thus new users do not have to start from scratch in using the language. Second, the graphics facilities permit the programmer to modify program code by operating on the concrete, visible results produced by the code. Suppose for example we have a program that draws a line, but one end of the line is not where we want it. In CMU Tutor we select the specification of that end point in our program, as if we were going to edit it. But then we indicate <u>in the screen area in which output appears</u> where that point should be. The system determines what coordinates specify that point, and replaces the original coordinates in our program code. CMU Tutor also provides incremental compilation, so that the results of such modifications are rapidly available.

Our second example is a direct outgrowth of our analysis. One of us (Lewis) was impressed by the merits of spreadsheets, as discussed earlier, and set out to extend the spreadsheet computational model to control interactive graphics. The resulting system, called NoPumpG, links graphical objects to an underlying spreadsheet via <u>control cells</u>, which hold the coordinates of the objects. This linkage is two-way, so that moving an object with the mouse causes the control cells to be updated, but placing a formula in a control cell causes the position of the object to be updated.

Thus graphical input to the spreadsheet, and graphical output from the spreadsheet, are both provided. By placing a clock in one cell of the spreadsheet animation can be produced: if a formula in a control cell refers to the clock cell then the corresponding coordinate, and hence the position of the graphical object on the screen, will change with time. NoPumpG aims specifically at suppressing the inner world, as we have phrased it: just as in an ordinary spreadsheet there is no inaccessible program world, but rather all objects are shared by user and program.

References

Anderson, J.R. (1987). Causal analysis and inductive learning. *Proc. Fourth International Machine Learning,Workshop*, 288-299.

Anderson, J.R. and Thompson, R. (1986). Use of analogy in a production system architecture. Paper presented at the Illinois Workshop on Similarity and Analogy, Champaign-Urbana, IL.

Balzer, R. (1985). A 15 year perspective on automatic programming. *IEEE Transactions on Software Engineering*, **SE-11**, 1257-1268.

Biggerstaff, T.J. and Perlis, A.J. (Eds.) (1984). Special issue on software reusability. *IEEE Transactions on Software Engineering*, **SE-10**.

Draper, S.W. (1986). Display managers as the basis for user-machine communication. In D.A. Norman and S.W. Draper (Eds.) *User Centered System Design: New Perspectives in Human-Computer Interaction*. Hillsdale, NJ: Erlbaum, 339-352.

Lewis, C.H. (1986). Why and how to learn why: Analysis-based generalization of procedures. Technical Report CS-CU-347-86, Department of Computer Science, University of Colorado, Boulder, CO.

Hutchins, E.L., Hollan, J.D. and Norman, D.A. (1986). Direct manipulation interfaces. In D.A. Norman and S.W. Draper (Eds.) *User Centered System Design: New Perspectives in Human-Computer Interaction*. Hillsdale, NJ: Erlbaum, 87-124.

Luhn, R. (1985). From the software desk. *PC World*, May, 97.

Norman, D.A. (1986). Cognitive engineering. In D.A. Norman and S.W. Draper (Eds.) *User Centered System Design: New Perspectives in Human-Computer Interaction*. Hillsdale, NJ: Erlbaum, 31-61.

Pirolli, P.L. and Anderson, J.R. (1985). The role of learning from examples in the acquisition of recursive programming skills. *Canadian Journal of Psychology*, **39**, 240-272.

Sherwood, B.A. (1985). An integrated authoring environment. *Proc. IBM Academic Information Systems University AEP Conference.*

Sherwood, B.A., & Sherwood, J.N. (1986). CMU Tutor: An integrated programming environment for advanced-function workstations. *Proc. IBM Academic Information Systems University AEP Conference.*

Spohrer, J.C., Soloway, E., and Pope, E. (1985). A goal/plan analysis of buggy Pascal programs. *Human Computer Interaction,* **1,** 163-207.

Swartout, W. (1983). The GIST behavior explainer. *Proc. National Conference on Artificial Intelligence AAAI83,* 402-407.

Zloof, M.M. (1977). Query by example: A database language. *IBM Systems Journal,* **4,** 324-343.